Antisemitism World Report
1993

305.892
ANT

D1314302

INSTITUTE
OF
JEWISH
AFFAIRS

79 WIMPOLE STREET   LONDON W1M 7DD   UNITED KINGDOM

© Copyright INSTITUTE OF JEWISH AFFAIRS 1993

ISBN: 0 901113 21 2
ISSN: 1350-0996

All rights reserved
No part of this publication may be reproduced, stored in a retrieval system, or transmitted in any form or by any means, electronic, photocopying, recording and/or otherwise without the prior permission of the publishers.

The INSTITUTE OF JEWISH AFFAIRS, established in 1941, is an international research body, concerned with contemporary political, social, legal, economic and cultural issues affecting world Jewry.

London office:
INSTITUTE OF JEWISH AFFAIRS
79 Wimpole Street, London W1M 7DD, United Kingdom
Tel: 071-935 8266   Fax: 071-935 3252

New York office:
501 Madison Avenue, 17th Floor
New York, NY 10022, USA
Tel: 212-755 5770 Fax: 212-755 5883

Printed by Woolnough Bookbinding Ltd.
Irthlingborough, Northamptonshire, United Kingdom

Contents

Preface

This *Report* documents antisemitism throughout the world in the year 1992. The absence of an entry on a country does not imply that antisemitism does not exist in that country. Equally, the fact that some entries are longer than others does not necessarily mean that antisemitism poses more of a problem in those countries where it is given lengthier treatment. The length of entries reflects to some extent the amount of data that were available. It is emphasized that *Antisemitism World Report 1993* is a report on *current* antisemitism: it is not intended as a survey of the general situation of the Jewish communities of the world. Population figures, both general and Jewish, are approximations.

Acknowledgements

The following individuals, organizations and institutes assisted in the preparation of this *Report*:

Manuel Abramowicz; Siegfried Adler; David Albahari; Lydia Aroyo; Amatzia Baram; Avi Beker; Werner Bergmann; Rolf Bloch; Jacques Blum; Henriette Boas; Judith Bokser-Liwerant; Peter Brod; Robert J. Brym; Centre de Documentation Juive Contemporaine, Paris; Centro di Documentazione Ebraica Contemporanea, Milan; Centrum Informatie en Documentatie over Israël, the Hague; Jerome A. Chanes; Mikhail Chlenov; Walter J. Citrin; Lea Cohen; Community Security Organization, Board of Deputies of British Jews; Delegation of Argentine Jewish Institutions; Sergio DellaPergola; Leonard Dinnerstein; Amanita Dufva; Rainer Erb; Bernie M. Farber; Marian Feldman; David Gingold; Kristoffer Gjotterud; Anne Godfrey; Adriana Goldstaub; Slavko Goldstein; Willy Guggenheim; Nelly Hannson; John Havercroft; Lukasz Hirszowicz; Inter-Parliamentary Council Against Antisemitism; Danko Ivin; Jeremy Jones; Joseph Klansky; Ignacio Klich; Seymour Kopelowitz; Joseph Kostiner; Jacobo Kovadloff; Jessica Kreimerman; Michael Leifer; Ronit Lentin; Jeff Lesser; Bea Lewkowicz; Maritza Lowinger; Victor Malka; Alice Marxova; Srdan Matic; Yossi Mekelberg; Bent Melchior; Rob Minshull; Richard Mitten; Sheldon Pine; Dina Porat and the Project for the Study of Antisemitism and the Roeters Van-Lennep Database of Contemporary Anti-semitism, Tel Aviv; Lisa Ronchetti; Eli Rosenbaum; Stephen J. Roth; William Rubinstein; Neil Sandberg; Joop Sanders; Dieter Schonebohm; Laslo Sekelj; Michael Shafir; Milton Shain; Lindsey Shanson; Henry Sobel; Paul Spoonley; Elan Steinberg; Swedish Committee Against Antisemitism; Leon Trahtemberg; Harold M. Waller; Rivka Yadlin; Eyal Zisser.

The Institute of Jewish Affairs gratefully acknowledges the help of: Jewish communal organizations and representative bodies throughout the world who reviewed entries concerning their communities; World Jewish Congress staff in Buenos Aires, Jerusalem, New York and Paris; and many individuals who wish to remain anonymous.

General Editors
Antony Lerman, Howard Spier
Section Editors
Hadas Altwarg, Julia Schöpflin, Lena Stanley-Clamp
Research and Editorial Team
Margaret Brearley, Nan Griefer, Jill Leuw, Lesley Levene, Krystyna Sieradzka
Technical Team
Tirzah Arenson, Christine Arthur, Frank Muller, Patricia Schotten, Catriona Sinclair

Introduction

The Balance Sheet for 1992

Last year's *Antisemitism World Report* noted a marked worsening of the antisemitic climate since the beginning of the 1990s. From the evidence of this year's *Report*, which covers the year 1992, the overall situation appears to have remained relatively unchanged. But since antisemitism reached a post-Second World War high point in 1991, there is every reason to be concerned and for urgent action to be taken in certain countries. Moreover, certain trends continue to give particular cause for alarm.

GENERAL BACKGROUND

Conditions conducive to the growth and spread of racism, xenophobia and antisemitism were more in evidence in 1992 than in 1991. And Europe remained the principal arena for manifestations of these phenomena.

In 1992, attention focused on the mounting violence against immigrants and asylum-seekers in Germany—and their inevitable echoes of Germany's Nazi past—which worsened towards the end of the year. These events gave rise to an international outcry, widespread calls for urgent action to be taken and to considerable soul searching, both in Germany and elsewhere, about the implications of the violence for Germany and for Europe as a whole. By March-April 1993, it appeared that the violence in Germany had peaked and that the action finally taken by the German authorities, as well as the expressions of international concern, had had a positive effect.

But as this *Report* goes to press, such optimism seems decidedly premature.

At the end of May 1993, the German Bundestag abolished the automatic right of refugees to asylum. Within days, an arson attack on the home of a Turkish family in Solingen resulted in the deaths of two women and three children.

With over 400,000 asylum-seekers arriving in Germany in 1992, there may well have been good reason to alter Germany's liberal asylum provisions. But whatever the motive for the change, many will see it as a sign that foreigners are not wanted in Germany. In fact this message emanates not only from Germany but from the European Community as a whole, which is taking measures to restrict the entry of non-EC nationals, and from other countries individually, such as France and the United Kingdom.

Governments claim that the steps being taken to limit the numbers of immigrants and asylum-seekers entering Western Europe are specifically designed to prevent the spread of racism, xenophobia and antisemitism. But many observers argue—pointing to incidents like that at Solingen—that such measures only fuel anti-foreigner feeling, provide legitimacy to far-right groups and exacerbate the climate of intolerance which increasingly prevails in Europe as a whole. If this is the case, then expressions of antisemitism, which are clearly a by-product of hatred of foreigners, can be expected to increase.

There are other circumstances which were conducive to the growth and spread of racism, xenophobia and antisemitism in 1992.

First, in Western Europe, democratic institutions were increasingly tested by continuing, and in some cases deepening, recession and accompanying high rates of unemployment. This led to widespread disillusionment with established political parties, which were seen as increasingly out of touch with their electorates. In a number of member states of the European Community this disillusionment also manifested itself in opposition to the Maastricht Treaty, some provisions of which were seen as inimical to the preservation of national identity and sovereignty, as well as to economic recovery.

Second, in the post-Communist societies of Central and Eastern Europe, the pressure for radical free market reforms, with their attendant economic and social hardship, has placed a great strain on fledgling democratic institutions, many of which are fragile. In a number of these countries, there is relatively little democratic culture and developed state of law, particularly in relation to minority groups.

Third, nationalist and ethnic antagonism intensified, particularly in Central and Eastern Europe. The appalling situation in the former Yugoslavia, where "ethnic cleansing"—a process reminiscent of the Nazi era—and dismemberment of the state of Bosnia-Herzegovina could not be prevented by the international community, served as a tragic warning of the extremes to which ethnic warfare could descend.

In the last few years, there has been an unprecedented eruption of nationalism in Europe. Much of this nationalism does not stem from liberal impulses. In many respects it is based on race and ethnicity, rather than on shared history and culture. It is exclusivist and intolerant. Because it is often espoused by national groups within existing nation-states, it poses a threat to the nation-state as we know it and threatens to break up Europe into increasingly fragmented parts.

It was once thought that the future would consist of the assimilation of minorities into a large integrated whole, but the opposite is occurring. It is becoming increasingly legitimate to base political demands on ethnicity (however distorted that concept of ethnicity may be). Because the interaction of such groups cannot readily be resolved, the result is all too often intolerance, the denial of human rights, the breakdown of political order, the decline of economic performance and escalation into civil and regional wars.

Fourth, developments in Europe, both East and West, reflect the breakup of traditional political and ideological structures which served both as a bulwark against extremism and as a means of integrating into the mainstream individuals predisposed to far-right ideas. As a result, people have been seeking solutions at the edges of politics, turning not only to far-right parties, but to green movements of various kinds, sects, new age philosophies, single-issue pressure groups and anti-politics parties (for example in Switzerland and Sweden).

Fifth, supranational organizations which are supposed to manage conflict and defend human rights—such as the United Nations, the European Community, the

Conference on Security and Co-operation in Europe (the "Helsinki Process"), NATO, the Council of Europe—do not appear to be adequate to the task. There was much hope that such bodies would increase in importance following the end of the Cold War, but the conspicuous failure to do little more than supply humanitarian aid in the conflict in former Yugoslavia has given encouragement to those who wish to use violence and the denial of human rights to gain control of territory and populations.

PARTIES, ORGANIZATIONS, MOVEMENTS

There are hundreds of groups throughout the world, mostly of a far-right, neo-fascist or neo-Nazi character, which are vehicles for the propagation of anti-semitism. For most of these groups, however, antisemitism is not at the forefront of their political or ideological activities. Their targets are principally immigrants, asylum-seekers, refugees, guest-workers—people who are perceived as racially or ethnically different from the mainstream. The vast majority are politically marginal and have negligible influence in the countries where they operate. Nevertheless, it remains true, as stated in our 1992 *Report*, that for many of these groupings, antisemitism is an overt element of their ideological outlook, and for others, even though they may eschew antisemitism in public, it clearly exists not far below the surface. Groups such as the Front National in France, the Freedom Party of Austria, the Vlaams Blok in Belgium, the Republikaner Partei in Germany, have concealed their antisemitism to gain public respectability, but it often emerges both in innuendo expressed by their leaders and at the local level where party members do not feel constrained to adhere to the parties' national imperatives.

Whilst it is difficult to say whether, overall, the membership of extremist antisemitic organizations has increased, some clear trends emerge. First, according to the German monitoring authorities, membership of extreme-right groups rose in Germany from 39,800 in 1991 to 65,000 in 1992, clearly a significant increase, especially since these figures may well be on the conservative side. Second, skinheads, who number at least 6,400 in Germany—there may be ten times as many—pose an "increasing threat" (again, according to the German authorities), and this is clearly mirrored in many other countries. More than ever, skinheads appear to be behind antisemitic incidents, and the phenomenon has spread from Western countries (originating in the UK, but found throughout Western Europe and North America) to Eastern Europe, and can be found in the former Czechoslovakia, Hungary and Poland. Third, extremist organizations are tending to be more highly organized, to develop increasing international links which enable them to organize and operate internationally, and to be more prepared to indulge in violent activities.

The electoral success of West European far-right groups, which was noted in last year's *Report*, continued in 1992, particularly in Germany, although overall fewer elections were held. In elections in Baden-Württemburg and Berlin, the Republikaner Partei won 10.9 per cent and 8.3 per cent respectively. The French Front National did not do as well as it hoped in the regional elections but still succeeded in securing almost 14 per cent of the vote, and achieved 12.5 per cent in the general election in 1993. In Turkey, the openly antisemitic Welfare Party, which has an Islamic fundamentalist orientation, gained 25 per cent support in elections in some provinces. Opinion polls and other data cited in this *Report* indicate that far-right parties appear to be holding on to their relatively high levels of support.

In Central and Eastern Europe, electorally significant nationalist groups with antisemitic leanings exist in Hungary, Poland and Russia. In Hungary, Istvan Csurka, who ceased to be a vice-president of the ruling Magyar Democratic Forum when all six vice-presidency positions were abolished following his antisemitic public statements, established a new grouping, Hungarian Way, which has to be watched very carefully. In Poland, two opposition groupings were formed after the collapse of the Olszewski government in June—the Movement for the Republic and the Third Republic Movement, which contain groups with an antisemitic record, and some of the leaders of which have been suspected of holding antisemitic views. In Russia, twenty members of the far-right National Salvation Front are Russian Supreme Soviet deputies.

MANIFESTATIONS

Antisemitic incidents—whether they be violence to persons, cemetery desecrations, arson attacks on Jewish property or the daubing of graffiti—are rightly scrutinized for what they tell us about levels of antisemitism. It must be emphasized, however, that, when considered on their own, they are a very imperfect indicator of whether antisemitism is on the rise, remaining static or in decline. Although some monitoring bodies, in the USA and the United Kingdom for example, have greatly refined the way in which they collect and analyse data on incidents, there remain problems of definition and interpretation.

Bearing in mind these problems, even a cautious approach to the figures reported here reveals some interesting developments. First, in some West European countries—Germany, the United Kingdom, Italy and Sweden—the number of incidents increased during 1992. In the USA, Canada and France, however, a decrease in incidents was recorded, although in the cases of France and Canada—and in many other countries—there was a sharp increase in such incidents towards the end of the year. This increase no doubt reflects both the impact of violence against asylum-seekers in Germany and the high level of racist attacks in Europe in general. (Figures produced by the Board of Deputies of British Jews show clearly that incidents increase in the UK following high-profile racist or antisemitic attacks elsewhere in Europe.) Second, although the systematic reporting of incidents in countries of Eastern Europe is in its infancy, our investigations show little evidence of serious antisemitic incidents (violence, bombing, firebombing, desecrations) occurring in large numbers. Third, in Latin America, where data collection is also not as fully developed as it should be, our evidence suggests that there has been no overall increase in incidents and probably a falling off in their number.

Concealed in the figures are three disturbing trends.

First, there is a greater propensity for the relatively few who express antisemitic beliefs to "act out" their beliefs in various forms of expression. This development is compatible with stable or declining levels of antisemitic sentiment and indicates that the immediate threat posed by antisemitism to Jews—in terms of the likelihood of personal injury, damage to property or the generation of a climate of fear in Jewish communities—can be relatively high even though antisemitism may not be a serious long-term threat.

Second, the degree to which Jewish cemeteries are attacked is of considerable significance. The clear impression from this *Report* is that, even in countries where manifestations have declined, there is a greater propensity to desecrate cemeteries. Whilst it would be an exaggeration to describe this as an epidemic, attacks on cemeteries are a particularly ugly form of antisemitism which play on the sensitivities of Jewish communities everywhere and their frequency gives great cause for concern.

Third, despite the apparent decline in the number of manifestations in some countries and the absence of any increase in many others, the increase in incidents towards the end of 1992 (noted above) in a significant number of places, is very disturbing. This may well be at least partly explained by the violent events in Germany which mounted in the latter part of the year and which led to "copycat" attacks elsewhere.

PUBLICATIONS

This *Report* shows that antisemitic publications—books, pamphlets, leaflets, greetings cards, periodicals—are now much more freely available in certain parts of the world, particularly Central and Eastern Europe, and some countries, particularly the UK, report an increased dissemination of such material. In some countries, periodicals with overt or covert antisemitic content are printed and distributed in large quantities (i.e. more than 50,000 copies)—for example, Russia (over fifty periodicals are listed), Turkey, France, Germany, the USA. In the Middle East, open expressions of antisemitism appear in publications in Iran, Syria, Egypt, the United Arab Emirates, Kuwait, Algeria and Iraq. The caricatures and images used (in cartoons and in print) run the gamut of antisemitic stereotypes: deformed Jews; Jews with money bags; Jews clutching the globe in their hands; Jews controlling the USA through finance; blood libels; claims that the Talmud is racist, that Jews undermine Islam, poison wells, bring AIDS. Even liberal Arab newspapers write of Jewish power in antisemitic terms. Other caricatures used include an octopus entwined with the Star of David; a hand marked with the Star of David stabbing the globe; and the devil with long nails, horns, fangs and Stars of David for eyes. Jews are referred to as Nazis and snakes, and the Star of David is equated with the swastika.

Among the themes of antisemitic propaganda generally, Jews are held responsible for the current economic problems faced by many states and for the problems of the past, particularly the introduction of Communism in Eastern Europe. The notion of a Jewish conspiracy to control the world, or at least the central institutions of societies—for example, the banks, the media, parliaments—is constantly repeated. So too is the view that Jews have profited from the Holocaust and that the Holocaust never occurred or its scope has been exaggerated. Traditional antisemitic themes appear in slightly different forms in different countries, sometimes cloaked in a special discourse. In Italy, widespread credence among far-right groups is given to *mondialismo*, a conspiracy theory which propounds that all the "world powers"—including Jews and Zionists—seek to "subdue" world populations economically, culturally and psychologically. In Russia, many on the far right adhere to the notion of "Russophobia": Russia is seen as being undeservedly despised by almost everybody, but especially by the Jews. Jews are therefore seen as the cause of Russia's misfortunes.

Most overtly antisemitic publications have very small circulations and make little impact. But copies of *The Protocols of the Elders of Zion* and other traditional antisemitic tracts are freely available in many countries, particularly in Eastern Europe and the Middle East. Much of this material originates from other countries. For example, CEDADE, the Spanish far right political organization, which has four publishing houses, is considered to be one of the largest producers of antisemitic publications in Europe and exports its material to Latin America and Austria.

MAINSTREAM POLITICS

Antisemitism remains relatively rare in mainstream political parties. In those countries where the far right, by virtue of its electoral success, can be judged to have entered the political mainstream—France, Austria, Belgium, Germany—there has been little change since 1991.

The role of antisemitism in mainstream politics in Eastern Europe is potentially the most dangerous. In Hungary, Romania and Poland, members of mainstream parties and some of those parties themselves are clearly antisemitic. Their antisemitism emerges most clearly during election campaigns, but not only then. Leading politicians in these countries are ready to make opportunistic use of antisemitism even if they are not antisemites themselves. In Russia, many members of the National Salvation Front, a loose alliance of extremist bodies which has twenty members in the Russian parliament, adhere to the notion that Russia's misfortunes are the fault of the Jews.

In the USA, the presidential candidacy bids of Pat Buchanan and David Duke undoubtedly brought antisemitism onto the national political stage. Duke is a veteran antisemite, former neo-Nazi and Ku Klux Klan leader who attracted considerable media attention during his short candidacy. Buchanan, a columnist, former White House staffer and a far more significant public figure, was seen by many as antisemitic.

RELIGION: THE CHURCHES

Since the Gulf War, manifestations of Christian antisemitism and anti-Zionism—which had increased markedly during the early years of the *intifada*—have declined in number and seriousness. During 1992, however, they remained a significant factor in antisemitism worldwide.

Roman Catholicism: Antisemitism was marked among small organizations of ultra-conservative Catholics representing pre-Vatican II theology, particularly among militant supporters of Monsignor Lefebvre. Some have links to far-right parties, and cite *The Protocols of the Elders of Zion* and contemporary antisemitic writers such as Henri Coston. Publications by such groups in Italy, France, Belgium, Australia and elsewhere contained antisemitic sentiments.

Certain single-issue lobby groups, such as Pro Vita (Belgium), also propagated religious antisemitism. Antisemitism is present in some Catholic-nationalist groups in France, Spain, Italy, Poland and elsewhere; the French Chrétienté-Solidarité has links to the Front National. Some Catholic fundamentalist publications (which number seventy-two in France alone) contained antisemitic material. Common themes are the power of Jewish finance and of a Jewish-Masonic conspiracy to unite all world religions in order to gain global domination. Pre-Vatican II anti-Judaism was reflected, particularly in Italy, in reiterations of Jewish guilt for the crucifixion of Jesus and for past ritual murders, in Christian triumphalism and the use of anti-Jewish stereotypes and language. A few Catholic clergymen openly expressed antisemitism, especially in Italy and Poland. Old antisemitic tracts attacking the Talmud continued to be reprinted in Poland and elsewhere, and new ones written (Italy). In Italy and Poland some antisemitic slogans of skinhead groups expressed Christian triumphalism. A Catholic antisemite in Norway published *The Protocols* and other anti-Jewish material.

Protestantism: In Germany, the United Kingdom, Australia and elsewhere some right-wing groups propagated anti-Judaism in their pamphlets (which generally have a small circulation). An alleged Jewish conspiracy of world domination was a common theme. In the USA the old Protestant fundamentalism in Ku Klux Klan ideology has been largely replaced by the racist pseudo-religion of "Identity". A few fundamentalist preachers and writers (New Zealand, the Netherlands) expressed virulent antisemitism and anti-Judaism. Common to both Catholic and Protestant anti-Judaism is the view that the Talmud is intrinsically evil and that *The Protocols of the Elders of Zion* is authentic.

Orthodox: Anti-Judaism was expressed by some clergy and in some unofficial Orthodox publications in Greece, Russia and Romania. Orthodox writers in Romania sharply attacked Romania's Chief Rabbi, Moses Rosen, using anti-Talmudic clichés and quoting from *The Protocols*. The Serbian Orthodox Church continued to publish antisemitic books by an anti-Jewish bishop. Charges of Jewish world supremacy and Jewish responsibility for creating Communism were common themes in Orthodox antisemitism.

Miscellaneous: A phenomenon of anti-Christian anti-Judaism exists (which urges return to pagan roots and blames Jews for having created Christianity). This was particularly noticeable among nationalist groups in Armenia and Belgium. Palestinian Christians are sometimes a source of antisemitism (Australia).

RELIGION: MUSLIM FUNDAMENTALISM

The problem of antisemitism stemming from Muslim fundamentalist sources clearly looms larger in this year's *Report* than it did last year. This form of antisemitism can be separated into two parts: antisemitic propaganda and literature in Muslim countries, and antisemitic propaganda and literature in non-Muslim countries with large Muslim populations, particularly in Western Europe and Latin America. In 1991, anti-Jewish activity and propaganda from Islamic fundamentalist sources emerged more as a potential than an actual threat. In 1992, there appears to more evidence of it as a present danger.

There is certainly very clear evidence of antisemitism in the writings and manifestos of organizations like Hamas and Hizbullah, and a strain of antisemitism in the Palestine Liberation Organization, which publicly makes every effort to eschew antisemitism. The Muslim fundamentalist organizations have international networks, are capable of mounting international terror campaigns and in 1992 and 1993 appear to have been behind two major incidents: the bombing of the Israeli embassy in Argentina and the bombing of the World Trade Centre in New York.

THE ARAB WORLD

Evidence of antisemitism in the Arab world remains somewhat uneven. This is partly connected with the problems of data collection. Not that there is any lack of evidence of antisemitic expressions but principally because so few experts have been monitoring developments in Arab countries from this angle. There is also genuine disagreement among expert observers as to how far expressions of antisemitism can be directly related to the political struggle of Arab states against Zionism and the state of Israel, and how deeply rooted antisemitism is in Arab societies. (For a fuller treatment of this problem, see the introduction to the section on the Middle East.)

The entry on Egypt in this *Report* provides disturbing evidence that antisemitism is becoming increasingly a grassroots phenomenon in that country. That this should be occurring in Egypt, the one Arab country that has concluded a peace treaty with Israel, is especially worrying. With other Arab countries, it may be possible to argue that the absence of peace fuels the use of antisemitic imagery and rhetoric in the political struggle. The corollary would therefore be that antisemitism would be reduced once peace was achieved. But if the case of Egypt disproves this thesis, antisemitism looks set to remain a serious factor in Arab societies.

EFFECTS OF ANTI-ZIONISM

Anti-Zionism does not emerge as a major factor in antisemitism in 1992. In some regions and countries—for example, Latin America and Greece—the use of anti-Zionism to mask antisemitic sentiments is more widespread, and anti-Zionism still has a greater antisemitic potency on university campuses, particularly in Western countries. Nevertheless, since the collapse of Communism, the end of the Cold War, the change in Arab attitudes following the Gulf War, the commencement of Middle East peace talks and the declining importance of Third Worldist international gatherings, anti-Zionism has ceased to be as important a factor as it was.

UNITED NATIONS

The one arena in which anti-Zionism remains a significant vehicle for antisemitism is the United Nations and some of its specialized agencies. For example, the Palestine Liberation Organization released a letter in December 1992, as part of documentation on alleged human rights violations in the occupied territories, which stated that the Israeli authorities, in observing Yom Kippur (the Day of Atonement), were "never fully happy on religious occasions, unless their celebrations, as usual are marked by Palestinian blood and the immolation of defenceless numbers of the Palestinian people." This is an obvious allusion to the blood libel and purports to show Jewish religious obsession with blood rituals and human sacrifice. The matter was taken up by Jewish representatives early in 1993.

A new body, UN Watch, was recently set up in Geneva by the World Jewish Congress to monitor activity of this kind.

HOLOCAUST DENIAL

Denial of the Holocaust—misleadingly referred to as "revisionism", which lends it a legitimacy it does not deserve—remained an important common denominator for both overtly and covertly antisemitic groups and individuals. There is still no evidence that Holocaust denial has had any impact on mainstream opinion although its major practitioners, like David Irving, Robert Faurisson, Fred Leuchter and Ernst Zundel, are nothing if not assiduous in attempting to spread their views worldwide. Holocaust denial developments in 1992 can more or less be traced by following the travels of Irving in particular. Fortunately, a number of countries either banned his entry or deported him once he had entered, signifying a greater awareness of the danger he represents and a greater willingness to take action to prevent his activities.

In Eastern Europe, Holocaust denial mostly takes a different form—the whitewashing and rehabilitation of former Nazi collaborators—which continues unabated. In Romania, open denial of the Holocaust occurred, adding to the seriousness of antisemitism in that country.

OPINION POLLS

Surveys of opinion can be useful indicators of the level of antisemitic sentiment, although social scientists have to find ways of compensating for the tendency of respondents not to admit to antisemitic prejudices. Comparisons of polls in different countries are difficult to make when different techniques and questions are used.

Polls conducted in Germany, Italy and Poland during 1992 showed higher than average levels of antisemitic prejudice among young people. In Germany, 14 per cent of 14-18 year-olds agreed that "Jews are Germany's misfortune", whilst only 1 per cent of 25-26 year-olds agreed. In Italy, among 14-20 year-olds, 13.4 per cent saw Jews as "foreigners". The importance of education emerges from the German poll: of the 14-18 years olds, 29 per cent of apprentices agreed with the statement, whilst 11 per cent of students agreed.

LEGAL MATTERS

The *Report* indicates a widespread desire to use the law to combat antisemitism and to punish antisemites, but in many cases legislation is found wanting or the authorities are unable or unwilling to prosecute or secure convictions. In a number of cases, attempts to prosecute foundered when legal protection of freedom of speech was considered more important.

In Eastern Europe and the former USSR, legislation against racial incitement, or at least provisions in constitutions, allow for the prosecution of those preaching racial or ethnic hatred, but in practice measures are somewhat crude and ineffectively applied. In Hungary, the Constitutional Court found the outlawing of offensive or derogatory statements against racial groups to be unconstitutional. In Poland, a number of significant cases against politicians accused of antisemitic propaganda were dropped. The authorities are clearly not over-enthusiastic to prosecute. In Romania, the authorities constantly blocked attempts by the Jewish community to prosecute attacks on Jews by the magazine *Europa*. And in Russia, although a number of cases were being investigated under Article 74 of the Russian Criminal Code, many regard it as too narrow and in need of a replacement. The authorities are also sometimes indifferent to calls for prosecutions.

In Western Europe, the failure to secure convictions in what appear to be open and shut cases has led to calls for the strengthening of legislation and for the harmonization of anti-racist legislation in Europe. Austria amended its laws to make it easier to convict for neo-Nazi activities; a law against denial of the Holocaust was put before the Belgian parliament; Germany toughened up its sentencing of young offenders responsible for attacking asylum-seekers; a new anti-racist bill was introduced in Italy at the end of 1992; Spain's Socialists proposed reforms that would strike at neo-Nazi or racist gatherings and symbols; and in Switzerland a new law accepted by the lower house would prohibit racist and religiously prejudiced actions, including Holocaust denial.

In the USA, despite the constitutional protection of free speech, forty-seven states and the federal government have some form of "hate-crime" legislation. However, constitutionally many of these laws have been called into question by a 1992 decision of the US Supreme Court. In Canada, some long-running cases were brought to conclusion, at least temporarily. Elsewhere, in countries like Brazil and Australia, existing anti-race hatred laws are not considered effective. France, Germany and Austria have legislation against denial of the Holocaust, and at least two other countries are actively considering such legislation. In Canada, Ernst Zundel's conviction for Holocaust denial under a law against spreading false news, was reversed because the Supreme Court found the law to be unconstitutional on grounds of freedom of expression and vagueness. However, many feel that the laws which prohibit Holocaust denial are not the way to combat the phenomenon.

COUNTERING ANTISEMITISM

The heightened concern about antisemitism, noted in last year's *Report*, was translated in 1992 into increased activity to counter antisemitism and other manifestations of racism. There has been widespread mobilization of people to protest racism and antisemitism. Germany is the prime example, with hundreds of thousands taking to the streets towards the end of the year to call for an end to racial violence. But such activity also increased in, among other places, Austria, France, Italy, Sweden, Mexico, Peru and Czechoslovakia. There are reports of new alliances being formed with other groups affected by racist attacks, expressions of solidarity with Jewish communities affected by antisemitic incidents and so on.

In Eastern Europe, many political leaders remain equivocal in their statements on antisemitism. Nevertheless, in some of the former Soviet republics, Poland, Hungary and even Romania some important activities condemning antisemitism were undertaken.

Branches of the Council of Christians and Jews and other Jewish-Christian friendship associations continued to oppose antisemitism and anti-Judaism in many countries during 1992, and undertook joint action with Jews. Religious leaders took part in demonstrations against racism in France and on the anniversary of Kristallnacht in Italy, and in other countries. Catholic and Protestant dignitaries in Germany denounced antisemitism, as did Pope John Paul II, the Archbishop of Canterbury, and the Conference of Catholic Bishops in both Hungary and Switzerland. Missionary campaigns targeted at Jews in Germany and the UK were opposed by church leaders. In Spain, 1,000 supporters of the International Christian Embassy held an act of public repentance for the expulsion of Jews from Spain. The desecration of Jewish cemeteries in several countries was condemned by Christian leaders.

It is difficult to assess the effectiveness of such activity but there would of course be much greater cause for alarm if no such mobilization took place.

OVERALL ASSESSMENT

Of the fifty-two entries in this *Report* (taking former Yugoslavia, former USSR and the Gulf states as one entry each), thirty-three show evidence of little change from 1991. Among some of the countries in which there appeared to be little change—for example, Iran, Iraq, Syria, Poland, the former USSR, France, Austria—the range and depth of antisemitic expression is nonetheless very disturbing. The impact of that antisemitism on Jews and the threat it represents to Jews is not uniform. In Iran, Iraq, Syria and Poland, there are tiny or non-existent Jewish communities. But in France and Russia, antisemitism has the potential to affect large numbers of Jews.

The situation looks to have the potential to become more serious in a number of countries, although in different ways. In the Ukraine, Russia and Slovakia, political and economic instability prevail and may worsen, thereby opening the door to the intensification of antisemitism which is already at high, or relatively high, levels. In the United Kingdom, the threat from Islamic fundamentalism, the increased dissemination of antisemitic literature and the tendency towards more extreme activity as exemplified by Combat 18, seems to point towards some intensification of antisemitism, even though, in comparison to some other European countries, antisemitism in the UK is generally minimal.

The countries where antisemitism markedly worsened, although not necessarily in the same ways, were Germany, Italy, Sweden, Switzerland, Turkey, Hungary, Romania, Canada and Egypt.

Countries where the situation appeared to improve were Belgium and Argentina, and possibly one or two Arab countries, Morocco and Tunisia.

PRINCIPAL TROUBLE SPOTS

Whilst there is an increasing desire to look at Europe as a whole, from the point of view of antisemitism it remains essential to differentiate between West and East. With very few elections in 1992, antisemitism could not be as significant a factor in the electoral process as it was in 1991. Nevertheless, in most former Communist countries, antisemitism remains a potent political force. This can be seen most clearly in Romania, Hungary and Russia.

In **Romania**, antisemitism certainly intensified between 1991 and 1992. With the ruling party being dependent for governance on the extremist parties, which espouse virulent antisemitism, the prospects for Romania's small Jewish community have considerably worsened and there are legitimate fears for its safety.

In **Hungary**, with the antisemite and leading figure in the main ruling coalition party, Istvan Csurka, still wielding considerable influence, antisemitic tendencies are growing. They may find fertile ground in the economic crisis and the general malaise and distrust of politicians that exist in Hungary today. Furthermore, there is reason to fear the agitation that will begin in 1993 in preparation for the 1994 general elections.

In **Russia**, there remain numerous grassroots chauvinistic and anti-Jewish groups and publications, and in the **Ukraine** a worrying antisemitic fringe movement has emerged. Whilst there was no indication that anti-Jewish sentiment was endemic among the rank and file of any of the populations of the former USSR, with the continuing economic, political and social dislocation accompanied by strong nationalist sentiments throughout the area, the threat posed by antisemitism to Jewish communities and to the prospects for democracy could become much more serious. The situation in these countries gives serious cause for alarm.

In the **Baltic states**, and **Moldova**, a problem causing considerable concern among Jewish communities is the continuing rehabilitation of Nazi collaborators.

The widespread and mounting violent attacks on asylum-seekers and foreigners in **Germany** led to an international outcry and, given Germany's Nazi past, considerable attention was paid to the role played by antisemitism in the events. Serious antisemitic incidents increased by approximately 20 per cent over 1991 (from 84 in 1991 to 104) but most of that increase was concentrated in the second half of the year, in the wake of the violence against asylum-seekers. This clearly indicates that antisemitism is an adjunct to hostility towards foreigners and that Jews are not the principal targets in Germany today.

The violence witnessed during 1992 was of grave proportions and there is no doubt that the government did not respond with sufficient resolution. Even now, the German situation remains of great concern, especially following the murder of five Turkish people in Solingen at the end of May 1993. Whilst the federal president and leading members of the government speak out forcefully against anti-immigrant violence and neo-Nazism, and attend the funerals of victims, Chancellor Kohl's failure to give a firm public lead and to visit the sites where violence has been at its worst has been conspicuous.

However, this *Report* finds no evidence to support comparisons between Weimar and Germany today. The German government does have the means at its disposal to act against violence, and with tougher sentencing and the banning of some key militant neo-Nazi organizations, it finally demonstrated that it was prepared to take tough action. Monitoring of this activity is not in itself a guarantee that action will be taken against it, but Germany certainly has a very efficient monitoring system which plays a significant public role and without which it would be impossible to take appropriate action. In addition, the hundreds of thousands of Germans who took to the streets to demonstrate their opposition to the violence showed that Germany's liberal democratic system commands very wide support. Again, demonstrations in large numbers are no guarantee that a system will survive or that minorities will be properly protected. But, since democratic governments generally pay considerable attention to public opinion, such demonstrations have an important role to play.

The phenomenon of **"antisemitism without Jews"** was more acutely apparent in 1992 than in 1991. The current size of Jewish communities appears to bear no relation to the degree of antisemitism in a country. In Poland, where levels of antisemitic sentiment are high, the organized Jewish community numbers less than 10,000. Yet, an opinion poll found that 10 per cent of Poles thought the Jews numbered between 4 and just over 7 million, and 25 per cent put their numbers between 750,000 and 3.5 million—astonishing results by any standard. But the phenomenon can also be found in Romania, Slovakia, many Arab countries and Japan.

Like last year, no one could seriously argue that the contemporary Jewish situation is remotely comparable to that of the many non-white minority groups for whom discrimination, violence and abuse are a daily occurrence. However, complacency would be entirely misplaced. What emerges clearly from this *Report* is that violent expressions of antisemitism follow in the wake of general anti-foreigner violence and racist attacks. The combination of a worsening racist and xenophobic climate, the increasing tendency towards politically-motivated violence, disillusionment with established political parties and continued economic recession has opened up a social and political space which organizations propagating sanitized versions of racism, xenophobia and antisemitism can exploit. The potential for increased expressions of antisemitism therefore remains high.

The number of serious antisemitic incidents, the range of antisemitic publications available, the appetite for antisemitic literature, the readiness of some politicians to make cynical use of antisemitism to further their political aims, the high levels of antisemitic sentiment among less-educated young people—none of this augurs well for human rights and democracy. As is plain from this *Report*, measures to combat antisemitism are insufficient in many countries and much needs to be done—on the levels of legislation, education and political action. And that action must be taken within the context of the general tightening of measures to combat racism and xenophobia.

Methodology

While many organizations are devoted to combatting antisemitism and many individuals are engaged in researching its history and current manifestations, until the appearance last year of *Antisemitism World Report 1992* there had been no internationally accepted "barometer" against which the current level of anti- . semitism could be measured. Last year seemed therefore the right moment to attempt to create just such a "barometer" in the form of a world survey of antisemitism, country-by-country, produced as far as possible according to common criteria and categories. Following the pattern set by the major human rights monitoring organizations, the latest volume, *Antisemitism World Report 1993*, is intended to provide:

1   an internationally recognized means of monitoring the advance or decline of the phenomenon worldwide;
2   a means of judging whether government and juridical authorities are taking appropriate action to combat antisemitism in their respective countries;
3   a tool for use by organizations and Jewish representative bodies whose task it is to combat antisemitism in pressing government and juridical authorities to take action;
4   a yardstick for judging the overall democratic health particularly of those societies where democratic institutions are at an early stage of development.

Antisemitism World Report 1993 is based on a wide variety of sources: specialist authors; Jewish communal organizations; monitoring organizations; research institutes; academic researchers; and the expertise and archives of the Institute of Jewish Affairs. Whenever a statement raised doubts and independent corroboration was impossible to obtain, the statement was not included.

Since one of the main purposes of this *Report* is to serve as a research-based tool for those engaged in combatting antisemitism in specific countries, it was decided to structure the survey country-by-country, within regions. There are other ways of producing such a survey and some phenomena—for example, antisemitism within international Islamic fundamentalist groups, antisemitism in international organizations like the UN—cannot be dealt with fully in a country-by-country treatment. However, overall assessments of world trends and consideration of some of the main expressions of antisemitism that transcend national boundaries were included in Part I of the Introduction to this *Report*.

In regard to the question of defining antisemitism, a strictly common-sense approach has been adopted. It was found that when those who concern themselves with the phenomenon in a serious manner were asked to report on it, there was a remarkable degree of unanimity about what was being described. The only significant area where differences emerge is on the question of the relationship between anti-Zionism and antisemitism. Here, we have erred on the side of caution, including only those elements of anti-Zionism which are patently antisemitic or had antisemitic effects.

Since no single index presents a reliable way of judging the state of anti-semitism, contributors to this volume were asked to organize their data in accordance with the categories listed below, which were intended to be as exhaustive as possible:

1 General and Jewish population figures
2 Past history of antisemitism
3 General political, social and economic conditions prevailing in country
4 Antisemitic political parties, organizations, movements, groupings, and estimates of their numbers and influence
5 Antisemitic manifestations/incidents (violent and non-violent)
6 Antisemitic publications (books, newspapers, magazines, etc.) and in the electronic media
7 Antisemitism in mainstream political life
8 Antisemitism in cultural (high and popular) life
9 Antisemitism in the business/commercial world
10 Antisemitism in education and at grassroots (e.g. leisure activities, including sport)
11 Religious antisemitism
12 Denial of the Holocaust, Holocaust "revisionism"
13 Antisemitic effects of anti-Zionism and the campaign against Israel
14 Opinion polls
15 Legal matters (including prosecutions under anti-incitement and anti-discrimination legislation)
16 Countering antisemitism (e.g. statements by non-Jewish political, religious and other leaders, educational initiatives, demonstrations)
17 Special factors (if any)
18 Overall assessment

It was clear that some of these categories were overlapping and that their application might vary considerably from country to country. In addition, contributors were encouraged to introduce categories of their own choosing to reflect special circumstances in the countries on which they were reporting, and in some countries certain categories do not apply. In some cases, no assessment has been given since this would merely have repeated the brief information already provided in the entry concerned. In the text of this *Report* the category headings have been shortened and renamed for reasons of space.

The *Report* should also be seen as a contribution to the attempt to refine our techniques of assessing the significance of antisemitism and not the last word on the matter. It is hoped that, apart from fulfilling the need for an authoritative survey, the volume will also stimulate discussion about the whole problem of measuring antisemitism. Naturally, the Institute of Jewish Affairs welcomes any comments or criticism from readers of the *Report*. Whilst every effort has been made to ensure accuracy, errors of fact may have crept in, and for these we apologize.

Western Europe

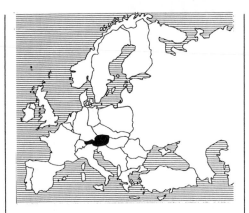

Austria

General population: 7,900,000
Jewish population: 8,000-15,000 (mostly in Vienna)

GENERAL BACKGROUND

Austria is a parliamentary republic currently governed by a coalition between the Social Democratic Party (SPÖ) and the Austrian People's Party (ÖVP). The two other parties represented in parliament, the far-right Freedom Party of Austria (FPÖ) and the Greens, enjoy the support of approximately 18 per cent and 8 per cent of the population respectively.

Austrian political life in 1992 was dominated by the issue of immigration from Eastern Europe, compounded by the influx of refugees from the war in former Yugoslavia, and by debates on Austria's application for membership of the European Community. The governing coalition continued to be challenged by the leader of the FPÖ, Jörg Haider, who sought to mobilize the opposition on the emotive issue of immigration.

In May, Austrians chose a new president to succeed Kurt Waldheim. The election of the ÖVP candidate, Thomas Klestil, as president not only marked the end of a period of diplomatic isolation for Austria, but his victory (with 57 per cent of the vote) also served to restore the presidency to its former status as a source of independent moral-political leadership.

The worldwide recession affected Austria's economy less severely than those of most other countries in Europe. Growth slowed to 2 per cent, unemployment rose to 6 per cent and inflation rose to 3.8 per cent (3.3 per cent in 1991).

HISTORICAL LEGACY

Historically, antisemitic prejudice in Austria is a combination of beliefs and suspicions for the most part impervious to attempts to introduce sectarian "rigour". This lack of clear differentiation between racial and non-racial forms of antisemitism continued into the Austrian First Republic, whatever other real political differences might have existed among its proponents.

In the 1930s, the Christian Social Party's diffuse amalgamation of religious, economic, cultural and racial prejudices, together with its reluctance to introduce discriminatory measures against Jews, could not withstand Hitler's racial "antisemitism of reason" and the Nuremberg laws. Yet the stated objectives of these two politically disparate types of antisemitism were fundamentally similar. In 1938, the Austrian Republic was absorbed into the Third Reich, and Nazi racial policies were applied to the inhabitants of the new areas.

The Austrian Second Republic, founded in 1945, completely repudiated National Socialism, including its racial policies. Antisemitism was re-defined officially as the relic of a hated regime. The juridical independence of Austria brought forth a corresponding explanation of the new Austria's ideological *tabula rasa*. The official negative connotations associated with the term antisemitism did not eliminate the problem of anti-Jewish prejudice in Austria after the war. Nonetheless, any open public expression of hostility towards Jews was seen to transgress, at least implicitly, the recognized normative expectations of post-Auschwitz Austrian political debate, and as such was considered largely unrelated to the wider political culture.

The election of Kurt Waldheim to the presidency in 1986, following disclosures that he had lied about his wartime service in a German army group which was responsible for the massacres of civilians and the deportation of Jews and other civilians to Nazi death camps in Yugoslavia and Greece, represented a watershed in the post-war "Jewish question" in so far as it witnessed the willingness of a major political party to appeal to antisemitic prejudice—coded in an appropriate post-Auschwitz idiom—for political ends. A 1991 poll showed that, even after five years of Waldheim's presidency, whose unprecedented diplomatic isolation was by no means limited to the Israeli government's stance, a significant percentage of Austrians still held "the Jews" accountable for the Waldheim affair. The same poll revealed an alarming adherence to certain anti-Jewish stereotypes in contemporary Austria.

PARTIES, ORGANIZATIONS, MOVEMENTS

The only openly antisemitic parties and organizations in Austria are those on the extreme right. In 1992, there was greater public awareness of groups professing neo-Nazi aims, but it is unclear whether this was due to the extent or imminence of the danger of a Nazi revival or merely to heightened and visible police activity. The Austrian state police have estimated the hard core of neo-Nazis to be around 300, although those on the periphery may number as many as 20,000. It is difficult to keep track of the various organizations since many are transitory and undergo constant splits and fusions. The most visible of the groups are the Volkstreue Ausserparlamentarische Opposition (VAPO) and the Aktionsgemeinschaft für Politik (AFP), but many lesser-known paramilitary associations, such as Kameradschaft Langenlois, Wehrsportgruppe Trenck, Kameradschaft Prinz Eugen, also exist in the shadowy network of Nazi groups.

The main organizational link between the FPÖ and the extreme right seems to be the Political Academy of the AFP. Recent appearances of some leading individual members of the FPÖ at the AFP Academy suggest shared ideological affinities between the pan-German nationalist wing of the FPÖ and the politically marginalized extreme right. As many as thirty-seven FPÖ dignitaries are reported to have had recent contacts with this milieu of the extreme right.

MANIFESTATIONS

Asylum-seekers and other foreigners, rather than Jews, were the principal victims of most organized neo-Nazi activity, although this was a matter of political priorities not of ideological substance. Virtually without exception, pro-Nazi, anti-Jewish and anti-foreigner ideology was linked in the slogans and statements of those arrested for "hate crimes" in 1992. According to a 1992 report on far-right extremism by the ministry of the interior, forty-five people were detained or arrested for far-right and xenophobic activities, twenty-four of whom were kept in pre-trial detention. The Austrian police also carried out sixty-four searches of homes and offices in 1992, seizing over 700 extreme right-wing posters and approximately 28,800 additional pieces of propaganda material.

On 16 January 1992, a temporary residence for refugees in the town of Traunkirchen was fire-bombed, the first incident of its kind in Austria. Five members of the Kamaradschaft-Gmunden group, including Alexander Tischler, who had been convicted in 1989 for spraying "Saujud" (Jewish swine) on a wall, were indicted for the attack. All five were found guilty of destruction of property at the trial in November; three were also convicted of Nazi activities and received prison sentences. Three of the five defendants had previously been convicted for assault, and all were either members or fellow travellers of the VAPO.

The day after the attack on the refugee home, police arrested three members of the neo-Nazi group Wehrsportgruppe Trenck on suspicion of plotting to overthrow the government. In raids on members' homes, the police seized a large cache of weapons as well as antisemitic and anti-immigrant literature.

In mid-April, twelve youths severely vandalized an apartment house in Linz, daubing slogans against foreigners and Jews. By August, however, the Linz police had not made any arrests, and the officer in charge of juvenile crime, Herbert Weishar, speculated that the attack had been the work of "young ruffians".

During the final week of October, eighty gravestones in the Jewish cemetery in Eisenstadt were daubed with swastikas, SS insignia, and the slogans "Foreigners Go Home!" and "Heil Haider". A letter sending "Aryans' greetings to our idol Jörg

Haider" and signed by the previously unknown Aryan Socialist Resistance Movement, was found at the cemetery. A special task force to investigate the desecration set up by the Austrian interior minister found that it had been organized and executed with help from abroad. To date, the police have not found the culprits.

PUBLICATIONS

Various levels of antisemitic prejudices appear in print or public discourse, ranging from open denial of the Holocaust to more subtle anti-Jewish sentiments found in such mainstream papers as *Neue Kronenzeitung* (see **Denial of the Holocaust**).

Deutsche Wochenzeitung and *National-Zeitung*, both published in Germany but widely circulated in Austria, Gerd Honsik's *Halt!* (see **Legal Matters**) and, to a lesser extent, *Aula*, the magazine of the FPÖ union of university graduates, are vehicles for both crude and more sophisticated attempts to challenge either the fact or the extent of the Holocaust. Antisemitic literature of various kinds has also been seized in police raids and neo-Nazi literature produced abroad circulates underground.

Propaganda in this primitive form is effectively excluded from all Austrian national newspapers—including the *Neue Kronenzeitung*—both because of editorial self-image and because of the public taboo on the subject. However, this does not mean that sophisticated attempts to trivialize the Holocaust do not appear from time to time in conservative newspapers or that examples of the use of more general prejudiced language do not appear occasionally in even "liberal" Austrian newspapers when discussing issues relating to Jews.

MAINSTREAM POLITICS

In mid-March, at an informal meeting of the heads of the four caucuses represented in the municipal council in the town of Hollabrunn in Lower Austria, Manfred Schuster of the ÖVP said that he could not vote for Robert Jungk, the presidential candidate of the Greens, because Jungk was "one-half Jewish" and had citizenship in three countries. Schuster added, "Yes, I am an antisemite". The three opposition parties attempted to bring in an emergency motion in the municipal council, but it was voted down by the ÖVP majority. Though the national ÖVP disavowed him, Schuster's local party defended him, and his action had no personal political consequences.

In April, Jörg Haider was censured by a Kärnten court after he had accused Robert Jungk of writing a "pamphlet of praise" for the Third Reich while in exile in Switzerland in 1942 and had called him a "base Nazi-flatterer".

All political parties represented in parliament explicitly oppose discrimination against Jews, and all categorically condemn every act of antisemitic violence. At the national level at least, flagrant expressions of anti-Jewish prejudice like Schuster's also elicit rebukes. At the same time, the affinity between contemporary hostility to foreigners and anti-Jewish hostility on the one hand, and the rehabilitation and/or praise of National Socialism, on the other hand, suggests that tendencies indicating an increase in political intolerance towards foreigners or of linguistic indulgence towards ideas redolent of the ideology of the Third Reich, give cause for concern for the Jewish community as well.

In this respect, developments in 1992 were not particularly encouraging. Racialist notions of ethnic groups were accorded quasi-official legitimacy in the FPÖ with the appointment of Andreas Mölzer as head of its education department. Mölzer has long been linked with the pan-Germanist right and is on record as lamenting the "partial reunification" of Germany (that is, without Austria); he recently became FPÖ leader Jörg Haider's primary policy adviser. Addressing a meeting of party academics in Salzburg on the subject of "National Identity and the Multicultural Society—a Fateful Question for our Nation [*Volk*]" in February, Mölzer argued that the hitherto secure "biological potency of the Germans" was, in the face of the influx of more "dynamic immigrants", threatened with the danger of *Umvolkung* (a word with Nazi connotations meaning ethnic transformation). Though Mölzer's appointment was widely criticized inside Austria, even from within the ranks of the FPÖ itself, a commission established by Haider concluded that Mölzer's views were compatible with the

FPÖ programme.

Haider also proposed concrete political measures to hinder the feared *Umvolkung* of what the FPÖ calls the "German cultural community". Haider had already demonstrated the electoral potential of fomenting social fears and reinforcing ethnic prejudices, and throughout the summer and early autumn, he continued to set the pace, and largely the terms, of the debate on foreigners.

In late October, Haider issued an ultimatum to the government: if it would not agree to FPÖ policies on immigration, his party would launch a petition to force its hand. (Under Austrian law, any petition that attracts more than 100,000 signatures must be debated in parliament.) The SPÖ and the ÖVP condemned the planned petition as "irresponsible incitement", at the same time stressing the restrictiveness and efficiency of the government's own new asylum and "residency" laws, and appropriating elements of Haider's propaganda for themselves. President Klestil, for example, saw nothing wrong in principle with Haider's plan—he merely thought it "superfluous"—while Chancellor Franz Vranitzky instructed foreigners "that some aspects of their behaviour are not approved of by the Austrians". For his part, Vice-Chancellor Erhard Busek of the ÖVP demanded the deportation of all illegal aliens.

In the end, Haider and his party launched a twelve-point petition entitled "Austria First". Some of its provisions duplicated existing government policy, but others—such as establishing segregated classrooms for foreign school children under certain circumstances, restricting foreigners' access to housing, curbing the practice of "prematurely naturalizing foreigners", and targeting foreign social clubs specifically for a crackdown on illegal commercial transactions—attempted to ascribe ethnic significance to social problems of a very different provenance. The gathering of signatures was scheduled to begin in early 1993.

DENIAL OF THE HOLOCAUST

At the beginning of the year, VAPO leader Gottfried Küssel, in television programmes broadcast in Germany and the United States, denied that the Holocaust had taken place, advocated the restoration of the Nazi party to power and the creation of a Fourth Reich, described Hitler as a "great man" and said that removing Jews from Austria and Germany would be "no problem". Police reacted swiftly and Küssel was arrested on 7 January, at the start of a major crackdown on Nazi organizations.

In February, shortly after the adoption of legislation outlawing denial of the Holocaust (see **Legal Matters**), it became known that the president of the Austrian Chamber of Engineers, Walter Lüftl, had described the mass extermination of the Jews in concentration camps as "technically impossible". Lüftl, whose remarks had been published in Gerd Honsik's journal *Halt!*, resigned under pressure on 13 March.

In the wake of the verdict in Gerd Honsik's trial (see **Legal Matters**), Richard Nimmerrichter, probably Austria's most widely-read newspaper columnist, published an article, "Methods of a Mass Murder", in the *Neue Kronenzeitung* on 10 May. According to Nimmerrichter, "only relatively few of [all] Jewish victims were gassed"; the others, he claimed, had died of starvation, exposure, disease or other physical abuse. In any case, Nimmerrichter claimed, conditions in the Nazi camps were "desperately similar" to Russian prisoner-of-war camps. Yet anyone who dared to challenge the notion that six million Jews had been gassed, he argued, "refuting" a claim entirely of his own making, would be "brought to court on charges of 'denying the Holocaust'". "The third generation of surviving Jews", Nimmerrichter suggested, "needs to retain the saga of martyrdom of the so barbarically gassed victims of Hitler for the same reasons that Christians have continued to commemorate the crucifixion of Jesus Christ—certainly a more barbaric death—for the past 2,000 years".

In the view of the Austrian Jewish community, Nimmerrichter's article violated the anti-Nazi law which prohibits "crude trivialization[s] of the National Socialist genocide and other National Socialist crimes against humanity", and it filed a complaint with the public prosecutor. The preliminary investigation had not been completed by the end of the year, but the prospects for an indictment did not seem encouraging, since Nimmerrichter's trivialization was nothing if not sophisticated.

OPINION POLLS

An opinion poll published in the weekly magazine *Profil*, following the police crackdown on neo-Nazi groups in January, found that 78 per cent of those questioned agreed that right-wing extremism was a problem "which should be fought with every possible means" and two-thirds thought that neo-Nazis were a threat to Austrian democracy.

A survey conducted by the American Jewish Committee, which was released in October, found that 39 per cent of Austrians maintained that "Jews have caused much harm in the course of history"; 37 per cent believed "Jews exert too much influence on world events"; 28 per cent contended "Jews have too much influence" in Austrian society; 20 per cent wanted the "entry of Jews into influential positions controlled"; and 19 per cent said "it would be better for Austria not to have Jews in the country".

LEGAL MATTERS

Austrian legislation dating from 1947 prohibits open National Socialist activity and public advocacy of Nazi objectives. In February, the Austrian National Assembly voted unanimously to amend this legislation in two important respects: the minimum sentence for such convictions was reduced from five years to one, and the denial of the Holocaust, or even the "crude trivialization" of Nazi genocide, became specific criminal offences.

Proponents of the amendments argued that the milder minimum sentence would increase the number of successful prosecutions for neo-Nazi activities, since in the past, juries had been unwilling to convict defendants if it meant an automatic five-year sentence (there have been fourteen such convictions since 1980). The new amendment brought Austrian law into line with legislation in Germany, but it seems likely to open up Austrian courts to countless defence motions demanding "expert" investigations of irrelevant technical minutiae about the gas chambers.

In May, Gerd Honsik, publisher of the neo-Nazi monthly magazine *Halt!* and author of a book entitled "Acquittal for Hitler", was sentenced to eighteen months' imprisonment for fourteen breaches of the laws against neo-Nazi activities, including having claimed that the gas chambers were not used to kill Jews but to de-louse them. In response to earlier cases of this type, the court had asked Austrian historian Gerhard Jagschitz to produce an accurate account of how the Holocaust was organized. After five years of gathering documents and eye-witness reports, Jagschitz concluded that Jews and others had indeed been murdered in Auschwitz-Birkenau by means of poison gas. The five-day trial debated painful details of the scale and efficiency of the Holocaust.

The court ordered Honsik to serve two earlier suspended sentences for similar offences consecutively with this new penalty, subjecting him to up to three years' imprisonment. Honsik's conviction set a precedent of sorts in Austrian law: he was the first person to have been convicted for having denied the Holocaust.

On 10 October, Simon Wiesenthal held a press conference at which he accused Egon Sabukoschek, a prominent retired dentist living in Graz, of having been involved in the deaths of Yugoslav Jews in Belgrade on 27 July 1941. According to eye-witnesses, Sabukoschek had been the "Jewish commissar" in Belgrade and had been involved in the selection of Jewish hostages who were eventually killed in retaliation for an alleged act of sabotage ostensibly committed by a Jew. Sabukoschek's lawyers unsuccessfully attempted to have the case dismissed on health grounds, and Sabukoschek himself has denied the charges, claiming to be a victim of mistaken identity. One possible obstacle to bringing a prosecution against Sabukoschek in Austria is that the statute of limitations for capital offences in former Yugoslavia, the scene of the crime, has expired.

COUNTERING ANTISEMITISM

Whether the climate of general ethnic intolerance and openness to authoritarian measures, which under certain circumstances could rebound to the disadvantage of Austrian Jews, retains its salience into 1993, depends to a high degree on the ability and willingness of enough people to speak out and act against the renewed climate of intolerance. For the most part, Austria has been spared the violence which occurred in Rostock and Mölln in Germany, spawning a kind of complacency on the part of many politicians (beyond the somewhat ritualized partisan denunciations of the FPÖ and its leader) to the potential dangers such attitudes pose. However, Austria has also witnessed the emergence of significant independent voices who have spoken out against intolerance, hostility to foreigners and antisemitism.

During the presidential election campaign, Thomas Klestil announced: "Let us prove to the world that Austria is not a land of old or new Nazis, and not a land of antisemitism or xenophobia". The Social Democrat candidate Rudolf Streicher, stating that Austria had yet to cure itself of antisemitism, warned "this sickness is not only latent, but resurfaces on all possible occasions".

In June, a festival in Vienna against racism and antisemitism attracted around 30,000 participants. The highlight was the appearance of Elie Wiesel on the balcony of Vienna's Hofburg palace, where Hitler proclaimed the Anschluss. Wiesel offered to rescue the Heldenplatz, where Hitler addressed the Viennese masses following the annexation of Austria in the Anschluss, from its Nazi associations and reclaim it for humanity.

Opposition to the increasingly emotional debate on "foreigners", especially to a perceived waning patience with Bosnian refugees, crystallized into a concerted drive to defeat the FPÖ petition. Though the deaths in Mölln probably played some role in galvanizing this opposition, a more immediate impetus was the desecration of the Jewish cemetery in Eisenstadt in October, which seems to have been read by many as a symptom and a warning. Austrian Chancellor Franz Vranitzky led a vigil at the Eisenstadt cemetery, which was attended by leading personalities from the arts and the church, to warn against antisemitism and anti-foreigner sentiments.

In early November, a number of writers, artists and other intellectuals launched SOS-Mitmenschen (SOS: Fellow Human Beings), an initiative expressing solidarity with all victims of hatred and intolerance. The broadly-based movement has assumed a *de facto* role of counter-weight to Haider and his petition. Dignitaries from all walks of life, and across a wide political spectrum, have criticized the petition campaign and associated themselves with the aims of the movement. SOS-Mitmenschen called for a candle-lit march against racism and neo-Nazism to be held in Vienna in early January 1993.

Rudolf Scholten, Austria's minister of education and arts, introduced a number of measures to raise awareness of Austria's Nazi past and to combat attempts by neo-Nazi groups to gain influence in Austrian schools. He issued booklets countering the denial of the Holocaust and explaining the amendments to the legislation against Nazi activities and launched a national essay competition on antisemitism. In April, Scholten and several Austrian film-makers boycotted the Austrian Film Festival in Wels after the local mayor, Karl Bregartner, refused to change the names of streets and public buildings honouring Nazi collaborators.

ASSESSMENT

The outcome of both the FPÖ petition and the planned demonstration against racism will play a major role in determining the tenor of the debate on "foreigners" in Austria in the near future. In a wider sense, Austria's political culture will be tested to see whether, and to what extent, expressions of prejudice against Jews or other minorities, which are less immediately threatening than physical violence or open espousal of National Socialism, elicit a spontaneous revulsion on the part of the general public. There seems to be no reason to doubt the Austrian government's resolve to prosecute grievous instances of antisemitic behaviour or its willingness to combat conspicuous challenges to fundamental democratic values. Yet if the Waldheim affair showed anything, it was the ephemeral nature of moral conviction in the face of hard psephological facts.

Belgium

General population: 9,800,000
Jewish population: 35,000-40,000 (mainly
in Brussels and Antwerp)

GENERAL BACKGROUND

The inconclusive results of the November
1991 parliamentary elections led to a long
period of coalition-building. A coalition of
the Flemish Christian Social Party (CVP),
the Flemish Socialistische Partij (SP), the
French-speaking Parti Social Chrétien
(PSC) and the French-speaking Parti
Socialiste (PS) was finally formed in March,
with Jean-Luc Dehaene of the CVP
becoming prime minister.

The coalition partners reached agreement on a number of constitutional
reforms in September, including devolution
to the regions, reduction in the numbers of
representatives in the two parliamentary
chambers and direct elections for the
Flemish and Walloon parliaments. These
reforms, which will transform Belgium into
a federal state, were aimed at diffusing the
tension between the Flemings and the
Walloons over language, social and economic issues, which have affected the
country for most of the century.

In the economic sphere, GDP grew by
1.5 per cent in 1992, inflation fell to 2.2 per
cent (2.8 per cent in 1991) and unemployment rose to 8.4 per cent (8.1 per cent in
1991).

HISTORICAL LEGACY

There has been a Jewish community in the
lands which constitute modern Belgium
since the Middle Ages, principally in
Antwerp. During the Middle Ages,
following an accusation of desecration of
the host, Jews in Brussels and Leuven were
burnt at the stake. Portuguese Jews sought
refuge in Antwerp in the fifteenth century.
A large Jewish population fully established
itself during the eighteenth century,
composed of immigrants from Holland,
Galicia, Lithuania, Moldavia and the
Ukraine. Antwerp was the refugees'
principal place of settlement.

Antisemitism in Belgium was most
virulent in the 1930s. At that time, the
Jewish population was made up of immigrants and refugees fleeing the antisemitism
and dictatorships of Germany and Poland.
The far-right parliamentary parties REX
(French-speaking) and VNV (National
Flemish Union) attacked Jews in their
electoral propaganda. Of 25,257 Belgian
Jews deported, mostly to Auschwitz, only
1,205 survived.

In 1952, the first French work denying
the Holocaust (author: Maurice Bardèche)
was translated into Dutch by Karel Dillen,
current president of the anti-immigrant
Vlaams Blok (VB). Antisemitic articles
denouncing an alleged Jewish-Communist
conspiracy were published during the Cold
War years in the Flemish Catholic daily *De
Standaard*.

Since the war, a home-grown far right
which espouses antisemitic ideas has
developed. Some groups have had a violent
paramilitary character.

PARTIES, ORGANIZATIONS, MOVEMENTS

The far right in Belgium, in pursuit of
political respectability and electoral success,
has to some extent eschewed overt antisemitism in favour of an anti-immigrant
platform. However, many far-right groups
are known for their virulent racism and
antisemitism.

The most prominent far-right party is
Vlaams Blok (VB), founded in 1978 with a
nationalist, populist programme. Its origins
and financial support come from militant
former members of the SS-Vlanderen
leagues. Extreme in its anti-immigrant
stance, it directs its propaganda against the

"establishment" and also demands a total amnesty for Belgians who collaborated with the Nazis. Electoral support for the VB has been increasing since the 1984 general election. It is represented at all political levels—municipal, provincial, national and European (one MEP). Its historical heartland is Antwerp, where it has 10 representatives and 18 seats on the provincial council. In the 1991 general election, the VB won 10 per cent of the Flemish popular vote (25 per cent in Antwerp), gaining 12 seats in the 212-member Chamber of Deputies and six seats in the 184-member Senate. Opinion polls carried out in 1992 showed its support in Antwerp to be running at 25-40 per cent.

Founded in 1985, the Front National Belge (FN) draws support from a number of neo-Nazi antisemitic groups. Between 1989 and 1991, some leading members of the racist Parti des Forces Nouvelles (PFN) joined the FN. The election results of the FN in Brussels increased from 0.5 per cent in 1985 to 4.2 per cent (33,534 votes) in 1991. In Wallonia, the party won 1.7 per cent of the vote (31,000 votes) in the 1991 general election. It has had one municipal councillor since 1988, two regional councillors for Brussels since 1989, and two provincial councillors and one parliamentary representative since 1991.

In the general election of November 1991, the "party of popular opposition", AGIR (a Walloon splinter of the PFN, founded in 1989), won between 3.4 per cent and 4.7 per cent of the vote in Liège. AGIR has links with Vlaams Blok, the French Front National, the Deutsche Liga (a splinter group of the German Republikaner Party) and the Brussels-based neo-Nazi group L'Assaut. Several antisemitic activists are members of this party.

Other extreme nationalist groups include the Jonge Wacht, which is based in Antwerp and Ghent. It is made up of former members of the neo-Nazi militia Vlaamse Militanten Orde (VMO—active in the 1970s and 1980s until it was banned in 1984), and has links with the French-speaking group L'Assaut. With approximately thirty members between them, L'Assaut (founded in 1988) and Jonge Wacht are openly antisemitic. Their programme includes fighting for a "White Europe" and "against Zionists". Both

groups have contacts in Vlaams Blok, AGIR and Vrij Historisch Onderzoek (VHO, a Holocaust-denying "think-tank") and links with former Walloon and Flemish SS members, including the Holocaust-denier Léon Degrelle. L'Assaut and Jonge Wacht have infiltrated the skinhead culture and are in contact with the group Blood and Honour-Belgian Division. In addition, they have relations with neo-Nazi extremists in France (Parti Nationaliste Français et Européen and KKK-France), in Germany (ex-ANS, FAP), in England (BNP and Blood and Honour), with the Swiss-based Nouvel Ordre Européen (NOE) and in the United States (NSDAP-AO). Several members of L'Assaut were arrested for commando-style attacks on immigrants and anti-fascists in March and September of 1992.

The French Ku Klux Klan receives support from Belgium. In October 1992, posters for KKK-France appeared in Brussels. The American organization NSDAP-AO also has contacts in Belgium. In December 1992, Harald Neubauer MEP, the president of the Deutsche Liga and a former member of the NSDAP-AO, attended the congress of the VB youth organization. In August 1992, a concert by the British neo-Nazi skinhead band Screwdriver, due to take place at a Flemish nationalist fête, was banned by the local authorities.

The Parti Communautaire National-Européen (PCN), a small but very active group founded in 1984 in Charleroi, spreads propaganda against "American-Zionist imperialism" and "cosmopolitanism". The PCN is not a far-right organization, but it follows the revolutionary nationalist ideas of Belgian theoretician Jean Thiriart. The PCN, which is also active in Brussels, has links with the European Liberation Front, a pan-European, anti-American movement, the French far-right group Nouvelle Résistance and the Russian National Salvation Front, on whose behalf it has been issuing press releases.

PUBLICATIONS

In 1992, antisemitic sentiment was expressed in a number of publications. *L'Assaut*, a monthly with a print-run of 200, has been published since 1988 by the far-right paramilitary group of the same name. The September edition of *Le National*, the monthly magazine of the Front National which has been on sale in bookshops since 1989, featured antisemitic caricatures. *Altaïr*, a privately-circulated periodical devoted to the expression of pre-Vatican II doctrines, is distributed to about 250 people by Jean-Pierre Hamblenne, an editor of Holocaust-denying and neo-Nazi pamphlets with close links with the VB and the FN. It was founded in 1974 and is also distributed in France, Holland and Switzerland.

Other antisemitic publications include *Vox Vitae*, the monthly magazine of Pro Vita, the traditionalist Christian anti-abortion lobby, which has a circulation of 18,000; *Bec et Ongles*, published by Rex National and linked with L'Assaut; and *Blind Justice*, a skinhead "fanzine" (a short-lived, mimeographed underground magazine with a limited circulation) from Liège, which also has links with L'Assaut.

Le Bulletin Célinien is a monthly magazine devoted to the antisemitic writer Céline. Founded in 1979, it is privately circulated and available only through subscription. It has 317 subscribers and 80 per cent of its readership is French. French Holocaust-denier Robert Faurisson is a regular contributor, as are leaders of the intellectual "New Right" from both the francophone and Flemish communities. Other collaborators in this enterprise include pre-Vatican II arch-traditionalist and "revisionist" contributors to the Dismas publishing outlet (founded by former directors of Editions de Baucens—see **Denial of the Holocaust**), and Marc van Besien and Daniel Gilson, former activists in the Parti des Forces Nouvelles and the Association pour l'Indivisible Liberté d'Expression (AILE), which distributes the writings of Léon Degrelle and the principal Holocaust-deniers in Belgium. In May, van Besien jointly organized the third *Bulletin Célinien* conference in Brussels.

The French Ku Klux Klan journal *L'Empire invisible* (formerly *Croix de Feu*), has been printed in Belgium since 1991. Its editor, L. van den Bossche, a former member of the SS-Vlanderen, also directs VHO propaganda.

Several Belgian authors collaborate with foreign antisemitic publications, such as *Le Choc du mois, Militant, Nationalisme République, Lutte du Peuple* in France and *Orion* in Italy. French publications which carry antisemitic material such as *National-Hebdo, Minute-La France, Rivarol* and *Le Choc du mois* are on sale in most bookshops in Belgium.

The Antwerp-based Flemish weekly *'t Pallierterke* claims to be apolitical, but is in fact close to Vlaams Blok. Founded in 1945, it is opposed to the prosecution of Nazi collaborators and peddles a camouflaged antisemitic line in anti-Zionist articles.

In October 1992, the chief editor of *Télémoustique*, which is one of Belgium's most widely-read French-language weeklies with a circulation of 216,000, published an article which gave support to Holocaust denial propaganda. For several years, *Télémoustique* has published articles which seek to deny the existence of the gas chambers. However, the mainstream press is otherwise free of overt antisemitism.

RELIGION

Religious antisemitism is constantly present in the bodies which maintain links with the parties of the far right. Militant supporters of Monsignor Lefèbvre, a pre-Vatican II arch-traditionalist, are organized in Antwerp, Brussels, Ghent, Liège and Namur and maintain contact with the Front National Belge. They draw their propaganda from *The Protocols of the Elders of Zion* and the works of the French antisemite Henry Coston. Religious antisemitism can be found in the single-issue lobby groups such as Pro Vita, the Prieuré du Christ-Roi and the cultural association Racines et Civilisation (which has links with the Dismas bookshop). The bookshop Librairie Jacques in Brussels is close to these religious groupings and provides an outlet for anti-Jewish propaganda, including Coston's books and his monthly revue, *Lectures françaises*, the French far-right writer François Brigneau, and others.

Several neo-fascist groups have adopted paganism and reject the concept of "Judeo-Christian civilization". Certain splinter groups, including the skinheads, affect to follow "Odinism"—the worship of the Germanic god Woden. This religious current has a significant following among the members of Vlaams Blok and the revolutionary nationalist trend of the FN.

DENIAL OF THE HOLOCAUST

In 1979, Léon Degrelle (founder and former leader of REX and a former SS general living in exile in Spain since 1945) wrote an article denying the Holocaust which was widely circulated in Belgium. From 1976 to 1991, militant Holocaust "revisionism" flourished, with the creation in 1976 of Editions de Baucens, a publishing house based in Wallonia, the establishment of the Flemish monthly *HARO* in 1977, the Antwerp magazine *Taboe* in 1983, the Flemish group VHO in 1985, and the French-speaking associations AILE and CER (Centre d'Etudes Révisionnistes) in 1991. Holocaust-denying circles are made up of former members of the Belgian SS and neo-Nazi elements on the fringes of the VB and the racist PFN.

Nineteen-ninety-two saw a decline in Holocaust-denying activities. This is partly due to the fact that several Holocaust-deniers were tried and sentenced in France, Canada and elsewhere. The work of the Holocaust-deniers was confined to the obscure magazine *Achtergronddossier*, which is edited by Jos Rogiers, a former leader of Vlaams Blok.

On 24 October 1992, at a conference organized by an organization of free-thinkers, the leader of the Norman Association for the Awakening of the Citizen, a French Holocaust "revisionist" group, attempted to deliver a speech protesting at the planned Belgian legislation against denial of the Holocaust (see **Legal Matters**).

LEGAL MATTERS

Since 1981, anti-racist legislation has been in force but it has been rarely used. A draft law against denial of the Holocaust, proposed by the Socialists and supported by most other parties, has been put before parliament. The proposal has been strongly attacked by several historians on the grounds that it will give publicity to those who deny the Holocaust.

COUNTERING ANTISEMITISM

In so far as antisemitic activity in Belgium

is currently in decline, there was in 1992 little protest by either Jewish or non-Jewish organizations. Most Belgian anti-racist campaigns were directed at the racist parties following their success in the November 1991 elections. They hoped to increase public concern over the prospect of the Vlaams Blok taking control of Antwerp in the 1994 local elections. Several organizations, including the Anti-Fascism Front in Liège, Charta 91 in Flanders, Charte 91 in Brussels, Young People Against Racism and Blok Buster, were founded.

Jewish youth organizations have taken steps to ensure that their members are aware of the danger represented by the far right. The Belgian Jewish Students' Union plans to organize exhibitions and conferences on the Nazi origins of the far right in Belgium in 1993.

ASSESSMENT

The level of antisemitic manifestations appeared to have fallen in comparison with 1991. The far-right political parties, Vlaams Blok and the Front National Belge, directed their electoral propaganda solely against immigrants and the "establishment". However, the fact that the two parties were supported by openly antisemitic and neo-Nazi groups was a cause of concern.

Denmark

General population: 5,100,000
Jewish population: 8,000 (mainly in Copenhagen)

GENERAL BACKGROUND

The last decade has been stable politically but less stable economically. A liberal-conservative government (in various coalitions) has been in power during this period. Inflation remained low at 2.5 per cent but unemployment, at a rate of 11 per cent, was growing.

In June, Danish voters sent shock waves throughout the European Community when a slim majority rejected the

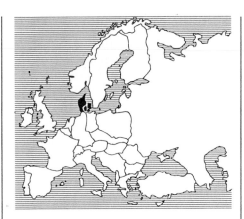

Maastricht Treaty on European Union in a referendum.

HISTORICAL LEGACY

Denmark's reputation for being free of serious anti-Jewish sentiment is only partly true. An anti-Jewish riot in 1819 was effectively stopped by the King, who five years earlier had granted civic equality to the Jewish community. At the turn of the century, modern political antisemitism prospered. Jewish financiers played an important economic role during this period and were subject to harsh accusations, especially during and after the First World War. Most Jewish financiers lost their money and influence in 1921-24 due to the post-war recession. Subsequently, antisemitism played only a peripheral role in public debate.

Like most other Western countries, Denmark permitted only a few German Jews to settle in Denmark from 1933 onwards. Following the German occupation of Denmark in 1940, hundreds of Jews who sought to use Denmark as a country of transit were rescued in a remarkable operation by sea to Sweden in October 1943. The year 1993, the fiftieth anniversary of the rescue, is to be celebrated in Denmark, the United States and Israel.

After the Second World War, there was considerable sympathy for the Jews and antisemitism virtually disappeared.

The so-called Blekingegade group (named after the Copenhagen street where the group was based) was established in the 1970s by left-wing sympathizers of the Palestinian cause. The group committed several crimes, including bank robberies and the murder of a policeman. All Jews were considered potential Zionists and, consequently, enemies. The group established a so-called "Z-file" of Danish Jews and non-Jews said to be sympathetic to Israel. The police exposed the group in 1989 and members received heavy prison sentences. The revelation was a shock to the Danish public and such virulent anti-Zionism must be considered exceptional.

PARTIES, ORGANIZATIONS, MOVEMENTS

The Danmarks Nationalsocialistiske Bevegelse (DNSB, Danish National Socialist Movement) is considered better organized than any of its counterparts in Scandinavia. Its leader, Poul Riis-Knudsen, also heads the World Union of National Socialists (WUNS), which has a broad international network. The DNSB has between 300-1,000 members in eight Danish towns. They march openly in Nazi uniform, reprint old antisemitic literature and submit anonymous articles denying the Holocaust to the mainstream press. Their actions have had little, if any, effect on public debate.

Den Danske Forening (Danish Society), which has 4,000 members, has in recent years achieved a fairly important position as a popular voice against immigrants (primarily Muslims) and refugees. Individual members of this group have made anti-Jewish statements. Many public meetings have been stopped by anti-racist demonstrations.

The Danish National Party has approximately 300 members and is led by a former member of the DNSB. It demands a total ban on Third World refugees and rejects legislation perceived to curtail Danish sovereignty.

The National Party, which has 500-700 members, rallies under the motto "Denmark for the Danes". It is believed to be behind violent attacks on immigrants.

While it does not espouse antisemitism, the Fremskridtspartiet (Progressive Party) has for years called for a ban on both immigration and refugees. The party currently holds twelve out of 179 parliamentary seats. Danish legislation on refugees has been strengthened considerably in recent years as a result of increasing antipathy towards foreigners, but this antipathy does not affect the Jewish community. Registered incidents against Jews have not risen but researchers have detected a tendency towards increasing day-to-day harassment.

MANIFESTATIONS

In March, Jewish communal leaders were sent a Danish version of a Holocaust-denying leaflet, *66 Questions and Answers on the Holocaust*, produced by the US-based Institute for Historical Review (see **United States** entry). Also in March, antisemitic posters, including a caricature of the Danish Chief Rabbi, appeared at a shopping centre near Copenhagen. In May, a DNSB sticker was attached to the door of a Jewish old people's home in Copenhagen. In October, DNSB leaflets were thrown through the gate of the Copenhagen Great Synagogue and delivered to the homes of well-known Jews.

ASSESSMENT

Increasing antisemitism did not appear to be a side-effect of the growing antipathy towards foreigners. However, the economic slow-down, growing unemployment, housing shortages, and Denmark's acceptance of a large number of refugees from former Yugoslavia (although they were generally received sympathetically), led to public concern that immigration may be becoming as "out-of-control" as it was perceived to be in Germany.

Finland

General population: 5,000,000
Jewish population: 1,000 (mainly in Helsinki and Turku)

GENERAL BACKGROUND

Since April 1991, Finland has been governed by a coalition government composed of the Centre Party, the Coalition Party, the Christian Union and the Swedish People's Party.

At 17 per cent in 1992, unemployment was exceptionally high (in 1990, it was 3 per cent). Public opinion was divided both in regard to Finland's application for EC

membership in March 1992 and over solutions to the economic situation. There was considerable optimism that the economy would soon improve.

HISTORICAL LEGACY

Jews were granted full civil rights in 1918. Antisemitism appeared among ultra-right circles in the 1920s-1930s mainly in written form, but there was no serious threat to Finnish Jewry. During the Second World War, despite Finland's status as a Nazi satellite state, no anti-Jewish legislation was enacted and Jews fought in the national army.

There have been minor threats to the Jewish community at times of crisis in the Middle East, although Finland's pro-Arab orientation since the Six-Day War in itself has not affected Jews domestically. Many Jews are involved in Finnish public life and their Jewishness has not been an issue.

PARTIES, ORGANIZATIONS, MOVEMENTS

There are no antisemitic organizations as such but two registered groups and additional small groupings have displayed an antisemitic attitude. Their influence is marginal.

The first, Nova Hierosolyma, was established in 1987 and claims to be a religious organization. Membership is estimated to be in single figures. Its chairman, Erkki Kivilohkare, wrote to newspapers in support of Iraq's invasion of Kuwait and attacking Israel and Jews. Following complaints by Jews and non-Jews, the newspapers ceased publishing his material.

The second organization, which has

called itself Kansallinen Radikaalipuolue (National Radical Party) since April 1991 (it was known as the Organization of the National Unity when it was founded in 1985), has imported ideas from other countries in Europe where intolerance towards foreigners and asylum-seekers (although in Finland there have been relatively few of the latter) has been a feature of the resurgence of the far right. The organization's leader, Tapio Linna, has gained little publicity and there are estimated to be only a handful of young people in the National Radical Party.

There are some anti-immigrant groups which support racial purity slogans. In Helsinki, a Skullhead-Skinhead movement was founded in July 1991. The editor of the group's magazine, Mark Parland, has written newspaper articles condemning Nazi crimes. However, he is in conflict with other members of the group, who favour Nazi ideology.

In the southern Finnish town of Lahti, a neo-Nazi group called Lahden Arjalainen Germaaniveljeskunta (Aryan German Brotherhood Community of Lahti) was found to be disseminating Nazi ideology in school neighbourhoods. The group's members are thought to be copying other such groups of young people in Germany. Finnish law prohibits the registration of such groups.

A few candidates from these groups were fielded in local elections in October 1992. In Helsinki, they received 500 votes and in Turku, 200. None was elected.

MANIFESTATIONS

The rise of xenophobia in Europe had echoes in Finland. During the year, there were several violent attacks on foreigners and the synagogue in Turku was stoned by three teenagers. Swastikas and other anti-Jewish graffiti were daubed. There were few such incidents and they were mainly carried out by young people seeking excitement spraying "fashionable" graffiti.

PUBLICATIONS

During 1991-92, the National Radical Party published five editions of its paper, *Uusi Suunta* (New Direction), with a print-run of about 500 each time. The paper carried antisemitic articles, apparently translated

from material published by neo-Nazi sources in Central Europe.

LEGAL MATTERS

The Finnish Criminal Code prohibits incitement to ethnic hatred—publication of *The Protocols of the Elders of Zion* was banned by a court decision in 1977. There are no specific laws regarding antisemitism. This may be explained by the fact that there is a small Jewish community and there has never been serious antisemitism in Finland.

Following a request by the Finnish Jewish community, the Ministry of Justice decided in 1992 to prosecute those responsible for *Uusi Suunta* and to confiscate its print blocks. The Helsinki City Court was due to give its verdict in 1993.

ASSESSMENT

Concern at the incidence of racist violence in Europe was expressed in the Finnish media. However, the racist and xenophobic groups in Finland are little known and have marginal influence. Economic crisis, rising unemployment, the issue of asylum-seekers—phenomena new to Finland—have stirred up intolerance towards immigrants and minorities, especially during the past two years.

France

General population: 57,000,000
Jewish population: 500,000-700,000
(over half in Paris area)

GENERAL BACKGROUND

Voters went to the polls three times in 1992. The regional and cantonal elections in March resulted in gains for the centre-right alliance of the Gaullist Rassemblement pour la République (RPR) and the Union pour la Démocratie Française (UDF), but they also reflected growing support for the ecology parties (13.9 per cent) and showed the stability of the Front National (FN) vote (12-14 per cent in national terms). A small majority voted in favour of the Maastricht Treaty on European Union in

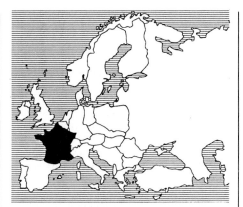

the September referendum. The result was interpreted as a manifestation of French distrust of closer European unity, a new phenomenon in a country that had previously been strongly pro-European.

All three votes showed the weakness of the Socialist government in a climate created by rising unemployment (10.3 per cent) and various political scandals. Inflation fell to 2.4 per cent from 3.1 per cent in 1991. From September, the franc came under intense pressure in a major European currency crisis, but retained its strength with support from the German Bundesbank. In foreign affairs, French involvement in Cambodia, Somalia and former Yugoslavia, the rise of Muslim fundamentalism in Algeria and increasing xenophobia in Germany, all contributed to a general feeling of anxiety about the future.

HISTORICAL LEGACY

The first Jews settled in what is now France during Roman times. Following the first crusades, their situation deteriorated: religious antisemitism and the royal desire to appropriate the wealth of the Jews led to a series of expulsions. With the integration of new lands into the realm, France "acquired" Jews together with its new territories (for example, Alsace and Lorraine). In the sixteenth century, Marranos (covert Jews) from Spain and Portugal found shelter in France.

While some called for the emancipation of the Jews, a trend within the eighteenth-century Enlightenment initiated a non-Christian tradition of antisemitism, making the Jews the symbol of the obscurantism and fanaticism of religion and equating them with financial power.

At the time of the French Revolution, the Jewish minority was highly stratified: the small group of former Marranos enjoyed a high level of culture and wealth and, being well integrated, increasingly resented the special status and limitations imposed on them. However, most of French Jewry, in the eastern part of the country, were very poor and subject to a virulent popular antisemitism. In 1791-2, French Jews were emancipated.

The nineteenth century brought new trends in antisemitism—the identification of the Jews with the harshness of industrial society and xenophobia towards Jews coming from abroad (mainly Germany and, at the end of the century, the Russian Empire), as well as distrust of assimilated Jews. A new conservative nationalism developed, drawing on the ideas of race-science and "aryan" mythology. In 1886, Drumont published *La France juive*, the first antisemitic "bestseller" in France, which raised the myth of the Jew to the status of an ideology.

The Dreyfus case in 1894 took place at a time of intense antisemitic agitation and seriously affected the position of assimilated French Jews. But it also led to the mobilization of forces committed to human rights, creating a polarization of opinion according to a pattern that was valid at least until the Second World War and perhaps 1967. For several decades, antisemitism was a characteristic of the ultra-conservative right.

The 1930s saw a wave of antisemitism nourished by the mass immigration of Jews from the East at a time of economic crisis, by the fears aroused by the rise of a Socialist government (led by a Jew) in 1936, and by Nazi propaganda.

The wartime Vichy government introduced anti-Jewish legislation and helped its administration to identify and arrest the Jews. Some 74,000 Jews who were deported from France died in the concentration camps.

After the war, the far right was reduced to tiny groups. In 1954, however, a wave of antisemitism marked the appointment of Pierre Mendès-France as prime minister. A new phase in antisemitism began in 1967: some felt that de Gaulle's remark in November 1967—that the Jews were "an élite people, sure of itself and domineering"—opened the gates to a new antisemitism. What is indisputable is that Israel's victory in the Six-Day War and the subsequent anti-Zionist propaganda created a feeling of unease in the 1970s and 1980s.

In the past decade, attention has been focused on two main problems: the rise of the Front National and the rise and growth of so-called "revisionism"—the denial of the facts of the Holocaust.

PARTIES, ORGANIZATIONS, MOVEMENTS

Both the number of antisemitic groupings and their membership seem to have remained stable during 1992. Their influence (if the Front National is excluded) on public opinion may be considered negligible. There are no exact figures for the membership of these groups, but in most cases, it does not exceed several hundred. Among these groups are:

The Maurrassian royalists of the Restauration Nationale, founded in 1955, equate Jews, Protestants and freemasons with the Republic, which they consider to be "anti-French".

The ultra-right Parti Nationaliste Français et Européen (PNFE), founded in 1985, had in 1989 some 400 members distributed over a third of French territory. Several activists were involved in bomb attacks in 1988 in south-eastern France against foreign workers. One of these attacks, "signed" by a non-existent "Groupe Massada", was aimed at creating tension between Jews and immigrants.

The neo-Nazi Faisceaux Nationalistes Européens (FNE) was founded in 1980. The group openly proclaims its neo-Nazi orientation and organizes parties, which attract approximately thirty participants, to commemorate Hitler's birthday.

Troisième Voie (TV), founded in 1985, was formerly the main group in the revolutionary nationalist trend of the French far right. A split in 1991 led to the formation of Nouvelle Résistance, while its leader, Jean-Gilles Malliarakis, supported the Front National. In 1992, Nouvelle Résistance attempted to infiltrate Ecolo J, the youth movement of the French Greens, and seems to have forged links with neo-fascist ecologists in Italy. It also has contacts with several revolutionary nationalist organizations elsewhere in

Europe, including the National Salvation Front in Russia.

The Groupe Union Défense (GUD) was founded in 1968 and is based in Assas Paris Faculty of Law. Its current activities appear to be restricted to propaganda.

The Parti Nationaliste Français (PNF) was founded in 1984 by members of the neo-Nazi trend of the Front National, but now seems to be in decline.

L'Oeuvre Française, founded in 1968 by the sons of a French pro-Nazi activist executed in 1946, is mainly based in the Paris area.

Nationalisme et République, founded by the successors of the late number two of the Front National, Jean-Pierre Stirbois, feels the present direction of the Front National is insufficiently doctrinal.

The Alliance Populaire was founded in April 1992 by dissidents from the Front National and the Comités d'Action Républicaine (CAR—which is close to the FN) and by leaders of the PFN. They claim to have 3,000 sympathizers and thirty-eight local federations and have denounced FN leader Le Pen's presidental ambitions as "utopian".

Among the Catholic fundamentalist movements, Chrétienté-Solidarité was founded in 1982 and its leader, Romain Marie ("Bernard Antony"), plays a prominent role in the Front National. It is very active in building international links with other Catholic-nationalist organizations.

La Contre-Réforme Catholique is a religious-political, fiercely anti-Jewish movement led by an abbot named Georges de Nantes. Its models are Franco, Salazar and Pétain, although the movement seeks an absolutist hereditary monarchy.

The skinheads started to develop in France in 1987. After a period of sharp increase in acts of violence (17 in 1987, 48 in 1988, 52 in 1989, 47 in 1990), the clampdown on their activities (70 arrests in 1987, 175 in 1988, 154 in 1989) led to a decrease in violence (24 acts of violence in 1991, 18 in 1992). The police estimated the number of skinheads in France to be approximately 1,000 by the end of 1992. The skinheads have a record publishing house, Rebelles Européens, founded at the end of 1986 in Brest, which specializes in the production of "skin" music groups such as Légion 88, Bunker 84 and Skin-Korp. It issued a compilation of Légion 88's music, *Thulé*, dedicated to Rudolf Hess.

The Front National may be added to the above list of antisemitic groupings, although antisemitism is not an openly declared part of the party's anti-immigrant platform. The FN's membership is estimated to be 50-60,000 but its influence goes far beyond this, as its results in elections have shown. It would be a mistake to assume that voters opt for the FN either because they believe it is antisemitic, or because they are antisemites. However, without being antisemites themselves, these voters do not seem to object to the latent antisemitism of the party and its leader, Jean-Marie Le Pen. Moreover, the FN sets the far-right agenda and groupings define their platforms in terms of their agreement or disagreement with FN policies.

In the regional elections, the FN undoubtedly benefited from the fact that the ballot employed a single-round proportional representation system. It gained 13.9 per cent of the votes (against 9.7 per cent in 1988), although Le Pen had announced that he was expecting some 20 per cent. The number of FN regional councillors rose from 137 in 1988 to 239 (out of a total 1,829). The FN came second in two regions: in Provence-Alpes-Côte d'Azur, it received 23.3 per cent and 34 seats out of a total of 123, and in the Ile-de-France, it won 37 out of 209 seats. The FN was able to embarrass the Socialist government when government ministers Jean-Pierre Soisson and Jean-Marie Rausch were elected regional presidents with the support of FN regional councillors—Soisson had to resign from the government, while Rausch renounced the presidency of the Lorraine regional council in order to remain in his government post.

Soon after the regional elections, the collaborationist activities of Roland Goguillot (also known as Gaucher), an FN member of the Franche-Comté regional council, were exposed by the weekly *Le Canard Enchaîné*. In consequence, his fellow FN members in the regional council left the party.

The cantonal elections, which used a two-round, "first-past-the-post" ballot, were less favourable to the FN. With 12.18 per cent of the vote in the first round, and

6.35 per cent in the second, the FN suffered from the refusal of all parties to form an alliance with it and only managed to get three of its members onto the general councils (out of a total 2,025 councillors).

It is impossible to assess support for the FN in the September referendum, since the Communists, some of the Greens and members of all the mainstream parties campaigned with it against the Maastricht Treaty.

MANIFESTATIONS

According to the ministry of the interior, 1992 saw a decrease in the overall number of violent antisemitic incidents (23 against 40 in 1991). Nevertheless, there was a sharp increase in such incidents towards the end of the year: 5 violent actions were recorded between January and September, but there were 8 in September, and 10 between October and the end of December. The incidence of threats (including Holocaust "revisionist" publications) was fairly similar: 80 in 1992 (184 in 1991, 372 in 1990), with a sharp rise in the autumn-winter period. Jewish community sources confirmed these figures: they reported 98 "hostile acts" in the Paris area in 1992 (152 in 1991), almost half of which (46) occurred between September and the end of the year. Violent incidents tended to be concentrated in three main geographical areas: the Ile-de-France, Rhône-Alpes (Lyons area) and Provence-Alpes-Côte d'Azur (Marseille and Nice area).

There was a sharp increase in the number of desecrations of Jewish cemeteries: 2 occurred in March and April, but there were 6 between 30 August and the end of December, including Herrlisheim in Alsace, where 193 graves were profaned, and at 2 cemeteries in Cronenbourg, near Strasbourg, which were vandalized within days of each other.

There was also a notable increase in the number and gravity of attacks against synagogues in the second half of the year. Synagogue walls were daubed in Nogent-sur-Marne on 19 August; in the Paris rue Sainte-Isaure synagogue on 19 September; and in the Paris rue Vergniaud synagogue on 30 September. Vandals attacked the synagogue of La Mainau in Strasbourg on 30 November, and the Bischheim synagogue in Alsace on 31 December. The synagogue in Saint-Avold was set on fire on 1 September. When arrested, the 21-year-old perpetrator declared his motivation had been "hatred of capitalists and Jews". Molotov cocktails were thrown at the Villepinte synagogue in Paris on 31 December.

PUBLICATIONS

In their 1992 book, *Les Droites nationales et radicales en France* (The Nationalist and Radical Right in France), Jean-Yves Camus and Olivier Monzat counted 87 periodicals expressing FN views, 72 Catholic fundamentalists, 5 Holocaust-deniers, 18 of the neo-Nazi trend, 17 Nouvelle Droite (New Right), 7 defending the memory of Pétain, 23 of the royalists, 14 of the nationalist-revolutionaries, and 5 of the skinheads.

Most of these publications have only a local circulation, many of them are not published regularly, and antisemitism is not necessarily their main purpose. Circulation figures are difficult to evaluate as most publications are distributed through individual subscriptions and in specialized bookshops. The figures listed below are only a very rough estimate.

All the far-right groupings mentioned have their own publications. The following publications included examples of antisemitic and virulently anti-Zionist utterances:

During 1992, the weekly *L'Action Française* replaced *Aspects de la France* as the press organ of the Maurrassian royalists of the Restauration Nationale. Its circulation is estimated to be 2,000-3,000. In December, former journalists of *Aspects de la France* announced the creation of a new royalist bi-monthly, *Vu de France*. The local branches of PNFE publish about ten bulletins, with circulations ranging between tens and a few hundreds. *Notre Europe Combattante*, the bulletin of the FNE, has an estimated circulation of a few hundred. The PNF produces a monthly publication, *Militant*. *Le Soleil* is the organ of l'Oeuvre Française. The Alliance populaire publishes *Espace Nouveau*, which has an estimated circulation of 1,000-2,000. Troisième Voie publishes the monthly *Révolution Européenne*, while Nouvelle Résistance publishes the monthly *Lutte du Peuple* and the bi-monthly *Première Ligne*, which denounce "US-Zionist imperialism". All of

these have estimated circulations of a few hundred. *La Contre-Réforme Catholique*, with a circulation of 3,000 copies, is the monthly publication of the Catholic antisemitic movement of the same name. Skinhead publications include *Le Côté Obscur*, which is published by Serge Ayoub (also known as "Batskin").

Antisemitic allusions appear in the press close to the FN, such as the fundamentalist Catholic daily *Présent*, which claimed a circulation of 15,000 in 1992, the weeklies *National Hebdo* and *Minute-La France*, and the monthly *Le Choc du Mois*. All of these publications have much higher circulations than those of the other groups and can easily be found at newsstands.

According to the weekly *Le Canard Enchaîné* on 8 April, a number of Minitel connections (computer terminals linked to the telephone) were used for spreading antisemitic propaganda (for example, accusing the Jews of spreading AIDS) or as letter boxes for such neo-Nazi organizations as the White Aryan Resistance.

MAINSTREAM POLITICS

There was no overt antisemitism in mainstream political life in France in 1992 but innuendoes were to be found in the propaganda of the Front National. An address by Jean-Marie Le Pen in La Trinité sur Mer on 23 August denounced the "obscure powers and the lobbies against the nation" involved in the "Maastricht plot", "cosmopolitanism and its religion of human rights" and "the globalist [*mondialiste*] and internationalist plot whose promoters do not hide their hatred of the nation and national values". Le Pen continued, "It is anyway strange that those who claim secure and guaranteed borders for Israel are also those who want to destroy the borders of France."

When, in November, the far-right weekly *Minute-La France* published an antisemitic cartoon of former Prime Minister Laurent Fabius on its front page, Le Pen commented, "It is difficult to make Fabius look like a Viking!".

DENIAL OF THE HOLOCAUST

Publication of the quarterly *Revue d'Histoire Révisionniste* under the editorship of Henri Roques was interrupted after its sixth issue in the spring of

1992, following a ban, imposed by the ministry of the interior, on publicizing the journal, exhibiting it and selling it to minors.

On 25 December, an association was established calling for a "national amnesty for the prisoners and victims of the Gayssot law" (the July 1990 law prohibiting the denial of the Holocaust). There was some surprise and dismay at this development since the stated aims of the association—"opening a contradictory debate on the question of the gas chambers" and "campaigning for the indemnification and moral rehabilitation of the victims condemned for not believing in the gas chambers"—appeared to be illegal. Two of the promoters of the association, Vincent Reynouard and Rémy Pontier, had themselves been condemned for denial of the Holocaust and were active in a local organization, the "Norman Association for the Awakening of the Citizen", which published a magazine denying the Holocaust, *Nouvelle Vision*.

EFFECTS OF ANTI-ZIONISM

Indications of increasing fundamentalism and anti-Zionism among first- and second-generation Muslim immigrants, such as the creation, revealed by the weekly *Le Point* in December, of a Hamas cell in Nancy under the cover of an association aiming at "ensuring a spiritual training for young Muslims", and the publication of a fiercely anti-Zionist essay, *Islam, the Soul of Mankind*, led to fears of a possible anti-Jewish radicalization in the North African Muslim community. An association of North African youngsters in the Paris suburb of Sartrouville which distributed cassettes on "the massacres in Palestine" was also thought to have daubed anti-Jewish slogans. Second-generation North African immigrants were apparently responsible for stones thrown at a number of synagogues in 1992.

On 30 October, *L'Hebdo Libéré*, an Algerian weekly distributed in France (with a total estimated circulation, in Algeria and abroad, of 120,000) was banned in France on the grounds of "praising Nazism and inciting to racial hatred" after it published, in the summer, Hitler's political will as part of a series of important political texts.

Israel's expulsion of 415 Islamic fundamentalist activists to Lebanon at the end of the year led the Communist daily, *L'Humanité*, to compare them to "the Polish Jews who were expelled from Germany by Hitler". A demonstration with the slogan "Israel: fascist" was organized in Paris by the Inter-University Committee for Co-operation with the Palestinian Universities, but attracted only 500 participants. One of the two cemeteries desecrated in Cronenbourg in December was defaced with anti-Israeli slogans protesting Israel's expulsion of the Hamas activists.

OPINION POLLS

The annual opinion poll on intolerance and racism conducted by the Commission Consultative on Human Rights of the office of the prime minister, which includes questions on the Jews, showed a degree of continuity. Nineteen per cent of those questioned expressed antipathy to the Jews (16 per cent in 1991, 18 per cent in February and October 1990); 22 per cent "rather" or "totally" agreed that there were too many Jews in France (21 per cent in 1991, 24 per cent in February and October 1990).

LEGAL MATTERS

There were a number of trials under the 1972 law prohibiting racial libel and incitement to racial or religious hatred or discrimination. One involved Alain Guionnet, whose publication *Révision* combined denial of the Holocaust with virulent antisemitism. Guionnet was sentenced to two months' imprisonment for having publicly shouted "Death to the Jews" and having made the Nazi salute. Guionnet appealed against the sentence to the Court of Cassation, the French court which rules on legal technicalities. An Alsatian FN member was given a suspended sentence and deprived of his civil rights for racist and antisemitic articles in *L'Alsacien-Der Elsasser*. The sentence was appealed. Jean-Dominique Larrieu, manager of the Ogmios bookshop and publishing house, which specialize in the distribution of Holocaust denial and antisemitic literature, was fined for having given illegal publicity to the *Revue d'Histoire Révisionniste* and the *Annales d'Histoire Révisionniste*. Roland Goguillot (also known as Gaucher) and Emmanuel Allot (also known as François Brigneau) were cleared of racial libel for an article in *National Hebdo* on 21 February 1991, which warned of "the Jewish International", but were fined for incitement to racial discrimination. They have appealed against the ruling. The Court of Cassation overruled the 1991 acquittal of Le Pen for his "Durafour-crématoire" pun, which linked a government minister with the extermination camps crematoria.

There were appeals against a number of convictions under the 1990 law prohibiting denial of the Holocaust. The following were confirmed in 1992: French Holocaust-denier Robert Faurisson was fined for his 1990 interview in the far-right monthly *Le Choc du Mois*, in which he described "the myth of the gas chambers" as "rascally"; Guionnet's two prison sentences for various papers in *Révision* (in one of the cases, Guionnet lodged an appeal with the Court of Cassation); and Vincent Reynouard and Rémy Pontier's suspended sentences for the distribution of a tract denying the Holocaust (they have appealed to the Court of Cassation).

Several sentences passed in 1992 were under appeal: Alain Guionnet's three-month prison sentence for a paper in *Révision*; Philippe Costa and Laurent Gentel's fine for the distribution of "revisionist" tracts in Nancy; Fabrice Robert and Pierre Gauzère's fine and deprivation of civil rights for having distributed "revisionist" material in Nice. Pierre Guillaume and Michel Gaudilhon were fined for distributing "revisionist" tracts in Caen, but did not appeal.

FN leader Jean-Marie Le Pen was also involved in a number of other trials in 1992. A local newspaper, which called Le Pen "Le Pen-Pétain" and described his supporters as "small Nazis, nostalgic for the gas chambers, defenders of the white race, hunters of Jews and Arabs", was cleared of libel by the Chambéry Court of Appeal but was condemned for "public insults". A Paris court ruled that the depiction of Le Pen in a cartoon as an SS officer or an Italian fascist was not defamatory in the framework of "political polemics" but condemned other cartoons as obscene because "they offend the human being in his dignity". Former Prime Minister Michel Rocard was found guilty of libel for having alleged on television that Le Pen had cheated in student elections in 1952.

The former minister of the interior, Charles Pasqua, raised the question of whether the implementation of existing measures prohibiting antisemitic phenomena was adequate and cited several local publications which had infringed the anti-racist legislation without being sued. A visit by a bailiff to two specialist bookshops in Paris revealed that publications, which should not have been distributed under the existing laws, were being sold freely.

COUNTERING ANTISEMITISM

The struggle against antisemitism was implicit but not central in public statements made by religious and political leaders. The same was true of statements by some members of the Jewish community. For example, before the local elections, Jean Kahn, the President of the Representative Council of French Jewish Organizations (CRIF), appealed to "all the republican parties not to look for the support of an irresponsible and demagogic far right".

There were several demonstrations against racism and the FN, including a rally on 9 November in Paris by all the major anti-racist organizations on the anniversary of Kristallnacht, which was attended by 1,000 participants. In the cultural arena, a Paris theatre staged four plays on the subject of racism over two days in June, which were followed by a debate on "theatre as a tool for combatting the far right". On an academic level, the French Jean Jaurès Foundation and the German Friedrich Ebert Foundation held a symposium on ways to stop the growth of racism. In the spring, students, teaching trades unions and anti-racist groups organized a week of education against racism in some 3,000 schools during which 50,000 booklets and posters were distributed.

Religious leaders were involved in initiatives against racism and the Front National. On 6 September, the Bishop of Reims cancelled all services in the city's cathedral after the FN decided to hold a mass meeting against the Maastricht Treaty in front of it. On 28 September, the Council of Christian Churches in France launched an ecumenical campaign against racism.

The Movement for the Manifesto Against the Front National launched an "appeal of a thousand citizens" against Le Pen's party and drew up a list of arguments to counter the Front National. Twenty political leaders from parties across the mainstream political spectrum made an appeal against racism, stating that "the rebirth of xenophobia cannot and should not be ignored any longer". A European Day of Reflection and Action Against the Far Right, called by fifty-one organizations, took place on 13 December in Nancy with 2,000 participants attending.

SPECIAL FACTORS

The issue of the French Republic's official attitude towards the wartime Vichy regime remained a constant factor, enhanced in 1992 by the fiftieth anniversary of the mass arrests of Jews in Paris on 16-17 July 1942. The debate acquired a new resonance in June, when a committee of 200 intellectuals demanded that "the President of the Republic and head of state recognize and officially proclaim that the French state of Vichy was responsible for persecutions and crimes against the Jews of France". The French Republic has never accepted responsibility for the Vichy government's crimes against the Jews. President Mitterrand had previously declared that "the Vichy regime was not the Republic" and that the Republic should not be held accountable for its actions. The committee then addressed its appeal to parliament, asking deputies to endeavour to make 16 July "a national day of commemoration for the persecutions and the crimes perpetrated against the Jews by the French state of Vichy".

The issue arose again in November when President Mitterrand laid flowers on the tomb of Marshal Pétain, head of the Vichy regime, in tribute to his role as a soldier in the First World War, despite calls for him to refrain from such a gesture. As a consequence, appeals were made for the "tradition" to be stopped, and for a "symbolic gesture" to be made, marking the recognition of Vichy's responsibility for the fate of the Jews. On 13 November, Mitterrand disclosed that he was thinking of a way to "manage differently the contradiction between the glory of Verdun

and the shame of 1942".

New preliminary investigations were lodged against Maurice Papon, the former secretary-general of the Bordeaux district prefecture, and René Bousquet, former secretary-general of the Vichy police, for their involvement in the deportation of Jews from Bordeaux between 18 April 1942 and 13 May 1944.

The case of Paul Touvier, head of the Lyons Milice (the pro-Nazi paramilitary militia) during the war and a close collaborator of the SS lieutenant Klaus Barbie, continued during 1992. The commission of seven historians, which had been appointed by Cardinal Decourtray to investigate relations between Touvier and the church between 1944 and 1989, presented its report in April. The report, which confirmed that certain French church dignitaries had given Touvier help, was added as evidence to Touvier's file in court.

In April, a Paris high court decided that because of lack of proof Touvier had no case to answer on five charges of crimes against humanity. A sixth charge was dropped on the grounds that the offence could not be classified as a crime against humanity because the Vichy state which Touvier served was not committed to ideological racial genocide. The decision met with widespread protest—President Mitterrand declared that he was "surprised, to say the least". The case was taken to the Court of Cassation, which ruled in December that Touvier could be tried for crimes against humanity for a massacre of Jewish hostages and referred the case for trial in a lower court.

The controversy over the *Fichier des Juifs*, a list of Jews in the Paris area drawn up during the Nazi occupation which was "discovered" in 1991 in the archive of the ministry of veterans, arose again at the end of the year when a commission of historians declared that it was not the census ordered by the Germans during the Occupation, a conclusion disputed by French lawyer Serge Klarsfeld.

ASSESSMENT

A number of general trends, which have been present in France for several years, were confirmed in 1992. As demonstrated by opinion polls, there appears to be a fair degree of social integration and acceptance of the Jews which co-exist with a persistent feeling of psychological unease towards the Jews.

There is an absence of antisemitism in mainstream political and cultural life, yet at the same time, there is a degree of tolerance of the latent antisemitism of the Front National. The switch to immigrants as the main target for intolerance, although not directly affecting the Jews, may lead to the development of a climate unfavourable to all minorities.

Concern remains over the potential development of two issues in the future. First, the degree of penetration of anti-Jewish feelings among the Muslim immigrant population, particularly younger members. Second, following CRIF President Jean Kahn's questioning of a possible "contamination" from Germany after the desecration of the Jewish cemetery in Herrlisheim, the degree of permeability of France to more general movements of intolerance in other European countries.

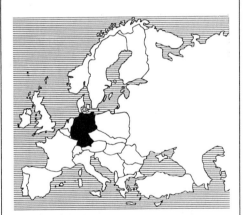

Germany

· General population: 77,600,000
Jewish population: 54,000-64,000
(including approximately 20,000-24,000
immigrants from the former Soviet Union)

GENERAL BACKGROUND

The hope of an economic upswing in the eastern German states was not fulfilled in 1992. Indeed, the decrease in industrial production and the cut-back of jobs

continued and, from the middle of 1992, the beginnings of an economic recession became apparent throughout the Republic. This situation caused conflict over the distribution of the financial burden, cuts in public spending, especially in the social services; and tax increases. *Politik-verdrossenheit*—public disillusionment over the policies of the government and the opposition—grew to mammoth proportions.

In domestic politics, there was much debate about changing the constitutional right of asylum. In 1992, the number of applications for asylum (438,000) reached a new peak. The wave of violence against asylum-seekers increased in strength in 1992 and reached a high-point after the excesses in Rostock-Lichtenhagen in August 1992.

After a long period of hesitation, a public counter-reaction was mobilized in the autumn, and, following a mass demonstration in Berlin on 8 November, candle-lit chains and demonstrations against violence and hostility towards foreigners took place in several cities. On the one hand, the Federal Republic was in the midst of its greatest internal political crisis, sharpened by a militant wave of extreme right-wing violence; on the other, a broad liberal consensus embracing all social groups, churches, trades unions, industries, arts and sciences, developed in opposition.

HISTORICAL LEGACY

The conservative élites of the German Kaiserreich were heavily tinged with antisemitism and regarded the Weimar Republic with great reservations. These élites did not recognize their own responsibility for Germany's defeat in the First World War, but explained it as an act of "Jewish betrayal". For this reason, and the November Revolution of 1918, which was seen as inspired and directed by Jews, conservative forces denounced and opposed the Weimar Republic as a "Jewish republic" from its inception in 1919.

To a considerable extent, influential elements in the political and economic élites offered no resistance to the storm of *völkisch*, militaristic and anti-democratic movements which found a favourable environment in Germany's domestic problems and the world economic crisis of the 1920s and 1930s. In 1933, Hitler's National Socialist movement was seen to offer a solution to Germany's economic and political crisis. Its radical antisemitic programme was not taken seriously by some, while others sympathized with a fundamental "solution of the Jewish question".

Immediately after seizing power, the National Socialist government began to put its antisemitic programme into effect. German Jews were discriminated against in stages: with their exclusion from public service and the boycott of Jewish businesses, their economic existence was limited; with the 1935 Nuremburg Laws, they lost their civil rights. The increasingly restrictive legislation drove them into social isolation or emigration. With the pogrom of November 1938 (Kristallnacht), the public use of force was added to legislative discrimination.

The first murders of Polish Jews occurred after the German occupation of Poland. From February 1940, Jews were deported from Reich territory to occupied Poland where the Jewish population was ghettoized. Before the start of the Russian campaign, *Einsatzgruppen* were formed which, from the summer of 1941, began the systematic murder of the Jews. From the autumn of 1941, this programme of murder was carried out by means of gassing facilities created for this purpose in death camps. The Wannsee Conference of January 1942 served to co-ordinate the destruction of European Jewry, which by 1945 had claimed six million victims.

Following the defeat of the Third Reich, the Allied powers sought to eradicate racism and antisemitism in the Federal Republic of Germany. The newly-emerging democratic parties followed this policy. In 1960, anti-Jewish incitement was made a criminal offence. In 1985, denial of the Holocaust was criminalized. Today, antisemitism in what was West Germany exists as a personal prejudice (as shown by opinion polls) and in an organized form on the political far right.

In the former German Democratic Republic (GDR), racism and antisemitism were regarded as having been overcome by the introduction of socialism. Following a brief period of "political cleansing", responsibility for the crimes of the Third Reich was placed on the Federal Republic. Despite the policy of anti-fascism, far-right and antisemitic groups began to appear in the early 1980s. The fall of the Berlin Wall in November 1989, and the subsequent freedom of reporting, brought the existence of right-wing extremism in the GDR to the attention of the world. Media concentration on the phenomenon resulted in the false impression that it was more widespread in the East than in the West.

PARTIES, ORGANIZATIONS, MOVEMENTS

The public discrediting of antisemitism obliged far-right, populist parties, such as the Republikaner Partei (with a membership of 23,000 in 1992), to dispense with it in public statements. Hostile attacks on foreigners in party propaganda focussed on asylum-seekers and immigrants from Eastern Europe; expressions of antisemitism appeared in party publications less frequently and in the form of innuendo. Commentaries on current events relating to Germans and Jews had an anti-Jewish slant.

After electoral defeats in 1991, the Republikaner Partei gained high returns in elections in 1992: 10.9 per cent in the Baden-Württemburg state parliamentary elections and 8.3 per cent in Berlin's communal elections. That the Republikaner Partei only received 1.2 per cent of the vote in Schleswig-Holstein was attributed to the Deutsche Volksunion's (DVU) splitting the far-right vote.

In contrast to the Republikaner Partei, antisemitism was more publicly voiced by the neo-Nazi parties, the Nationaldemokratische Partei Deutschlands (NPD) and the DVU. The DVU saw its numbers increase from 22,000 in 1990 to 24,000 at the end of 1991. In the 1992 elections, the DVU concentrated its efforts exclusively on Schleswig-Holstein and won 6.3 per cent of the vote. In contrast to the Republikaner Partei and the DVU, the NPD achieved neither electoral success (0.9 per cent in the Baden-Württemberg state parliamentary elections) nor a growth in membership (7,300 in 1990, 6,700 at the end of 1991).

All three parties have intensified their activities in the new federal states, building up local party organizations and running membership drives. While the DVU and the NPD have been classified for decades as anti-constitutional organizations and kept under close observation by the Verfassungsschutz (Office for the Protection of the Constitution), the Republikaner Partei only received this classification this year, following a decision by the Federal Minister of the Interior in December 1992.

The total membership of all extreme right-wing organizations rose from 39,800 in 1991 to 65,000 in 1992. The Verfassungsschutz counted 81 organizations, excluding the Republikaner Partei, with 35,500 members (not taking multiple membership into account) and 6,400 militant right-wing extremists, particularly skinheads, in less organized groups at regional and local levels. Of the 81 organizations, there were at least 33 neo-Nazi groups with a total of 1,200 members. An additional 800 neo-Nazis belonged to banned groups which are currently dormant.

An increasing threat is posed by right-wing, xenophobic youths, particularly skinheads. In 1992, the Verfassungsschutz counted 6,400 skinheads (2,600 in West Germany and 3,800 in East Germany) who were responsible for the majority of acts of violence against foreigners. Since skinhead groupings are poorly organized and the statistics only include those who are known to the police, 6,400 is considered the minimum estimate and the actual total may be five to ten times higher.

MANIFESTATIONS

According to figures released by the Verfassungsschutz in February 1993, incidents of far-right violence increased from 1,483 in 1991 to 2,506 in 1992, including 697 cases of arson. The rise in the number of deaths (from 3 to 17) and severe injuries (from 449 to 687) is an indicator of the growing brutality of the perpetrators of violence. These acts of violence, which have been increasing since 1990, are primarily aimed at asylum-seekers and immigrants from Eastern and South-Eastern Europe, but foreign workers, women, disabled people and Jewish properties have also been targeted. The fact that anti-Jewish incidents increased markedly only in the second half of the year indicates that antisemitism is an adjunct to hostility towards foreigners; that is, only within the framework of far-right

ideology do Jews and memorials to Jewish persecution become targets of attack—seven attacks on Jews have been recorded. In the case of the manslaughter of a fifty-three-year-old man by two skinheads in a Wuppertal restaurant on 13 November 1992, antisemitic motives were suspected because the proprietor called the man a Jew during a bout of drinking and fighting. However, in the view of the public prosecutor, the evidence showed that this remark did not influence the culprits.

It is reported by Jewish communities that their children have been provoked into fights by other pupils at school.

On 30 August, the monument, on the Putlitz Bridge commemorating the deportation of the Jews from Berlin, was bombed. After their arrest, the two perpetrators expressed their intentions to continue the wave of violence unleashed by the Rostock attacks and stated that they had been motivated by "hatred of foreigners and Jews". On 25-6 September, the Jewish section of the memorial at the Sachsenhausen concentration camp was the object of an arson attack. This was followed on 20 October by an arson attack on the Ravensbrück concentration camp memorial by four teenagers. A large number of Jewish cemetery desecrations and other antisemitic defacements also occurred. The Verfassungsschutz counted 104 known desecrations of Jewish cemeteries, synagogues and communal facilities, in addition to memorial sites (84 in 1991). The number of Nazi and antisemitic slogans defacing houses and public transport is incalculable. These incidents and, according to the Jewish communities, the growing number of abusive and threatening letters and telephone calls show that the general hostility towards foreigners has been extended to Germany's Jews.

Evidence suggests that the antisemitic activities of neo-Nazi groups are co-ordinated. For example, on 21 September, three skinheads, under the leadership of Thomas Dienel, the head of the neo-Nazi Deutsch-Nationale Partei (DNP), desecrated a synagogue in Erfurt with two halves of a pig's head and threatened the Jews with death in an accompanying note. This group is probably also responsible for cemetery desecrations in Thüringen.

The far-right press and neo-Nazi

circles were jubilant at the death of Heinz Galinski, the former chairman of the Central Council of Jews in Germany. Jewish journalist Ralph Giordano received death threats following an open letter to Chancellor Kohl in which he criticized the government's failure to stem far-right terror and declared that German Jewry could not rule out armed self-defence. On 21 December, following discussion in Israel of a boycott of Germany, the Jewish cemetery in Leipzig was desecrated with swastikas and antisemitic graffiti.

PUBLICATIONS

The far right publishes a number of weekly and irregular periodicals which contain antisemitic materials, primarily asserting Jewish conspiracies to influence leading politicians and journalists. These periodicals include: *Deutsche Nationalzeitung*, the weekly publication of the DVU, which was established in 1950. With a self-declared circulation of 130,000, it is the most widespread publication of the German far right. *Deutsche Stimme*, which claims a circulation of 250,000, is the monthly journal of the NPD. *Deutsche Rundschau*, which claims a circulation of 50,000, is the monthly journal of the Deutsche Liga für Volk und Heimat, a small neo-Nazi party which split from the Republikaner Partei in 1991. Founded in 1951, *Nation und Europa* appears monthly with a circulation of 10,000. It is associated with the NPD and the Deutsche Liga.

Founded in 1975, the "revisionist" *Historische Tatsachen* has appeared bi-monthly since 1985. Edited by Udo Walendy, the journal has connections with the Institute for Historical Review in California (see **United States** entry). Another Holocaust "revisionist" publication, *Recht und Wahrheit*, is the monthly journal of the Deutsche Freiheitsbewegung and has a circulation of several thousand. *Deutschland in Geschichte und Gegenwart* is a quarterly "revisionist" magazine with a circulation of 3,000.

Deutscher Jahresweiser, a quarterly with a circulation of several thousand, is edited by the neo-Nazi lawyer Manfred Roeder. *Klartext*, which appears irregularly, is the journal of the Nationalistische Front, a small aggressive neo-Nazi group which was banned in December 1992. *Code*, a

monthly publication with an estimated circulation of several thousand, has links with *Spotlight* and *New American View*. *Elemente*, which appears twice a year, is produced by Thule-Seminar, a racist think-tank. *Der Scheinwerfer* appears monthly with an estimated circulation of 1,000. *Der Schulungsbrief* is a neo-Nazi monthly with a circulation of 100.

There are also a number of skinhead magazines which propagate racism and antisemitism and a multifarious skinhead music scene whose records include antisemitic lyrics. In the autumn of 1992, German officials began to institute sharper controls and prosecutions. In Bonn, the Federal Investigative Office for Publications Dangerous to Youth has banned several records and magazines, and a number of bands and their recording companies have been prosecuted for incitement.

The series *Explosiv: der heisse Stuhl* (Explosive: the Hot Seat), on the independent television channel RTL, scheduled a debate in November on the subject "The Germans hate Jews. We have to defend ourselves". The broadcast was cancelled when G. B. Ginzel, a researcher on antisemitism, exposed his opponent in the debate, "Professor Horst J. Andel", as Aharon Moshel, a far-right publicist with links to the Republikaner Partei.

MAINSTREAM POLITICS

Public figures who express antisemitic sentiments put their political careers at risk. This was the experience of Karl-Heinz Schmidt, a Rostock city councillor who resigned after questioning the patriotism of Ignatz Bubis, the Chairman of the Central Council of Jews in Germany. During a press conference in November, Schmidt asked Bubis: "You are a German citizen of Jewish faith. Your homeland is Israel. Is that right? What do you think about the daily acts of violence between Palestinians and Israelis?"

CULTURAL LIFE

A sub-culture of skinheads which includes antisemitism along with militant hostility towards foreigners has emerged. Their ideology is disseminated primarily through magazines, concerts, records and computer games.

A radio editor who gave an antisemitic commentary during a nationwide religious broadcast was obliged to resign following protests.

BUSINESS AND COMMERCE

Anti-Jewish resentment was reported in the areas of construction and real estate in connection with the restitution of Jewish property in the former GDR. The bankruptcy of a Berlin property development corporation, partly owned by Jews, revived the cliche of "Jewish speculation".

RELIGION

Some Catholic and Protestant fundamentalist and evangelical groups propagate anti-Judaism in their leaflets and ascribe efforts to bring about the co-operation of all religions to a Jewish-masonic conspiracy.

Prominent Protestant theologians continued to criticize attempts by missionary groups to convert Jews. The Catholic fundamentalist theologian, Johann Baptist Metz, criticized the books of two Catholic laymen, Eugen Drewermann and Franz Alt, as "trendy, antisemitic chit-chat". He accused them of separating Christianity from its Jewish roots.

DENIAL OF THE HOLOCAUST

The so-called *Leuchter Report* (see **United States** entry) and similar texts and videos which deny the Holocaust continued to be distributed. In those cases where the public prosecutor was able to identify the originator, charges were preferred (see **Legal Matters**).

Despite his prohibition from entering the country, the British Holocaust-denier David Irving continued to appear in Germany. Irving's invitation to deliver a lecture, attended by Fred Leuchter, Ernst Zundel and other Holocaust-deniers, issued by a Christian Democrat member of the Pforzheim district council, led to a public scandal and to preliminary proceedings against the councillor for defamation of Jewish citizens. The proceedings were later dropped due to insufficient evidence.

EFFECTS OF ANTI-ZIONISM

Following Israel's deportation of 415 Islamic fundamentalists in December, the Republikaner Partei tried to turn a candle-lit chain in Berlin against violence and right-wing extremism into a demonstration against the "racist politics" of Israel.

OPINION POLLS

No specific study on antisemitism was conducted in 1992, but questions asked about the "portrayal of Jews" by the Allensbach Institute for Opinion Research in an April poll showed a more negative picture than a 1987 study of antisemitism. Fifty-four per cent thought Jews cunning (42 per cent in 1987), 28 per cent as unpredictable (15 per cent in 1987), 23 per cent as ruthless (15 per cent in 1987), and 19 per cent as sinister (7 per cent in 1987). Significantly, these statistics applied equally to Eastern and Western Germans. This contrasted with sample surveys conducted in 1990-1 which had presented Eastern Germans in a more favourable light.

Studies about young people, which were undertaken individually for the new federal states of Brandenburg, Lower Saxony and Saxony-Anhalt, contained three or four questions about antisemitism. The answers of the young people, aged between fourteen and twenty-five years, showed a negative trend. Eleven per cent of pupils and 29 per cent of apprentices agreed with the statement "the Jews are Germany's misfortune". Overall, 14 per cent of those between fourteen and eighteen agreed with the statement, while only 5 per cent of those aged between twenty and twenty-four, and only 1 per cent of those aged twenty-five to twenty-six, agreed.

LEGAL MATTERS

In Berlin, fines and prison sentences were imposed for public incitement in two cases in December. In the first case, a woman who attempted to intervene in an attack on a black person was called a "dirty Jewess" by the attackers. In the other, a woman was accused of being a "Jewish sow who ought to be gassed". In Frankfurt, a man was fined for including with the repayment of a loan a demand that the money "only be used for Germans and not for asylum-seeking or Zionist pigs".

During the year, several prominent right-wing radicals were convicted for incitement, instigation of racial hatred and reviling the memory of the dead. The

Munich publisher Alfred Detscher was given a suspended sentence of one year and fined 10,000 marks. In Schweinfurth, the veteran Nazi, former Major General Otto Ernst Remer, received a prison sentence of twenty-two months for denying the Holocaust; in Munich, he was given a suspended sentence of four months for distributing video cassettes in which the gassing of Jews in Auschwitz was denied. In Mannheim, the federal chairman of the NPD, Günther Deckert, was fined 10,000 marks and given a year's suspended sentence for appearing publicly with American Holocaust-denier Fred Leuchter in November 1991 and endorsing his so-called *Report*.

In the numerous court proceedings against those who had set fire to refugee shelters and assaulted foreigners (resulting in deaths in some cases), verdicts were constrained by the juvenile code, leading to criticisms that the penalties were too light. Following the wave of racist violence in the autumn, verdicts became harsher.

In November and December, three militant neo-Nazi organizations—the Nationale Offensive (NO), the Nationalistische Front (NF), and the Deutsche Alternative (DA)—were out-lawed by the Federal Minister of the Interior and their financial assets were sequestered. Other groups suspected of forming right-wing terrorist organizations were also investigated.

COUNTERING ANTISEMITISM

The numerous demonstrations against racism and right-wing extremism were also directed against antisemitism. The small and little-publicized protests throughout the Republic had, by the end of the year, become mass demonstrations with hundreds of thousands of participants. After the attack on the Jewish Holocaust memorial at Sachsenhausen, a national protest was organized on 8 November in Berlin, which an estimated 300,000 people attended. Both this attack, and the resulting criticism from abroad, alarmed many politicians, who demonstrated their abhorrence of the crime by visiting Sachsenhausen.

The arson attack on the Mölln apartment house, in which three Turkish women met their deaths, caused wide-spread public revulsion which resulted in mass candle-lit chains not previously experienced in the history of the Federal Republic and led to an intensified action by the state against right-wing extremists.

Politicians of the democratic parties, Protestant and Catholic dignitaries, prominent figures in the arts, sport, the sciences and the media, the top economic organizations, the trades unions and the professional associations, all made public proclamations against hostility to foreigners and antisemitism.

The newly-elected President of the Central Committee of Jews in Germany, Ignatz Bubis, used his inaugural visits to high-ranking politicians in Bonn and the regions, as well as the media attention given to his appointment, to call on Germany's politicians to take energetic measures against violence and xenophobia. In a series of interviews and television appearances, Bubis called on Germans to oppose right-wing violence actively. At the same time, he defended democracy in the months of crisis and rejected as exaggerations all comparisons of the situation with the final phase of the Weimar Republic.

ASSESSMENT

Attacks on Jews and Jewish properties occurred less frequently in comparison with the number of abuses committed against asylum-seekers and their dwellings. However, as witnessed in the second half of 1992, Jewish properties became targets for attack by increasingly mobilized right-wing extremists and Jewish communities felt increasingly threatened in comparison with the previous year. However, police protection of the communities was considered to be good and, due to its social and professional status, the Jewish minority is integrated into the mainstream of society and is specially protected by the law.

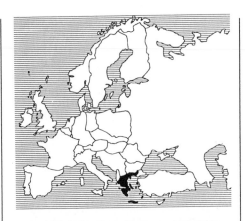

Greece

General population: 10,000,000
Jewish population: 5,000 (mainly in
Athens and Thessaloniki)

GENERAL BACKGROUND

The conservative New Democracy party
won the 1990 general election, replacing the
socialist Pasok party which had been
plagued by scandal. Former prime minister
Andreas Papandreou was acquitted of
embezzlement in January 1992.

Greece is one of the poorest EC
countries in terms of gross national product
per capita. In 1992, inflation fell to 14.4 per
cent from 17.5 per cent in 1991, but it
remained four times higher than the EC
average. Unemployment for 1992 was
officially just below 9 per cent. In December, Prime Minister Konstantinos
Mitsotakis dismissed his entire cabinet on
account of its hostility to his austerity
policies.

HISTORICAL LEGACY

Jews have lived in Greece since at least the
third century BCE. When Greece became
part of the Ottoman Empire in the fifteenth century, many Jews who had fled
from the Inquisition in Spain and Portugal
settled in the Balkan peninsula.
Thessaloniki became the largest centre of
Jewish population.

During the Greek struggle for independence in the nineteenth century,
relations between the Christian Orthodox

Greeks and the Jews deteriorated considerably, the Jews being well known for their
support of the Ottoman Empire. The
Turkish police had to intervene to quell
outbreaks of violence against Jews which
occurred in Smyrna in 1872 and in Con-
stantinople in 1874. In 1872, a synagogue
on the island of Marmara was destroyed.
During this period, Jews also became
victims of blood libel accusations.

In 1931, in the atmosphere of fierce
economic competition between refugees
from Asia Minor, who were settled in
Greece after the population exchange with
Turkey in 1923, and the Jews, the Jewish
neighbourhood of Kampel in Thessaloniki
was burned down.

Following the Nazi invasion of Greece
in 1941, 65,000 Jews—85 per cent of the
Greek Jewish population—were deported
to concentration camps. Protests against the
deportations by Greek intellectual and
religious leaders were in vain.

Since the Second World War, antisemitism has not been displayed in any
institutionalized form. Nevertheless,
unofficial antisemitism appears in three
contexts: the Arab-Israeli conflict, anti-
Jewish theological discourse (see below),
and, more recently, in the context of
Macedonian independence.

PARTIES, ORGANIZATIONS, MOVEMENTS

The following are current right-wing
groups which hold antisemitic views. All
are small and have no parliamentary
representation:

Enieo Etnekistiko Kinima (United
Nationalist Movement), which was
founded in 1979. It maintains a bookshop
and publishing house in Athens called Nea
Thessis (New Position) which circulates a
Greek version of *The Protocols of the Elders
of Zion* in small numbers.

Founded in 1981, Laikos Syndesmos
(Popular League), one of whose leaders is
Nikolas Michaloloakos, maintains connec-
tions with foreign far-right organizations,
including Pamyat in Russia, CEDADE in
Spain and the Front National in France.
This very active neo-Nazi organization
held its third congress in April 1992 in
Athens and runs offices in Thessaloniki,
Volos, and Patras.

Ethniko Metopo (National Front),
founded in 1987 and led by, among others,

M. Konstas, publishes the magazine *Metopo* (Front).

The recently-founded OEN Megas Alexandros (Alexander the Great Organization) has links with the weekly *Stochos* (see **Publications**).

MANIFESTATIONS

There have been occasional incidents of antisemitic graffiti in schools and outside Jewish shops in Athens and Thessaloniki. The Jewish monument in Lianokladi, built in 1988, was defaced with swastikas several times in 1992. The Central Jewish Board launched a complaint against the far-right weekly paper *Stochos* for having encouraged this vandalism (see **Publications**).

PUBLICATIONS

All the following antisemitic or anti-Zionist publications (anti-Zionism in Greece often reflects antisemitic attitudes) have low circulations:

Stochos (Target) is a far-right weekly paper published by Ghiorgos Kapsalis. Its circulation has increased over the past few years from 5,500 to 7,500. Following several successful complaints by the Greek Jewish community, the paper has been obliged to print a number of apologies under the Greek law on incitement to hatred against citizens. *Stochos* has sought to launch a campaign against the erection of Jewish monuments in Greece.

Laikos Syndesmos publishes the monthly magazine *Chrissi Avgi* (Golden Daybreak) and intends to publish a weekly magazine in 1993.

Other publications include: the dailies *Avriani* (Tomorrow's Press) and *Elephteri Ora* (Free Time); the weekly *Nei Anthropi* (New Man); *Christinaniki* (Christian) and *Nea Tassis* (New Position), which appear irregularly; and the monthly *Antidoto* (Antidote).

Two unofficial ecclesiastical publications—*Agathangelos* (Archangel), and *Orthodos Typos* (Orthodox Press)—circulate in religious and army circles.

Greece has refused to recognize the independence of the former Yugoslav republic of Macedonia, arguing that no other country has the right to claim the name of Macedonia, which is also the name of Greece's northern region. In this context, the celebration of 500 years of Jewish life in Macedonia by Greece's Jewish communities in 1992 was depicted by the far-right press as an attempt to undermine the "Greekness" of Macedonia. Criticism was directed at a medal, issued by the Jewish community in Thessaloniki, which depicted a menorah on one side and the star of ancient Macedonia on the other. The far-right press argued that the Jews, as a religious minority in Greece, had no right to use Greek "ethnic symbols" which represent the whole of Greece.

GRASSROOTS

Covert discrimination and anti-Jewish remarks in the army have repeatedly been reported by Jewish soldiers.

On the popular level, Jews are often portrayed in stereotypical terms as wealthy and omnipotent.

RELIGION

While the Christian Orthodox Church has never adopted an overtly antisemitic stance, some members of the clergy have played a considerable role in shaping a negative image of Jews. The most common religious allegations concern the murder of Christ. The custom of burning a Judas puppet on Easter reinforces this image.

Anti-Judaism expressed by Christian Orthodox circles is a function of internal struggles within the clergy and the church's general struggle against other religions.

DENIAL OF THE HOLOCAUST

Six or seven publications on this subject have appeared in Greece, including Greek versions of Robert Faurisson's *Is the Diary of Anne Frank Genuine?* and Richard Harwood's *Myth or Holocaust*, which have been produced by the Elepheri Skespsis (Free Thought) publishing house. While most are translations, the book *O Mythos* (The Myth) was written by the Greek author Kostas Plevris. References to the denial of the Holocaust frequently appear in articles published by *Stochos* and *Chrissi Avgi*. The Holocaust and Greek Jewish history in general are largely ignored by Greek educational institutions and the media.

EFFECTS OF ANTI-ZIONISM

While anti-Zionist attitudes do not necessarily stem from antisemitic sentiments, in specific circumstances the two phenomena may be closely related. Greece was the only European country which voted against the UN partition plan in 1947 and has traditionally maintained close ties with the Arab states. But when the socialist Pasok party came to power in 1981 and the Lebanon war broke out the following year, criticism of Israel grew dramatically. Some right-wing political groups called for a boycott of Greek Jewish shops. The *intifada* and the presence of many Palestinian and Arab students in Greece have contributed to the persistence in the country of strong anti-Israeli sentiments, in which Greek Jews are often identified with Israel in public opinion.

ASSESSMENT

Although the scope of organized anti-semitism and far-right activities in Greece appears to be rather small, the rise of nationalism in the Balkans, the Macedonian issue and the influx of Albanian immigrants have created an atmosphere in which far-right organizations and publications could gain wider support.

In this political climate, in so far as the manifestation of a minority identity is perceived as a threat to the Greek state, Greek Jewry maintains a low profile.

Irish Republic

General population: 3,520,000
Jewish population: 1,200-1,400 (mainly in Dublin)

GENERAL BACKGROUND

In February, Charles Haughey resigned as Ireland's prime minister and leader of the Fianna Fail party after having been implicated in a telephone tapping scandal. He was replaced in both roles by Albert Reynolds.

In a referendum in June, 68.7 per cent of voters approved the Irish Republic's ratification of the Maastricht Treaty on European Union.

In November, the governing coalition

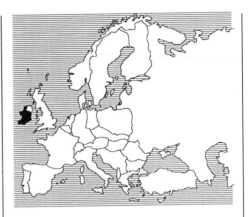

of the Fianna Fail and Progressive Democrat parties collapsed after losing a confidence motion. In the ensuing general election, the Labour Party made sweeping gains, mainly at the expense of Fianna Fail. However, no party gained an absolute majority and Albert Reynolds headed a caretaker administration while coalition negotiations took place.

Ireland's previously stable economy was weakened during the year: interest rates rose and the currency was in crisis. Unemployment was high, with some 300,000 people (18 per cent of the working population) out of work, although mass emigration more or less ceased.

HISTORICAL LEGACY

Jews have lived in Ireland since the seventeenth century, but the majority of Jews came to Ireland, mainly from Lithuania, in the 1880s. By the early twentieth century, the Jewish community in Ireland numbered some 4,000 people, living peacefully in Dublin, Cork and Limerick. Many since emigrated to Britain, Israel and the United States.

In 1904, a "pogrom" took place in the southern city of Limerick when Father Creagh, a priest of the Redemptorist order, incited the local population against "bloodsucking" Jewish money-lenders and travelling peddlers. His explicit sermons brought about a trade boycott of Jewish businesses which lasted two years. The boycott was accompanied by intimidation, abuse, harassment and beatings (although there were no fatalities) and resulted in the almost total departure of the 150-strong Limerick Jewish community.

The issue of "pogrom" resurfaced three times in the past thirty years, when various individuals sought to justify it *a posteriori*. In 1965, a correspondence resulted from an RTE television programme on the incident. In 1970, the then Lord Mayor of Limerick, Stephen Coughlan, declared his support for Father Creagh's "saving the impoverished Limerick population against the exploitative Jews". This resulted in a controversy in the letters pages of the newspapers. The controversy flared up again following the publication of an article in *The Irish Times* in September-October 1984, with the Jews being defended mainly by left-wing politicians. Only in 1990 did Limerick make formal amends to its Jews by restoring the city's eighty-eight-year-old Jewish cemetery.

In the Republican movement, Arthur Griffith, the founder of Sinn Fein, wrote many antisemitic articles in the nationalist paper the *United Irishman* at the turn of the century. In 1943, Oliver J. Flanagan, a Dail member for the Fine Gael party, the founder of which had belonged to the quasi-fascist Blueshirts movement (which fought on Franco's side in Spain), proposed to the House to "rout the Jews out of this country". None of his fellow Dail members protested.

Attempts to settle Jewish refugees in neutral Ireland during the Second World War met with consistent government opposition. There is no wartime evidence that the prime minister, Eamon de Valera, who was primarily concerned with Irish territorial integrity, uttered any condemnation of German atrocities. In January 1939, de Valera, in a recorded discussion with Eduard Hempel, the German minister to Eire, agreed that Nazi procedures against the Jews "must primarily be explained by the behaviour of the Jews after the [1914-18] war". Historian Dermot Keogh pointed out that the [high] "number of visa refusals by the Department of Justice had tragic consequences. The Irish must live with that guilt." In 1991, a claim by writer and former Labour cabinet minister, Dr Conor Cruise O'Brien, that Ireland's 4,000 Jews would have been handed over to the Nazis had Germany won the war, was the subject of much controversy.

PARTIES, ORGANIZATIONS, MOVEMENTS

No race relations legislation was enacted in Ireland until 1989. Previously, the National Socialist Irish Workers' Party (NSIWP) openly distributed Nazi literature which had been illegally published elsewhere in Europe. The NSIWP also printed its own publications, including business-type cards with slogans denying the Holocaust, Nazi, antisemitic and anti-Gypsy slogans, a monthly magazine and pamphlets. Some of its literature found its way into secondary schools. The NSIWP was possibly responsible for a series of attacks in 1986 on a Dublin Jewish butcher's shop. The party has not been heard of since, and there has been no evidence of the existence of similar groups. There is a consensus that organizations such as the NSIWP are tiny and insignificant.

PUBLICATIONS

In December 1992, an Irish-language publishing company released an openly antisemitic and pro-Nazi book, *Cè Hì Seo Amuigh?* (Who Is That Outside?), which asserted, among other things, that there was "no proof that the Germans intended to exterminate" the Jews and that pictures of Nazi concentration camp victims were corpses exhumed after the 1945 Allied bombing of Dresden. The book, by Roisin Ni Mheara, an Irishwoman who spent the war years in Germany, married two Nazi officers and was an associate of Rudolf Hess, was not banned under the Incitement to Racial Hatred Act and, like all Irish-language publications, received a government grant of Ir£1,000. There was only one protest in the press when the book was first published, but Mervyn Taylor, the (Jewish) minister for equality and law reform, has since denounced it as "reprehensible that a book of that nature should be aided from public funds".

In a series of articles in the *Irish Times* in August-September 1992, Dr Brian Maye of University College Dublin praised the leadership qualities of Sinn Fein founder Arthur Griffith. In an article entitled "Griffith objected to money-lending, not Jews", published on 11 September 1992, Dr Maye referred to the Limerick "pogrom", stating: "the Jew in Limerick has not been boycotted because he is a Jew, but because he is a usurer". Regarding the relationship between Griffith and the Dreyfus affair, Dr Maye wrote: "in 1904, Griffith still mistakenly believed that Dreyfus was a criminal and what he was bemoaning when he wrote 'attack a Jew—and all Jewry comes to his assistance', was what he perceived as a tendency among Jews to rally behind the bad eggs of their race. What must be appreciated is that it was to Jews as wrong-doers, and not to Jews as Jews, that he was referring." In reply, *Irish Times* columnist Fintan O'Toole stressed Griffith's antisemitism and demanded that Ireland face up to its past. This too resulted in a lengthy controversy.

LEGAL MATTERS

In 1989, the Prohibition of Incitement to Racial Hatred Act was passed, making it a criminal offence to incite against any minority. An equality law, with measures to combat racial discrimination and discrimination against women, gays and lesbians and the disabled, is in the early stages of consideration.

ASSESSMENT

With the election in November 1992 of the first Muslim member of parliament, and with several recent publications on racial hatred in Ireland, racism has been discussed more openly. It should be stressed that overt antisemitism in Ireland is minimal in comparison with other European countries: there were no recorded incidents of desecration of Jewish cemeteries or antisemitic daubings in 1992.

Italy

General population: 57,103,000
Jewish population: 35,000 (mainly in Rome and Milan)

GENERAL BACKGROUND

The results of the Italian general election on 5 April reflected growing voter disenchantment with Italy's traditional governing coalition. The Christian Democrats (DC), the Socialist Party (PSI), the Socialist

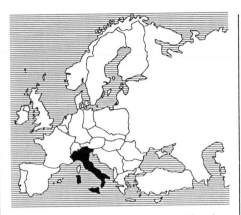

Democratic Party (PSDI) and the Liberal Party (PLI), together received less than half of the votes.

The beneficiaries were small parties representing territorial interests, such as the Lega Lombarda-Lega Nord (Lombard League-Northern League) which made the largest gains, increasing its share of the vote by 8 per cent and pushing the Christian Democrats into second place in Lombardy, Italy's wealthiest region.

A series of economic and political scandals which shook the country during the year made the political class appear even less trustworthy. In June, Giuliano Amato of the PSI was appointed prime minister.

The Italian economy remained in recession in 1992. GDP only grew by 1 per cent, compared to 1.4 per cent in 1991. Industrial production fell slightly compared to 1991, but, unlike the previous year, this was not balanced by an increase in the service sector in 1992. Thus, unemployment rose from 10.9 per cent in 1991 to 11.2 per cent in 1992. Inflation fell from 6.4 per cent in 1991 to 5.4 per cent in 1992.

In September, the lira was devalued against other EC currencies in the Exchange Rate Mechanism. The government introduced a series of measures aimed at reducing the country's huge public-sector deficit, including cuts in public spending, ending the index-linking of salaries and increasing privatisation to reduce the role of the public sector. But, with 10-15 per cent of Italians living in poverty, the public spending cuts only increased popular discontent.

HISTORICAL LEGACY

Jews have lived continuously in the Italian peninsula for over 2,000 years. Their treatment has differed according to the areas in which they have lived. Times of relative tolerance and fruitful growth have alternated with times of serious anti-Jewish prejudice.

From the middle of the sixteenth century onwards, the attitude of the Popes towards the Jews became more ambiguous. This attitude culminated in 1555 with the issuance of the Bull *Cum nimis absurdum* by Pope Paul IV, which marked the beginning of a harsh policy towards Jews living in the Papal state, with the closing of the ghettos, the exclusion of Jews from many cities and villages, and forced baptisms.

Since the unification of Italy in 1861, the Jews have had full civil and political rights.

The fascist period (1922-45) may be divided into three periods: up to 1938, the regime was indifferent to the Jewish problem; in 1938, anti-Jewish legislation deprived Jews of their rights; and in 1943-5, the collaboration of the authorities of the Repubblica Sociale Italiana with the Nazi occupation led to the deportation of 8,566 Jews from Italy and Italian territories in the Aegean basin.

The 1970s saw a return to anti-Jewish prejudice both among the general population and in the political arena. This was traced to the influence of the far right, and to the moderate left and the far left as a by-product of anti-Zionism. The most violent antisemitic action was the attack by international terrorists on the Rome synagogue in October 1982 in which a child was killed and thirty-six people were injured.

PARTIES, ORGANIZATIONS, MOVEMENTS

There are no overtly antisemitic parties in Italy, but roughly twenty-five far-right groups and organizations are scattered throughout the country. No figures exist on the number of supporters they have. While antisemitic attitudes may not be displayed openly, widespread credence is given to *mondialismo*, a globalist conspiracy theory which propounds that all the "world powers"—including Jews and Zionists—seek to "subdue" world populations economically, culturally and psychologically. Many groups are *antimondialista* in that they seek to combat the "world powers" of the *mondialismo* theory.

The Movimento Sociale Italiano-Destra Nazionale (MSI-DN, Italian Social Movement-National Right), led by Gianfranco Fini, is a neo-fascist, anti-immigrant party. In the April elections, the MSI-DN won 5.4 per cent of the vote and thirty-four out of a total 630 seats in the Chamber of Deputies, and 6.5 per cent and sixteen out of 315 seats in the Senate. Support for the party has been drawn both from those nostalgic for the fascist regime and from young people.

Despite its xenophobic platform, members of the MSI-DN have condemned antisemitism. The MSI-DN has described the anti-Jewish legislation introduced by Italy's fascist government in 1938 as an "error" and a "horror". The party's daily paper, *Il Secolo d'Italia*, has published articles against antisemitism and leaders of the MSI-DN's youth movement, the Fronte della Gioventù, have openly taken a stand against antisemitism. However, the party has an ambiguous relationship with such far-right groups as the skinheads who, although officially disavowed as fascists by the MSI-DN, attend party demonstrations. Furthermore, some party politicians, such as Teodoro Buontempo from Rome, a former leader of the Fronte della Gioventù, have displayed a sympathetic and tolerant attitude towards them.

The skinheads are the biggest and most active grouping of the far right. Their historical references are Nazism and the fascist Salò Republic of 1943-45. As elsewhere, the majority of skinheads are violently opposed to "aliens" and foreign immigrants and are anti-Zionist and antisemitic. Their propaganda concerns include the struggle against racial mixing, the defence of aboriginal populations, the rejection and expulsion of foreign workers, denial of the Holocaust, and the fight against Zionism and *mondialismo*.

There are 1,000-1,500 skinheads, aged between fourteen and twenty-five, mostly belonging to the working or lower middle classes. A skinhead movement appears to be evolving, made up of twenty or so, often disorganized, micro-groups scattered all over the country. Such groups are often formed at "Nazi-rock" concerts, in bars and sports fan clubs. These groups are particularly active in the Lazio region, with 300-500 supporters under the leadership of the Movimento Politico Occidentale (MPO, Western Political Movement); in Lombardy, with 300 people rallying under Azione Skinhead and in the Veneto region, where Veneto Fronte Skinhead has 150-300 supporters. These twenty or so groups are organized in a federation called Base Autonoma (Autonomous Base) and attempts have been made to form a national association called Skinhead d'Italia. The MPO leader, Maurizio Boccacci, is a member of the CISNAL, a trade union with close ties to the MSI party. MPO, which has its headquarters in Rome and a base in Frascati, has sought contacts with the political leadership of all these groups.

The exchange of information and shared organizational frameworks are customary among these movements and similar movements in other countries, such as Germany, Belgium, England, Greece, Poland and the United States.

There is less information on a number of other far-right organizations, which include:

Lega Nazional Popolare (People's National League) operates mainly in Rome and in Southern Italy. Its leader, Stefano delle Chiaie, was once active in right-wing subversive organizations. He and another leader, Adriano Tilgher, belonged to one of the two major right-wing subversive organizations of the 1970s called Avanguardia Nazionale (National Vanguard).

Fronte Nazionale (National Front), which is modelled on the French party of the same name, operates on the neo-Nazi fringes. It was founded by Franco Freda, leader of the Gruppo Ar, which controls the Edizioni di Ar publishing house (see **Publications**). Fronte Nazionale operates with very small groups of supporters in the Lombardy, Veneto, Emilia Romagna, Tuscany and Calabria regions. Fronte Nazionale is opposed to foreign workers, *mondialismo*, Zionism and the United States.

Following Gianfranco Fini's election as secretary of the MSI and the party's move towards mainstream political

credibility, a clustering strategy among the various far-right movements appears to have emerged. Such movements have also sought to attract dissident fringes from CISNAL and Fronte della Gioventù.

Cultural links have recently been established between a few far-right groups and some Muslim organizations.

MANIFESTATIONS

Manifestations of antisemitism increased by 50 per cent in comparison with 1991. The majority of incidents were carried out by far-right groups and were particularly numerous between September and November.

Most antisemitic incidents were either verbal or written: Jewish institutions and private citizens received threatening letters and telephone calls, graffiti was daubed on synagogues, Jewish-owned shops and city walls, and antisemitic leaflets were distributed. However, in May, a Jewish high school student in Rome was insulted and beaten by a classmate. In November, Zuhir Sayad, a Palestinian student, was beaten by classmates for defending Jews.

In February 1992, approximately fifty skinheads marched in Milan against immigration and shouted anti-Israeli slogans. On 29 February, nearly 600 skinheads took part in a demonstration in Rome organized by the MPO. On 17 October, the MSI held a demonstration in Rome against the government's austerity measures, which was attended by 20,000 people. Some of the demonstrators marched making Nazi salutes. After the demonstration, a small group of skinheads rode past the ghetto area shouting antisemitic slogans, but were chased away.

After *L'Espresso* magazine erroneously suggested in November that 10.5 per cent of Italians believed that "Jews are foreigners and should leave Italy" (see **Opinion Polls**), members of the MPO daubed yellow Stars of David imprinted with "Zionists get out of Italy" on Rome's Libyan synagogue and dozens of Jewish-owned shops. In retaliation, on 5 November, seventy younger members of the Jewish community attacked the MPO's offices in Rome.

Following the attack on MPO headquarters, a nine-metre-long banner reading "Jews, you will never win. Long Live

Christ the King" appeared near a highway entrance in Rome. Its authors were thought to be members of the MPO. Leaflets against Jews and Zionists signed by the Movimento Politico per le Comunità di Popolo (Political Movement for the People's Community) and the Movimento Antisionista Italiano per la Base Autonoma (Italian Anti-Zionist Movement for the Autonomous Base) were handed out in Rome and Naples in December (see **Legal Matters**).

There incidence of vandalism in Jewish cemeteries increased, a phenomenon unusual in Italy. In September, Jewish tombstones in a cemetery in San Remo and the Jewish cemetery in Livorno were desecrated with swastikas and Nazi slogans. The Jewish part of the cemetery in Finale Emilia, a village near Modena which has been without Jewish inhabitants for some time, was desecrated in May and again in early November. Two other cemeteries, one in Modena and one in Salemi, were also damaged in early November. At the end of November, the Jewish cemetery in Naples was vandalized and two small cemeteries near Como were daubed with Nazi slogans.

Over the past few years, there has been an increasing use of antisemitic stereotypes in everyday conversation and a rising incidence of tasteless jokes about the Holocaust. There also appears to be a growing trend, especially among young people, to use the word "ebreo" (Jew) against any adversary with the disturbing meaning of "someone who must be destroyed".

PUBLICATIONS

Magazines reflecting far-right views regularly focus on the Jewish question in terms of antisemitism, anti-Zionism, Holocaust denial theories and the controversy surrounding the concept of *mondialismo*.

L'uomo libero (The Free Man) is a quarterly produced in Milan since 1980 by the publishing house of the same name with a circulation of 5,000. The editor-in-chief is Mario Consoli, and Sergio Gozzoli and Piero Sella, who are considered the ideologues of the skinhead movement, are members of the editorial staff. It has published articles denying the Holocaust.

Avanguardia, which describes itself as the "militant monthly for the national community and its people", is published in Trapani, Sicily. It has approximately 400 subscribers and is distributed in Emilia, Tuscany, Abruzzi and Sicily. It has contacts with Islamic fundamentalists and has argued that "Europe" and "Islam" have a common enemy in *mondialismo*. also supports the skinhead movement

Various skinhead "fanzines" (short-lived, mimeographed underground magazines with limited circulations) exist, many with titles reflecting National Socialist themes, such as *La mia battaglia* (My Battles), *Blitzkrieg*, *Risveglio Europeo* (European Awakening). Others include:

Azione Skinhead (Skinhead Action), published in Milan, is the official mouthpiece of the Skinhead d'Italia organizations and the only "fanzine" distributed on a national level. *Nuovi Orizzonti* (New Horizons), the mouthpiece of neo-Nazi MPO, is the most politically-oriented fanzine. *Azione Patavium* (Patavium Action), the "skinzine" published in Padua, cites its "enemies" as "*mondialismo* and economic lobbies as well as the Zionist movement".

Orion, the former organ of the anti-Zionist and Holocaust-denying Fronte Europeo di Liberazione, is a monthly magazine published in Milan by Società Editrice Barbarossa. It is distributed in far-right bookshops in twenty-seven Italian cities, as well as in many newsstands in Milan, and with a circulation of 2,000, is the most widely read publication among young far-right sympathizers. It seeks out political debates on right-wing and left-wing political issues and is anti-Zionist, antisemitic and propounds theories of Holocaust denial.

Bollettino Novità NS (NS Bulletin) is produced by the NSDAP/AO. The mimeographed Italian edition is distributed among a small group of neo-Nazis (versions are also published in English and German).

Sentinella d'Italia (Italian Sentinel) is a monthly magazine published in Monfalcone (near Trieste), which was founded in 1947. The editor-in-chief is Antonio Guerini. It is an extremely radical, antisemitic magazine in favour of historical denial with strong references to the fascist regime and the 1943-45 Italian Republic of Salò.

Candido, the bi-weekly neo-fascist magazine owned by MSI senator Giorgio Pisanò, has devoted considerable space to articles denying the Holocaust. Following Pisanò's resignation from the MSI and the failure of his attempt to found a new Fascism and Liberty party, the magazine apparently closed after the December 1992 issue.

Ideogramma, published every four months in Milan, was a pre-Vatican II Catholic traditionalist, antisemitic, *antimondialista* publication, but, following the transfer of its headquarters to Turin in March, it seems to have abandoned its neo-fascist outlook.

The anti-capitalist economic and financial review, *L'antibancor-Rassegna periodica di economia e finanza*, was first produced by the Fronte Nazionale in September 1992 and published by Edizioni di Ar in Salerno (see below). It analyses the economic situation from the same ideological viewpoint as the other magazines produced by this publishing house.

The main far-right publishing houses which produce anti-Jewish material are the Padua-based Edizioni di Ar, which has a bookshop in Salerno; the Parma-based Edizioni La Sfinge, which focuses on denial of history; and Edizioni dell'Uomo Libero. There were approximately forty antisemitic books and pamphlets available in 1992, fifteen of which focused on Holocaust denial, almost exclusively produced by far-right publishing houses.

The following are a few of the 1992 publications: *Il Talmud e i non ebrei* (The Talmud and non-Jews) by H. De Vries De Heekelingen, Edizioni La Sfinge; *Studi sul Talmud* (Studies Concerning the Talmud) by J. Pohl, K. G. Kuhn, H. De Vries De Heekelingen, Edizioni All'insegna del Veltro; *Il Genio d'Israele* (The Israeli Genius), *L'Azione distruttrice dell'ebraismo* (The Destructive Actions of the Jewish Faith) by J. Evola, Edizioni Il Cinabro; and *Il mondialismo capitalista* (Capitalist Mondialism) by Lello Ragni, Edizioni dell'Uomo Libero.

Claudio Mutti's pro-Islamic group in Parma revolves around the small All'insegna del Veltro publishing house, which has published a number of anti-Jewish books.

A reprint of Hitler's *Mein Kampf*, published by Varese-based La Lucciola, was on sale in major Italian bookshops and has even been displayed in a kiosk inside the Palace of Justice in Milan.

Published some time ago by the Giuseppe Nascimbeni Cultural Centre in Verona, the pamphlet *Cristianesimo, democrazia, capitalismo nel nuovo ordine mondiale* (Christianity, Democracy, Capitalism in the New World Order) by Gino Oliosi, remained in circulation. The pamphlet expresses *antimondialismo* and traditional, pre-Vatican II Catholic positions. Edizioni Il Cerchio published a book in 1992 entitled *I fanatici dell'apocalisse. L'ultimo assalto a Gerusalemme* (The Fanatics of the Apocalypse. The Latest Attack against Jerusalem) by Maurizio Blondet, who has written several anti-Jewish articles in Catholic and right-wing publications in the past.

There were very few anti-Jewish articles in mass media magazines and newspapers. However, an article by Monsignor Ernesto Pisoni entitled "La passione di Gesù" (The Passion of Jesus), appeared in an April issue of the weekly television guide, *Telesette*. After quoting the reference to the crucifixion of Jesus in the Book of Luke, the author alluded to the guilt of the Jews as the cause of future persecutions throughout history.

In another article, published in the widely-read Catholic magazine *Famiglia Cristiana* (Christian Family), theologian Franco Pierini, writing on the subject of persecutions suffered by the Jews, dismissed the fact that Jews had been accused of ritual murder as "unfounded for the most part".

An article entitled "Un tabù in banca. La finanza ebraica e i suoi rapporti con la Germania" (A Bank Taboo: Jewish Finance and its Relationship with Germany) in the Catholic weekly *Il Sabato* (Saturday), a magazine which has previously published numerous controversial articles, outlined how the power of Jewish finance operated in the past and suggested that it was still functioning.

MAINSTREAM POLITICS

Antisemitism in mainstream politics is rare. Irene Pivetti, a Lega Nord member of parliament, wrote an article in the November issue of *L'Indipendente*, a newspaper close to the Lega, entitled "I raid antisemiti: solo un polverone" (Antisemitic raids: just raising some dust), which denied the existence of antisemitism in Italy today and cited several Jewish characteristics as the cause of Jewish persecutions in the past.

In September, Gianfranco Miglio, the ideologist of the Lega Nord, commented that Hitler had only committed some "stylistic errors".

CULTURAL LIFE

In Soncino, a town which was renowned in the fifteenth century for its Jewish printers and where visitors can still visit The House of the Printers Museum, a museum guide in May described the Jewish family who had lived there using traditional antisemitic stereotypes.

GRASSROOTS

Antisemitic expressions by sports fans have occurred during and after soccer matches. While some fans do not technically belong to the skinhead "movement", they nonetheless imitate the skinhead style. These youths use the word "Jew" as a term of abuse against journalists who criticize them, opposing teams, individual players, and so on. In June, Aron Winter, a Dutch player for Lazio, who is erroneously assumed to be Jewish, was the subject of far-right graffiti in the Rome area, including "Winter raus, razza pura vogliamo" (Winter out, we want the pure race) and "Gli ebrei non li vogliamo" (We don't want any Jews).

Scholars and researchers have found inaccurate descriptions of Jewish history in Italian textbooks. These deficiencies have led to concern that students may not be sufficiently prepared to counter the stereotypes concerning Jews which they are exposed to outside of the classroom.

RELIGION

Even though the Papal position towards the Jews has become more open, there were still examples of ambivalent attitudes in 1992.

In April, the Cardinal of Rome and president of the Italian Episcopal Conference, Camillo Ruini, wrote an article for the Roman newspaper *Il Messaggero* for Easter. The theme of the article was the coming of Christ and the decision by Jewish leaders to eliminate him. In May, Sicilian Cardinal Salvatore Pappalardo was forced to apologize for describing the killers of an anti-Mafia judge as members of the "synagogue of Satan". The Archbishop of Vicenza, Pietro Nonis, wrote an article in December for the city's newspaper *Il Giornale di Vicenza* which concluded by suggesting that antisemitism continued to exist because the Jews did not want to recognize Jesus as the Messiah.

There were also two examples of antisemitic materials distributed among church-goers. A supplement to the Sunday service distributed in several Roman parishes included the figure of Jesus surrounded by stereotypical depictions of Jews holding money and knifes dripping with blood. In the church bulletin of the Poirino-Sud parish, near Turin, the priest employed several Christian writings as well as presumed passages of the Talmud to demonstrate Jewish contempt for Christianity, and described Jews as power hungry and haters of the church.

DENIAL OF THE HOLOCAUST

Theories denying the Holocaust are gradually gaining legitimacy and publicity, if not credibility. Skinhead and MPO leaders gained media coverage in 1992 when they outlined these theories. British Holocaust-denier David Irving was interviewed in the magazine section of the mainstream paper *La Repubblica* in July and French Holocaust-denier Robert Faurisson was accorded a full-page interview in the leading Italian newspaper, *Il Corriere della Sera*, in November.

Booklets and leaflets denying the Holocaust were distributed in Italian schools and universities during the year.

On 13 June, the MPO held a meeting in Rome focusing on Holocaust denial entitled "Olocausto Fuori" (Out with the Holocaust). The organizers invited Robert Faurisson, who did not come, and David Irving, who was refused entrance at the border for "reasons of public order".

Both Italian translations of foreign Holocaust denial material and works by Italian authors were available. In 1992, Edizioni di Ar published *La Soluzione finale. Problemi e polemiche* (The Final Solution: Problems and Controversies) by Carlo Mattogno. Mattogno has written approximately fifteen books and booklets denying the Holocaust, produced by such far-right publishers as Edizione La Sfinge in Parma, Edizioni dell'Uomo Libero in Milan, Edizioni Ar in Padua and La Sentinella d'Italia in Monfalcone.

Cesare Saletta, a supporter of the Gruppo Comunista Internazionalista (Internationalist Communist Group) wrote, printed and distributed three booklets denying the Holocaust in the past. *Lo sterminio mancato: la dominazione nazista nel Veneto orientale 1943-45* (The Extermination That Never Was: Nazi Domination in the Eastern Veneto 1943-45), a book by Pier Arrigo Carnier, was reprinted this year by Editore Mursia, a publishing house which has not previously been known to produce far-right material. The author did not specifically focus on the Holocaust but, by re-evaluating Nazi policy in Italy, defended the actions carried out on the Adriatic Coast and at the San Sabba concentration camp in particular.

EFFECTS OF ANTI-ZIONISM

During a demonstration against racism in Milan, a leaflet by the "Partito Marxista-Leninista Italiano" (Italian Marxist-Leninist Party) was distributed. Entitled *Razzismo, antisemitismo e sionismo* (Racism, Anti-semitism and Zionism), it stated that since Zionism was a chauvinistic, racist and fascist ideology, responsible for horrible crimes throughout history, a person could not be truly against racism if he or she was not also an anti-Zionist.

OPINION POLLS

Early in October, 1,064 adults were interviewed by telephone for an opinion poll on antisemitism. This poll was carried out by the firm AstraDemoskopea, at the request of *L'Espresso* magazine, which printed the results in early November.

The results showed different degrees of intolerance. Only 4 per cent demonstrated a marked intolerance against Jews that often turned into an aggressive attitude. They agreed with such statements as "Jews should leave Italy", "I don't like them and I don't trust them" and "They lie when

they say that Nazis exterminated millions of them in the gas chambers".

Thirteen per cent of interviewees agreed with the statement that antisemitic episodes in Germany and France were "a protest against Jewish power and the Jewish lobby"; 15 per cent of those interviewed thought that Jews were not "real Italians". Roughly 10 per cent of interviewees would "try to persuade their son/daughter not to marry a Jewish woman/man"; 9 per cent claimed that the extermination of the Jews was "overemphasized by the media", and 18 per cent stated that the Jews "should stop feeling sorry for themselves about the Holocaust".

The level of traditional prejudice towards Jews was high: 25 per cent of those interviewed thought that Jews had "a special relationship with money"; 31 per cent associated the word "Jew" with "money", 27 per cent with "race" and 17 per cent with "power".

Two main trends emerged. First, Jews were seen as outsiders and strangers by people with a higher level of education. Second, the young, aged between fourteen and seventeen, showed a higher-than-average rate of antisemitic prejudice.

Another opinion poll conducted in June 1992 sought to assess the degree of friendliness or dislike towards twelve minority groups. Jews ranked ninth (with 10 per cent) on the list of the most disliked people after gypsies, homosexuals, drug-addicts, Arabs and immigrants from non-EC countries. This level of negative feeling was the same as that registered in 1986, 1988, and 1990—indicating a rate of dislike that has remained unchanged over the years.

The widely read Catholic magazine *Famiglia Cristiana* commissioned the SWG Institute to carry out a survey focusing on attitudes towards Jews, antisemitism and the Holocaust among 701 young people between the ages of fourteen and twenty: 76.2 per cent of those interviewed either totally or partially agreed with the statement that "antisemitism is still present in Italy" (this percentage was considerably lower among adults), while 19.3 per cent found the statement to be an exaggeration and 3.2 per cent believed it to be untrue.

Only 32 per cent of the young people

included in the sample considered the Jews to be "Italians like everyone else", while 52.6 per cent saw Jews as "Italians with different cultural characteristics", 13.4 per cent saw them as "foreigners" and 1.7 per cent as "undesirable foreigners". SWG researchers reported that they found that young people who were studying were significantly less extreme in their views than those already working.

LEGAL MATTERS

In mid-December 1992, the cabinet passed a bill against racism which was still being discussed in parliament at the end of the year. The bill contained seven articles condemning the encouragement of discrimination as well as ethnic, nationalistic, racial and religious hatred. The provisions recommended official actions and police investigations similar to those employed against the Mafia and terrorists, proposed one- to five-year prison sentences for the incitement to racial hatred and suggested recourse to other punishments such as internal exile and special surveillance.

There has been some controversy over the need for new legislation in this area since several arrests have been made and charges preferred on the basis of laws already in existence. For the first time, a 1975 law against incitement to racial hatred was applied to the distribution of leaflets in December. Giorgio Cola, a nineteen-year-old skinhead member of the Movimento Politico per le Comunità di Popolo (Political Movement for the People's Community) was arrested as he handed out leaflets which contained statements against "abortion and the defence of the race" and which accused "the world's most criminal and murderous religion, Zionism" of being in favour of abortion in order to promote non-EC immigration and therefore destroy Catholic civilization.

COUNTERING ANTISEMITISM

Reaction against racism and antisemitism has been widespread in Italy. The president of the republic, Oscar Luigi Scalfaro, condemned antisemitism on several occasions during the year. The president of the Senate condemned these phenomena when introducing the session on 15 September and there have been numerous

motions condemning antisemitism proposed by regional and city councils and various party organizations.

In a report to an Italian Senate commission in November, interior minister Nicola Mancino warned that "the phenomenon of antisemitism should not be minimized" and expressed concern that any appearance that the authorities were "lukewarm" in reacting to antisemitism and skinhead activities might be seen as "tacit approval" and lead to "more significant actions against the Jewish community".

A large number of high schools, cultural and leisure associations requested lessons, documentary exhibits, conferences and talks on the history of antisemitism, the deportation of Italian Jewry and the current problem of antisemitism in Italy. In November, the minister of public education, Rosa Russo Jervolino, promised to produce and facilitate distribution to schools of an audio-visual presentation featuring Jewish history, a project that had been urged for some time by the Unione delle Comunità Ebraiche Italiane (Union of Italian Jewish Communities).

In a November address to German bishops, the Pope condemned racism and antisemitism and warned that the "indifference and apathy" of Christians in the face of racist violence was no less dangerous than the violence itself. Representatives of the Catholic community have sought to have the Pope's statements against antisemitism included in national school programmes on the Catholic religion.

On 9 November, the anniversary of Kristallnacht, 30,000 people marked the "European Day Against Racism, Xenophobia and Antisemitism" in thirty-one Italian cities with parades, candle-lit vigils and meetings. On 28 November, thousands of people marched through Rome, Milan, Bari and other cities to protest against racism and antisemitism. Many marchers wore yellow Stars of David and held banners proclaiming "Never Again" and "We are all Jews". On 29 November, 4,000 people marched to the old ghetto area in Rome to demonstrate solidarity with the Jewish community. There were further demonstrations against antisemitism and racism throughout Italy on 12 December. On 13 December, the Italian Soccer Players Association organized a "Footballers' Day of Protest against Violence and Racism", during which Italy's professional footballers staged pitch demonstrations against the mounting number of racist and antisemitic incidents and the increasing violence by extreme right-wingers and skinheads at matches. The Players Association and the Football Federation also initiated a television advertising campaign.

ASSESSMENT

As was the case last year, there were two overall trends in antisemitism in 1992: that of antisemitism as a by-product of neo-fascism and racism, and antisemitism linked to the Middle East conflict, which was less dramatic but more diffuse. It also emerged in democratic and "right-thinking" environments as well as on the political left and among arch-traditionalist Catholics.

The new factor this year was the improved organization and determination of the far right and the skinhead movement in particular. If at the beginning of the year the skinheads focused their propaganda and violent actions on the immigrant work force, during the second part of the year, they shifted their attention towards the battle against Jews and Zionism. There were no direct attacks against individuals, although the escalation of negative propaganda produced by this movement led to fears of future violence towards Jews.

Fortunately, the climate of intolerance gradually relaxed during the final weeks of the year and reports of antisemitism returned to levels consistent with preceding years.

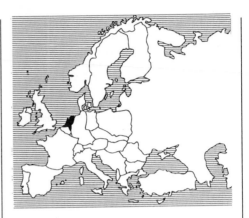

The Netherlands

General population: 15,000,000
Jewish population: 25,000 (mainly in Amsterdam)

GENERAL BACKGROUND

The present centre-left coalition of Christian Democrats and Labour has been in power since 1989. In 1992, the country's strong economy continued to experience a slow downturn particularly in the export market which suffered from the falling value of the American dollar and competition from Eastern Europe. The inflation rate remained stable at 3.6 per cent and unemployment fell to 4.3 per cent.

HISTORICAL LEGACY

In the 1930s, several National-Socialist parties emerged, some more antisemitic than others. During the Nazi occupation, contrary to what is generally believed abroad, social antisemitism increased sharply. In the early post-war years, anti-Jewish sentiment continued in certain circles, despite the fact that some 100,000 of the Netherlands' 140,000 Jews had perished in the Holocaust. Though social anti-semitism has by no means completely disappeared, it remains publicly unacceptable.

PARTIES, ORGANIZATIONS, MOVEMENTS

There are no overtly antisemitic parties in the Netherlands. The extreme right-wing parties, the Centrumpartij and the Centrumdemocraten party (which has one seat in parliament), are both insignificant and direct their propaganda mainly against the influx of Third World immigrants. Moreover, both parties are plagued by internecine rivalries, which this year resulted in two members leaving to establish their own parties.

The far-right Aktiefront Nationaal Socialisten (ANS) is the Dutch-Flemish branch of the banned German organization Gesinnungsgemeinschaft der Neuen Front, which was established in the 1980s by the late Michael Kühnen. In the Netherlands, the ANS is estimated to have between twenty-five and fifty members and is led by a thirty-five-year-old resident of Groninguen who, in November 1990, was sentenced to five months' imprisonment for distributing racist propaganda. The Groninguen public prosecutor is closely watching the ANS.

MANIFESTATIONS

In March, three graves in the Jewish cemetery in Beek, near the Belgian border, were desecrated and eight tombstones were daubed with swastikas. At the same time, a monument to Jewish deportees in Meerssen, near Beek, was defaced with swastikas. In a letter to a local newspaper, an unknown group called the Nationaal Socialistisch Volksfront (National Socialist People's Front) claimed responsibility for the violations.

Also in March, the synagogue in Haaksbergen in eastern Holland was daubed with a Star of David containing the words "kanker Jood " (Cancer Jew).

The antisemitic outbursts in Germany in the autumn were not accompanied by any physical violence against Jews or Jewish property in Holland. But CIDI (Centre for Information and Documentation on Israel) reported that it had received many complaints from Jews about antisemitic remarks during that period, although it added that the events in Germany may have increased Jewish sensitivities towards antisemitism in Holland. According to the CIDI, there was a 20 per cent increase in reported antisemitic incidents and verbal anti-semitism in Holland increased in 1992, although not alarmingly.

PUBLICATIONS

The German neo-Nazi paper *Neue Front Widerstand*, published by the banned German organization Gesinnungs-gemeinschaft der Neuen Front, has a circulation of about 400, of which about forty copies are sent to subscribers in the Netherlands. It is distributed through a post office box number in Delfzijl, a port in the Groninguen province, by a female resident who allegedly has contacts with the ANS.

Dutch police intercepted neo-Nazi material from the American NSDAP/AO which was addressed to a post office box used by the ANS in Assen.

MAINSTREAM POLITICS

Antisemitism in mainstream politics is rare because of the taboo on it in Dutch society. However, Jan Sonneveld, a Dutch Chris-tian Democrat member of the European Parliament, reportedly expressed anti-Jewish sentiments in June in the weekly newspaper *Vrij Nederland*. He was said to have dismissed criticism of Syria's human rights record as "Jewish slander".

CULTURAL LIFE

In April, a compact disc, which featured an antisemitic version of *Little Red Riding Hood*, reached no. 3 in the popular music charts. The song, entitled *Joodskapje* (Little Jewish Riding Hood), told of a Jewish girl's visit to her wealthy grandmother who had an exceptionally large hooked nose. At the CIDI's request, the record company, Polydor, removed the song from the compact disc and the performer, Frank Paardekoper, apologized.

When "house" music with a chorus which included words ending in-*oden* were played in teenage discos, both in large cities and in small villages with no Jewish populations, some club-goers reacted by yelling "*Joden, Joden* " (Jews, Jews). Some also wore leather jackets decorated with SS insignia.

GRASSROOTS

Antisemitic prejudice came to light at football matches, particularly against the Amsterdam club Ajax, which is considered to be a "Jewish" club by some supporters of rival clubs—notably those of Rotter-dam's Feyenoord team—because the team's players and management have in the past included members with Jewish origins. Some of Ajax's supporters, although not Jewish, nickname themselves "Jews", wear Ajax scarves emblazoned with the Star of David, wave Israeli flags and inscribe the word "Jew" on their jackets.

At a match between Feyenoord and the Israeli team, Hapoel Petach Tikvah, in Rotterdam on 16 September 1992, some of Feyenoord's supporters shouted "Joden" and imitated the hissing sound of gas escaping from the gas chambers. Because of the difficulty in isolating the people responsible and fearing an exacerbation of crowd violence, the match was not stopped. On 17 January 1993, nearly 1,000 supporters of FC Utrecht arrived in Amsterdam for a match with Ajax. Some of them shouted antisemitic slogans, made Nazi salutes and sang an antisemitic song, the words of which had been distributed beforehand. All 1,000 supporters, including the majority who had not participated in the incident, were sent back to Utrecht immediately, the first time that such a measure had been taken. In Breda, two supporters who had shouted "Auschwitz was a Lie" were banned from attending football matches for a year.

Black football players were also targets of abuse by some football supporters. These racist and antisemitic manifestations were part of the general hooliganism by some football supporters who, when attending matches, vandalize trains and shops. A report by the Royal Netherlands Football Association (KNVB) noted, however, that during 1992 vandalism by supporters in general had diminished while manifestations of racism and antisemitism had increased.

DENIAL OF THE HOLOCAUST

Leaflets denying the Holocaust were delivered to many people with "Jewish-sounding" surnames in five Dutch cities. The leaflets were published by the Antwerp-based Foundation Vrij Historische Onderzoek (Foundation for Free Historical Research), a "revisionist" organization whose spokesperson is Siegfried Verbeke, a member of the far-right Vlaams Blok in Belgium. Entitled *The Six Million Holocaust* and *American Expert Exterminates the Legend of the Gas Chambers*, the leaflets asserted that the Holocaust was "a pack of lies" designed to be "an endless source of income for the survivors and their descendants" and claimed that the gas chambers were used only "to combat lice that transmit typhoid". The CIDI, the Anne Frank Foundation and the Landelijk Bureau Bestrijding Racisme (Countrywide Bureau Combating Racism) filed a civil suit against the foundation under Dutch legislation

which outlaws racist and discriminatory acts (see **Legal Matters**).

OPINION POLLS

An opinion poll conducted in December showed that 3.2 per cent of those questioned would vote for one of the extreme right-wing parties because of their anti-immigration platforms. This would translate to five (out of 150) parliamentary seats. Among young people, the percentage of support for the far-right parties was 6 per cent.

LEGAL MATTERS

In November, the Hague District Court forbade the distribution in the Netherlands of two leaflets which denied the Holocaust on the grounds that they denied the existence of a crime against humanity and were likely to foster racism and discrimination. The banning followed a civil suit filed against the Belgian Foundation for Free Historical Research by the CIDI, the Anne Frank Foundation and the Landelijk Bureau Bestrijding Racisme. This may have been the first such ruling to cross international borders and was made on the basis of a European Community (EC) law which allows one resident of an EC country to sue a resident of another. Siegfried Verbeke, the spokesman for the Belgian foundation, appealed to the Hague Higher District Court.

In November, Nazi collaborator Jacob Luitjens was deported to the Netherlands from Canada. Luitjens was a member of the Landwacht, a local police force established by the Nazis to round up Jews and resistance fighters. Sentenced to life imprisonment *in absentia* for war crimes, Luitjens was immediately imprisoned on his arrival in Holland.

Jewish author Leon de Winter took action against the Amsterdam satirical students' weekly *Propria Cures* (which has 6,000 subscribers) over a cartoon which appeared in November depicting him in evening dress, leaning on a pile of emaciated dead bodies. This was a pastiche of an advertisement by the Libris chain of bookshops in which de Winter was shown leaning on a pile of books in evening dress with the caption "Do as I do. Buy your books with Libris".

De Winter lodged a civil action against *Propria Cures*, claiming damages of Fl 50,000 ($20,000) for the defamation of his good name and integrity as an author. He argued that the cartoon implicitly accused him of exploiting the Holocaust for personal financial gain. In the first week of December, he was awarded Fl 5,000 ($2,000) and *Propria Cures* was ordered to publish a full-page apology and forbidden to publish identical or similar material.

Leon de Winter again featured in a court case during the year following the publication in 1988 of a collection of writings by Theo van Gogh, a satirical newspaper columnist and television presenter. Van Gogh's original 1984 article accused de Winter of "parading" his Jewish identity and made questionable comments about the Holocaust, the gas chambers and Anne Frank. The reprinting of the article led the CIDI and the Foundation for Combatting Antisemitism (STIBA) to take criminal proceedings against van Gogh in the Amsterdam Lower District Court and, following van Gogh's appeal, in the Amsterdam Higher District Court.

Van Gogh argued that, as a satirical columnist, he was entitled to freedom of expression, but on 12 January 1993, he was fined Fl 2,000 ($1,200) and sentenced to a month's imprisonment, suspended for two years. He then announced that he would re-publish the column immediately and would be glad to go to prison for it. On 26 January 1993, the Amsterdam Higher District Court acquitted him, agreeing with his argument that he had made the same sort of "sick jokes" that are made by many columnists and cabaret performers in Holland.

COUNTERING ANTISEMITISM

On 18 November, the Senate unanimously adopted a resolution condemning all forms of racism and discrimination. The original motion, submitted by Hanneke Gelderblom, a Jewish senator for the Democrat 66 party, had also demanded a condemnation of antisemitism, but the resolution adopted omitted this word in order to extend its scope. In his New Year address to the second chamber of parliament in the first week of January 1993, chairman Dr Willem Deetman included antisemitism in a condemnation of racism and discrimination.

Also in November, the CIDI asked both the Interior and the Welfare and Culture Ministers to appoint an ombudsman in order to centralize complaints about racism and antisemitism and, if necessary, to allow centralized action to be taken against them. The CIDI's request was unsuccessful but, following the adoption during the year of a law against discrimination on grounds of race, religion and sexual orientation, a Commission for Equal Treatment was established which will pay special attention to complaints about racist and antisemitic discrimination. At a December conference of European Jewish organizations, the CIDI proposed that European Jewish communities should exchange information about antisemitic incidents so that protests could be made through the appropriate channels.

On Christmas Eve, over 10,000 persons, including many young people, demonstrated in Eindhoven and other towns against racism and xenophobia.

A report by the KNVB commission, established early in 1992, on the prevention of racist and antisemitic manifestations at football matches was published on 22 January 1993. It recommended a series of counter-measures including police intervention, the banning from matches of known trouble-makers and appeals by football players to stop racist and antisemitic crowd behaviour. The KNVB planned to register discriminatory expressions at football matches and to start an anti-discrimination campaign among supporters. A number of Feyenoord supporters have launched a campaign, Feyenoord Against Racism, to combat racist and antisemitic outbursts at football matches.

ASSESSMENT

There was no noticeable increase in racism or antisemitism in the Netherlands in 1992. Although antisemitism has not altogether disappeared at the grassroots, it remained under taboo in Dutch society and legal and political measures have been introduced to oppose it. However, it appeared to be essentially a residual phenomenon in the Netherlands and did not pose a serious threat to the Jewish community.

Norway

General population: 4,300,000
Jewish population: 1,400 (mainly in Oslo)

GENERAL BACKGROUND

Norway has a minority Labour Party government. The country's stable and prosperous economy relies heavily on oil revenue. In 1992, inflation remained at 2.4 per cent but unemployment was rising at approximately 5 per cent.

In October, parliament approved the European Economic Area agreement between the European Free Trade Association and the European Community. In November, Norway applied for membership of the EC despite such a move being opposed by more than half the population, according to opinion polls.

HISTORICAL LEGACY

Antisemitism and "scientific" racism had proponents in Norway since the beginning of the century, including John Alfred Mjoen, Eivind Saxlund and Mikal Sylten. Their writings were challenged by others and, in a few cases, by the courts. In the 1930s, the National Union Party led by Vidkun Quisling and other minor political groups advocated Nazi ideas and defended Hitler's actions against the Jews. The Labour press and two non-Socialist newspapers took a clear stand against Nazism and antisemitism. Most of the press sharply condemned the events of Kristallnacht and attacks on Jewish property in Oslo. But the Labour government was reluctant to receive refugees from Germany.

When Germany invaded Norway on 9 April 1940, the country's Jewish population was 1,800. During the Nazi occupation, persecution of the Jews began in 1941 and Quisling was elevated to the role of "minister president" in February 1942. In October 1942, Jewish property was confiscated and several hundred Jews were arrested. On 10 November 1942, the joint leadership of the Norwegian church and other Christian organizations wrote to Quisling protesting against these measures. On 26 November 1942, 530 Jews were deported to the Nazi extermination camps. Altogether, 760 Jews were deported from Norway and only twenty-four survived. About 930 Jews fled to Sweden and some sixty remained in hiding in Norway. After the war, the Norwegian government extended a special invitation to Jews who had survived the camps to settle in the country.

After a spate of swastika-daubing in early 1960, measures were introduced to combat antisemitism. For example, the ministry of church and education instructed schools to keep a close watch on possible anti-Jewish teachers. In 1963, parliament approved legislation outlawing actions or expressions offensive to a minority faith or ethnic group; in 1970, the legislation was amended and strengthened. The law has rarely been applied. In 1977, a teacher was given a suspended sentence of 120 days for making antisemitic statements in two Oslo newspapers.

In 1975, an antisemitic group called the National People's Party attempted unsuccessfully to enter mainstream political life. In 1985, it blew up a mosque in Oslo and sprayed Nazi slogan's on Oslo's synagogue. The party appeared to have disbanded in 1991.

PARTIES, ORGANIZATIONS, MOVEMENTS

In recent years, racist movements have appeared. While their principal targets are foreign immigrants, antisemitism is part of their programme. These groups have organized demonstrations against asylum-seekers and foreign workers. In November 1991, 10,000 Norwegians participated in a counter-demonstration against one of these movements, Norge mot innvandring (Norway Against Immigration).

Manifestations of neo-Nazism in Germany and Sweden have to some extent resulted in the growth of similar organizations in Norway. Three groups are known to be functioning: Zorn 88, the Boot Boys (skinheads) and Hvit arisk motstand (White Aryan Resistance). Zorn 88 (8 refers to H, the eighth letter in the German alphabet; 88=Heil Hitler), which was established in 1988, is the only self-declared neo-Nazi organization in Norway. It has an openly antisemitic programme, denying that the Holocaust took place and blaming the Jews for causing the Second World War. The group has approximately 100-250 members, several of whom were members of Quisling's National Unity party. The Boot Boys and Hvit arisk motstand are linked to, and collaborate with, the Swedish groups of the same names.

The Folkets Motstandsbeveglse (People's Resistance Movement) claims to be a Christian alternative to Marxism and Freemasonry and seeks to combat "racist Zionist violation". The organization is led by a Catholic, Alfred Olsen. The number of members or sympathizers of Folkets Motstandsbeveglse is unknown.

MANIFESTATIONS

Threatening telephone calls have occasionally been directed against persons who publicly condemn racism. Immigrant housing has been subjected to racist attack and arson. Antisemitic "chain letters" have been sent to non-Jews.

PUBLICATIONS

Alfred Olsen's Folkets Motstandsbeveglse put up antisemitic posters and circulated them to prominent individuals, officials, schools and newspaper editors. One poster threatened death to sixteen individuals, including two Jews, Salman Rushdie and a number of Christians sympathetic to Israel.

Norwegian academic Dagfinn Rian, in his book *The Great Lie. The Myth of Jewish Conspiracy and the Protocols of the Elders of Zion*, published in 1992, revealed that Alfred Olsen had privately published a Norwegian version of *The Protocols of the Elders of Zion*.

Zorn 88's periodical *Gjallarhorn* is published on an irregular basis with a print-run of 1,000.

DENIAL OF THE HOLOCAUST

Alfred Olsen invited Ahmed Rami, editor-in-chief of Stockholm's Radio Islam (see entry on **Sweden**), to Norway on two occasions in 1992. A planned meeting in March was banned by the police but, despite strong protests, Rami was allowed to speak at an open-air meeting in Oslo on 28 June.

LEGAL MATTERS

During 1992, a member of parliament and the Nansen Committee (the Norwegian Committee Against the Persecution of Jews) called on the director general of public prosecutions to investigate whether Alfred Olsen's antisemitic activities constituted sufficient violation of the law to merit prosecution. Their request is under consideration.

COUNTERING ANTISEMITISM

In June 1992, the government, the royal family and parliament paid respects to the Jewish community's centenary celebrations. Norway's Christian communities sent an open letter to the Jewish community condemning antisemitism.

On 26 November, the government organized a meeting, which was attended by King Harald and the speaker of parliament, to mark the fiftieth anniversary of the German deportation of the Jews of Norway. The prime minister promised her support in the fight against racism and antisemitism.

Between May 1990 and December 1992, Help the Jews Home, a joint Christian-Jewish committee, raised 25 million Norwegian kroner ($3,600,000) on behalf of immigrants to Israel from the former Soviet Union.

On 17 December, the Norwegian Group Against Antisemitism was founded to combat antisemitic manifestations in Norway and to monitor antisemitism worldwide.

ASSESSMENT

In 1992, antisemitism was a marginal phenomenon in Norway which posed little threat to the Jewish community, particularly when compared with racist sentiment against asylum-seekers.

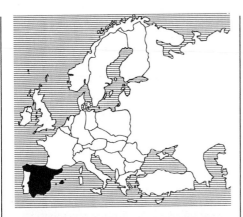

Spain

General population: 39,000,000
Jewish population: 12,000 (mainly in
Madrid, Barcelona and Malaga)

GENERAL BACKGROUND

Spain has been governed for a decade by
the moderate Spanish Socialist Workers'
Party (PSOE) under the leadership of
Felipe Gonzalez.

Violence perpetrated by the Basque
separatist organization ETA decreased
considerably in 1992, partly because of a
series of arrests of terrorists, and partly
because of a number of events, such as the
Barcelona Olympic Games, Expo '92 in
Seville and the 500th anniversary of
Columbus's voyage to the New World,
which led to a much heavier police presence than usual.

Spain witnessed a dramatic recovery
after a decade of economic uncertainty and
recession, culminating in the 1987-9 boom
that saw the fastest economic growth rates
in Europe. By 1990, the expansion had
slowed, but growth remained high, and
slower but sustained expansion is likely in
the medium term.

The domestic economy in 1992 was
plagued by two chronic problems—an
inflation rate (6.4 per cent) above that of its
main EC trading partners, and the highest
unemployment rate (20 per cent) in the EC.
The peseta was devalued twice in the final
quarter of the year, and the heavy government spending on the events of 1992 was

expected to rebound on the Spanish people.

HISTORICAL LEGACY

In 1992, Spain commemorated the 500th
anniversary of the expulsion of the Jews
who refused to convert to the Catholic
faith. The country remained without Jews
until 1869, when a new constitution, which
implicitly revoked the Edict of Expulsion
of 1492, allowed private religious practice.
It did not grant legal status to religions
other than Catholicism until 1992 (see
Legal Matters), thus curtailing the development of Jewish communities.

The small Spanish Jewish community
in existence during the civil war of 1936-39
was sometimes caught between the warring
sides, but most Jews fled the country
during the conflict.

Spain, under General Franco, remained
officially neutral during the Second World
War but sympathized with the German-
Italian axis. Spain's problems were often
blamed on the "Anglo-masonic-Jewish
conspiracy". During the war, however, the
Spanish government issued passports to
some 11,000 Sephardi Jews in Nazi-
occupied Europe. A further 35,000-40,000
Jews were permitted to pass through Spain
en route to other destinations. In 1967,
after the Six-Day War in the Middle East,
Jews in Egypt were issued with Spanish
passports and were thus able to leave for
the country of their choice.

Franco also provided shelter to Nazis
and Nazi collaborators after the war. Those
still alive include the Belgian Nazi collaborator Léon Degrelle, Dutch collaborator
Patiste Hawke and Mauthausen doctor
Aribert Heim. Other Nazis went to South
America via Spain with the assistance of
local bureaucrats.

Between the 1950s and 1970s, following the independence of Morocco and
adverse conditions in Argentina, Jews
settled in Spain in larger numbers.

PARTIES, ORGANIZATIONS, MOVEMENTS

The Barcelona-based Circulo Español de
Amigos de Europa (Spanish Circle of
Friends of Europe, CEDADE) is the most
prominent neo-Nazi organization in Spain.
Established in 1965, it is one of the oldest,
largest (with some 1,500 members) and
most active neo-Nazi group in Europe. It is

responsible for many of the antisemitic publications in Spain through its publishing houses and it sponsors lecture tours by Holocaust-deniers. CEDADE, which has adopted environmental concerns as a vehicle to express its xenophobic and racist theories, is especially interested in creating links with groups holding similar ideas elsewhere in Europe. Its leader, Pedro Varela, is in prison in Austria for neo-Nazi activities.

The Frente Nacional (FN), which has ties with Le Pen's French Front National, and Juntas Españolas (JE) are far-right nationalist parties. They have the support of some 1 per cent of the population, concentrate mostly on nostalgic memories of the Franco era and oppose liberalization, democracy and abortion. While they do not espouse antisemitism, their anti-immigrant platforms reflect a pro-white xenophobia. The leader of the FN, Miguel Bernard, said in November that he expected all the fringe groups to unite and become a strong enough force to gain ground in the 1993 elections. However, attempts to unite the FN and the JE have so far failed.

There are several other ultra-right groups, including Nacion Joven, Las Bases Autonomas, Coordinadora de Estudiantes Nacional Revolucionaria, Fuerza Nacional de Trabajo and Juntas Jovenes. While these parties are mostly fascist and racist, they operate on the fringe.

MANIFESTATIONS

In March, on the eve of the ceremony commemorating the 500th anniversary of the expulsion of Spanish Jewry and the visit to Spain of Israeli President Chaim Herzog, anti-Jewish graffiti appeared in some Madrid locations. All were signed by a youth group that is apparently controlled by CEDADE. Examples included: "Jews, murderers of the Palestinian people", "Death to Sepharad", "Holocaust lies", "We don't want Jewish visits" and "Juden Races [sic]". Some members of the Jewish community received antisemitic letters during this time as well.

The anniversary of Franco's death, 20 November, has become for European neo-Nazis the occasion of an annual pilgrimage to Madrid's Plaza de Oriente, where Franco's followers would gather to hear him speak, and to Franco's grave in the Valle de los Caidos. This year's pilgrimage took place in a climate of increased anti-foreigner violence following the racist killing of a Dominican woman by an off-duty Civil Guard and three right-wing teenagers, and the manslaughter of a Moroccan immigrant by a group of skinheads, as well as the attack on immigrants in Germany and other European countries.

PUBLICATIONS

The media devoted much coverage to the "Sepharad '92" activities and featured special supplements on the Sephardi Jews who were expelled 500 years ago.

The Barcelona daily paper *La Vanguardia* published a series of articles by its regular columnist Gregorio Moran. In one article, entitled "The Spirit of Masada", the author criticized visits by Israeli schoolchildren to Masada, where "after converting an inhospitable place where Herod the Great had palaces and mosaics, after adapting everything to fit a concentration camp for fanatics, they [the Jews] preferred to stab each other to death before falling to the impious Romans". Moran continued: "In the State of Israel, everything is artificial. From its cities, its myths, its museums . . . its sticky Torah students, with their herds of children and their lies to avoid the army and be paid for by the state for the simple fact that they serve as rabbits working to compensate the high birth rate of the Arabs and do not work because it is undignified for the spirit. . . . Even if they have all the money in the world, even if they are supported by all the financial 'lobbies' on the planet, nobody will be able to bury the centuries of Arab and Christian culture that made Jerusalem what it is today."

CEDADE, with its four publishing houses, is one of the largest producers of antisemitic publications in Europe. The publishing houses reproduce the bi-monthly magazine *Cedade*, Nazi books, pamphlets and other material (in Arabic as well as Spanish), some of which is exported to Latin America. Some 20,000 issues of the monthly neo-Nazi magazine *Halt!* are sent to Austria, where such publications are supposed to be banned.

DENIAL OF THE HOLOCAUST

In May, CEDADE national secretary Christian Ruiz told the Spanish state news agency EFE that in Spain as opposed to other countries, "there are no laws against denying the Holocaust". At that time, CEDADE organized a European neo-Nazi congress in which it demanded the legalization of Nazi parties. Although only a handful of people attended, speakers included such prominent Holocaust "revisionists" as Ernst Zundel, who was convicted for distribution of Holocaust-denying material in Canada, Manfred Roeder, who was sentenced to thirteen years' imprisonment in Germany for terrorist activities, and Thies Christophersen, a German who distributes Nazi pamphlets in Denmark.

In February, French Holocaust-denier Robert Faurisson visited Spain on a lecture tour sponsored by CEDADE, organized to coincide with a visit by Nazi war crimes investigator Simon Wiesenthal. Although Faurisson was prevented from delivering his speech at the University of Barcelona, he spoke instead at a local hotel. He also gave a lecture, entitled "The Holocaust—The Search for Truth", at the law faculty of Madrid's Complutense University. British Holocaust-denier David Irving cancelled a lecture he was scheduled to give in Barcelona.

GRASSROOTS

Some members of Ultrasur, the Frente Atletico, Boixos Nois and Brigadas Blanquiazules, the fan clubs linked to Madrid and Barcelona's main football teams, Real Madrid, Atletico de Madrid, Barcelona and Español, cheer their teams on with neo-Nazi symbols including swastikas and Hitler salutes. They are believed to be behind much of the recent skinhead violence. The Jewish community has called for the football clubs to stop supporting these groups.

RELIGION

The pro-monarchist Catholic Union Nacional Tradicionalista (National Traditionalist Union) circulates La Voz de España, a monthly news-sheet critical of aspects of Spanish society, including Jews. Following the conciliatory visit of King Juan Carlos to the Madrid synagogue, the March issue questioned the need for repentance for what was done to the Jews.

OPINION POLLS

There were no opinion polls directly related to antisemitism in 1992. A profile in La Vanguardia revealed that the "average Spanish racist" was over fifty years old, had a low educational and social level, voted for right-wing parties and had never travelled outside of Spain.

LEGAL MATTERS

In February, after years of failed attempts, Samuel Toledano, president of the Federation of Jewish Communities in Spain, signed an agreement which granted the Jewish community—along with the Muslim and Protestant communities—the same legal status as that of the Roman Catholic community. Under the terms of the accord, the Jewish community was granted tax-exempt status on property and other holdings, donations by members became tax-deductible, marriages performed by rabbis were considered valid in civil law, and Jewish education became available to pupils in public schools who requested it.

In May, a court in Barcelona sentenced Damian Carulla, director of Editorial Makoki, a publishing house which specializes in underground comics, to thirty-two days' imprisonment and a fine of 100,000 pesetas ($1,000 dollars) for publishing a Spanish version of Hitler=SS, a comic book that satirized the Holocaust. Carulla was also forbidden to publish further editions of the book in Spain. The court, which overturned a previous ruling that had absolved Carulla of any wrongdoing, observed that "Jews can find no humour in the disrespect and lack of consideration for their feelings or those of their relatives who lived through the concentration camps".

In November, two skinheads were prosecuted in Barcelona for a 1990 attack on a teenager who refused to kiss a photograph of Hitler. One of the aggressors was never found and, although the other failed to appear at the trial, the state attorney sought a six-year sentence for him in absentia.

In 1991, the Constitutional Court ruled in favour of a Holocaust survivor who claimed that Belgian Nazi collaborator Léon Degrelle, in questioning the existence of Nazi gas chambers, had injured her honour as a member of a group which had suffered from Nazi persecution, even though he had not mentioned her specifically. Despite this landmark ruling, there is a gap in Spanish legislation on incitement to race hatred and there is no legislation against Nazi or racist gatherings and symbols. In December, Socialist legislators proposed reforming the penal code to introduce "racist motivations" and "xenophobia" as elements that could lead to criminal charges.

COUNTERING ANTISEMITISM

In 1992, Spain's immigrant communities experienced manifestations of the wave of racism which occurred in many other European countries. When, in November, a Dominican woman was murdered by an off-duty Civil Guard and three youths, governmental and public condemnations made clear their opposition to racism and xenophobia.

The year was particularly important for Jewish life in Spain, "Sepharad '92", the 500th anniversary of the expulsion of the Jews of Spain, was commemorated with a series of congresses, concerts, special events, books and media attention which sought to analyse and create awareness of the role of the Jews in Spanish life before the expulsion.

The most important expression of conciliation came from King Juan Carlos who visited the Madrid synagogue on 31 March—the 500th anniversary of the edict of expulsion of the Jews—and welcomed the Jews back to their home. The King did not revoke the edict, as some people had hoped, since it was considered to have been revoked de facto in the 1869 constitution.

In October, in the presence of former Israeli President Itzhak Navon, some 1,000 members of the International Christian Embassy (ICE) held an act of public repentance in Toledo. According to organizer Samuel del Coso Román, the ICE's Spanish representative, the group felt that the King's reconciliation in the synagogue did not go far enough.

In November, seventy-six professors at Madrid's Complutense University signed a manifesto in opposition to the participation of Belgian Nazi collaborator Léon Degrelle in a lecture series organized by the law faculty on the subject "Precursors of the Fall of Communism". In December, some 300 students of various faculties at Complutense protested to the university authorities regarding the increase in neo-Nazi activities. Demanding a clear and official statement denouncing racism and xenophobia, the students handed in a petition with 4,000 signatures and complained against the "consent that is given by some of the faculties to activities by groups with fascist ideology".

The daily *El Mundo* reported that the national and municipal police had joined forces in order to combat the skinhead violence, which rose significantly in the second part of the year.

ASSESSMENT

Although there was a marked increase in violent incidents carried out by skinhead groups in comparison with last year, these remained at the fringe of society and did not constitute a serious threat to the Jewish community. There was much ignorance about Jewish matters but the events marking "Sepharad '92" helped to redress the balance.

Sweden

General population: 8,700,000
Jewish population: 16,000-20,000 (mainly in Stockholm)

GENERAL BACKGROUND

The liberal-conservative coalition government, which came to power in 1991, faced the worst economic crisis of the post-war period. Unemployment was 5.3 per cent (2.7 per cent in 1991) and the inflation rate was 2.4 per cent (9.4 per cent in 1991). The number of bankruptcies rose by 22 per cent. Economic growth was -1.8 per cent in comparison with the previous year.

HISTORICAL LEGACY

In the 1930s, anti-Jewish attitudes influenced Sweden's restrictive policy towards the immigration of Jewish refugees. In

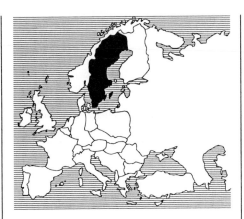

1938, widespread fear of massive Jewish immigration, including antisemitic protests at Uppsala and Lund universities, led Sweden virtually to close its borders to Jewish refugees from Nazi persecution. It was also due to Swedish and Swiss demands that in 1938 the German authorities began stamping "J" in the passports of Jews.

In the late 1940s and 1950s, veteran Nazi Einar Aberg, a founder and leader of the wartime organization Sveriges Antijudiska Kampforbund (Swedish Anti-Jewish Action Group), became a leading European antisemitic propagandist.

In the late 1970s, with the emergence of the neo-Nazi Dietleb Felderer and his Bible Researcher publishing-house, material denying the Holocaust began to circulate on a larger scale than before. During the Israeli campaign in Lebanon in 1982, traditional antisemitic accusations surfaced in articles, editorials and letters within the mainstream press.

In 1987, Radio Islam, headed by Ahmed Rami, a refugee from Morocco, started broadcasting antisemitic propaganda in the Stockholm area. It claimed, for instance, that there was a Jewish world conspiracy and that the Holocaust was a "Jewish hoax". In November 1989, the Stockholm District Court sentenced Rami to six months' imprisonment for broadcasting antisemitic propaganda and Radio Islam was forbidden to broadcast for one year. In October 1990, the appeal court in Stockholm upheld the conviction with minor changes and reaffirmed the prison sentence.

PARTIES, ORGANIZATIONS, MOVEMENTS

Riksfronten (Reich Front, formerly Foreningen Sveriges Framtid) is a racist and antisemitic organization with an estimated 200 members. In February 1992, its founder and leader, Leif Larsson, received an eighteen-month prison sentence for violent assault; the organization is headed by Torulf Magnusson in his absence.

Kreativistens Kyrka (Church of the Creator, COTC) is the Swedish branch of the American neo-Nazi organization of the same name. COTC, which is violently racist and antisemitic, is led by Tommy Ryden and has an estimated 100 members.

Nordiska Rikspartiet (Nordic Reich Party) is a neo-Nazi party headed by Assar and Vera Oredsson, with an estimated membership of 300. This organization, in particular its "storm troops" Reich Action Group, have previously been linked with neo-Nazi violence. During 1992, these activities decreased.

Nysvenska Roerelsen (New Swedish Movement) is led by veteran fascist Per Engdahl. It is a Mussolini-style movement with an estimated 300 members.

Radio Islam/Svensk-Islamiska Foreningen (Swedish-Islamic Association) is a group centred around the now-closed antisemitic radio station Radio Islam and includes editor-in-chief Ahmed Rami and David Janzon, a member of the neo-Nazi Sveriges Nationella Forbund (see below), who is legally responsible for the station. Rami has close ties with several neo-Nazi groups and Holocaust denial propagandists in Sweden and abroad. In October, he was one of the main speakers at the annual conference of the American Institute of Historical Review. According to a report in the Swedish daily *Expressen* in May, Radio Islam has for a number of years received funding from Iran.

In October 1992, Radio Islam closed down as a result of the Stockholm District Court verdict against David Janzon (see **Legal Matters**). Ahmed Rami has published several antisemitic books, among them *Vad ar Israel?* (What is Israel?) in 1988, *Israels makt i Sverige* (Israel's Power in Sweden) in 1989, and *Judisk haxprocess i Sverige* (Jewish Witch-hunt in Sweden) in 1990.

Sverigedemokraterna (SD, Sweden Democrats) is an extreme right-wing party, primarily hostile to non-European immigrants but also openly antisemitic in its internal propaganda. The party has been in internal conflict over policy issues, with one faction tentatively moving towards hard-core neo-Nazism and another wishing to continue the parliamentary "Le Pen-style" approach. The party won almost 5,000 votes in the September 1991 general election but did not gain any seats. There are SD representatives in the local councils of Dals-Ed and Hoor. SD leader Anders Klarstrom previously belonged to the Nordiska Rikspartiet. The SD has contacts with a number of far-right organizations in Europe including the German Republikaner Partei, whose leader, Franz Schönhuber, spoke at an SD meeting in Stockholm in 1991. Its present membership is unknown.

Sveriges Nationella Forbund (SNF, Swedish National League), a neo-Nazi movement, has an estimated 200 members, including David Janzon, who belongs to the SNF's Stockholm section. During the past two years, the Malmoe section of the SNF has linked up with Gerhard Lauck's US-based neo-Nazi organization NSDAP/AO.

Storm Network is an informal gathering of the most violent and militant neo-Nazi activists in Sweden, many of whom are skinheads, which openly voices support for Ahmed Rami and Radio Islam. It has an estimated 150 activists, with an additional 250-500 possible sympathizers nationwide, and maintains links with members of Riksfronten, COTC and the SD. Storm Network is centred around Vitt Ariskt Motstand (VAM, White Aryan Resistance), which is modelled on the US Nazi terror organization The Order and is promoted as the nucleus of the "Aryan Revolution". Activists have been sentenced for a number of violent crimes, including three cases of murder (in 1985, 1986 and 1990), several armed robberies, burglaries in military arms depots and violent assaults. During 1992, leading VAM activist John Christopher Rangne was imprisoned for planning an armed robbery. Another activist, Stefan Lund, was given a five-year prison sentence for armed robbery.

MANIFESTATIONS

On 24-25 November, more than 140 gravestones in two Jewish cemeteries in Stockholm were desecrated. The police linked the desecrations to the antisemitic propaganda spread by Ahmed Rami in connection with his "anti-Zionist congress", which was later cancelled. On 2 December, the Jewish cemetery in Karlskrona was desecrated.

Antisemitic expressions were common at most neo-Nazi meetings. At the annual neo-Nazi gathering in Stockholm on 30 November, commemorating the death of King Karl XII, a Jewish woman was physically attacked by neo-Nazis calling her a "Jewish swine".

The number of threats against, and antisemitic letters or telephone calls to, Jews or Jewish institutions increased during the year.

PUBLICATIONS

Radio Islam continued broadcasting its violently antisemitic propaganda in the Stockholm area until October, when it closed down during the trial of David Janzon in the Stockholm District Court (see **Legal Matters**).

Expressions of antisemitism were common in most neo-Nazi publications. Riksfronten publishes the quarterly magazine *Riksalarm* (Reich Alarm), which has a circulation of approximately 400.

RAHOWA (Racial Holy War), the journal of COTC, did not appear during the year, probably due to the imprisonment of its editor David Twaland (also known as David Emilsson) who in early 1992 was sentenced to eighteen months' imprisonment for burglary in a military arms depot. COTC also distributes the American English-language *Racial Loyalty*. Both publications are virulently antisemitic.

Nordiska Rikspartiet publishes the quarterly magazines *Nordisk Kamp* (Nordic Struggle), *Nordiska Rikspartiet*, (Nordic Reich Party) and *Solhjulet* (The Sunwheel), which appears sporadically.

Sverigedemokraterna's bi-monthly magazine *SD-Kuriren* (SD Courier) appeared only once during 1992. SD party ideologue Leif Ericsson, also known as Leif Zeilon, publishes the irregular semi-private magazine *Sveamal* which openly promotes both the views of VAM as well as those of Ahmed Rami and French Holocaust-denier Robert Faurisson.

The SNF and NSDAP/AO currently publish the joint paper *Sveriges Nationella Forbund,* which uses the resources of Gerhard Lauck's magazine *The New Order.* (The paper is also published in German, Hungarian, Dutch and French.)

The bi-monthly magazine *Storm,* from which Storm Network takes its name, promotes armed struggle against "racial enemies, Jews and the ZOG [Zionist Occupation Government] regime". The magazine has become the focal point for several activist organizations, of which VAM is the best known.

Antisemitism within the mainstream media was less frequent than in previous years. However, in June, the daily *Expressen* (circulation 600,000) published articles by two exiled Estonian antisemites, Jürl Lina and Alex Milits, which, among other things, blamed Estonian Jews for the Communist terror in Estonia in 1940-1. The daily *Dagens Nyheter* (circulation 400,000) published two letters from readers which defended Radio Islam and propagated Holocaust "revisionist" ideas. Other letters compared Israelis or the Israeli government with the Nazis. In June, the daily *Nerikes Allehanda* (circulation 70,000) carried an article claiming that the propaganda of Radio Islam had to be understood in the context of the "fascist and racist" nature of Zionism as well as the "criminal wars" pursued by the "Jewish state of Israel". On all these occasions, the papers published articles or letters protesting against the antisemitic statements which had been made.

GRASSROOTS

The refusal by the Rectorate of Uppsala University to dissociate itself from anti-Jewish statements made by Professor Jan Bergman, head of the Theology Department and a lecturer on Judaism, attracted criticism from international scholars. Bergman made the statements in connection with the 1989 trial of Ahmed Rami, on whose behalf he was also a witness.

In a March report on the main television news magazine *Aktuellt,* a former student of Bergman's revealed that the professor had warned students that Jews "in a position of power can be dangerous".

The minister of education, Beatrice Ask, condemned statements made by

Gunnel Wahlstroem, a religion and history teacher in a Stockholm secondary school, in an interview she gave to the *Judisk Korenika* (Jewish Chronicle). Wahlstroem, who belongs to Ahmed Rami's "inner circle", questioned the veracity of the Holocaust and claimed that media and finance in Sweden were controlled by the Jews.

DENIAL OF THE HOLOCAUST

The denial of the Holocaust was a major theme in Radio Islam broadcasts until its closure in October. A majority of neo-Nazi and far-right publications included propaganda denying the Holocaust.

In mid-March, French Holocaust-denier Robert Faurisson visited Stockholm at the invitation of Radio Islam's Ahmed Rami. Following massive protests, Faurisson failed to deliver any speeches in public. While in Sweden, members of the Riksfronten acted as Faurisson's body-guards. On March 20 and 21, Faurisson participated in two Radio Islam broadcasts entirely devoted to propaganda denying the Holocaust. During his visit to Sweden, Faurisson also made a video in which he presented his "revisionist" ideas (the video was placed on sale by Radio Islam and Sverigedemokraterna).

Faurisson returned to Sweden on 3 December as the sole guest of the "anti-Zionist World Congress" which, according to its organizer, Ahmed Rami, was to have taken place in Stockholm at the end of November, but did not do so. Faurisson did not make any public appearances, though a speech denying the Holocaust was broadcast on a Stockholm local radio station run by the near-defunct far-right Sverige Partiet (Sweden Party) on 5 December.

Forskningen om Förintelsen (Research on the Holocaust), a book denying the Holocaust, by a Rolf Du Rietz, was published during 1992. Very few copies of the book are thought to be in circulation.

LEGAL MATTERS

On 8 October, the Stockholm District Court sentenced David Janzon, who is legally responsible for Radio Islam's broadcasts, to four months' imprisonment for "agitation against an ethnic group" (that is, the Jews). The defence lodged an appeal, which will be heard in 1993.

The trial dealt with statements made on Radio Islam during 1991. Among the nine statements which the court found had violated the law against "agitation against an ethnic group" was the claim that "Jewish power is like cancer and AIDS, against which the Swedish society has no immunity and no defence", as well as several "revisionist" statements claiming that the Jews had invented the Holocaust for economic reasons. The verdict stated that Radio Islam "expresses the opinion that the Jews are lying about the Holocaust in order to gain economic profit. This accusation expresses contempt for the Jewish national group".

While the trial was in progress, Ahmed Rami announced his decision to close the radio station down. This decision was probably a tactical move, since the court would in any case have ordered Radio Islam to close down for a period of up to one year following the guilty verdict.

On 2 October, the Attorney General brought new charges against Radio Islam. But, under the new constitutional law regarding freedom of speech which came into force on 1 January 1992, charges were pressed against editor-in-chief Ahmed Rami, rather than David Janzon, who, although legally responsible for the station, has minimal influence on the broadcasts. It is uncertain whether these charges will result in a trial against Rami.

The new charges concern statements made on Radio Islam during April 1992 in which Jews were, among other things, accused of spreading pornography, crime, drugs, and moral and spiritual decay in order to "undermine" non-Jewish society. One of the statements included the assertion "Many great thinkers have also come to the conclusion that the Jewish Torah and Talmud are a testament of Satan. But also that *The Protocols of the Elders of Zion* represents a concretization of these Satanic scriptures. *The Protocols of the Elders of Zion* is an operative plan of action, meant for our time."

COUNTERING ANTISEMITISM

On 17 March, protesters organized a demonstration in Stockholm against Robert Faurisson's presence in Sweden and prevented him from delivering a speech in the Stockholm suburb of Enskede. Speakers included a former deputy prime minister, Per Ahlmark, founder of the Swedish Committee Against Antisemitism, and the Committee's chairman, Liberal MP Hakan Holmberg. In 1992, for the first time, the Committee received financial support from the Swedish government. During the year, Per Ahlmark addressed many international gatherings in several countries urging democratic governments to take a strong stand against antisemitism.

The desecrations of two Jewish cemeteries in Stockholm in November were strongly condemned by government and opposition leaders. Prime Minister Carl Bildt and opposition leader Ingvar Carlsson also visited one of the cemeteries with the chairman of the Stockholm Jewish community, Salomo Berlinger.

In Stockholm on 29 November, the Swedish Committee Against Antisemitism and other organizations organized a demonstration, which was attended by almost 1,000 people, against the cemetery desecrations and the planned "anti-Zionist World Congress". Speakers included the minister of culture, Birgit Friggebo, and the secretary general of the Social Democratic party, Mona Sahlin. A similar demonstration in Malmoe on 13 December was attended by 500-600 people. Archbishop Bertil Werkstroem expressed sorrow and outrage at the desecrations and said the deed reflected "an inability to learn from the most tragic crimes in history".

The aborted "anti-Zionist World Congress" led to strong condemnations by members of the government and leaders of the opposition.

The demand by the chairman of the Swedish Committee Against Antisemitism, parliamentarian Hakan Holmberg, that neo-Nazis and antisemites invited to Sweden should be prevented from entering the country under the immigration law, attracted cross-party support. When Robert Faurisson was later allowed into Sweden, the minister of culture, initiated a commission with the aim of strengthening the law on immigration. A five-party motion demanding a revision of the law against "agitation against an ethnic group" to include denial of the Holocaust was not approved by the parliament.

British MPs Greville Janner and David

Sumberg representing the Inter-Parliamentary Council Against Antisemitism met with members of the Swedish government and the Speaker of the House, Ingegerd Troedsson.

A Holocaust survivors' organization was established to promote education about the Holocaust.

ASSESSMENT

The prime targets of xenophobia and racism during 1992 were non-European refugees and asylum-seekers from the former Yugoslavia. A disturbing sign was that approximately 10 per cent of voters (according to opinion polls) supported Ny demokrati (New Democracy), a populist party openly hostile towards refugees and immigrants which had twenty-five parliamentary seats.

During 1992, there was an increase both in reported antisemitic incidents and in the distribution of anti-Jewish propaganda. Particularly worrying was that, in the propaganda of the increasingly violence-prone far-right and neo-Nazi groups, antisemitism had come to play a definitive dominant role. It should be noted that open expressions of antisemitism were relatively rare outside the extremes of the right and the left. However, anti-Zionist statements close to antisemitism and attempts to trivialize the Holocaust were occasionally made by persons who regard themselves as left-of-centre.

In 1992, much of the political establishment and the media, in contrast to previous widespread indifference, reacted strongly against antisemitism and neo-Nazism. The Swedish Committee Against Antisemitism received support from a large number of politicians and journalists. It remained to be seen if this positive development was temporary or marked a major change of attitude.

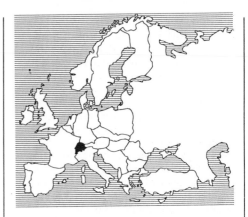

Switzerland

General population: 6,600,000
Jewish population: 18,300 (mainly in Zurich, Geneva and Basle)

GENERAL BACKGROUND

Switzerland has a federal constitution, under which the twenty cantons and six half-cantons retain considerable autonomy. The ruling coalition of the Christian Democratic People's Party, the Social Democratic Party, the Radical Democratic Party and the Swiss People's Party has been in power since 1959.

The collapse of Communism in Eastern Europe and moves towards greater European integration have led Switzerland to question its traditional neutrality and this issue dominated Swiss politics in 1992. Following a May referendum, in which a majority voted in favour of Switzerland's joining the International Monetary Fund and the World Bank, the government announced that it would apply for membership of the European Community. It experienced a setback when a referendum on 6 December rejected Switzerland's proposed membership of the free trade European Economic Area.

The Swiss economy was in recession during the first six months of the year but appeared to be on the way to recovery in the second six months. Inflation fell from 5.9 per cent in 1991 to 3.3 per cent and unemployment rose to 3.9 per cent from

1.3 per cent in 1991.

Switzerland has more requests for asylum than any other European country, relative to the size of its population. In 1991, applications were up by 16 per cent on 1990, and violent incidents towards asylum-seekers increased from 41 in 1990 to over 90 in 1991. Following changes in legislation and bureaucracy relating to asylum, the number of asylum-seekers fell from 42,000 in 1991 to 20,000 in 1992.

The number of xenophobic incidents also fell, to 40. Most were relatively minor; attacks on hostels for asylum-seekers on the whole caused little damage. Graffiti sprayed on hostels included Nazi slogans. Five died and several were injured in hostel fires; although arson was not proven in these cases, it has been suggested that police and judiciary were sometimes reluctant to recognize political motivation behind attacks. Nearly all attacks which were politically motivated stemmed from the far right; far-left groups are not believed to have carried out any attacks in the last three years.

HISTORICAL LEGACY

Switzerland's Jews were the last in Western Europe to acquire complete emancipation when the 1848 Swiss constitution was amended in 1866 to give them civic and legal equality and in 1874 to allow them freedom of religious expression.

Ritual slaughter was prohibited by the Swiss constitution in 1893. In 1974, this prohibition was removed from the constitution but introduced into a law for the protection of animals. Switzerland is today the only European country in which Jews and Muslims may not slaughter animals in accordance with their religious practices.

In 1933 and 1935, the Swiss Federation of Jewish Communities took legal action against the distribution in Switzerland of Henry Ford's *The International Jew* and *The Protocols of the Elders of Zion*.

The period from the end of the Second World War to the end of the 1970s saw only isolated incidents of public antisemitism. Christian and Jewish organizations united to fight all forms of xenophobia.

In 1978-9, the screening of the American *Holocaust* television series in Switzerland led to the desecration of cemeteries,

the daubing of graffiti and arson attacks on synagogues in Basle and Zurich. The war in Lebanon in 1982 brought about a renewed wave of anti-Jewish manifestations which subsided shortly afterwards. Apart from the activities of some small neo-Nazi groups, antisemitic incidents occur in Switzerland mainly as a reaction to events in the Middle East. In autumn 1992, however, following the events in Rostock, there was a marked increase in antisemitic incidents.

PARTIES, ORGANIZATIONS, MOVEMENTS

The number of skinheads and radical neo-Nazi activists remained constant, at around 100-200, with perhaps 200-400 sympathizers. Neo-Nazi parties, of which the largest is the Patriotische Front, have a fluid membership; members accused of criminal acts often distance themselves from their organization. Most far-right organizations are local and small, with rarely more than a few dozen members. The Patriotische Front, founded in 1988, grew from sixty or seventy members in spring 1989 to 400 members and several thousand sympathizers in 1992. Its members use neo-Nazi vocabulary and the greeting "Heil Hitler". Nationale Koordination acts as an umbrella organization for neo-Nazi groups; it is led by Gaston-Armand Amaudruz, a veteran racist of long standing who publishes neo-Nazi and antisemitic writings banned outside Switzerland, including *Die Auschwitz-Luge* (The Auschwitz Lie).

The xenophobia of neo-Nazi groups has exerted some influence on legitimate far-right parties such as Schweizer Demokraten (Swiss Democrats, formerly National Action for People and Homeland), and even on sections of the Swiss Peoples' Party, one of the governing coalition parties, particularly in encouraging more restrictive policies towards asylum-seekers. In the 1991 elections to the two chambers of the Swiss parliament, the splinter parties, including Schweizer Demokraten, gained ground by using anti-foreigner slogans.

MANIFESTATIONS

From January to September there was virtually no public manifestation of antisemitism, although some hotels in mountain resorts continued to refuse to accommodate groups of religious Jews. From October onwards, however, several incidents occurred in which Jews were verbally or physically abused, particularly in Zurich. In November, an armed man attempted to enter the offices of the Swiss Jewish community in Zurich, and there was increased verbal abuse of Jewish children on their way to and from school. In December, swastikas were daubed on at least six schools. On 19 December, eleven graves in the Bern Jewish cemetery were defaced with swastikas and other Nazi graffiti.

PUBLICATIONS

Memopress, founded in 1966, appears in the form of a press release. It is published in a print run of 40,000, six times a year by Emil Rahm, a businessman who lives near Schaffhausen. Topics covered by *Memopress* have included Holocaust "revisionism" and the fight against foreigners in Switzerland.

Eidgenoss (Swiss Citizen) is a monthly publication founded in 1977. Published by Max Wahl, who was fined in Munich in October 1991 for incitement to racial hatred, *Eidgenoss* has contained articles attacking "Jewish propaganda lies" about the Holocaust and news from the far-right scene in Germany and other European countries.

Advertisements for Hitler's *Mein Kampf*, placed by a sign-painter called Luigi Baitella, appeared in three city-owned free newspapers: in the *Berner Stadtanzeiger* in February and December, in the *Winterthurer Stadtanzeiger* in May and in the *Tagblatt der Stadt Zürich* in November.

DENIAL OF THE HOLOCAUST

Bernhard Schaub, a teacher at a Rudolf Steiner school, wrote and published *Adler und Rose*, a booklet denying the Holocaust. Two similar "revisionist" books, *Der Holocaust Schwindel* (The Holocaust Swindle) and *Der Holocaust auf dem Prufstand* (The Holocaust Examined), were published by the teacher Jurgen Graf.

LEGAL MATTERS

In December, the Nationalrat (the lower chamber of the Federal Assembly) voted to accept a revision of the penal law in order to permit adoption of the United Nations' Convention on the Elimination of all Forms of Racial Discrimination. The new legislation would prohibit racist and religiously prejudiced actions, including the denial of the Holocaust. The law is due to go before the Ständerat (the upper chamber) in 1993. However, after legislation has been passed by the Swiss parliament, it can be put to a referendum if 50,000 Swiss citizens demand it. Some right-wing and xenophobic groups are already mobilizing for such a referendum and there are fears that this could lead to an emotional campaign with an uncertain result.

A military tribunal ruled against a Swiss army commanding officer who subjected a Jewish soldier to antisemitic abuse. Since there is currently no legal redress against antisemitic remarks, the tribunal based its conviction on the fact that the soldier had also been called a "pig".

COUNTERING ANTISEMITISM

A parliamentary group against racism and xenophobia was formed. The group's membership, which exceeded 100 by the end of 1992, has been particularly active in getting the revision of the penal law through parliament (see **Legal Matters**).

In April, to mark the 500th anniversary of the expulsion of the Jews from Spain, Switzerland's Conference of Catholic Bishops and representatives of the Swiss Federation of Jewish Communities signed a joint declaration condemning antisemitism as a "crime against God and humanity".

ASSESSMENT

A central theme of Swiss politics during the year was hostility to foreigners. While there was a drop in racially motivated violence against asylum-seekers, and while manifestations of xenophobia and antisemitism remained more muted than in Germany or some other European countries, their seriousness should not be underestimated. The rise in antisemitic incidents towards the end of the year was significant, given the traditional taboo on antisemitism in Switzerland. Moves to close the borders to immigrants complicated the possibility of integration for Jewish immigrants too.

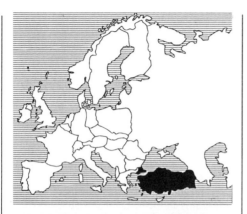

Turkey

General population: 57,000,000
Jewish population: 26,000 (mainly in Istanbul)

GENERAL BACKGROUND

Turkey is ruled by a coalition of the right-of-centre True Path Party and the left-of-centre Social Democratic Party, led by Prime Minister Suleyman Demirel.

Turkey has a free market economy. The liberalization and privatization processes which began in the 1980s have produced some positive results in terms of increased economic growth and a boom in exports but have not resolved the chronic problems of inflation (65 per cent) and unemployment (16 per cent).

The country has been the scene of political violence in the south-eastern provinces, near the Iraqi and Syrian borders, mainly conducted by members of the underground Kurdish separatist movement, the Kurdish Workers' Party (PKK).

HISTORICAL LEGACY

In 1992, Turkish Jews celebrated the 500th anniversary of the arrival of their Sephardi ancestors who were expelled from Spain in 1492. Although there were Jewish settlements in various parts of Anatolia under the Roman and Byzantine rule, the Sephardi Jews, who were welcomed by the Ottoman Empire after Spain's expulsion order, formed the majority of Turkish Jewry. Under the Ottoman administration, Jews in the Balkans and the area which forms present-day Turkey enjoyed a comfortable life.

After the establishment of the Turkish Republic in 1923, the constitution provided for equal rights for the Jews and other religious minorities. There has been little antisemitism since then, except during the Second World War, when neutral Turkey imposed discriminatory measures against the non-Muslim minorities, including the Jewish community.

Since the Second World War, there have been relatively few cases of anti-semitism and none of these came from official quarters. Since the 1960s, antisemitic newspapers and magazines have occasionally appeared. In some instances, the major dailies have expressed antisemitic views. In the 1970s, Turkey's first-ever antisemitic political party emerged: known originally as the National Salvation Party, it is now called the Welfare Party and is led by the pro-Islamic Necmettin Erbakan.

In September 1986, twenty-one worshippers were killed in an attack by the Abu Nidal terrorist group on the Neve Shalom synagogue in Istanbul.

PARTIES, ORGANIZATIONS, MOVEMENTS

The Welfare Party is the only political group in Turkey which has an antisemitic platform. In 1992, its leader, Necmettin Erbakan, repeatedly made antisemitic remarks in parliamentary debates, public meetings and television appearances. During a debate in parliament in April, he blamed the outburst of political violence in south-eastern Turkey on the Zionists and the Jews. In a panel discussion on state television in August, he claimed that the Jews were behind the "ethnic cleansing" in Bosnia-Herzegovina. In speeches and statements to the media, Erbakan has repeatedly referred to a Zionist-Jewish conspiracy with the United States and other "imperialist" forces against Turkey. He has alleged that the "Jewish lobby" in the US and Europe seeks to establish in the Middle East a "Greater Israel" which would encompass Turkish territory.

The Welfare Party received a boost in the local elections held in some provinces in October. It received 25 per cent of the total vote, in comparison with 17 per cent in the 1991 parliamentary elections.

In 1991, there emerged an antisemitic grouping, centred around the Bilim Arastirma Vakfi (Islamic Foundation for the Research of Knowledge). Founded by Adnan Oktar, who is also known as Adnan Hodja (a name which confers upon him the status of an Islamic religious teacher), the grouping continued to be active in 1992. Adnan Oktar, who draws his support mainly from university students with wealthy backgrounds, has expressed strong antisemitic sentiments in books and publications, including the newspaper *Son Mesaj* (see **Publications**).

MANIFESTATIONS

The Neve Shalom synagogue in Istanbul was bombed on 1 March by a terrorist group reported to be affiliated to the Hizbullah movement. Two terrorists threw two grenades in front of the well-guarded synagogue shortly after a wedding ceremony. One grenade exploded and injured a Jewish passer-by; the other failed to go off. One of the perpetrators was immediately apprehended and the other was later arrested in south-eastern Turkey. Two other accomplices were detained in Istanbul. The terrorists admitted that they had acted on instructions from the "Turkish Hizbullah" group in the south-eastern province of Cizre, which has links with the Lebanese Hizbullah.

PUBLICATIONS

There was an increase in antisemitic publications in 1992. Adnan Oktar circulated 600,000 copies of the second edition of the forty-page paper *Son Mesaj* (Last Message). The first edition, which was released in 1991, had an estimated circulation of 200,000. The paper was mainly devoted to antisemitic articles which, among other things, repeated mediaeval Christian blood libels; alleged that Hitler was financed by Jewish banks; asserted that Hess, Goering and Himmler were ordered by the Jews to eliminate European Muslims and Christians; explained how the swastika was derived from the Star of David; and outlined a Jewish-masonic world conspiracy whose emissaries included the Diners Club. There were also slanderous stories about the Quincentennial Foundation, which organized the series of events

celebrating the arrival of the Jews in Turkey five centuries ago.

Privately financed, *Son Mesaj* was not sold on news-stands, but was widely distributed by post. Many Jews received copies in their offices or homes. The similarity of the editorial material to antisemitic publications in other countries suggested that it was provided by foreign antisemitic sources.

A number of pro-Islamic dailies and weeklies have carried antisemitic articles. The Welfare Party's daily paper, *Milli Gazete* and the pro-Islamic *Zaman* have constantly published anti-Jewish material.

Anti-Jewish attacks have also appeared in Marxist and Maoist publications. The pro-Maoist weekly magazine *2000'e Dogru* (Towards the Year 2000) has on various occasions attacked the Quincentennial celebrations, the Turkish Jewish community, and prominent Jewish businessmen. During 1992, the magazine conducted a slanderous campaign against Jewish industrialist Jack Kambi, the president of the Quincentennial Foundation and an active member of the Jewish community. The magazine made systematic personal attacks on Jack Kambi and his son Jeffy, who is a partner in one of Turkey's top industrial companies. While many of the magazine's attacks were levelled at the Kambis' alleged dealings with Israel and the threat which the magazine perceived such dealings posed to Turkey, no such criticism was directed at non-Jewish firms which trade with Israel. The right-wing nationalist periodical *Yeni Dusunoe* (New Thought) made similar attacks on Jack Kambi.

Halil Ibrahim Celik, a Welfare Party parliamentarian and member of the parliament's Human Rights Commission, told the private Channel 6 Television in November that he believed the Jews should be annihilated and that this belief was in line with the Prophet's teachings. He said that his hatred of the Jews was due to the killing of Muslim Palestinians by the Israelis. When asked whether it was right for him to have laid a wreath at Auschwitz a few years earlier to honour the Nazi persecutors and not to commemorate the victims, Celik expressed his admiration for Hitler.

LEGAL MATTERS

As a result of representations by the Jewish community, the State Security Court prosecutor ordered legal proceedings against *Son Mesaj*. The prosecutor established that the antisemitic campaign conducted by the paper was contrary to the constitution and the penal code as well as to international agreements such as the Paris Charter, to which Turkey is a signatory. Court deliberations began in late 1992. This was the first time that the Turkish authorities had taken legal action against a publication on grounds of antisemitism.

In April, the four men arrested for the bombing of the Neve Shalom synagogue were put on trial at the state security court in Istanbul. In February 1993, the two assailants received sentences of ten years and ten months each, one accomplice was sentenced to ten months' imprisonment, and the fourth was acquitted.

COUNTERING ANTISEMITISM

The Quincentennial celebrations provided an opportunity for Turkish officials and other Turkish personalities to express their sympathy for the Jewish community. The occasion also gave the Jews a very good press.

ASSESSMENT

The rise in Islamic fundamentalist activity in Turkey, with its anti-Israel and anti-Jewish overtones, caused increasing concern within the Jewish community. The success of the Welfare Party in the 1992 local elections led to speculation that it might become a coalition partner in a future government, since none of the main parties had an overall majority. Although the legislative elections were not due until 1995, this possibility worried many Turkish citizens, particularly in the Jewish community.

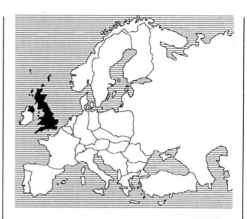

United Kingdom

General population: 57,200,000
Jewish population: 300,000 (two thirds in London; also in Manchester, Leeds and Glasgow)

GENERAL BACKGROUND

Three themes dominated the political arena in 1992—the general election; the worsening economic situation; and Britain's relations with its European Community (EC) partners and the Maastricht Treaty on European union.

The general election, held in April, saw the return of the Conservative Party to power, but with a depleted majority.

The primary focus of the government's economic strategy continued to be the reduction of inflation. However the decline of inflation to a year-end figure of 3.6 per cent reflected a deepening of the recession, with manufacturing output ending up below the 1991 figure and unemployment rising to just under three million or over 10 per cent of the workforce. A severe run on sterling in September forced Britain's withdrawal from the Exchange Rate Mechanism of the EC and resulted in an effective devaluation. The successive reductions in bank interest rates did not lead to the expected industrial recovery and by the end of year, the economic situation appeared to be one of the most troubled of the post-war era.

HISTORICAL LEGACY

Individual Jews were present in the British Isles in Roman times but organized settlement began after the Norman conquest of 1066.

Massacres of Jews occurred in many cities in 1190, most notably in York. The medieval settlement of Jews came to an end with their expulsion by King Edward I in 1290. After that date, only a few converts to Christianity or secret adherents to Judaism remained.

Following the expulsion of the Jews from Spain in 1492, a secret Marrano community became established in London, but the present community dates from 1656.

During the following three centuries, there were few serious outbreaks of antisemitic violence. By the early nineteenth century, Jews had achieved virtual economic and social emancipation. In the next eighty years, all barriers to political emancipation were removed.

The influx of refugees from Russia between 1881 and 1914 (when the British Jewish community rose in number from 25,000 to 350,000) led to antisemitic agitation both on the streets and in parliament.

The rise of fascism and Nazism encouraged the growth in Britain of the British Union of Fascists and the Imperial Fascist League. Mass antisemitic rallies and marches in the mid-1930s led to street battles between right-wingers on the one hand, and Jews and left-wingers on the other. At no time was there any likelihood of right-wing electoral success. The government, while often unsympathetic to those who resisted antisemitism, was ultimately concerned with the threat to public order and Britain's legislation banning overt paramilitary activity dates from this time.

Sir Oswald Mosley, the leader of the British Union of Fascists (later renamed the Union Movement), was interned for the duration of the Second World War together with other fascist and Nazi sympathizers.

In the post-war years, Jews were faced with attempts by antisemitic groups to re-establish themselves. In the 1960s, a younger generation of neo-Nazis agitated against the Jewish community. While there were several arson attacks on synagogues and physical assaults on Jews, the authorities again took action (if somewhat belatedly), and several leading neo-Nazi activists were imprisoned.

During the late 1970s and early 1980s, the forerunners of the groups now active achieved their widest support, but they were ultimately undermined by the changing political climate and their own internal divisions.

PARTIES, ORGANIZATIONS, MOVEMENTS

The far right grew both in size and scale of activities during the year, although it remained comparatively small, marginal to the mainstream political process and without influence on government or local authority policy.

The largest group, the neo-Nazi British National Party (BNP), consolidated its leadership position during the year, and its estimated membership grew to around 2,500 members.

The BNP contested thirteen constituencies in the April 1992 general election and won 7,005 votes, an average of 1.05 per cent in each constituency. Although insignificant in real terms, the BNP's support in the London constituencies of Bethnal Green and Stepney (1,310 votes) and Bow and Poplar (1,107 votes) were the highest nationalist votes since the National Front's watershed year of 1979. The organization was also greatly encouraged in October, when it gained 651 votes (20 per cent) in a local council election in Millwall (East London).

While presenting itself as a legitimate political party, the BNP is in fact dedicated to neo-Nazi ideology and the raising of racial tensions through its "Rights for Whites" campaigns. BNP members are widely regarded as being responsible for repeated desecrations of Jewish cemeteries and buildings, and Jews, blacks, Asians, homosexuals and "left-wingers" are regularly targeted for physical attack. BNP literature often contains thinly-veiled allegations of a Jewish conspiracy.

The BNP has increasingly strong links with European and North American neo-Nazi groups and members regularly attend international far-right gatherings. Recent months have witnessed the formation of a new clandestine group, based on the BNP, but including members of other groups, called Combat 18, which has already begun to harass members of the Jewish community.

The Blood and Honour movement provides a focus for violent neo-Nazi skinheads, and has approximately 1,500 members. The group organizes skinhead concerts throughout Europe, and its adherents are regarded as role models by their European and American counterparts.

It is this linking function with Europe and North America that makes Blood and Honour an important part of neo-Nazi youth culture. Skinheads pride themselves on their reputation for (violent) hooliganism, and skinhead concerts are regularly followed by assaults on blacks and Asians. However, it is Jews who remain the primary target, and its magazine, also called *Blood and Honour*, is filled with Nazi imagery and accusations of a Jewish conspiracy. There is little doubt that Blood and Honour supporters have been partly responsible for a number of antisemitic incidents, particularly cemetery desecrations and the daubing of communal buildings.

The National Front (NF) was Britain's leading far-right group for many years. Its membership has now declined to 150-200, and many of its more violent elements have now joined the BNP. The NF was further weakened by the loss of its powerful deputy leader, Steven Brady, who declared the NF's ideology to be obsolete and offensive.

Brady's move reflected the growing far-right demands for a British equivalent of Jean-Marie Le Pen's Front National. This trend is currently led by the Western Goals organization, which has unsuccessfully attempted entryist tactics into the Conservative Party. During the year, it sought to become the British representative of the Technical Group of the European Right, the umbrella organization of far-right groups represented in the European Parliament. Western Goals hosted Le Pen in December 1991, when both Steven Brady and Holocaust denial propagandist David Irving held meetings with him. Irving's links with Western Goals were illustrated in September 1992, when a Western Goals leader, Gregory Lauder-Frost, addressed one of Irving's Holocaust denial "seminars".

Western Goals failed in its attempts to hold meetings with Le Pen and Allessandra Mussolini of the Italian Movimento Sociale Italiano at the annual Conservative Party conference, and it appears that the group may now have ceased activity, to be replaced by the newly-formed Revolutionary Conservative Caucus.

Britain's leading Holocaust denial propagandist, David Irving, has nevertheless announced his interest in such a group, which he speculatively referred to as a "Christian Democrat" party. This is not the first time that Irving has attempted to become a national leader of the far right, but his popularity elsewhere has not been matched in Britain.

MANIFESTATIONS

Reported antisemitic incidents in 1992 rose by 9 per cent over 1991, indicating a continuing upward trend.

The most noticeable aspect of recent years has been the increased dissemination of antisemitic literature. This constitutes antisemitic activity in its own right and, by its very nature, incites further anti-Jewish activity.

Dissemination of antisemitic literature takes two forms—the mass distribution of publications among Jewish organizations and individuals, with the aim of having as widespread an impact as possible, and targeted abusive material, which is sent to specific individuals. The former type accounted for 14 per cent of the total, compared to 21 per cent in 1991; the latter type remained stable in 1992, representing 35 per cent of the total, compared with 33 per cent in 1991.

Nineteen-ninty-two produced what appears to be a new and disturbing change of emphasis, with assaults accounting for a higher proportion of total incidents than in previous years (11 per cent, compared with 6 per cent in 1991). Such incidents usually take the form of violent (but not life-threatening), unprovoked attacks on Jewish teenagers, perpetrated by youths.

PUBLICATIONS

The distribution of antisemitic leaflets and other publications emanating from the far right declined during the first three-quarters of 1992, although it began to rise again towards the year's end.

Two examples were hoax Chanukah cards containing anti-Jewish poems sent to prominent Jews in Britain and abroad, and a series of pseudo-academic monographs sent mainly to Jewish academics by Geryke Young, the elderly widow of the late George K. Young, a prominent far-right campaigner.

It is also usual for correspondents whose letters are published in the Jewish press, to receive antisemitic literature from far-right organizations.

Of growing concern is the increasing dissemination of anti-Jewish literature through Muslim sources. This falls into two categories. First, the sale of classic antisemitic texts, such as *The Protocols of the Elders of Zion* and *The International Jew*, by mainstream Muslim bookshops. The *Satanic Voices*, published during the year by David Pidcock, leader of the Islamic Party of Britain, quoted extensively from far-right sources, including *The Protocols*, in what was ostensibly an analysis of Salman Rushdie's *Satanic Verses*. The second category is religiously-inspired antisemitic articles in fundamentalist publications. Although they represent only a small minority within Britain's Muslim population, fundamentalist groups such as Hizb-ut-Tahrir (Liberation Party), the Murabitun European Movement and the Muslim Institute continuously publish, or voice, anti-Jewish propaganda. Islamic societies in British universities and colleges are increasingly subject to fundamentalist influences, and as a consequence, are becoming centres for anti-Jewish, as well as anti-Israel, activity.

Antisemitism seldom appears in the mainstream press, but occasional articles do betray lapses of taste, or go beyond political denunciation of Israeli government actions.

MAINSTREAM POLITICS

Antisemitism rarely surfaces in mainstream political life. Successive governments have acknowledged the significant role played by the Jewish community, its institutions, leaders and members in the country's political life. The Board of Deputies is recognized by the government as the representative body of the community and, over the past 100 years, has been accorded

statutory responsibilities for various matters affecting the community. Jews are represented in the highest offices of state, in parliamentary and municipal life, in the civil and armed services, the judiciary and universities and all professions and occupations.

BUSINESS AND COMMERCE

Certain small areas of the business world are affected by a residual (social) antisemitism, but these are of little account, and Jews are active, and often prominent, in all walks of commercial activity.

GRASSROOTS

Antisemitism is not a feature of education in Britain today. Teaching of the Holocaust, as part of the historical study of the Second World War, has recently been included in the National Curriculum.

Mobile exhibitions, such as *Anne Frank in the World* organized by the Anne Frank Educational Trust and the Board of Deputies' own Jewish Way of Life Exhibition, tour Britain on a continuing basis and are focused primarily at school children,

RELIGION

No religious antisemitism emanates from the major churches, and recent years have seen a growth in the dialogue between the Jewish community and church bodies. The Council of Christians and Jews, the Interfaith Network, and the Inner Cities Religious Council all play an important and growing role in promoting interfaith understanding, and numerous meetings have taken place between Jewish and Muslim religious leaders.

The community is concerned, however, by the growth of evangelical activity aimed at it, and on several occasions during the year sought meetings at the highest level with church authorities.

DENIAL OF THE HOLOCAUST

Holocaust denial, a common theme in far-right literature and activity, is now also beginning to appear within the Muslim community and fundamentalist leaders have recently spoken of their contacts with David Irving.

During the course of the year, Irving held three so-called "Historical Revisionist

Seminars", each attended by approximately 150 people, the majority of whom were BNP activists. Guest speakers at his meetings included the Canadian Ernst Zundel and the American lawyer Sam Dickson.

Irving himself embarked on several international tours in mid-1992. The tours were curtailed, following his deportation from Canada, the refusal of the American authorities to re-admit him, and his banning from Italy.

Almost without exception, Holocaust denial was limited to the political and religious fringes and did not intrude into the mainstream academic or political worlds, despite the widely criticized use of David Irving by the leading Sunday paper *The Sunday Times* in its publication of Goebbels's diaries.

EFFECTS OF ANTI-ZIONISM

Much organized anti-Zionist activity has traditionally been controlled by the London office of the Palestine Liberation Organization (PLO). The rescinding of the United Nations' resolution equating Zionism with racism, the loss of PLO funding after the Gulf War, and the start of the Middle East peace talks have drastically curtailed anti-Zionist activity in Britain. The most memorable action in the last year was the delivery of fake land confiscation orders to offices near the Israeli embassy. However, anti-Zionist articles in both the fringe and the mainstream press sometimes go beyond criticism of Israel and betray the anti-Jewish bias of the authors.

OPINION POLLS

No opinion polling on antisemitism was carried out in the United Kingdom.

LEGAL MATTERS

The primary legislation to counter incitement to racial hatred and discrimination is contained within the Public Order Act (1986), which incorporated the former Race Relations Act (1976) and the Malicious Communication Act (1988).

Following the conviction of seven people for distributing antisemitic literature in 1991, there was a temporary diminution in the scale and offensiveness of the literature distributed in 1992, and only two

cases came to notice during the year—Brian Arthur Leason in the Gateshead area and Michael John Green in Hull. Green was found guilty and given a suspended sentence; the other case has yet to be heard.

Charges against veteran neo-Nazi campaigner Colin Jordan were dropped in December for technical reasons, following a year-long judicial process. During and after the Gulf War, he had sent antisemitic leaflets to prominent members of the Jewish community.

The Board of Deputies continued to press for the strengthening of the legislation to counter antisemitic manifestations and meetings were held on the matter with relevant government departments.

During the course of the year, a number of far-right activists were convicted for crimes of violence, although they were not directed at the Jewish community; some arose out of violent clashes with anti-Nazi activists.

COUNTERING ANTISEMITISM

At the end of the year, the award of the Interfaith Medallion to the Papal Pro-Nuncio, HE Archbishop Luigi Barbarito, by the International Council of Christians and Jews was a significant event in the diplomatic, Christian and Jewish calendars. In his address, he referred to the Pope's recent condemnation of antisemitism.

Further significant statements were made by the Archbishop of Canterbury, the Anglican primate, at the Jubilee celebrations of the Council of Christians and Jews in December, and both the prime minister and the home secretary hosted meetings at which they were briefed on antisemitism by Board of Deputies' leaders (November 1991 and July 1992 respectively).

Significant meetings were also held during the year with religious and lay leaders of the Hindu, Sikh and Afro-Caribbean communities. The meetings led, in the case of the Hindu community, to a growing and close collaboration with the Jewish community.

ASSESSMENT

The Jewish community in Britain faced organized hostility from three main sources—the far right, Muslim fundamentalists, and Palestinian and Arab elements.

Other hostile groups included anti-Zionists (primarily on the extreme left), black separatists, and Christian fundamentalists. Anti-Jewish prejudice in business and social life was not a major factor.

The overall rise in European far-right activity, racism and xenophobia were reflected in Britain. However, the British far right has no influence on government policy.

The far right may lack "power" in the political process, but its impact on racial and political violence is manifest throughout Britain, and shows the growing confidence and strength of groups such as the BNP and Blood and Honour. The bulk of this "street" violence is directed against people of Afro-Caribbean and Asian origin, but Jews remain the primary ideological target. The growth in Holocaust denial propaganda is the most obvious example of this.

Antisemitism from Muslim fundamentalists continues to be the product of an aggressive anti-Zionism that attacks supposed Jewish and Zionist conspiracies to control the world and is increasingly expressed in far-right terminology.

Despite these concerns, the Jewish community in Britain was not subject to the scale of antisemitism which affected some other Jewish communities and antisemitism remained marginal.

Central and Eastern Europe

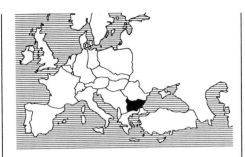

Bulgaria

General population: 8,472,724 (December 1992 census)
Jewish population: 2,200-7,000 (mainly in Sofia)

GENERAL BACKGROUND

Bulgaria's post-Communist phase is characterized by two major features. The first is the suspicion of many Bulgarians that the Turkish and Muslim minority of a million-and-a-half, whose human rights were abused in the 1980s, is seeking to impose a Turkish identity on Muslims who were ethnic Bulgarians. The second major feature is the relatively strong influence of the Bulgarian Socialist Party (BSP), former Communists, who are now playing on Bulgarian nationalist sentiment.

The Bulgarian government formed at the end of 1992 was officially sponsored by the Movement for Rights and Freedoms (MRF), the party which represents Bulgaria's ethnic Turks and Muslims in parliament. The government depended on a patched-together majority of the MRF with only 10 per cent of seats in parliament, a number of former Union of Democratic Forces (UDF) deputies, and over half of the deputies of the Bulgarian Socialist Party (Communists).

The process of economic reform slowed down. About 90 per cent of the economy was still state-owned. The decline in the GDP continued, with unemployment rising to 16 per cent. The rate of inflation was 80 per cent.

HISTORICAL LEGACY

There is no strong tradition of antisemitism in Bulgaria. There were no anti-Jewish laws in Bulgaria until the outbreak of the Second World War, although some discriminatory practices had begun to develop. For instance, there were practically no Jews in the state administration. Official persecution of the Jews began with the Law for the Defence of the Nation, which was modelled on Nazi Germany's Nuremberg laws and was adopted in January 1941. The Jews were stripped of basic human rights. As in other countries allied with Nazi Germany, the Jewish population was destined for deportation to the death camps. About 12,000 Jews from Bulgarian-occupied territories in Greece and Yugoslavia were deported to extermination camps under German pressure and with the authorization of the Bulgarian government. Jews who were Bulgarian citizens were rescued at the last moment. With the personal approval of King Boris III, their deportation was at first postponed and was later revoked altogether. Although at the time the antisemitic propaganda was backed and inspired by the authorities, antisemitism was never widespread. Anti-Jewish restrictions were abolished at the end of the Second World War.

At the time of Stalin's anti-Jewish measures in the USSR in the late 1940s and early 1950s, Jews in Bulgaria were expelled from the interior ministry and the security services. The Communist government installed in September 1944 conducted a policy of tacit assimilation but no systematic antisemitic policy on its part can be discerned.

PARTIES, ORGANIZATIONS, MOVEMENTS

There are no antisemitic political bodies as such but the following should be borne in mind. First, the Bulgarian National Front, founded and based in the USA, contains a number of former fascists (the most notorious of whom, Ivan Dochev, was, however, expelled). The organization began to transfer its base to Bulgaria in 1992. Second, there are numerous small nationalist organizations. If combined, their following could prove significant and, should the economic crisis deepen, their influence would be likely to rise. Third, hardliners in the main political forces—the UDF and the BSP—do not always shrink from nationalism. In an interview with the

BSP daily newspaper *Duma* on 27 August 1992 Rumen Vodenitcharov, a politician close to the former Communists, claimed that some Bulgarian parliamentary deputies and trade unionists were being used by the "Jewish-pro-Turkish lobby" in the US Congress.

MANIFESTATIONS

Political instability has given rise to isolated manifestations of antisemitism. In the last stage of the 1992 government crisis the then outgoing deputy prime minister, Ilko Eskenazy of the UDF, was widely expected to be the next prime minister in a government sponsored by the MRF. Privately, however, some UDF deputies said that Bulgaria could not have a Jew as head of a government sponsored by the Turks (i.e. the MRF). On 27 August Eskenazy was viciously attacked in the weekly *Novy den*, which has a limited circulation and claims to be centrist and independent, for opposing the move by some leading UDF members and deputies to repeal the Act of the People's Tribunal. This raised two issues. First, the People's Tribunal was set up after the Second World War to try persons suspected of having committed war crimes. The Communist regime, however, used it as a pretext to murder many of its opponents and many innocent people. The Organization of Bulgarian Jews, Shalom, and Eskenazy do not dispute these facts, but suggest that only innocent victims of the Tribunal should be rehabilitated. This proposal seems unacceptable to some and the *Novy den* article which attacked Eskenazy stated, among other things, that the Jews themselves provoked anti-semitism, the pogroms and even the Holocaust.

Second, the property of those sentenced by the Tribunal was confiscated. Many of them had acquired property confiscated from Bulgarian Jews under the anti-Jewish legislation. If the sentences passed by the Tribunal were to be revoked en masse, their heirs would acquire the property as the restitution laws in Bulgaria do not go beyond 1945. Thus much of the Jewish property confiscated during the Second World War may never be returned to its owners.

PUBLICATIONS

The antisemitic book *Svetovna konspiratsiya* (The World Conspiracy) was reprinted, though it was not in great demand. Writing in the weekly *Novy den* on 16 July 1992, Nikola Nikolov, the book's author, claimed that Lea Cohen, Bulgarian Ambassador to the EC and Belgium, was serving a Jewish "élite" which sought to rule the world.

COUNTERING ANTISEMITISM

In December 1992, President Zhelev, meeting with Bulgarian members of the International Committee set up to commemorate of the fiftieth anniversary of the rescue of Bulgarian Jewry, which falls in the spring of 1993, stressed the need for understanding and cooperation between ethnic and religious groups.

ASSESSMENT

Although a nationalistic trend—promoting the Bulgarian national identity despite the existence of a large Muslim minority—continued in Bulgarian politics, the country's post-Communist phase remained free of serious antisemitism.

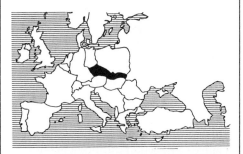

Czechoslovakia

General population: 15,600,000
Jewish population: 6,000-14,000 (half in Czech Republic and half in Slovak Republic)

GENERAL BACKGROUND

After four decades of Communist mismanagement Czechoslovakia was faced with serious political, economic and social problems. In the Czech Republic progress towards a stable democratic order and the introduction of a market economy proceded more quickly than in the less developed Slovak Republic. This was one of the reasons which led to the dissolution of the common state. The Czechoslovak federation ceased to exist at the end of 1992 and was replaced by two independent states.

HISTORICAL LEGACY

During the thousand years of Jewish history in Czechoslovakia, periods of prosperity for Jews (for example under the Czech King Premysl Otakar II, 1253-78) have alternated with periods of persecution (for example the pogrom of 1389 in Prague). Under President Tomas Masaryk (1918-36) Czechoslovakia was the most democratic country of Central Europe with a flourishing Jewish community of 255,000 (118,00 in the Czech lands, 137,000 in Slovakia). Of these, 192,000 died in the Holocaust. Slovakia and Croatia were the only two Nazi satellite states to accede voluntarily to the deportation of their Jews. Most Czechoslovak survivors of the Holocaust left the country after the Communist takeover in 1948 or after the Soviet occupation in 1968.

PARTIES, ORGANIZATIONS, MOVEMENTS

The Republican Party in the Czech Republic preaches racism and xenophobia. Gypsies and asylum-seekers are its main target; antisemitism is a by-product of its hate campaigns. In the presidential election on 26 January 1993 the party's leader, Miroslav Sladek, obtained the votes of fourteen members of parliament out of a possible 200. (109 votes were cast for Vaclav Havel and 49 votes for the candidate of the Communist-led Left Bloc. There were 28 abstentions.)

In Slovakia none of the groupings which declared their support for the pro-Nazi Tiso regime obtained sufficient votes in the June 1992 parliamentary elections to reach the 5 per cent threshold required. All political parties represented in the Slovak parliament, including the ruling Movement for a Democratic Slovakia, declared a commitment to democracy.

Among the rank-and-file of different political movements, however, a tendency to whitewash the pro-Nazi Slovak state survives. On 13 October, the 105th anniversary of Tiso's birth, the Tiso Society, including Stanislav Panis, a former federal parliamentary deputy and Holocaust denier, and Martin Savel, publisher of antisemitic pamphlets, met in Tiso's birth place of Bytca. In both republics groups of skinheads, several hundred in all, committed acts of hooliganism, usually aimed at Gypsies, but included also the spraying of anti-Jewish slogans and graffitti.

MANIFESTATIONS

No violent attacks against Jews were reported. There were few recorded instances of verbal abuse against Jewish individuals. Slogans at political meetings and Nazi symbols depicted on walls were rarely aimed at the Jewish community. Jewish cemeteries were vandalized in the Czech towns of Pribram and Golcuv Jenikov and synagogue walls and Holocaust memorials were desecrated in the Slovak towns of Nove Zamky and Nitra. In Pribram and Nitra the culprits were young hooligans.

PUBLICATIONS

The bulk of the Czechoslovak media are normally positive towards Jews and Jewish issues. Numerous articles commemorating the fiftieth anniversary of the deportations were published. The only Czech periodical which systematically fomented anti-Jewish hatred was the weekly *Politika*, whose editor, Josef Tomas, was compelled to cease publication in December pending completion of criminal proceedings. In one of its last issues the paper printed a "partial list of Jews and Jewish half-breeds in contemporary Czech culture" including the names of 158 prominent writers, actors, musicians and other artistic personalities. The list included such well-known non-Jews as Vaclav Havel and Jiri Grusa, Czech Ambassador to Germany. The list and other items in *Politika* were condemned by the entire Czechoslovak media with the sole exception of the Prague gutter daily *Spigl*, which itself occasionally publishes antisemitic articles.

In Slovakia the weekly *Zmena* and some low-circulation tabloids carried antisemitic material. The owner of Agres Publishers in Bratislava, Martin Savel, who specializes in printing and disseminating antisemitic periodicals, including *Politika* in Prague and pamphlets such as *The Protocols of the Elders of Zion*, was brought to court. His case was still under consideration.

MAINSTREAM POLITICS

There was no overt antisemitism in mainstream political life. However, the attitudes of politicians of different leanings to some problems—for instance, judicial action against publishers of racist publications, indemnification of Nazi victims, restitution of property, the Arab-Israeli conflict—frequently differ widely. In the June 1992 elections the writer Alexej Pludek, author of antisemitic novels, was elected a member of the federal parliament on the list of the Communist-led Left Bloc. The Slovak minister of culture, Dusan Slobodnik, a participant in a subversion course led in 1945 by SS officers, who later became a scholar specializing in Soviet literature, now claims that Slovaks are being slandered as antisemitic by a hostile foreign press.

EDUCATION AND GRASSROOTS

There remained a lack of school textbooks explaining the truth about the Holocaust: under Communism the fact that the overwhelming majority of victims of Nazism were Jews was concealed. Grassroots attitudes are often influenced by rumour-mongering about Jewish influence in big business and world politics. On the other hand, the pop singer Petr Muk, a non-Jew intending to convert to Judaism, wears the Star of David. His groups, "Shalom" and "Ocean", sing about Israel and are very popular among teenagers.

DENIAL OF THE HOLOCAUST

Some Slovaks seek to divert responsibility for the anti-Jewish policy of the Tiso regime. It is difficult to assess what proportion of the population believes that Tiso acted as he did under Nazi pressure and whether the fact that he exempted some Jews outweighs his guilt for deporting the majority. Views such as those expressed by Stanislav Panis—that the crematoria at Auschwitz could not have processed as many corpses as Jews claim

they did—are isolated and meet with general condemnation.

OPINION POLLS

According to an opinion poll carried out by the Prague-based AISA Sociological Research group in the second half of April 1992, 12 per cent of Czech and 52 per cent of Slovak respondents believed that Jews had too much influence in politics, while 16 per cent of Czechs and 27 per cent of Slovaks did not want to have Jewish neighbours. In November 1992, 35 per cent of those polled in the Czech Republic declared a positive attitude to Jews, 32 per cent had neither positive nor negative opinions, and 29 per cent had no attitude to them at all.

COUNTERING ANTISEMITISM

President Havel continued frequently to condemn all forms of racism, xenophobia and antisemitism. Leading politicians and clerics participated in commemorating Holocaust victims in both the Czech and the Slovak Republics.

Numerous books on Jewish topics were on the shelves of bookshops and plays about Jews were staged in several theatres, including a play by Karol Sidon who became rabbi of Prague and the Czech Republic in the autumn of 1992. Czech cultural associations condemned the weekly *Politika* and collected signatures on protest manifestos. The Slovak "Human Movement" of Bratislava intellectuals criticized the authorities for leaving fascist and xenophobic utterances without "appropriate civic and political answer".

ASSESSMENT

Although extremists on the right as well as the left did their utmost to exploit the popular discontent resulting from the difficulties of post-Communist transformation, the number of antisemitic incidents did not grow substantially. Initiatives countering antisemitism intensified not only among Jews but in society as a whole. In comparison with anti-Gypsy sentiment, antisemitism remains a marginal problem. The number of Jews in both republics was tiny and there was no serious threat to the Jewish community. But any worsening of economic or social conditions in either of the two republics or in neighbouring countries, accompanied by a substantial rise in the number of asylum-seekers, could give rise to serious problems for minorities, including Jews.

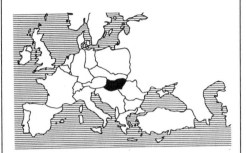

Hungary

General population: 10,000,000
Jewish population: 100,000 (mainly in Budapest)

GENERAL BACKGROUND

Since the peaceful change-over from Communism, Hungary has been struggling to build a democracy without having the benefit of a strong democratic tradition. The anti-Communist reaction is extremely strong; the former Communist Party plays no role in the country and the "reformed" communists have adopted a social democratic position. The country is ruled by a democratically elected coalition of three parties. The main party, the Democratic Forum, has declared itself a centrist party with a Christian-nationalist policy and is supported by the Smallholders and Christian People's Party. The opposition is mainly liberal, with a smaller socialist grouping.

The market economy continued to develop slowly and Hungary had by the year's end succeeded in attracting about half of all Western investment in the East European area. Nevertheless, unemployment was around the 13 per cent mark and, according to scholarly writings, the financial situation of 70 per cent of Hungarian families had deteriorated during the year. The budgetary deficit was approximately 7 per cent of GNP.

HISTORICAL LEGACY

Following the emancipation of the Jews in 1867, antisemitism became a serious issue only after the First World War (though there was a blood libel case in 1882). In 1920 Hungary adopted the so-called *numerus clausus* law, which restricted the admission of Jews to universities. In addition, the inter-war Horthy regime was characterized by social antisemitism as well as the *de facto* exclusion of Jews from certain positions in the civil service, judiciary, and similar areas.

Following Hitler's rise to power, and particularly after the Anschluss, Hungary adopted a series of anti-Jewish laws as well as a forced labour service for Jewish men (in which some 25,000 to 40,000 perished). Antisemitic agitation was rife. The Nazi invasion of Hungary on 19 March 1944 led to the destruction of Hungarian Jewry, in which close to 600,000 Jews were exterminated, with considerable collaboration by the Hungarian authorities.

After the Second World War there were some minor pogroms and, following the assumption of power by the Communists, anti-Zionist agitation became a regular feature in the press. But otherwise the Communist regime placed a taboo on antisemitism. Even anti-Zionist propaganda was milder in Hungary than in neighbouring Soviet satellite states.

PARTIES, ORGANIZATIONS, MOVEMENTS

No major political grouping in Hungary would today adopt an antisemitic programme. On the contrary, it would deny any taint of antisemitism if the charge were levelled against it on account of the behaviour of any of its members.

Early in the year a tiny neo-Nazi group calling itself the Hungarian National Socialist Action Group was discovered in Gyoer. The group had been maintaining contacts with neo-Nazi groups in Austria, Germany and Spain and was in possession of weapons and propaganda material from these countries and the USA. Six people were arrested and the group's leader was given a suspended sentence of one year's imprisonment. Nevertheless, the group continued its activities—under the new name of Hungarian National Front—demanding a "revision" of the attitude towards the war-time Hungarian Nazi movement and referring to "similar revisions" in Romania and Slovakia.

More dangerous is the growing band of skinheads. The targets of their aggression were at first mainly gypsies and Third World students studying in Hungary; a number of skinheads have been convicted of assault. Lately they have become more openly anti-Jewish. They support the ultra-nationalist elements, wearing the symbols and uniforms of the Nazi and Arrow Cross parties.

It is difficult to categorize the new political movement of Istvan Csurka, leader of the MDF's "*völkisch*-national" wing. In summer 1992 Csurka formed the Hungarian Way Foundation, which by the end of the year claimed 300 circles nationwide. The stated aim of the Hungarian Way is "to bring about a true change of the system based on national values". Csurka maintains that the old Communist *nomenclatura* still retains power or enjoys the spoils of its past misdeeds and that "vocal liberalism is as much a Bolshevik instrument as the dictatorship of the proletariat". He claims his group is neither right-wing nor left-wing but exclusively one of the "Magyar ethnicum".

Although Csurka has made numerous antisemitic statements (see below), the programmatic declarations of the Hungarian Way are not explicitly anti-Jewish. Csurka denies that the emphasis on Magyar national and ethnic values—which characterizes all other views and values as non-Hungarian or even anti-Hungarian and seeks to exclude them from public life—is potentially anti-Jewish. He claims that he wishes only to protect, and make a dominant factor of, Magyar ethnic and Christian values—almost suggesting that he is protecting the majority against the minority. However, ideology of this type is seen as antisemitic not only by Jews but also by all liberal elements in the country.

MANIFESTATIONS

Leaving aside the unquantifiable but consistent rumours of antisemitic abuse in the streets, in schools (between pupils), and discriminatory practices in professional life, there were few overtly antisemitic incidents in the year in question. One incident which deserves mention occurred at a football match in December when crowds shouted crude antisemitic slogans and some people were physically assaulted.

The most serious incident was a demonstration outside the parliament building on the national holiday of 23 October by several hundred youngsters, many of them skinheads, wearing symbols of the former Hungarian Nazi party. On this occasion hooligans heckled and ultimately silenced President Goencz, who was to deliver the festive address. The crowd then hailed Csurka. The police did not intervene. The demonstration was not in itself antisemitic but the tone, uniforms, and slogans were generally regarded as anti-democratic and potentially anti-Jewish. It should be remembered that President Goencz has been a constant target of press and political attacks by the right and that in his programmatic essay (see below) Csurka claimed that the president acted on instructions "from Paris, New York and Tel Aviv".

Perhaps the most serious aspect of this incident is that the authorities failed to respond effectively. The minister of the interior stated that there existed no legislation against the use of Nazi insignia (a bill was subsequently introduced—see **Legal Developments**). One far-right deputy of the Hungarian Democratic Front, Izabella Kiraly, received a delegation of the skinheads responsible for the mayhem and later defended them publicly as "decent kids with a patriotic feeling with whom one should talk and not condemn them".

PUBLICATIONS

Last year's *Antisemitism World Report* mentioned the publication of two antisemitic books, by Jozsef Szendi and Aron Monus respectively. Although both books were confiscated, it is reported that they were still openly on sale, for instance at meetings of the *völkisch*-national wing of the MDF. Legal proceedings were initiated but the authors escaped abroad. Monus returned and, although he gave a number of public lectures, the authorities claim they have been unable to find him for the purpose of serving a writ.

Two blatantly antisemitic periodicals,

Szent Korona (Holy Crown) and *Hunnia Fuzetek* (Hunnia Booklets) continued to appear in 1992 in spite of the fact that proceedings were initiated against *Szent Korona* for incitement to hatred against Jews and Romanians, and *Hunnia Fuzetek* was denounced for the same offence. In regard to *Szent Korona*, it should be recalled, the trial was suspended following a claim by the defence that the prohibition of racist incitement conflicted with the constitutional guarantee freedom of expression; the matter was referred to the Constitutional Court. In May 1992 the Constitutional Court confirmed the legality of the ban on incitement to race hatred and the trial went ahead. A conviction was made in 1993. But this did not prevent the continued appearance of *Szent Korona*, which claims to have 3,000 subscribers in the USA alone and receives considerable funding from Hungarians abroad. Investigations against *Hunnia Fuzetek* have, as far as is known, not yet begun.

More disturbing is the fact that some members of the government parties unashamedly support *Hunnia Fuzetek* (which is on a far higher level than *Szent Korona*) by frequently contributing articles to it. *Hunnia Fuzetek* also caused an incident in parliament when a deputy excluded it from among press publications freely available to deputies. This action, which provoked a complaint from the right, was supported by the coalition parties.

It would surely not be correct to include the MDF daily *Uj Magyarorszag* or even Csurka's own *Magyar Forum* in the same category as the openly antisemitic papers. Yet it must be noted that even *Uj Magyarorszag* and *Magyar Forum* frequently carry unpleasant articles and slanted innuendos with anti-Jewish undertones—or worse. *Uj Magyarorszag*, for instance, published a long interview with *Hunnia Fuzetek*'s chief editor, Ferenc Kunszabo, who was quoted as saying that, due to their long persecution, "Jews everywhere try to break up and destroy the communities around them". Another journal, *Ring*, is in a similar category.

MAINSTREAM POLITICS

The government can in no way be regarded as antisemitic. Members of the government, particularly Prime Minister Antall, repeatedly made positive statements about the Jews, assuring them of full protection, and denounced extremism—always emphasising, however, that they were denouncing extremism of the right and the left with equal force. When the leaders of Hungarian Jewry, after the 23 October disturbances mentioned above, complained of signs of growing antisemitism, Antall invited them for a long talk to reassure them.

Anxiety regarding antisemitism in political life arises rather from the fact that even within the coalition parties of the current government there are groups—or at least individuals—who make dubious and sometimes unequivocal pronouncements of an anti-Jewish, anti-minority, anti-liberal flavour. They indicate a willingness to "exclude" these elements from the mainstream of Hungarian life. (It should be noted that the MDF is split into three groups—Antall's Christian-democratic centre, the *völkisch*-nationalist wing of Csurka on the right, and a small left-of-centre "national-liberal" group.)

A second complaint is that the centrists are too tolerant of the extremists—that they are ready to dissociate themselves from offensive views voiced within their own parties but would not unambiguously condemn them, let alone expel the culprits from their party. Frequently the centrists dismiss these extremist or antisemitic outbursts as individual views or as journalistic activities which are best ignored.

A watershed in both general political life and antisemitism in Hungary was Istvan Csurka's 10,000-word programmatic essay which appeared in the weekly *Magyar Forum*, which is his mouthpiece, on 20 August. The essay, anti-Western, anti-market economy, anti-alien and racist, criticised the government and the MDF for not instituting a more resolute "change" of the past regime and not pursuing a clearly nationalist policy. But the essay's main thrust was antisemitic: Csurka blamed the Jews for every ill in Hungary's history since the First World War, effectively charging them with being engaged in an anti-Hungarian conspiracy.

Not only members of the opposition but even liberal members of the MDF described the essay as the basis of a new Hungarian National Socialist ideology. However, the government's and the MDF's reaction was initially lukewarm; it was probably only due to the strong impact the incident caused abroad that Prime Minister Antall gradually distanced himself more explicitly from Csurka's views and got rid of Csurka as a vice-president of the MDF by abolishing the positions of all six vice-presidents. While Antall was able to preserve the unity of his party, many people see this continued unity as a victory for Csurka.

Csurka has carried on his campaign in preparation for the MDF National Congress in January 1993 and the general election, which is due in spring 1994. He has said among other things, that he hoped that after the 1994 elections "the opposition in parliament will be Hungarian". He also remarked that the (present) opposition elements "are no longer to be seen as opponents but as enemies". This was said in response to the publication by a Jewish historian of a collection of antisemitic articles under the title *Kirekesztoek* (Excluders), which contained, together with excerpts from the writings of Hitler, Eugen Dühring, Eduard Drumont and Ferenc Szalasi (leader of the war-time Hungarian Nazis), articles by Csurka, the editors of *Szent Korona* and *Hunnia Fuzetek*, and people of their ilk.

Another incident which caused controversy was a statement in August by Jenoe Fonyai, chairman of the Association of Former Political Prisoners and recently elected vice-president of the World Federation of Hungarians, that "those who condemn fascism are lowly, despicable Bolshevik henchmen".

Some statements by members of the government, such as assertions by the interior minister that he could not act against the skinheads and their Nazi uniforms (even though he condemned them) or that of the minister of justice that Hungary bears no responsibility for the Holocaust following its occupation by the Nazis (even though the fact of intensive Hungarian collaboration is not disputed), often undo the government's and particularly the prime minister's efforts to conduct a fair policy towards the Jews.

LEGAL MATTERS

The principal legislation of Jewish concern adopted in 1992 was a series of six laws on the subject of indemnification. On the one hand, it must be recognized that of all the post-Communist democracies in Eastern Europe only Hungary has introduced legal measures not only on the return of property (reprivatization) but on the compensation of individuals who suffered loss of life, deprivation of liberty or damage to health. On the other hand, it must be noted that in compensating both the victims of Nazi and of Communist persecution, serious discrimination was made against the victims of Nazism (i.e. the Jews) in comparison to the compensation accorded to political victims of Communism. The Jewish community and others have brought this discrimination before the Constitutional Court, which has power to annul discriminatory laws.

Another important development was the judgment of the Constitutional Court on the constitutionality of the provisions of the Hungarian Penal Code regarding race hatred (see **Publications**). On 26 May the Court decided that the ban on *incitement* to hatred was constitutional because the inherent curtailment of freedom of expression was justified to protect other equally important rights and values, but another clause of the Penal Code outlawing merely *offensive or derogatory statements* against racial or other groups could not be upheld.

Following the disturbances on 23 October (see **Manifestations**), members of the MDF introduced a bill outlawing the use of Nazi and Communist insignia and uniforms. The bill has not yet been debated.

At their meeting with the prime minister, Jewish leaders (see **Mainstream politics**) also requested legislation against the denial of the Holocaust. Although the prime minister was sceptical, he asked the Jewish leaders to submit a draft.

COUNTERING ANTISEMITISM

Apart from the legal measures contemplated (and described above), the most important initiatives in this field were strong statements by both the Catholic and the Protestant churches against antisemitism. These were made in the wake

of the Csurka affair. First, the joint
organizations of Christians and Jews (there
are two such bodies in Hungary) were
hesitant to condemn Csurka outright-
which led to a strong protest and withdrawal of the Jews from one of these
bodies; but later more helpful councils
seem to have prevailed. Particularly
appreciated was the declaration of the
Hungarian Catholic Bishops' Conference
of 26 October, which repeated the words
of the Pope that "antisemitism and racial
discrimination are a sin against God and
humanity".

ASSESSMENT

President Goencz has stated that antisemitism exists in Hungary but has not
assumed dangerous proportions. This is
probably a correct assessment for the
present. However, antisemitic tendencies
under the leadership of a strong personality
such as Csurka are growing. They may find
a fertile ground in the economic crisis and
the general malaise and distrust of politicians that exist in Hungary today. One
must particularly fear the agitation that will
begin in 1993 in preparation for the 1994
general elections. The threat to Jews will
not necessarily appear in direct references
to them but in pronouncements against
"aliens", "liberals", "cosmopolitans", and
"not-true-Magyars".

Poland

General population: 38,000,000
Jewish population: 4,000-10,000 (mainly
in Warsaw)

GENERAL BACKGROUND

The year 1992 saw further movement
towards a fully-fledged market economy,
with accompanying malpractices and social
tensions. The political situation was
characterized by a power struggle between
the presidency on the one hand and the
government and parliament on the other. In
June the right-wing government of Jan
Olszewski was toppled and was followed
by a coalition government headed by

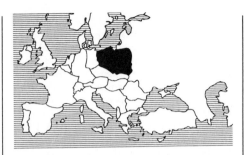

Hanna Suchocka, a devout Catholic
member of the Democratic Union. The
Christian National Union, a mainstay of
the toppled government, continued to play
a key role in the new coalition. The new
governing coalition abandoned the extremism of its predecessor but was rather shaky.
Its policy consisted of a continuation of a
free market policy combined with acceptance of the demands of the Christian
National Union, a party which followed
the concepts of the Catholic hierarchy,
which is critical of Western society.

A marked characteristic of public life
was the decline of authority, both moral
and political. This applied to political
groupings with roots in Solidarity and to
most political leaders (including President
Walesa), parliament, government, and the
Catholic Church. The latter scored
victories on several fundamental issues-the
teaching of religion in school, anti-abortion
legislation, and legislation on "Christian
values" on radio and television. These
successes, together with the church's
attempt to enhance its political and material
standing, generated among the public a
feeling of unwarranted interference by the
church in both public and private life.

The power of conservative Catholicism, fears that the Polish economy was
being taken over by foreigners and the
country's policies dominated by foreign
interests (primarily American, German and
Jewish), the activating of groups among the
population claiming German ethnicity and
an influx of immigrants from the CIS,
Romania, the Balkans and the Third
World-all this contributed to a shift of the
political spectrum to the right. Unemployment, pauperization and a feeling of lack of
better prospects among wide sections of the
Polish population combined with an
atmosphere of nationalist and religious

parochialism and intolerance. These factors clashed with strong countervailing forces—the quest for modernization, the desire to join the affluent West and the strong tradition of liberalism, especially among the intelligentsia.

HISTORICAL LEGACY

The Jewish community in Poland today is a tiny remnant of an ancient community which became established in the Middle Ages and numbered 3.500,000 million on the eve of the Second World War.

Until the seventeenth century the situation of the Jews in Poland was, on balance, better than in most countries of Europe but it deteriorated as the Rzeczpospolita declined. With the emergence of modern Polish nationalism, antisemitism was incorporated into the platform of the National Democracy (Endecja) under its foremost ideologist, Roman Dmowski (1864-1939).

The predominant Catholic Church has adhered almost continuously to its antisemitic tradition. This state of affairs has, however, begun to change as a result of the dissemination, albeit slow, of the teaching of *Nostra Aetate*. Nevertheless, for the new approach to prevail, much work still needs to be done.

Deeply ingrained in the historical memory of the Jewish people is the hostility the Jews encountered from large segments of the population, a wide section of the Polish social and political establishment and most governments in independent Poland. Then followed the trauma of the Holocaust, when the Jews felt that they went to their deaths in the face of indifference, and in some cases hostility, on the part of the Poles.

Post-war hopes of a more amicable relationship between Poles and Jews were thwarted first by the murderous grassroots antisemitism of the immediate post-war period, which reached its apogee in the Kielce pogrom of July 1946, and then by Communist-inspired antisemitism, which culminated in the antisemitic campaign of 1968. The overthrow of Communism did not put an end to antisemitism, either at the grassroots level or as a political instrument.

PARTIES, ORGANIZATIONS, MOVEMENTS

On 4 March *Gazeta Wyborcza* reported that 128 political parties were registered. Most of these parties were minuscule—including the extreme nationalist groupings with antisemitic tendencies. These latter claim a link to the pre-war Endecja and the legacy of its leader Roman Dmowski. Dmowski's ideological legacy, which includes antisemitism, anti-Germanism, clericalism and authoritarianism, is also invoked by some of the more respectable bodies which are represented in parliament.

The Senioral National Party is led by Maciej Giertych, a science professor at the University of Poznan and son of the late Endek leader Jedrzej Giertych. It claims a membership of 4,000. The party has a strong clerical tinge, Giertych having close connections with Primate Glemp. The party's activities are publicized through the Catholic media and protected by the conservative wing of the church, though official support has been less in evidence since 1990. The party's organ is *Slowo Narodowe*, which is edited by Giertych and Jan Engelgard.

The leader of the National Democratic Party is Jan Zamoyski, scion of an old aristocratic family. The party, established in 1991, is closely linked to the London-based National Democrats and, like most of the "respectable" right-wing parties, avoids overt antisemitic expression.

Offshoots of Giertych's National Party are the National Party Szczerbiec (named after the coronation sword of the Polish kings) and the National Democracy Party. The National Party Szczerbiec was founded in 1989 following a split in the National Party; its leaders are Marian Baranski and Jan Majewski. There are no data about its membership, which cannot be substantial. Also, its affiliated organizations—Memorial Committee for the Victims of Stalinism, Committee to Prosecute Crimes against the Polish Nation and the Roman Dmowski National Association—are tiny. The party's organ, *Glos Narodu*, is edited by Majewski, M. Skorupka and J. Janowski. Szczerbiec condemned the January 1990 episcopal letter on relations between Catholics and Jews. Its virulent antisemitic propaganda gave rise to a (fruitless) complaint to the authorities from the Warsaw-based Jewish Historical Institute.

The National Party Fatherland split

from Szczerbiec in 1990. Its leaders are Stefan Jastrzebski, Boguslaw Jeznach, Jedrzej Dmowski and Boguslaw Rybicki. Jastrzebski and Rybicki held high office under the Communists. Its press organ is *Ojczyzna*, which in 1992 reprinted a tract by the antisemitic clergyman Stanislaw Trzeciak, *Zydzi w swietle Talmudu* (The Jews in the Light of the Talmud). The membership of the party, according to Rybicki, is 3,600 which, like many other party membership figures, is considerably inflated. The party has close links with conservative priests.

The most active of the extremist nationalist groupings is the Polish National Community-Polish National Party. Its leader is Boleslaw Tejkowski who in the 1950s was a Communist Party official in the Cracow region and was subsequently linked to the secret police. Antisemitic and anti-German, the party believes in a strong political centre and promotes traditional values but, unlike the nationalist groups mentioned above, is opposed to the Vatican and the church hierarchy. The party maintains that the number of Jewish victims of the Holocaust is grossly exaggerated and that most Jews survived, continue to live in Poland under different names, and are to be found in high state and church offices. The party claims 4,000 members and 67,000 sympathizers. In its activities, such as demonstrations and acts of violence, the party mobilizes skinheads (see below). It has branches in several Polish cities and boasts contacts with France's Front National, Russia's Pamyat, the Pan-Slavic Movement in Kiev, neo-Nazi organizations in Canada, and the North Korean and Libyan embassies (and possibly other Arab embassies).

There are several other extreme nationalist groups of lesser and/or local importance. The National Front of Poland is based in Gdansk. Its leaders, Wojciech Podjacki and Wojciech Bala, are in their early twenties and most of the members (probably several hundred) are eighteen to twenty years-old, about a third of them unemployed. The party sees the nation as a community of race and culture and post-1989 governments as agents of Western—in particular American—finance, which is allegedly dominated by Jews and Germans. Its organ is *Szaniec*, which is edited by

Marian Jastrzebski and Andrzej Wojciechowski.

Other small nationalist groups are the National Revival of Poland, the Organization Of Polish Youth Wszechpolak, the All-Polish Youth Bastion-Home Federation of Fighting Youth, the Polish National Club and many others.

There is in Poland a skinhead movement of perhaps several thousand individuals. Unlike the organizations listed above, it is not an officially registered body. The skinheads provide bodyguards at meetings of nationalist groups and commit acts of violence on behalf of the more militant groups such as Tejkowski's Polish National Community. According to the police, they are the most dangerous of the extreme nationalists. Their strongholds are Nowa Huta, Lodz, Katowice, Wroclaw, Poznan, Czestochowa and Legnica.

Another element in the antisemitic camp are the former hardliners of the Polish United Workers' Party who played a militant role in the official antisemitic policies and sponsored the nationalist and antisemitic Grunwald Patriotic Association (established in 1980-1). Many of them, including Grunwald supporters, have emerged in Party "X". Its leader, Stanislaw Tyminski, who emigrated from Poland to Canada in 1959, gained the second largest number of votes in the 1990 presidential election. His second-in-command is Jozef Kossecki, an antisemitic propagandist under the Communist regime. Party "X" spokesmen have frequently resorted to antisemitic propaganda. For instance, Tyminski declared in February 1992 that he was not antisemitic but believed Poland was being manipulated by the Jewish minority.

A splinter group under Jozef Ciurus, who is reportedly opposed to the party's antisemitic slogans, was registered as the Labour Party in January 1992. Another splinter group under Zdzislaw Zaleski, an author of several antisemitic tracts, registered as Party "X"-Polish Faction in February 1992.

Party "X" claims 5,000 members. It has a youth branch, the Organization of the White Eagle. Its publication is *Listy X*. Its three representatives in parliament ceased to function as a parliamentary group in mid-1992. This may signal a decline in the fortunes of the party, whose populist appeal was feared by the Polish political establishment.

A new phenomenon is the appearance in Poland of German neo-Nazi groups, a fringe companion to the surfacing of a German minority in certain regions, especially Silesia. It was reported in *Stern*, no. 3, 1992 and *Zycie Warszawy*, 21 October 1992, that the monthly *Schlesien Raport* is sponsored and supplied with technical means and press materials by the right-wing Nazionale Partei Deutschlands and that emissaries of the Nazionale Offensive operated in some Silesian towns. The Nazionale Offensive is hostile to Jews, Africans and homosexuals. Also, Swedish neo-Nazis, namely the White Aryan Resistance of Erik Rundquist, have established themselves in Szczecin.

MAINSTREAM POLITICS

The toppling of the Olszewski government in June 1992 led to certain shifts on the Polish political scene. The more militant figures in that government, including the prime minister himself, the minister of the interior (Antoni Macierewicz) and the minister of defence (Jan Parys), established the Movement for the Republic and the Third Republic Movement. Their primary objective is to undermine President Walesa alleging that he, his entourage and many figures in the establishment have been Communist agents. Some leaders of these groupings attempt to dispel possible foreign suspicions of antisemitic attitudes. But some groups which belong to the new opposition movement—for instance, the Polish Independence Party led by Romuald Szeremetiew, deputy minister of defence in the Olszewski government—have a record of antisemitism.

The Centre Alliance, which was a part of the Olszewski coalition, distances itself from antisemitism. Its leader, Jaroslaw Kaczynski, declared at a meeting at the Warsaw Technical University that antisemitism was both stupid and impractical. This rather mild statement met with the disapproval of the audience, as did similar statements by leaders of the Olszewski groups.

The Confederation of Independent Poland, led by Leszek Moczulski (who participated in the 1968 antisemitic cam-paign), is regarded by many as xenophobic and anti-democratic. But its leadership attempted to distance itself from anti-semitism: in 1992 they wrote twice to the Jewish journal denying that the Confedera-tion was hostile to national minorities and that it harboured Endek antisemites as members.

The Solidarity splinter factions Fighting Solidarity (leader Kornel Morawiecki) and Solidarity-80 (leader Marian Jurczyk) continue to uphold their antisemitic stance. Their influence is concentrated in working-class centres such as Lodz, Szczecin, Silesia and the steel-works of Cracow and Warsaw.

Antisemitic features are also apparent in the pronouncements of the peasant Polish People's Party which sometimes claims the government's economic policies are subservient to New York, Bonn and Tel Aviv.

The Christian National Union represents small-town, parochial Poland and is the most influential of the national groups. Its leaders are Professor Wieslaw Chrzanowski, who is on the more moder-ate wing of the party, Jan Lopuszanski, Stefan Niesiolowski and Henryk Goryszewski. Their view is that the national-religious character of the country is more important than democracy. Party spokesmen and propagandists, including members of the clergy, often resorted to antisemitism in the parliamentary elections. In 1992 they generally desisted from direct antisemitic attacks. But some of their actions and statements, though probably not prompted exclusively by antisemitism, keep the suspicion alive. For instance, party deputies opposed naming a hall in the parliament building after the first Polish president, Gabriel Narutowicz, who was assassinated by a nationalist fanatic in 1922, because he was elected by a majority which included national minority votes. CNU leaders sponsored celebrations in honour of the National Armed Forces, an extremist faction whose record includes collaboration with the Nazis and murdering Jews under German occupation and in the first post-war years.

MANIFESTATIONS

A number of demonstrations typically combining anti-Jewish and anti-German slogans took place. In some cases the Israeli and German flags were burned. Many of the demonstrations were organized by Tejkowski's Polish National Community; skinheads were the main participants.

On 15 February a demonstration against Jews and Germans was held in the border town of Zgorzelec. Early in April there were antisemitic incidents in Auschwitz and Treblinka during visits by Israeli secondary school pupils. On 10 April skinheads from several cities shouted antisemitic slogans in Czestochowa in an attempt to disrupt the unveiling by the Israeli ambassador of a plaque commemorating the anniversary of the establishment of the ghetto. More serious was a protest later in the year by a group of inhabitants which included nationalist personalities against the erection of commemorative plaques for the Jewish community of Czestochowa; the protestors argued that these Jews were brethren of the Stalinist tormentors of the Polish people. On 13 June several hundred supporters of the Freedom Party and Fighting Solidarity demonstrated in the centre of Wroclaw under the slogan "Down with Judeo-Communism". In August the inscription "Skinhead territory. Non-believers and Jews keep out" appeared on a building in Kruszwica where skinheads were holding a training course. In September, at a Solidarity manifestation against government policies in Warsaw (which, unlike the extremists' demonstrations, rallied several thousand participants) there were shouts of "Down with Jews and Communists". On 11 November, the anniversary of Poland's resurrection as an independent state after the First World War, about 150 young people demonstrated in Cracow under the slogans "Poland for the Poles", "Jews and Germans out of Poland", and "Tejkowski for president"; the demonstrators also opposed Poland's joining the European Community and burned the EC flag. On 9 December a demonstration in support of a referendum on a law criminalizing abortion was attacked by skinheads shouting "Sieg Heil, Catholic Poland and Christ the Lord" and antisemitic slogans.

There were also demonstrations in front of the diplomatic missions of Israel, Germany and the United States. On 12 March forty young nationalists shouting

"A good Jew is a dead Jew" and "Poland for the Poles" and displaying a banner reading "Put an end to Jewish-German occupation" demonstrated in front of the Israeli embassy. In early April demonstrators against a visit to Germany by Walesa in front of the German embassy and the German consulate also carried antisemitic slogans. On 30 May over a hundred members of Tejkowski's party marched to the German consulate in Szczecin and burned the German and Israeli flags. In July it was reported that Party "X" picketed the US embassy shouting slogans "Bush-yes, Mossad—no".

The influential *Polityka* (11 April 1992) and *Gazeta Wyborcza* (21 April 1992) drew attention to the inactivity of the police in the face of law-breaking by extremists. The latter paper contrasted this stand-off policy by the police with its vigorous action when a peaceful demonstration against religious instruction in schools attempted to gather in front of the seat of the Papal Nuncio.

There were a number of desecrations of Jewish cemeteries. In January youngsters damaged the Jewish cemetery in Warsaw. On 3 April forty Jewish tombstones were seriously damaged at the Wroclaw Jewish cemetery. Some put the blame on Tejkowski's skinheads; others maintained that pupils from local schools were responsible. On the night of 2-3 October there was an incidence of vandalism at the Zabrze Jewish cemetery in the Katowice region; a Polish television commentator remarked that graves were vandalized in that area "every month". A report on the desecration of Catholic, Protestant and Soviet cemeteries referred to an order by the minister of the interior on action to prevent and investigate such acts of vandalism.

There were several acts of violence of an antisemitic character. In the summer taxi drivers attacked Jews wearing traditional garb in Warsaw's Central Railway Station; the police were slow in coming and reluctant to intervene. The worst case of nationalist violence against individuals was an assault on German lorry drivers, one of whom was killed, in Nowa Huta on 3 October. One of the skinheads held for this attack told legal officials that their training as members of the Polish National Party had included instruction on how to combat

Germans, Jews and blacks. In riots that followed in Cracow nationalist extremists shouted slogans against Jews, coloured people and Arabs.

The experience of recent years shows that manifestations of antisemitism tend to be linked to electoral campaigns. There were no such campaigns in 1992.

PUBLICATIONS

Jewish subjects are popular in Poland at present. In so far as publishing is now a commercial venture, this reflects the demand of the Polish reading public. Only a tiny fraction of the hundreds of books and items in the periodical and daily press are antisemitic.

Publications by extremist groups for which antisemitism and other kinds of xenophobia play a central role were mentioned above. Publications such as *The Protocols of the Elders of Zion* are still available and the re-issuing of old antisemitic tracts continues. Examples are a work by Justin Pranajtis of Beilis trial notoriety entitled "Christians in the Jewish Talmud" (St Petersburg 1892) and "The Programme of World Jewish Policy" by another well known antisemite, the priest Stanislaw Trzeciak (in addition to his "Jews in the Light of the Talmud" which was mentioned above). Another such publication which appeared in 1992 is "Satan the Greatest Enemy of Man" by Bonifacy Gunther. The Warmia Diocese Publishing Co brought out a book by Peter Raina, a non-Pole living in the West, entitled "The Controversy Over the Convent of the Barefoot Carmelites in Auschwitz". Raina alleged that the Pope was manipulated by Jerzy Turowicz (the editor of the progressive Catholic *Tygodnik Powszechny* of Cracow) and Archbishop of Paris Jean Lustiger, both persons of Jewish ancestry.

DENIAL OF THE HOLOCAUST

The Holocaust is a major factor in Polish-Jewish relations. Both peoples suffered greatly under the Nazi occupation but they were unequal victims—which is not recognized by many Poles. Widespread among the Polish public is the image of the selfless, heroic Pole who, irrespective of the mortal danger facing him and his family, rescues the Jew, who for the most part accepts his fate passively. Many Jews feel that the extent of the assistance provided by Poles has been exaggerated and that the hostility or indifference of the Polish population to the Holocaust is either minimized or ignored. The tendency to reject the uniqueness of the Holocaust is also resented by the Jews.

Except on the fringes of Polish extreme nationalism (see above for Tejkowski's views on the subject) there is no outright denial of the Holocaust. However, the phenomenon of relegating the experiences of the Nazi occupation to the background and emphasizing the crimes of Stalinism was clearly noticeable in 1992 not only in journalism but also in school textbooks. A new phenomenon is instances of white-washing Polish collaborators with the Nazis. The fiftieth anniversary of the National Armed Forces was marked by the distribution of medals to their surviving leaders and the holding of a military parade in Warsaw (see above). Cracow's Ignacy Fik Street, named after an anti-Nazi literary critic, journalist and poet executed by the Gestapo, was re-named after Jozef Mackiewicz, a Polish writer who cooperated with the Polish-language Nazi press in Vilnius. These acts, sponsored by right-wing elements and firmly opposed by liberal and democratic opinion, are not comparable to what is happening in post-Communist countries where nationalists cooperated with the Nazis.

OPINION POLLS

Tygodnik Solidarnosc (3 April 1992) remarked that racist excesses can rely on the lenient attitude of the majority and on the approval of many Poles. Half of the population, according to an opinion poll devised by the Jewish Historical Institute and sociologists from Warsaw University, regard antisemitism as a marginal phenomenon. Many who condemn antisemitism usually assume an apologetic stance, raising the issues of alleged Jewish anti-Polishness and Jewish support for Communism. But several influential writers reject the view that antisemitism is a marginal phenomenon in Polish society. Professor Tadeusz Zielinski, the Civil Rights Ombudsman, stated that his office receives numerous letters which reflect a dangerous combination of religious intolerance and racialism;

he sees the danger of an escalation of antisemitism when Jewish property is returned, to its rightful owners. In fact, popular antisemitism is kept alive by its cynical use for political purposes, as was evident during electoral campaigns in recent years.

Observations by many writers and opinion polls drew attention to the issue of xenophobia. In May 1992 a poll conducted by the Centre of Public Opinion Research of a representative sample of the adult population showed that the Poles regard all their neighbours (with the exception of Hungarians and Slovaks) and Israelis, many of whom originate in Poland, as unfriendly. This attitude is accompanied by a decline in sympathy towards the countries of Western Europe and the United States.

A comparative study of attitudes to foreigners of youths in the fourteen-seventeen age range in Warsaw and Berlin conducted by the Berlin Zentrum fur Europaeische Bildungsforschung and the Warsaw Institute of Educational Research in the spring of 1992 showed that only 47.8 per cent of the Warsaw respondents regarded foreigners as trustworthy, and 54.8 per cent saw their presence in the country as a disadvantage. The respective figures for West Berlin were 82.2 per cent and 22.8 per cent. There was also less awareness of the issue of hostility to foreigners in Warsaw than in Berlin: 81.1 per cent of West Berlin youth and 77.9 per cent of East Berlin youth were worried by the phenomenon, as compared with 58.6 per cent in Warsaw.

In June the Sopoty Workshop of Social Research conducted a poll among pupils of post-elementary schools (i.e. teenagers over fourteen) who were asked the simple question: Whom would you prefer not to sit next to in school? Possible objects of rejection were the mentally ill, homosexuals, AIDS victims, Jehovah's Witnesses, children of known Communists and alcoholics, or members of a non-Polish ethnic group. A third of the respondents rejected gypsies, under a fifth—Russians and Jews, under an eighth—Germans, and under a tenth—English and Japanese. These percentages were much larger in the case of pupils of vocational schools—twice as large for Germans and Jews. The least prejudice was displayed by secondary school pupils.

At the beginning of May a poll conducted by the Centre for Public Opinion Research showed that 37 per cent of a representative sample thought that participation of foreign firms in the management of Polish enterprises would bring more harm than good, 20 per cent thought the disadvantages would equal the advantages, and 17 per cent expected positive results on balance. Between 8 and 11 per cent of the sample opposed the sale of shares in Polish enterprises to American, French, British and Japanese, 18 per cent opposed selling to Germans, 30 per cent to Jews, 36 per cent to Russians.

The Demoskop Market and Social Research organization compared the results of three polls conducted in January 1991, April 1992 and September 1992 on the extent of Jewish influence on (i) cultural, (ii) economic, and (iii) political life in Poland:

Table
The Jews enjoy excessive influence on:
[+ agree, - disagree, 0 uncertain]

	Jan 1991			Apr 1992			Sep 1992		
	+	-	0	+	-	0	+	-	0
(i)	20	56	24	29	55	16	29	63	8
(ii)	26	49	25	40	46	14	37	52	9
(iii)	31	45	24	40	44	16	41	49	10

The table is a very rudimentary summary of the Demoskop enquiry, which differentiated between degrees of agreement and disagreement and correlated responses with sex, age group, educational level and income per head of family.

The above-mentioned poll, whose questionnaire was designed by the Jewish Historical Institute and sociologists from the University of Warsaw, addressed the issue of Polish attitudes to Jews. Forty-six per cent of the respondents agreed that the Poles disliked the Jews, but only 14 per cent of those thought the dislike was strong. About a quarter of the respondents opposed the view that the Poles dislike Jews, and about a third were uncertain.

Polish views on the causes of Poles' dislike of Jews are distributed as follows, according to an opinion poll conducted by the Sopoty Workshop of Social Research and presented to the President's Council for Polish-Jewish Relations in November:

17 per cent regarded the killing of Christ as the reason, 35 per cent saw the reason in the alleged excessive influence of the Jews in Poland, and 55 per cent in the Jews' allegedly excessive international influence.

A Demoskop poll on Polish ideas of the numerical strength of the Jewish minority in Poland yielded an astonishing result. Ten per cent thought the Jews numbered between 3,800,000 and 7,200,000, and 25 per cent put their numbers between 750,000 and 3,500,000. *Dos Jidisze Wort* (no. 22, 1992) commented that a side effect of the antisemitic propaganda was the impression that the Jews were omnipresent.

What seems to emerge from all these polls is that in 1992 about half of the Polish population displayed a general dislike of foreigners and Jews and a belief that their presence was to the country's detriment. A considerable percentage of Poles (between one-fifth and one-third) shared distinct antisemitic prejudices. About one-seventh was strongly antisemitic.

COUNTERING ANTISEMITISM

There were no major statements or acts of state concerning Jews and antisemitism in 1992 comparable to the Episcopate's pastoral letter of 20 January 199, Walesa's statement during his visit to Israel in May 1991 and the establishment of the Council on Polish-Jewish Relations in March 1991. In April 1992, during a visit to America, the then prime minister, Jan Olszewski, met Jewish leaders and gave a promise that the Holocaust would be taught in Polish schools. (No mention of the meeting was made when Olszewski was interviewed on his visit to America by Polish Radio several days later.) Foreign Minister Krzysztof Skubiszewski visited Israel in November. Among matters discussed was a Polish cultural centre, antisemitism and the Auschwitz convent. In October Tadeusz Zielinski, the civil rights ombudsman, warned against religious intolerance, racism and antisemitism (see above). The contents of textbooks and the combating of anti-semitism and prejudice were discussed with top state officials during the late Heinz Galinski's visit to Poland as a guest of President Walesa. The Polish State Treasury created the Eternal Memory Foundation for the preservation and reconstruction of Jewish monuments and earmarked a

modest sum for this purpose. The issue of rights as veterans for individuals who rescued Jews during the Nazi occupation was raised but it encountered difficulties in parliament.

A number of conferences and symposia took place in Poland and Israel on Polish Jewish history. In May the Fourth Theological Symposium "The Church, Jews and Judaism" was organized by the Academy of Catholic Theology and the Episcopal Commission for Dialogue with Judaism. There were also grassroots initiatives such as an event on the Jewish festival of Simhat Tora at the Catholic church in the Zoliborz quarter of Warsaw organized by the Polish Council of Christians and Jews on 18 October. The Council participated in the work of a twenty-seven person delegation of the American Center for Christian-Jewish Dialogue which visited Poland in July. Only a minority of clergymen were involved in the improvement of Polish-Jewish relations. They have been continued mainly by a handful of prominent priests and bishops striving for the implementation of the *Nostra Aetate* declaration. Many Polish clergymen preferred to ignore this declaration.

Dos Jidisze Wort (no. 2, 1993) complained that the Polish daily press, when discussing *Nostra Aetate*, never referred to its teachings on the Jews and antisemitism, while *Gazeta Wyborcza* (12-13 September 1992) remarked that "everyday practice in some Polish churches gives rise to painful reflection"

A pro-tolerance march in Poznan at Easter organized by Polish non-Communist left-wing groups attracted about 1,000 participants but also groups of skinheads who distributed antisemitic and anti-German leaflets. A demonstration was held in Wroclaw on the anniversary of Kristallnacht.

A noticeable phenomenon was the publication of numerous books, both scholarly works and works of fiction, on Jewish subjects, television programmes and many articles on antisemitism in the press. The authors of these articles sought to analyse the reasons for the widespread antisemitic prejudice in Polish society and its material and psychological condition; the position of the Catholic Church and political parties on the subject was criticized.

Another noticeable phenomenon was attempts by some right-wing activists to distance themselves from antisemitism and/or to explain away previous statements. Also, attempts by the more important nationalist groups to distance themselves from Tejkowski's Polish National Community and other extremists should be recorded. One reason may have been the perception that the extremists' militant antisemitism was harmful to them at a time when no electoral campaigns were in progress.

An important countervailing factor to antisemitism is the developing relations with Israel. Many Israelis now visit Poland and many Poles visit Israel. A high point in Polish-Israeli relations was the visit to Poland of President Herzog at the end of May. Cultural relations are now a fact of life. Co-operation agreements between Warsaw and Tel Aviv and Lodz and Haifa were signed in 1992. A Polish-Israeli commission on textbooks was established. In October a Centre for Education and Information on Jewish Culture was initiated by the Joint and the Jewish Agency in Warsaw. The Israeli ambassador appears relatively often in the media and comments on Polish-Jewish relations.

LEGAL MATTERS

The implementation of the law against racism, including antisemitic propaganda and of profanation of religious objects and places of worship, leaves much to be desired. The court case of the anti-gypsy pogrom in Mlawa in June 1991 was concluded on 23 October 1992 when individuals most active in the riot were sentenced to various terms of imprisonment and fined. However, no juridical action was taken against the ministry of the interior on account of police inaction when faced with the pogrom—a potential encouragement of passive police behaviour in similar circumstances.

In March 1992 the case against Boguslaw Jeznach and Maciej Giertych for conducting antisemitic propaganda during the parliamentary election campaign was dropped. The prosecuting authorities concluded that attacks made during the campaign were not sufficiently concrete

and that it was unclear who was the target of objectionable statements.

In a similar instance, the Gdansk Provincial Court found the National Front of Poland, which had been taken to court for describing the Democratic Union as "the party of the Jewish minority" not guilty of racial incitement.

The trial of Boleslaw Tejkowski, also for conducting antisemitic electoral propaganda, took place in March. The trial was a focus for disorderly behaviour by skinheads. Tejkowski countered the indictment by declaring his hostility to "imperial talmudic nationalism". The court decided to send him for psychiatric investigation. The authorities proved unable to carry out this decision, though Tejkowski remained active and appeared several times in public during the year. Enlightened public opinion criticized the handling of the prosecution against him as well as that against Giertych and Jeznach.

In June the editor of the Kielce edition of *Gazeta Wyborcza*, Bogdan Bialek, took legal action against leaders of Party "X" Stanislaw Tyminski and Jozef Kossecki for distributing the pamphlet "Poland Needs a Caretaker" in which they alleged that his newspaper employed over 1,000 Jewish nationalists as informants. The sequel to this judicial action is not known.

In certain cases the authorities acted resolutely to prevent the occurrence of antisemitic incidents. But as far as prosecutions are concerned, they seemed not to be over-enthusiastic in applying the law, partly out of fear of providing publicity to antisemitic events and thus creating martyrs out of the extremists, and partly with an eye to the possible adverse reactions of important sections of the Polish public.

Another legal problem which came to the fore in 1992 was the restitution of Jewish property, in particular that of the property of Jewish communities and public bodies. In the positive solution of this problem the Jewish Polish community sees a foundation for its normal functioning, since most state finance has been withdrawn.

ASSESSMENT

There was considerably less antisemitic propaganda and other manifestations of antisemitism in 1992 than in the two previous years. Mainstream political bodies which encouraged antisemitic expression during the election campaigns of 1990 and 1991 were on balance disinterested in active antisemitism. Antisemitic activities were carried out mainly by the extremist nationalist groups, in particular Tejkowski's Polish National Community. Skinhead gangs, which are used by several extremist groups, are a growing danger to the democratic process: the combination of social frustration and xenophobia is an explosive mixture.

Opinion polls leave little doubt that these dangers need to be taken seriously.

Books, television programmes and newspaper articles demonstrated the existence of considerable interest in Jewish matters in Poland , including soul-searching in respect to antisemitism. But the prevailing opinion of the man-in-the-street seemed to be that antisemitism was a marginal problem. This may have been true as far as practical attitudes to Jews were concerned, at least as long as property restitution did not affect vested interests, but it did not seem true with regard to Polish public life, in which the "Jewish card" still had a role to play.

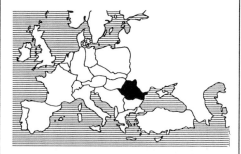

Romania

General population: 22,760,449 (January 1992 census)
Jewish population: 9,107 (January 1992 census); 17,000-18,000 (estimate by Romanian Chief Rabbi)

GENERAL BACKGROUND

Since autumn 1992 the prime minister, Nicolae Vacaroiu, has headed an executive based on the Democratic National Salvation Front (DNSF), a party formed in mid-1992 following a split in the National Salvation Front (NSF). The NSF, formed after Ceausescu's overthrow in December 1989, was headed by Ion Iliescu, a former Communist official. The NSF won a large majority in the first free elections in May 1990. Iliescu became the country's president and the first post-Ceausescu government was headed by Petre Roman who, though of partial Jewish descent, attaches little importance to this fact.

Roman's attempt to reform the Romanian economy brought him into conflict with Iliescu and conservative elements of the NSF. Against a background of social unrest brought about by the attempted reform, Roman was ousted in October 1991 and, as indicated above, the NSF split into the pro-Iliescu DNSF and the NSF, which is still headed by Roman. Roman's replacement as premier, Theodor Stolojan, headed the government till the general and presidential elections of September-October 1992. In these ballots Iliescu was re-elected president and the DNSF emerged as the largest (but not a majority) party in parliament.

The DNSF government had the parliamentary backing of the extreme nationalist parties, which were not, however, part of the coalition. To this category belong the Greater Romania Party, whose president is Corneliu Vadim Tudor; the Party of Romanian National Unity (PRNU), which is basically anti-Hungarian but has close connections with antisemitic trends; and the Socialist Labour Party (SLP), the heir of the former RCP, which remains faithful to the nationalist line of its predecessor.

Economic conditions deteriorated during the year. Inflation ran at over 200 per cent and by early 1993 over 10 per cent of the population were unemployed.

HISTORICAL LEGACY

In the nineteenth and early twentieth centuries Romania was generally considered one of the most antisemitic countries in Europe. Following foreign pressure, citizenship was granted to Jews on a collective basis only after 1923, but this step was resented by many political parties as well as large segments of the general population.

Antisemitism emerged as a powerful factor in the country's political life in the third decade of this century with the establishment of the Legion of the Archangel Saint Michael by Corneliu Zelea Codreanu in June 1927. Many points included in the antisemitic programme of the Legion (also known as the Iron Guard) were legislated by the Goga-Cuza government, which lasted only from 27 December 1937 to 11 February 1938. On 14 September 1940 General (later Marshal) Ion Antonescu set up, together with the Iron Guard, the National Legionary State. In January 1942, following an abortive rebellion against Antonescu, the Guard was banned. Under Antonescu's rule, much of the legislation of the Goga-Cuza government became even harsher. A part of the Jewish population was deported to the Transdniester region during Romania's occupation of this territory after the outbreak of the Second World War, and many of those deported met their death. There were pogroms against the Jews in Romania proper.

The number of Romanian Jews exterminated in the Holocaust is subject to dispute between Romanian historians of non-Jewish origin and those of Jewish origin. The former have never produced a specific figure but regard estimates by Jews as grossly exaggerated. According to Jewish historians, between 250,000 and 300,000 Romanian Jews perished in the territories that were under Romanian jurisdiction during the Second World War. This figure does not include the approximately 150,000 Jews from Northern Transylvania who were exterminated in 1944 either by the Hungarian authorities or by the Germans, who deported them to concentration camps with the collaboration of the Hungarian government.

After the war several Jews were prominent in the leadership of the Romanian Communist Party (RCP). Of these the best known are Ana Pauker and Iosif Chisinevschi. At no point after the Communist takeover, however, was the RCP's leadership composed of a majority, or even a plurality, of Jews. Pauker was a victim of Stalin's antisemitic campaign, which was shrewdly exploited by the RCP's First Secretary, Gheorghe Gheorghiu-Dej (who

was no less of a Stalinist than Pauker) in order to remove a political adversary. Chisinevschi survived politically until 1958, when he was caught attempting to strike an "unholy alliance" with some Stalinists-turned-liberal elements in the party in an effort to emulate the Khrushchev line in the USSR.

In 1964 Dej adopted a neo-nationalist policy, which reached a new peak under Nicolae Ceausescu, who succeeded him as party leader in March 1965. Although under Ceausescu antisemitism was never officially endorsed, it was condoned and occasionally appeared in the press and in literary works by authors closely associated with the presidential couple. The most prominent of these authors, the Ceausescu hagiographers Eugen Barbu and Corneliu Vadim Tudor, re-emerged in prominent positions in Romania's antisemitic circles in 1990-1.

PARTIES, ORGANIZATIONS, MOVEMENTS

No political party in Romania openly admits to being antisemitic. However, two broad categories of radical parties in which antisemitism plays an overt or covert role can be differentiated. The first category is made up of the parties of "radical continuity" which advocate a continuation of the Ceausescu line in foreign and internal policy but with a stronger emphasis on the xenophobia of the former regime. This category includes the GRP, the PRNU, the SLP and the Party of Social Democratic Unity (PSDU).

The second category, which may be labelled "radical return", advocates a revival of the nationalist ethos based on interwar political and social values.

Unlike the others, the PSDU is not represented in parliament. In the general elections of 1992 the GRP obtained 3.89 per cent of the vote for the Chamber of Deputies and 3.85 per cent of the vote for the Senate, as a result of which it is represented by twenty-two deputies and senators. (Romania has a bi-cameral system: parliament is composed of 341 deputies and 143 senators).

Tudor put the membership of the GRP at 28,000 card-carrying members and about 40,000 sympathizers in summer 1992. The GRP was set up in May 1991 with Tudor as president and Barbu as vice-president and, from its foundation, has had a clear anti-Jewish orientation. The basis on which the party was established was laid down by *Romania mare*, a weekly published by Tudor since May 1990, which regularly contains viciously antisemitic articles.

The GRP is close to both the former secret police and the SLP, which was set up in 1991. After the 1992 elections the GRP and SLP founded in the Senate the National Bloc. The most prominent member of the SLP in the Senate is Adrian Paunescu who, like Tudor, is a former "court poet" of the Ceausescu family. Paunescu owns both the weekly *Totusi iubirea* and *Vremea*, a newspaper printed on alternate days which often carries antisemitic articles, sometimes under Paunescu's signature. No official figures for membership in the SLP are available. In the 1992 elections the SLP obtained 3.03 per cent of the votes for the Chamber of Deputies and 3.18 per cent of those for the Senate. It is represented in parliament by thirteen deputies and five senators.

In late 1992 the GRP suffered a major blow with the resignation of Radu Theodoru, its vice-president and ideologist. Although Theodoru tried to present the extreme nationalist posture of the GRP as the outcome of Tudor's domination of the party, this was certainly not the case. Theodoru had been a major factor behind these positions and a particularly ferocious antisemite. In fact, after his resignation from the GRP his written contribution to the weekly *Europa* remained the same. Theodoru was immediately named president of the PSDU.

Both GRP and SLP are close to the Romanian Cradle (Vatra romaneasca), an extremist anti-Hungarian organization founded in early 1990, whose political arm is the PRNU. The honorary president of Romanian Cradle, Iosif Constantin Dragan, who has an Iron Guardist past and is reputed to have amassed a fortune in the West, is known for his close links with the former regime. Dragan now heads the Europa Nova publishing trust, which is suspected of being behind a weekly even more viciously antisemitic than *Romania mare*, namely *Europa*.

Dragan also heads the Marshal Antonescu League and the Marshal Antonescu Foundation. Along with other organizations, the Marshal Antonescu League has demanded that the prosecutor general seek nullification of the death sentence pronounced on Antonescu and some members of his government. The demand remained under examination in late March 1993. In an interview with the independent weekly *22* in April 1992 the PRNU's president, Gheorghe Funar, expressed his approval of the "patriotic" articles which appear in *Europa* and *Romania mare* and described complaints about antisemitism in Romania as "a lie spread by those who pursue anti-Romanian interests". This statement was clearly directed at Chief Rabbi Rosen, whose repeated complaints about growing antisemitism provoked (as in 1991) a strong reaction from the antisemites.

Vatra romaneasca claims a membership of six million, but this figure is not credible. Total membership of the PRNU is unknown, but the party emerged relatively strongly in the 1992 elections. It obtained 7.71 per cent of the votes for the Chamber of Deputies and 8.12 per cent of the votes for the Senate, and is represented by 30 deputies and 14 senators.

None of the "radical return" parties has been able to obtain parliamentary representation. The New Christian Romania (NCR) did not run in the elections, having been set up only in November 1992, on Codreanu's birth date. Its leader is Serban Suru, a thirty-year-old teacher, and the party has both very young members and very old former members of the Iron Guard. The NCR openly calls for Codreanu's rehabilitation.

The National Legionary Party, led by former policeman Ionel Catanescu, was launched in September 1992. Most observers believe this was a diversionary move by the DNSF, which wished to raise the specter of the extreme right in order to bring back voters disillusioned with its performance but wary of a revival of the extremist parties. Catanescu seemed to know little about Iron Guardist ideology and nothing more was heard of his party.

The same cannot be said about the Christian Democratic Union-Sibiu Convention (CDU-CS). Its members were expelled from the Christian Democratic Union in 1990 precisely on account of pro-Iron Guard sympathies. Membership of the

CDU-SC is unknown but the party had intermittently published the journal *Puncte cardinale* (a reference to a book of the same name by Nichifor Crainic, a well-known antisemite). The journal demands the rehabilitation of the Legion and calls for the younger generation to step into its shoes.

The Movement for Romania (MFR), headed by the young Marian Munteanu, has an organizational structure resembling that of Codreanu's organization. Although it claims to be democratic it refuses to condemn the Iron Guard and openly identifies itself with some of its ideals. The MFR obtained only 13,000 votes in the 1992 elections but its popularity is reported to be growing among tomorrow's electorate—college students and schoolchildren.

The "radical return" category should also include the Party of National Right (PNR) established by Radu Sorescu in April 1992. Although antisemitism does not appear to be on the party's agenda (Sorescu has said the "Jewish problem" is no longer "relevant" in today's Romania), the PNR's agenda puts it squarely among the extremist parties. Its agenda includes the internment of gypsies in camps and a renewed "Axis" of Berlin, Tokyo and Rome to be joined by Bucharest and based on "economic interest". The PNR obtained 7,000 votes in the 1992 elections but, as with the MFR, it appears to gain in popularity among the younger generation.

Two non-party organizations deserve particular attention for having adopted antisemitic postures. One is the Cluj-based Zalmoxis Cultural Society, which in July-August 1992 published in *Europa* a venomously anti-Jewish "appeal" to members and sympathizers. The other is the Romanian Institute for Romanianism and Roman Studies, which was founded in early 1992 and includes many sympathizers of the GRP.

MANIFESTATIONS

In March Chief Rabbi Rosen disclosed that he had received death threats in the wake of the intensification of the antisemitic campaign led by *Europa*. A prominent member of the NSF who claimed to have a double agent among sympathizers of the Iron Guard warned him that an assassination attempt was being prepared.

Also in March the monument in Iasi to victims of the June-July 1941 pogrom was desecrated by anti-Jewish graffiti. In the same month sixteen tombstones were desecrated in the Jewish cemetery of Suceava, one of Romania's oldest Jewish cemeteries. In June the German daily *Suddeutsche Zeitung* reported that "paranoid" anti-Jewish graffiti could be seen in Bucharest. In October the press carried reports about the first skinhead manifestations in Romania, which were mainly directed against the gypsies. The skinheads daubed a swastika on a deserted building in Bucharest and a member of the group in the same town expressed admiration for Hitler. The existence of a skinhead group was also reported from the town of Ploiesti.

PUBLICATIONS

The electronic media are essentially free of antisemitism although programmes with antisemitic undertones have occasionally been broadcast. For example, in September the independent Channel Two carried an interview with a university professor who attempted to exonerate the Iron Guardist ideologue Nae Ionescu. Also, a television series on Communist prisons repeatedly failed to differentiate between democrats and former Iron Guardists, presenting them all as martyrs.

It is expected that antisemitic programmes will be aired more often in future on some channels. This is due to the fact that Dragan's Europa Nova has been granted by the newly-established Council on the Audiovisual licenses in several Romanian towns, including Timisoara (where Dragan is backing another extreme nationalist publication, the daily *Renasterea banateana*) and Iasi. Previously television channels he owned broadcasted illegally, and many of the programmes shown were overtly antisemitic.

In addition to *Romania mare*, *Europa*, *Totusi iubirea*, *Vremea*, *Natiunea* (a Dragan-owned weekly serving Romanian Cradle), and *Puncte cardinale*, a plethora of other publications (whose weekly circulation was estimated in 1992 by the weekly *22* at one million) often carry antisemitic articles. More blatant are the weeklies *Spionaj-Contraspionaj*, which is apparently financed by members of the former secret police, *Politica* (owned by Tudor and mouthpiece of the GRP youth organization), *Timpul* (edited by the well-known nationalist Adrian Rizea), *Flacara* (whose editor, Ion Goia, is a member of the pro-Marshal Antonescu League), and *Phoenix* (Oradea). The Bucharest daily *Universul romanesc* belongs to this category but other dailies (among them the independent *Adevarul* and *Tineretul liber* and the pro-Iliescu *Dimineata*) occasionally published articles with antisemitic undertones in 1992. These may not have been as vitriolic as those carried by *Europa* (whose editor-in-chief, Ilie Neacsu, often employs the pejorative *jidani* when referring to Jews and who in 1992 called for Rabbi Rosen's expulsion from Romania) but they are not very far behind. In the same category as *Europa* is the Timisoara weekly *Gazeta de vest*, which is overtly pro-Iron Guard. The editor-in-chief of this publication, Ovidiu Gules, is known to have ties with the half-brother of Horia Sima, who inherited Codreanu's mantle as leader of the Guard and is still alive in Spain. From December 1991 to May 1992 *Gazeta de vest* serialized Sima's memoirs. Also reflecting a pro-Iron Guard line is the MFR monthly *Miscarea*. Contributing to the re-rehabilitation of the Iron Guard in the public eye are also publications which, mainly for commercial reasons, publish week after week articles claiming to be a contribution to understanding the "Legionary phenomenon". Leader in this field is the weekly *Baricada* but this magazine (or the weekly *Formula AS*) is by no means an exception. Even *Tinerama*, a weekly owned by a Jew who returned to Romania from exile, indulged in this practice.

Many books seeking to rehabilitate Antonescu were published in 1991 and 1992. The chief ideologists of the Iron Guard were also re-edited, some of them at respectable publishing houses. These houses apparently wish to fill a gap created by many years of silence on Romanian rightist thought but, by putting on the market a product lacking any critical scientific apparatus, they contribute wittingly or unwittingly to the rehabilitation of interwar antisemitism.

Paul Everac, who was appointed president of Romanian television in January 1993, published in 1992 a volume—the Reactionary—which was full of anti-Jewish and anti-gypsy venom. In the same year Everac published an article approvingly quoting *The Protocols of the Elders of Zion* and another tract evincing admiration for the "achievements" of the totalitarian regimes. The independent daily *Romania libera* labelled the latter tract Paul Everac's "*Mein Kampf*".

MAINSTREAM POLITICS

It is possible to differentiate two major categories affecting antisemitism in mainstream political life in Romania. The first deserves the label "opportunist antisemitism" and relates to political personalities who, though not antisemites themselves, are ready to accept tacit collaboration with antisemites when their interest is served by it. The second category includes antisemites who are members of political parties and movements that are not antisemitic as a whole.

Heading the first category is undoubtedly President Iliescu. Although on several occasions in 1992, at the urge of Rabbi Rosen, Iliescu dissociated himself from antisemitism, he accepted the endorsement of the GRP, the SLP and the PSDU in the presidential campaign. Also, in November 1992 *Europa*, celebrating its 100th issue, gave Iliescu its "distinction" and the president accepted it through an envoy who attended the ceremony. The category also includes Radu Campeanu, the former president (since early 1993 vice-president) of the National Liberal Party (NLP), who stated in April 1992 that he could not see why his party should not enter into an alliance with the MFR. Apparently driven by the urge to increase electoral appeal among the pro-nationalist public, several prominent DNSF personalities, such as senators Vasile Vacaru, Ion Solcanu and Oliviu Gherman, agreed to be interviewed by *Europa* (Iliescu himself agreed to a similar interview in early 1993). In December 1992 the DNSF minister of health, Iulian Mincu, accepted a distinction offered by the weekly *Romania mare*.

Several parliamentarians representing the DNSF have expressed, both inside and outside parliament, views that reflect an antisemitic outlook. Foremost among these is the priest Simeon Tatu who, in a veiled attack on Petre Roman, suggested in 1991 that parliamentarians produce evidence of their Romanian ethnic purity going back at least two generations; Tatu was also present at the *Europa* anniversary. A second parliamentarian who has expressed anti-Jewish views is Senator Romulus Vulpescu, who contributes a weekly column to *Romania mare*.

That many extremists are members of other parties was demonstrated in mid-1992 when eleven parliamentarians (mostly from the DNSF but also from the NSF and the NLP) became representatives of the GRP, on whose lists many of them were re-elected to the legislature several months later.

Senator Adrian Motiu, representing the PRNU, suggested in 1992 that the house invite Romania's former Chief Rabbi, Alexandru Safran, for a visit. The house approved the initiative. The purpose of the invitation (which was accepted) was to counter Rabbi Rosen's arguments on the Holocaust. Motiu and his friends obviously hoped to build on the animosity known to have existed between Safran and Rosen. But the invitation was cancelled when Rosen produced evidence (based on Safran's memoirs) showing that the former Chief Rabbi confirmed his own statements on the Holocaust of Romanian Jewry.

BUSINESS AND COMMERCE

No evidence of anti-Jewish discrimination in the business and commercial world is available. The antisemitic publications, however, warned repeatedly against Israelis who did business in Romania, who were said to be committing "genocide" against the Romanian people, among other things through economic enslavement.

The anti-Jewish publications were full of venom when it was learned, in late November 1992, that Romanian-born Israelis had asked Israeli Foreign Minister Shimon Peres to back their demand for restitution of property confiscated from the Jews by the fascist and Communist regimes. To Tudor this was "an absurd claim, which is suspiciously reminiscent of the abusive policy of Israel towards Germany, from which it squeezed immeasurable values after the war".

RELIGION

As in 1991, *Romania mare* and *Europa* published many articles reflecting religious antisemitism. These were not, however, the only publications to do so. In June 1992 the daily *Tineretul liber*, for example, carried an article by a Professor Petre Dogaru on the history of Communism in Romania. According to Dogaru, Karl Marx simply put into practice the ancient teachings of Judaism for achieving world domination. These teachings, according to an item in *Spionaj-Contraspionaj* in August 1992, included the "Talmudic principle" that "the best among the Christians must be killed". It was not surprising, therefore, that *Romania mare* and *Europa* accused Rabbi Rosen of what was tantamount to ritual murder. It was he, according to several tracts in these publications, who had engineered the deaths of several Romanian patriotic intellectuals who had opposed his failed endeavour to re-issue the antisemitic writings of the national poet Mihai Eminescu in the 1980s. In support of their claim, authors such as Radu Theodoru and Nicolae Radu (who had specialized in religious antisemitism since 1991) allegedly quoted the Talmud (an 1866 antisemitic commentary on which was re-issued by the Zalmoxis publishing house in 1992) and *The Protocols of the Elders of Zion* (parts of which were serialized in *Europa* in 1992). Claiming that in his insistence on the Holocaust of Romanian Jewry Rosen was in fact attacking the Romanian Orthodox Church, Florian Popa Micsan wrote in *Romania mare* in April 1992 that the Jews wished to crucify the Romanian people just as they had crucified Christ. According to Micsan, in a long serial published in *Europa* entitled "Chief Rabbi Rosen is the spring of anti-Romanianism", Romanian Jews had "entered into a coalition with the object of crucifying Jesus Christ—the Romanian people—once again". This cabal, Tudor wrote, could also be proved by the fact that Ceausescu "had been shot on the very holy day of the birth of Jesus Christ". Only the "mean Zionist intrigues", wrote Theodoru in *Romania mare*, could explain the "assassination of a president on the Holy Days of the birth of the Lord".

Rosen was not the sole target of these attacks. According to Ilie Neacsu—"under the influence of the Talmud, the Torah and other doctrinaire works of a racist character"—Petre Roman—this "little Jew-boy"—had claimed from childhood that one day he would be prime minister. In January *Europa* claimed that "in the spirit of the Talmud, which designates the Jewish people for ever-greatness, Mr Petre Roman began to elbow his way to the top of the Romanian pyramid". But in order to achieve this purpose, Roman had been helped not only by the Talmud, but also by foreign secret services such as the CIA and the Mossad, which were bent on transforming Romania into a colony dominated by international Jewish money.

DENIAL OF THE HOLOCAUST

Continual references by Rabbi Rosen to the Holocaust of Romanian Jewry triggered not only denials of these facts by the extremists but also assertions that the "circus of the Holocaust" (Theodoru) or the "so-called Holocaust" (Mircea Cernatescu in *Romania mare* in March 1992) was a diversion whose "diabolical aim" (according to an unsigned article in *Romania mare*, also in March) was to enable "world Jewry to squeeze whatever can still be squeezed out of this country".

In December Micsan wrote in *Europa* that the "scenario" in which Rabbi Rosen was involved aimed at "recolonizing Romania with a number of Jews equal to the number of those fictitiously killed between 1940 and 1944". Under the title "Genocide, Holocaust, Shoah—one big kike diversion" Nicolae Radu placed the entire Holocaust of European Jewry under a question mark. In December he wrote in the same weekly that the purpose of the unending "campaign", in which one false notion after another was invented, was to "maintain the obligation of the German people to allow these ever-hungry leeches to go on sucking from the Teutonic body".

In March, against this background, *Romania mare* told Roman he had nothing to fear in Romania for "nobody is going to gas you here, at most you might die from suffocating on that garlic smell inherited through genealogy". It was also against this background that Senator Vulpescu demanded in the house that Rosen apologize to the Romanian people: as Micsan put it in February, the Romanians "owed nothing to the Jews", but Rosen "owed them an

apology, for which he should kneel down and beg for forgiveness". Finally, it was against this background that in October-December the scholarly journal *Studii de drept romanesc* (Studies in Romanian Law) published an attempt to rehabilitate George Alexianu, the governor of the Transdniester region during the war, who had been shot together with Antonescu. After all, as the weekly *22* remarked in February, when visiting Jerusalem's Yad Vashem memorial in 1991, President Iliescu was the only East European head of state who avoided apologizing for his countrymen's part in the Holocaust.

EFFECTS OF ANTI-ZIONISM

Europa, Romania mare, Politica and other antisemitic publications referred repeatedly to Mossad's alleged involvement in Romanian affairs and to politicians of Jewish origin (Roman and Silviu Brucan being the ones most often mentioned) as serving the interests of "world Zionism"—whose aim was to subdue Romania economically and politically—and to Israel's "fascist-like" behaviour in the occupied territories. The alleged Zionist plot was "shown" to be linked to the Hungarian irredenta in Transylvania, particularly in several articles by Theodoru. Tudor wrote in January 1992 that the Romanians "wanted to be Jews" and emulate *in toto* the behaviour of the Israelis in the occupied territories, applying it to Hungarians residing in Transylvania.

There also appeared several articles supporting Iraq and denouncing Western policies towards Saddam Husseyn as serving Zionist purposes. The independent daily *Romania libera* reproduced photocopies of a letter to Tudor by an Iraqi diplomat showing that Tudor had been paid for services rendered to the Iraqis. Both Tudor and the Iraqi embassy in Bucharest claimed the letter was a forgery. There is no evidence that the anti-Zionist campaign had any impact on the Romanian public at large.

OPINION POLLS

No polls on antisemitism were published in 1992. On a related issue, a survey conducted by the Romanian Institute for Public Opinion Survey in late November on a representative sample of 1,074

Romanians aged seventeen and over found that 8 per cent of the respondents thought the "danger that extremist forces will become very powerful in the next five years" was "very great"; 20 per cent were persuaded that the danger was "great"; 28 per cent thought it was "not very great"; 21 per cent thought there was "no such danger at all"; and 23 per cent either had no opinion or did not reply to the question.

LEGAL MATTERS

In May 1991, in the wake of several ferocious antisemitic attacks by *Europa*, the Federation of Jewish Communities in Romania asked the prosecutor general to investigate the matter on the basis of the appropriate legislation. In place of a reply two weeks later the prosecutor's office wrote to Rabbi Rosen inviting him to "reconcile" himself with Neacsu. Rosen met with the prosecutor general himself, who claimed to have no knowledge of the communication and promised a reply to the complaint within two weeks. Twenty-six weeks later there was still no reply. On 18 December 1991, at a further meeting with the prosecutor general, a reply (due to be received, according to the letter of the law, within thirty days after the launching of a complaint) was again promised "soon"; four months later it had still not arrived.

Meanwhile, in March 1992, a representative of the prosecutor's office told Rosen that he should produce "historical evidence" for his arguments on the Holocaust (as if this were the matter under discussion) and that the Penal Code could not be applied because it had been legislated under Ceausescu. But all other legal proceedings were still being conducted under the provisions of this code. At a meeting with President Iliescu (see below) in the same month representatives of the Federation were promised that the investigating organs would pursue the matter and a government declaration (see below) released soon thereafter spoke in the same spirit. On 4 May, however, a reply from the prosecutor general's office rejected the complaint on the basis of a Penal Code article giving leeway to the prosecutor general to decide on certain matters. In November 1992 Rabbi Rosen launched an initiative for parliament to legislate a new law. (A further letter in November to the

prosecutor general, in the wake of the publication in *Europa* of a letter signed "Itzik Strul" containing material offensive to Romanians—which Rosen deemed a forgery—proved fruitless).

COUNTERING ANTISEMITISM

On several occasions, President Iliescu (and on one occasion the government) issued statements denouncing antisemitism in the country. Nevertheless, the president was constrained by his party's "unwritten alliance" with some of the extremist forces such as the GRP, the PRNU and the SLP. The first such encounter took place in March, when the NSF had not yet split into a Roman wing (still called NSF) and an Iliescu wing (the DNSF). At that time Iliescu expressed his "full disapproval and condemnation of manifestations of antisemitism in some publications, in *Europa*, *Romania mare*, and others". These manifestations, he added, were not only insulting to the Jews of Romania but also to the Romanian people, who had always "rejected extremism of any kind, chauvinistic manifestations, hatred, and violence". Iliescu said he was "perplexed to remark that *Gazeta de vest* vindicates the Iron Guard and its Captain, Corneliu Zelea Codreanu". This, he added, was particularly dangerous since the younger generation was not aware of "what fascism, the Legionary movement, had represented in the country". The rehabilitation of the movement was said to be "an attempt to assassinate that democracy which we want to build in Romania". The Stolojan government's declaration, issued on 25 March, "disapproved and condemned" the dissemination in the press of "extremist, Legionary or fascist-like views". In an allusion to the campaign against Rosen and Israel ambassador Zvi Mazel personally, the government said these publications were printing "unacceptable attacks *ad personae* and on diplomats representing countries with which Romania has friendly ties". It was further stated that these attacks were particularly dangerous in the transition period from Communism to democracy.

No declaration by the country's leaders condemning antisemitism, however, was issued during the electoral campaign or when discussions on the setting up of the new coalition were conducted, although the antisemitic campaign had meanwhile grown unashamedly. The explanation for this silence was obvious—Iliescu and his DNSF depended on the support of the parties of "radical continuity". Indeed, the GRP and *Europa* had threatened to withdraw support for Iliescu after his March declaration, an idea that was eventually dropped.

On 30 October, at his swearing-in ceremony in the parliament, Iliescu said he was determined to "continue to take a position against ethnic, religious, or any other form of intolerance, against extremism, xenophobia, antisemitism and other forms of racist hatred ... that can seriously affect the national interest". Yet he refrained on this occasion from specifying who was guilty of these manifestations; it was clear that his party was dependent on the support of people like Tudor and that any mention of *Romania mare* might have entailed high political costs. In a speech to parliament on 21 December, on the occasion of the anti-Ceausescu uprising anniversary, Iliescu walked a political tightrope. On the one hand, he said, "xenophobic, chauvinistic, antisemitic manifestations" were "unacceptable"; on the other hand, he condemned "anti-Romanian attitudes". This was clearly an attempt to appease the parties of "radical continuity", which had been accusing both the Jewish and the Hungarian ethnic minority leaders of "anti-Romanianism".

One other prominent Romanian political personality, Minister of Defence Nicolae Spiroiu, condemned antisemitism in early December, assuring Rosen at an encounter that "the Romanian army was combating antisemitism and defending all Romanian citizens, without distinguishing between their religious or ethnic affiliation".

In an interview with the weekly *22* in February and in an article in the daily *Adevarul* in March two prominent NSF leaders, George Stancov and Adrian Severin respectively, firmly condemned antisemitism. Also, in a declaration read in parliament in early December the entire NSF faction condemned "positions of extreme nationalism ... antisemitism and xenophobia".

In early November eight parties—the Party of Civic Alliance, the National Peasant Party Christian Democratic, the Social Democratic Party, the Ecologist Party, the Hungarian Democratic Federation of Romania, the New Liberal Party, the Socialist Democratic Party and the Republican Party)—rallied to what Rosen termed an "SOS appeal" and attended a meeting at the Choral synagogue in Bucharest to discuss ways of combating the growing tide of antisemitism. The parties promised to support the initiative to introduce special legislation combating racism launched by the Chief Rabbi.

In November in what was probably an attempt to appease Rosen and the Jews, the Romanian Academy elected the Chief Rabbi an honorary member of the academy.

On several occasions in 1992 Romanian intellectuals rallied against antisemitism. A debate on the phenomenon was organized by the Writers' Union in April. Following the publication of Rosen's book *The Martyrdom of Romanian Jews* in 1991, Cornel Nistorescu, a prominent journalist, denounced in the weekly *Expres* in January the "silence" on the atrocities and the attempt to cast Antonescu as a national hero. Nistorescu, together with the television journalist Mihai Tatulici, was the main driving force behind a television debate on antisemitism in Romania in late March. Several other intellectuals published articles denouncing antisemitism and the attempt to rehabilitate Antonescu. Of these the most prominent was the historian Andrei Pippidi.

Assessment

Antisemitism intensified between 1991 and 1992. Rabbi Rosen held that the safety of Romanian Jewry could no longer be guaranteed by the authorities. While this may be somewhat overstated, there can be no doubt that the intricate political map of Romania, which has resulted in the ruling party being dependent for governance on the extremist parties, has considerably worsened the prospects for the vestiges of Romanian Jewry.

Equally worrying is the growth in popularity, particularly among the younger generation, of parties and movements openly identifying with the Iron Guard and its ideology. Against the background of growing social unrest triggered by the transition period, the popularity of both left-wing (a trend that continues to enjoy the backing of former Communists and the former secret police) and right-wing antisemitism, which share the endeavour to "externalize the guilt" for the nation's problems rather than search for it in their own past and near present, may yet grow, and Romanian Jewry's traditional "scapegoat role" has certainly not seen its end.

It should, however, be borne in mind that the Jews are not the only national nminority targeted by the extremists. The Hungarians and the Gypsies, were it only for their significantly larger numbers, also come under constant attacks.

Former Soviet Union

GENERAL BACKGROUND

Following the final collapse of the USSR in December 1991, the fate of the former Soviet republics, in common with that of other post-Communist societies in East-Central Europe, was directly linked to the speed and efficacy of economic and political reform. Russia, by far the most important country of the area in terms of territory, size of population, economy and, of course, military power, showed signs of continuing economic and political disintegration, with minority nationalities increasingly audacious in testing Moscow's will. Owing to the interdependence that had built up over several decades of Soviet power, the problems experienced by Russia were present in varying degrees in all the former Soviet republics. Jewish communities in the Muslim republics faced the additional problem of increasing "Islamization".

As Russia's economic and political situation deteriorated, there were signs that, while many citizens were indeed benefiting from the reforms, wide sections of the population were disillusioned; pauperization was a growing problem. An associated problem was the ongoing political and constitutional struggle between President Yeltsin and Communist and nationalist forces in the country, a struggle centred in the conservative-dominated parliament. Elements of the far right united in October to found the National Salvation Front. As the year wore on President Yeltsin appeared to lose some of the political credit he had gained at the time of the failed coup against Gorbachev in August 1991.

A further intractable problem was the existence in the former Soviet minority republics of approximately 25,000,000 ethnic Russians, many of whom now found themselves the target of an increasingly assertive anti-Russian nationalism. In addition, important political and economic differences remained between Russia and some other members of the increasingly shaky Commonwealth of Independent States.

With many Western countries, including the United States, in recession, with the United States additionally involved in a presidential campaign, and with the West's attention fixed for much of the year on the violent disintegration of the former Yugoslavia, the promised Western financial aid was slow in coming and, when it did come, it was frequently lost to bureaucrats and the quickly burgeoning criminal gangs in the former USSR.

The governments of the former Soviet republics remained generally favourably disposed towards Jews and sought good relations with Israel. The large-scale emigration of Jews continued, though many Jews were content to wait and see how successful the government's reform programme would turn out to be.

HISTORICAL LEGACY

The institutionalized Jewish disabilities of the tsarist period were overturned by the Bolshevik Revolution, and the revolutionary transformation of society under Communist rule gave Jews unprecedented equality of opportunity. However, antisemitic policies were introduced in Stalin's last years, culminating in the so-called "Doctors' Plot". A disproportionate number of Jews appeared to figure in the "economic" trials which took place in the 1960s.

The movement for emigration to Israel which emerged among Soviet Jews in the late 1960s was triggered by a growing sense of Jewish identification fuelled by, *inter alia*, frustration with widespread discriminatory practices, inadequate recognition of Soviet Jews' participation in the Great Patriotic War and their suffering in the Holocaust, and the impact of Israel's crushing victory in the 1967 Six Day War. In response to this movement, the Soviet authorities launched a powerful political and ideological campaign against Zionism and Israel. An influential group of Soviet anti-Zionist propagandists introduced traditional antisemitic themes into this propaganda, including the spectre of a world Jewish conspiracy which variously served, inspired or controlled "imperialist" policies aimed at subverting the Soviet Union and the Soviet Bloc.

Gorbachev's policy of *glasnost* was welcomed by liberal elements in the Soviet Union, including the Jewish population. There was a renaissance of Jewish cultural and religious life throughout the country. It soon became clear, however, that "openness" provided a platform for reactionaries and extremists too. As the official anti-Zionist and antisemitic campaign of the Brezhnev era ceased, a new phenomenon— Russian chauvinist and hardline Communist organizations appealing to grassroots antisemitism—appeared on the scene as the country experienced growing chaos and demoralization.

With the collapse of the Soviet Union and its replacement by fifteen independent states, the revival of Jewish life continued apace. At the same time, the economic and political environment in the former Soviet republics was in varying degrees increasingly unstable.

THE NATURE OF ANTISEMITISM IN THE FORMER USSR

The position of the Jewish minorities in the former USSR has always differed from republic to republic. With the country's break-up into separate entities, a process far advanced before the final collapse of the Soviet Union in December 1991, these differences became more pronounced.

In most parts of the former USSR there exist varying degrees of popular antisemitism—the substratum of the more "modern" antisemitic concepts and movements. These phenomena are linked almost everywhere to the revival of nationalism, in particular its extremist forms, and to the anti-Communist antisemitism widely propagated in the 1920s and later by the Nazis and pro-Nazi elements.

In Russia antisemitism is strongly linked to parochial nationalism, which is manifested in the political struggle and intellectual debate. In the minority republics the anti-Russian backlash affects the situation of the Jews in so far as many of them acted willy-nilly as a Russifying element. In some of the former minority republics, first and foremost the Baltic states, the nationalist revival entails, among other things, attempts to rehabilitate the anti-Soviet nationalists, including their pro-Nazi component and individuals who were directly involved in the Holocaust.

Another manifestation of nationalism is the eruption of ethnic unrest. The Jews find themselves caught up in the cross-fire of the unrest with each side demanding their support. One example was the Armenians, and the situation in Moldova, where the Russian and Ukrainian minorities refused to surrender the Trans-Dnestr region to the Romanian-speaking authorities in Kishinev.

Armenia

General population: 3,376,000
Jewish population: 1,000 (mainly in Yerevan)

PARTIES, ORGANIZATIONS, MOVEMENTS

It was reported in March that the nationalist groups, Hydet and Tsaharon had put out antisemitic propaganda, the former blaming the Jews for the Armenian genocide of 1915 and the latter blaming the Jews for having brought Christianity into the world.

Belarus

General population: 10,260,000
Jewish population: 120,000 (mainly in
Minsk, Gomel and Bobruisk)

PARTIES, ORGANIZATIONS, MOVEMENTS

In December a number of tiny ultra-
nationalist groups met on the initiative of
the Slav Assembly (Slavyansky sobor).
Reportedly, "misanthropic and antisemitic
rhetoric" was voiced. Generally, the shrill
anti-Jewish invective found in Russia and
the chauvinism and xenophobia characteristic of Ukrainian extremists were absent
from political life in Belarus.

MANIFESTATIONS

In October it was reported that, immediately following the unveiling of a monument to Jewish victims of the Nazis in the
town of Lida in Grodno Region, vandals
had knocked down the memorial stone
from its base and broken its marble
headstones.

PUBLICATIONS

With television and radio and a large
proportion of the press either directly
controlled by, or under the close scrutiny
of, the government, nothing which could
be considered incitement to ethnic strife
was permitted even in such hitherto openly
antisemitic periodicals as the former
Communist Party organ *Politichesky
sobesednik* or the weekly *7 dney*, which had
previously carried an article by the well
known anti-Zionist and antisemitic agitator
Alexander Romanenko.

Slavyanskie vedomosti, which was not
subject to government control, was not
characterized by the same forbearance.
Although criminal proceedings had been
initiated against the paper in autumn 1991
by the procurator-general, in January 1992
it was claiming that "the Torah enjoined
Jews to lie on oath", that "Hassidic Jews
engaged in ritual slaughter in order to drink
Christian blood", and that "Jewish masons
infiltrated the Bolshevik Party and were
responsible for the reign of terror".

In July the legal action against

Slavyanskie vedomosti was dropped after
the Philosophy and Justice Institute of the
Belarus Academy of Sciences claimed it
was unable to find in the paper "any
ideological or political material which
could qualify as spreading racism or
national hatred". The Belarus Jewish
journalist Yakov Bassin observed that the
Institute "has long had a reputation for
demagoguery, hysterical accusations against
Jews, and falsification paraded as scholar-
ship and can boast such alumni as [the anti-
Zionist and anti-Jewish agitators] Vladimir
Bovsh and the late Vladimir Begun".

RELIGIOUS ANTISEMITISM

In April a pile of copies of *Pamyat*, the
newspaper of the antisemitic group of the
same name, were seen, apparently awaiting
distribution, in the premises of the Metropolitan Filaret of Minsk, the Exarch of
Belarus of the (Moscow-Patriarchate)
Russian Orthodox Church.

DENIAL OF THE HOLOCAUST

It was reported that organs of the ultra-
nationalist press such as the magazines
Nioman and *Byelorusskaya dumka*,
vigorously campaigning for the rehabilitation of Nazi collaborators, had claimed that
Jews had lied about the Holocaust and, in
particular, had exaggerated the number of
Jewish victims.

COUNTERING ANTISEMITISM

In December Mikhail Slemnev, Chairman
of the National Politics and Inter-ethnic
Relations Committee of the Belarus
Supreme Soviet, and his deputy Mikhail
Zhebrak assured representatives of the
American Jewish Committee of the
government's intention to combat antisemitism and maintain good relations with
the Jewish community.

Estonia

General population: 1,565,000
Jewish population: 3,000 (mainly in Tallinn)

PARTIES, ORGANIZATIONS, MOVEMENTS

At a meeting of the ethnic Russian organization Baltic Russia in Tallinn in July, the principal speaker, Nina Bondareva, claimed Jews were responsible for Russia's ruin and were "living off Russian blood". On 16 July Bondareva, reputed to be a former inmate of a mental institution, was given time on Estonian television and again attacked Jews as being responsible for the destruction of the Soviet Union.

MANIFESTATIONS

There was an outbreak of antisemitic incidents in the first half of 1992. Both old and new Jewish cemeteries in Tartu were vandalized, Jewish buildings were daubed with swastikas, and Jewish activists received death threats. On 13 August a bomb exploded at the Jewish school in Tallinn (there were no casualties).

REHABILITATION OF NAZI COLLABORATORS

As with the other Baltic states, the issue of Nazi collaborators remained a cause for concern. Rallies of former Nazi collaborators during the year evoked protests from Jewish organizations both in Estonia and in the West. Alarm was also expressed at the government's sanctioning and financial backing of re-created veteran's organizations such as Fighters for Estonian Freedom which, Estonian Jewish survivors claimed, included mass murderers.

In December 1991 the Swedish parliament, having heard a report that neo-Nazism was rampant in Estonia, debated whether or not to curtail dealings with Estonian trade missions. The Estonian Jewish community was blamed by the Estonian government for deliberately spreading such misinformation and vilified in the ultra-nationalist press.

Georgia

General population: 5,464,000
Jewish population: 23,000-24,000 (mainly in Tbilisi)

MANIFESTATIONS

In Tbilisi there was a spate of child kidnappings in which children of Jewish families were involved. While Georgian Jewish leaders considered such crimes were indicative only of the general lawlessness, the procurator general was nevertheless instructed by the government to pay particular attention to crimes against Jews. A decision by young Jews to form a Jewish self-defence group was deferred.

PUBLICATIONS

In November it was reported that the pro-Gamsakhurdia Russian-language papers *Respublika Gruziya* and *Voskresenye* had carried material alleging a "Jewish-masonic plot" against Georgia.

Latvia

General population: 2,681,000
Jewish population: 16,000-18,000 (mainly in Riga)

PARTIES, ORGANIZATIONS, MOVEMENTS

The most important ultra-nationalist group during the year was Fatherland, which was part of a coalition with the 18 November Society, the Radical Association, and the Anti-Communist Association. The coalition, For Fatherland and Freedom, targeted its attacks on the Russian minority but some Jewish activists suspected a number of its supporters of being antisemites.

In December, following the publication of a prominent article by the American magazine *Life* accusing Latvia of turning a blind eye to anti-Jewish sentiment in the country, the Latvian authorities immediately denied the charge. Also, leaders of the Latvian Jewish community claimed that

"There positively is no state antisemitism in Latvia at the present time". An investigation carried out by the New York-based National Conference on Soviet Jewry noted that "The current official view of the Riga Jewish community is that there is no physical danger to Jews in Latvia and there is no official antisemitism".

MANIFESTATIONS

At the end of November Juris Boars, a Latvian Supreme Soviet deputy and Director of the Institute for International Relations, wrote in the ultra-nationalist paper *Dyona* that Latvians had no need to apologize to Jews for what had occurred during the war as the Jews had slaughtered Latvians; he named "the Jew Beria" as the principal killer. Boars repeated this charge on Latvian television.

In November, speaking in parliament, Supreme Soviet deputy Juris Debelis attacked "Russian Yid-loving journalists" as being responsible for Latvia's difficulties.

On 10 December the car of Yevgeny Livshits, a Riga businessman who, among other things, imported medicines from Israel, exploded when he started it up. Several days later his home was daubed with swastikas.

PUBLICATIONS

The Moscow-based *Jewish News Weekly* of 28 December 1992 reported that white-washing of Latvian crimes against Jews under the Nazi occupation was common in the ultra-nationalist press.

On 19 December 1992 the widely-read Riga evening newspaper *Rigas Balss* published an item stating that a local bookshop claimed it had been forced to close as a result of the high rent charged by its Jewish and Israeli landlords.

Latvian Jews complained about the publication by the firm Zvaigzne of a school history textbook portraying the Jews as the principal oppressors of the Latvian people. The book, written by Oddissey Kostanda, a Latvian member of parliament and a teacher, was published at the end of 1991 and used in schools in 1992. One of the offending phrases read "In order to crush, suppress and humiliate the population of the Latvian Republic, the Soviets came and began their work. Simon Shustin, a Jew, was their organizer."

COUNTERING ANTISEMITISM

In a statement issued on 15 December 1992 in response to an article in the American *Life* magazine which claimed that anti-semitism was widespread in Latvia (see above), President Gorbunovs stated that "I would like to announce that the Republic of Latvia in its legislation, official documents and policy firmly adheres to the September 19, 1990 Declaration 'About the Condemnation and Unallowability of Genocide and Anti-Semitism in Latvia', as well as condemns and firmly stands against any possible anti-Semitic forms or manifestations. The State of Latvia will continue to be intolerant towards any manifestations of anti-Semitism and ethnic discrimination in Latvia as these are counter to our national traditions."

Lithuania

General population: 3,700,000
Jewish population: 9,000 (mainly in Vilnius)

PUBLICATIONS

Early in 1992 the government banned the import of antisemitic Russian periodicals such as *Molodaya gvardiya* and *Nash sovremennik*.

On 18 March, in reaction to a speech by the rabbi of Vilnius, the yellow press newspaper *Respublika* commented: "Just because [former President] Landsbergis treats the Jews so well, do not circumcise him." This remark was condemned forthwith by President Landsbergis and in a Supreme Soviet Presidium declaration.

REHABILITATION OF NAZI COLLABORATORS

As in 1991, the principal source of contention between the government and the Jewish community was the rehabilitation of at least 25,000 alleged Nazi collaborators. The government continued to claim that collaborating with the Nazis arose from patriotic, anti-Soviet motives and that those rehabiliated had not been given a fair trial. Western Jewish organizations accused the government of rehabilitating individuals known to have participated in the creation and subsequent liquidation of ghettos in Vilnius and Ponary.

In 1992 a further six rehabilitations were annulled. Moreover, the genocide of Lithuanian Jews was commemorated by the issuing of special stamps and the hoisting of national flags with black ribbons.

Moldova

General population: 4,367,000
Jewish population: 60,000-70,000 (mainly in Kishinev)

REHABILITATION OF NAZI COLLABORATORS

A campaign by an extremist group, the National Christian Party, to rename a principal thoroughfare in Kishinev after Romania's pro-Nazi dictator Ion Antonescu evoked an outcry from Jewish activists. The proposal attracted the support of the Writers' Union and the ultra-nationalist newspaper "Voice of the Nation". "Voice of the Nation" ran a series of articles in support of former Romanian fascist leaders including Codrianu, head of the infamous Iron Guard. After strong protests, the Jewish leaders were given assurances that the thoroughfare would not be re-named.

GRASSROOTS ANTISEMITISM

A report issued by the World Jewish Congress in October claimed that Jews had been obliged to leave a shelter in central Kishinev and move to the outskirts as a result of anti-Jewish agitation.

Russia

General population: 148,000,000
Jewish population: 500,000 (mainly in Moscow and St Petersburg)

PARTIES, ORGANIZATIONS, MOVEMENTS

It was increasingly difficult to obtain a clear picture of the constantly shifting relationships throughout the political spectrum. The far right (see below) was no exception. In broad terms, in domestic affairs the far right was fundamentally opposed to Yeltsin's reform programme, although there was a virtual consensus that the clock could not be turned back to the Soviet period. In foreign affairs the far right was preoccupied with Russia's perceived beggar's status and pro-American shift and advocated most vocally policies more favourable to Russia's traditional allies such as Serbia and Iraq.

The founding in Moscow in October 1992 of the **National Salvation Front** (NSF)—an "unholy coalition of former communists, chauvinists and self-described fascists", as the London *Times* described it—split Russia's far right. The NSF, a loose umbrella organization of extremist bodies, was the result of many attempts to achieve unity. Having made the first attempts to form a joint platform on the eve of the 1990 Russian parliamentary elections, the nationalist and Communist elements in Russian politics came together in 1992 under the aegis of the Russian National Assembly, which was formed in June, and subsequently with the formation of the NSF. Gennady Zyuganov was instrumental in forming both coalitions. These forces had strong representation in the Russian legislature in the form of the Russian Unity bloc, which united national-ists and Communists from four parliamen-tary factions—Rossiya, Communists of Russia, Fatherland and the Agrarian Union.

The NSF, which numbered among its membership twenty Russian people's deputies and three former USSR people's deputies, endeavoured to present the "respectable" face of the far right. The founding of the NSF was a progression of the "red-brown alliance"—as its detractors labelled it—of hardline Communists and Russian nationalists which had originally emerged around 1987. In their opposition to Gorbachev's policy of *perestroyka* and, later to Yeltsin's reform policies, both groups ascribed much of the blame for Russia's misfortunes during this century to, *inter alia*, Jews.

According to the NSF's own Russian Information Agency, the founding meeting, which took place in a cinema in Moscow, attracted over 1,400 delegates from 103 Russian cities and observers from many of the former Soviet republics—a total gathering of around 3,000.

As far as can be ascertained, speeches at the congress were not overtly antisemitic—apart from the obligatory condemnation of the "Zionist/Western conspiracy" to destroy Russia and the fact that leaflets and a brochure entitled "Lenin's Jewish Forefather" were distributed in the cinema foyer. At the same time, the steps to the platform were guarded by teams of men wearing black uniforms and berets. On the fringes of the congress and at a separate street protest by a militant Communist faction, black-shirted youths distributed overtly pro-fascist literature.

Some of the leading members of the NSF—for instance, Sergei Baburin, Albert Makashov, Valentin Rasputin and Igor Shafarevich—were well known personalities in Russian public life.

President Yeltsin immediately moved to ban the new organization on the grounds that it was unconstitutional despite its proclaimed intention to act within the law. On 30 November the Russian Constitutional Court began hearings called by Front activists to decide whether Yeltsin's decree dissolving the NSF was constitutional or not. On 12 February 1993 the Constitutional Court deemed his decree unconstitutional.

Remaining outside of the NSF were the "less respectable" fringe groups, the numerous **Pamyat-type neo-Nazi and neo-fascist groups** as well **as neo-Stalinist groups** of the type of Nina Andreeva's St Petersburg-based All-Union Communist Party of Bolsheviks and Viktor Anpilov's Russian Communist Workers' Party and his Working Russia movement. The so-called **Liberal Democratic Party** of Vladimir Zhirinovsky (who obtained 6,000,000 votes when he stood against Boris Yeltsin in the 1990 Russian presidential elections), also remained outside the NSF. (In September Zhirinovsky—said by some to be half-Jewish— met in Paris with Front National leader Jean-Marie Le Pen, a meeting which, he said, confirmed that they had common ideologies and a unity of views.)

Many extremists made clear their belief in the authenticity of *The Protocols of the Elders of Zion*. They also looked back with pride and admiration to their forbears from the beginning of the century, the *pogromshchiks* popularly known as the Black Hundreds and their principal political grouping, the Union of the Russian People. The fringe groups were frequently at odds with one another on both doctrinal and personal grounds.

Far-right activists, both those belonging to the NSF and to "less respectable" fringe groups, frequently brandishing anti-Jewish placards and shouting anti-Jewish slogans, joined in several large demonstrations organized against Yeltsin in the Russian capital and elsewhere.

Although there were reports from Jewish activists around the country to the effect that anti-Jewish statements had been made by Cossacks, there appeared to be no concrete evidence of this. While it was understandable that Jews, with their bitter memories of pre-revolutionary Cossack antisemitism, should be perturbed about the revival of the Cossacks, all the indications were that the Cossacks were backing the Yeltsin camp.

MANIFESTATIONS

Although antisemitic demonstrations in Moscow, St Petersburg and elsewhere were fairly commonplace, there were relatively few violent incidents.

On 1 February a bitter, long-running legal dispute between the New York-based Lubavicher (Hassidic) movement and the Russian State Library (formerly the Lenin Library) over the ownership of a 12,000-volume collection of books and manuscripts—besides the collection's spiritual value, widely different financial values were placed upon it by both parties—turned violent. On that day hardline Communists who were regularly picketing the library attacked a Lubavicher rabbi who crossed their line. Five days later a busload of Hasidim forced their way into the library, overturning cabinets and tables. On 17 February members of the Lubavich movement were beaten up in the library. In April the synagogue and Moscow headquarters of the Lubavicher movement were firebombed; there was extensive damage but there were no casualties. No one claimed responsibility for the attack. The dispute over the collection, which received extensive media publicity in Russia, was the subject of many antisemitic remarks by the "patriotic" press.

In April during during Passover a home-made bomb exploded in a synagogue in Rostov-on-Don.

In June, amid much media publicity, a two-week-long picket of Ostankino television centre in Moscow by hardline Communists over its alleged anti-Russian bias was forcibly brought to an end by the authorities. A number of "anti-Zionist" and undisguised anti-Jewish placards were in evidence during the picket. This event too became a *cause celebre* of the "patriotic" press.

In October about twenty-five black-shirted members of Dmitry Vasilev's Pamyat group burst into the offices of the liberal Moscow newspaper *Moskovsky komsomolets*, a paper well known for its criticism of Pamyat societies and pro-Communist organizations. The men held the editor hostage and videotaped the staff before leaving after twenty minutes. President Yeltsin strongly condemned the action and on 16 October signed an order to investigate it.

Also in October, following the arrest of its leader, Alexei Andreev, it was reported that the St Petersburg-based neo-Nazi National Social Party had set up an armed unit and established contact with neo-Nazi groups in the West.

There was a number of incidents of vandalism and desecration of Jewish monuments. For instance, on 6 January 1993 twenty headstones were broken by unidentified persons in a Jewish cemetery in Yekaterinburg.

"RUSSOPHOBIA"

In an interview with the Russian newspaper *Megapolis-Express* (no. 26, 1992), Vladimir Zhirinovsky, the leader of the so-called Liberal Democratic Party, denied that he was an antisemite: "It was not the Russians who created antisemitism. This is a defensive reaction to anti-Russian senti-ments. Most editorial boards in newspa-pers, radio and television are composed of people of Jewish nationality. Let the Jews adopt a patriotic line and say that they wish to see Russia rich and cultured and let them help to make this a fact. But in reality they say something else—that Russia is a barbaric country, that Russians are bad people, and that they are occupiers and are oppressing someone."

This statement provides an example of the concept of "Russophobia", a relatively recent addition to Russian reactionary ideology. According to the former dissi-dent Igor Shafarevich, the originator of the concept, the Russians are undeservedly despised by everybody—by nationalists in the minority republics, by Western-oriented liberals, and, first and foremost, by the Jews. In the view of Shafarevich, the Jews' hatred of Russia is tied to "their faith in the 'Chosen People' and in the world dominance to which it is destined". Essentially, "Russophobia" is an expression of the humiliation felt by many conserva-tive Russian nationalists at the state to which their country has been reduced and of their need to find a ready scapegoat for its troubles.

During 1992 Shafarevich himself was asked to resign his position as a foreign associate of the US National Academy of Sciences mainly on account of the anti-Jewish views expressed in his tract "Russophobia". In a long-running dispute with the US organization, Shafarevich, currently head of the mathematical institute of the Russian Academy of Sciences, refused to resign, rejecting the charge of antisemitism. "This work [Russophobia]", Shafarevich wrote to the US academy, "contains criticism of a certain literary trend in which strong Jewish nationalist emotions are combined with equally strong Russian emotions, as well as criticism of radical Jewish groups which actively participated in the [Bolshevik] Revolution."

PUBLICATIONS

In August the Moscow Jewish newspaper *Yevreyskaya gazeta* listed fifty-six Russian newspapers and journals which, it said, had published antisemitic materials (including cartoons and caricatures) between August 1991 and July 1992. The data given by *Yevreyskaya gazeta* were supported by further sources. First, on 25 June Yevgeny Proshechkin, chairman of the Moscow-based Anti-Fascist Centre, stated that over thirty newspapers and six journals of a fascist and antisemitic inclination were being regularly published in Moscow; he claimed that the total monthly circulation of these publications exceeded 1 million copies. Second, in August the influential

Russian daily *Nezavisimaya gazeta* reported that overtly racist and antisemitic material was being carried by 35 "national-patriotic" newspapers in Moscow, 14 in St Petersburg, and 13 in other cities of Russia and Belarus, as well as in 7 thick journals in the Russian cities of Moscow and Krasnodar and the Belarus capital of Minsk. Third, in September the Moscow daily *Vechernyaya Moskva* noted that there were around forty antisemitic newspapers and periodicals in Russia.

Several of these anti-Jewish publications—in particular *Sovetskaya Rossiya, Literaturnaya Rossiya, Nash sovremennik* and *Molodaya gvardiya*, which express the views of Russian conservative nationalists and neo-Stalinists—were long established titles. Other publications, which were less widely known (many of them had sprung up in the period of *glasnost* and were no doubt ephemeral), contained antisemitic materials of varying degrees of virulence.

Perhaps the most influential organ of the "patriotic" press in 1992 was the relatively new weekly *Den* which, together with *Sovetskaya Rossiya*, became the house organ of the National Salvation Front. Another new paper, *Al-Qods*, published and edited by Saaban Khafiz Saaban, a Palestinian businessman and self-styled head of the "Palestine Government-In-Exile", appeared in Moscow in Russian and Arabic and carried material praising in extravagant terms "martyrs" of the 1970s-80s Soviet anti-Zionist and antisemitic propaganda campaign.

The "patriotic" press has created in the last few years a list of "martyrs" said to have been slain by the "Zionists". These "martyrs" include the anti-Zionist and antisemitic propagandist Yevgeny Yevseev, who was killed in an automobile accident in Moscow; Minsk propagandist Vladimir Begun, who died of a heart attack; Konstantin Smirnov-Ostashvili, an anti-Jewish activist who committed suicide while serving a two-year prison sentence for leading an anti-Jewish provocation; and Igor Talkov, a nationalist pop singer who was shot dead in mysterious circumstances.

The Soviet Anti-Zionist Committee, a body set up by the Communist authorities in 1983 but since the days of *glasnost* pushed firmly to the sidelines, co-operated increasingly closely during the year with the "patriotic" press, in particular *Den* and *Al Qods*. (Its chairman, Colonel David Dragunsky, died in October.)

Much anti-Jewish literature, including "classics" of antisemitica such as *The Protocols of the Elders of Zion*, was freely on sale in Russia's cities, in particular close by some of Moscow's metro stations.

Dmitry Vasilev's faction of Pamyat filed a libel suit in a Moscow court against *Yevreyskaya gazeta* for describing his newspaper as antisemitic. Vasilev claimed damages of 20 million roubles.

Newspapers

The following list of Russian newspapers and periodicals said to have published antisemitic materials between August 1991 and July 1992 appeared in *Yevreyskaya gazeta* in August 1992. The data includes, where available, the name of the editor of the publication in question, the place of publication, the print run, and a description of the publication's orientation (in many cases that given by the publication itself).

Borba (Struggle), Motto: "The socialist fatherland is in danger!", Moscow

Veche (Popular assembly in old Russia), quarterly newspaper pub. by Novgorod writers' organization , Editor V. Slepenchuk, Novgorod

Volya Rossii (Russia's Will), Russian newspaper, Yekaterinburg

Golos Rossii (Russia's Voice), issue-oriented political bulletin of National Republican Party of Russia, St Petersburg

Delo (The Cause), workers' and peasants' newspaper, Editor A. A. Rumyantsev, print run 2,040, Moscow

Den (The Day), weekly "Newspaper of spiritual opposition", Editor Alexander Prokhanov, print run 120,000, Moscow

Domostroy (Household Order), international newspaper, Editor L. Kalinina, (member of Russian Communist Party), print run 100,000, Moscow

Zemlya (The Land), Motto: "Democracy is hell, Tsardom is heaven", Editors A. Zhmurov and V. Demin, Magadan or Irkutsk

Zemshchina (Boyar Domain), all-Russian newspaper of Union of Christian Revival, Editors A. Zhmurov and V. Demin, Moscow

Istoki (Sources), independent military newspaper, Editor Vyacheslav Blaznin, print run 20,000, Moscow

Istoricheskaya pamyat (Historical Memory), Russian patriotic newspaper, St Petersburg

Kulikovskaya bitva (The Battle of Kulikov), pub. by Russian National and Patriotic Centre, Vologda

Kunak (Friend), Editor A. P. Magomedov, Makhachkala

Literaturnaya Rossiya (Literary Russia), weekly newspaper of Russian Writers' Union, Editor Ernst Safonov, Moscow

Molnya (Lightning), newspaper pub. by workers' movement, Moscow

Moskovsky traktir (Moscow Tavern), newspaper of Russian National Liberation Movement, Editor Oleg Gusev, Moscow

Na strazhye (On Guard), organ of Chief Directorate of Internal Affairs, Moscow

Nakanunye (On the Eve), Russian newspaper, Zlatoust

Narodnaya pravda (The People's Truth), Russian public and political newspaper, St Petersburg

Narodnoye delo (The People's Cause), People's Social Party, Editor Aleksey Andreyev, print run 20,000, St Petersburg

Nashe vremya (Our Times), newspaper of National Republican Party of Russia, Editor E. E. Sokolov, print run 40,000, St Petersburg

Nashe pokolenye (Our Generation), founded by Vologda Region Union of Youth Organizations, Vologda

Nashe slovo (Our Word), pub. by guard corps service of Orthodox Russia, Moscow

Otechestvo (Fatherland), opposition newspaper of Russian Patriotic Movement, Editor E. A Shchekatikhin, print run 25,000, St Petersburg

Otchizna (Fatherland), bulletin of Otechestvo Leningrad Russian Patriotic Movement, Editor Yury Belayev, St Petersburg

Pamyat (Memory), newspaper of Pamyat Patriotic Association, Editor Viktor Pakhomov, Novosibirsk

Polozhenye del (The State of Affairs), irregular publication by Trustee Fund of Kazan Holy Mother Patriot Centre, Editor N. V. Filimonov, print run 100,000

Pravda (The Truth), daily former central organ of Soviet Communist Party,

Editor Gennady Seleznev, print run 1,010,000, Moscow

Puls Tushina (Tushin Pulse), newspaper pub. by Pulse Centre, Tushin district of Moscow, Editor V. T. Fomichev, print run 5,000, Moscow

ROD. Russkoye osvoboditelnoye dvizhenye (RLM—Russian Liberation Movement), pub. by St Peterburg Men's Club, St Petersburg

Rodnye prostory (Native Lands), historical and cultural newspaper of the Wise Men [*sic*], Editor Aleksey Boikov, print run 5,000, St Petersburg

Russkiye vedomosti (Russian Gazette), motto: "Russia for Russians only", Editor V. N. Korchagin, print run 8,000, Moscow

Russky vestnik (Russian Herald), weekly newspaper, Editor A. A. Senin, print run 100,000, Moscow

Russkaya gazeta (Russian Newspaper), Editor [Valery?] Skurlatov, Moscow

Russky zov (Russian Call) , Russian Orthodox patriotic newspaper, Nizhny Tagil

Russky puls (Russian Pulse), Editors V. V. Stepanov and V. T. Fomichev, print run 7,000, Moscow

Russky styag (Russian Banner), ultranationalist publication, Editor A. Barkashov, Moscow

Russkoe voskresenye (Russian Revival), pub. by Russian National Liberation Movement, Editor Aleksey Batogov, print run 40,000, Moscow

Russkoye delo (The Russian Cause), pub. by National Democratic Party, motto: "No retreat—Russia stands firmly behind us", Editor Oleg Gusev, print run 20,000, St Petersburg

Russkoye znamya (Russian Banner), first published in 1991, Arzamas 16, Nizhny Novgorod region

Sergiev Posad (Sergiev Settlement), Russian Orthodox patriotic bulletin pub. by Brotherhood of the Revered Sergey Radonezhsky, print run 10,000, Sergiev Posad

Situatsiya (The Situation), weekly founded by Ministry of Internal Affairs, Editor V. I. Filatov, print run 100,000, Moscow

Sovyetskaya Rossiya (Soviet Russia), independent national daily, Editor V. Chikin, print run 910,000, Moscow

Tyumen Literaturnaya (Literary

Tyumen), pub. by Russian writers and Russian emigrants, first pub. 1989, Tyumen

Chto delat (What Is To Be Done?), opposition newspaper pub. by Working Russia movement, Moscow

Ekho (Echo), pub. by Vologda writers' organization, Vologda

Journals

Voenno-istorichesky zhurnal (Journal of Military History), monthly pub. by Ministry of Defence, Editor V. S. Yeshchenko, print run 9,290, Moscow

Kuban, founded 1945, since January 1991, published by Russian Writers' Union, Krasnodar

Molodaya gvardiya (Young Guard), conservative nationalist and neo-Stalinist monthly, Editor Anatoly Ivanov, print run 32,000, Moscow

Nash sovremennik (Our Contemporary), conservative nationalist and neo-Stalinist monthly, published by Russian Writers' Union, Editor Stanislav Kunyaev, print run 164,782, Moscow

Politichesky sobesednik (Political Interlocutor), monthly political illustrated journal published by editorial collective, Editor N. D. Astanevich, Minsk

Probuzhdeniye (Awakening), N/D, Moscow

Russky vestnik (Russian Herald), weekly newspaper of religious orientation, Strunino, Vladimir region

Radonezh, N/D, Moscow

Sever (The North), N/D,

RELIGION

Exclusively belonging to this category was an article which appeared in the neo-Stalinist newspaper Sovetskaya Rossiya on 10 October. In the article Metropolitan Johann of St Petersburg wrote that after the destruction of the kingdoms of Israel and Judea the Jews "misinterpreted" their holy books by linking the restoration of Israel to the coming of the Messiah. "The fact that Jesus Christ revealed the mistakes of their 'prophets' and destroyed the myth that they were the 'chosen people' caused them to hate him bitterly", he wrote. In regard to modern times, the cleric, the spiritual leader of Russia's second largest city, saw a connection between Communism, which he described as a "united international political structure", and the Jews' "centu-

ries-old dream of world supremacy". Metropolitan Johann wrote that chief among the tools of those working "to destroy Christian feeling and nation states" have been "heretic sects, philosophers' groups and masonic lodges".

A spokesman for the Russian Orthodox Church stated that the article was the personal opinion of Metropolitan Johann alone and did not reflect the views of the Russian Orthodox Church.

There was a religious element in a two-day conference held at the Central House of Actors in Moscow in October by the National Patriotic Front faction of Pamyat led by Dmitry Vasilev. A priest denounced the Patriarch of the Orthodox Church, Aleksei II, as "a devoted Leninist and friend of New York freemasons". The meeting, at which a group calling itself Christian Revival was also present, was attended by about 1,000 people.

COUNTERING ANTISEMITISM

Racist and antisemitic groups and organizations were repeatedly condemned in the mainstream news media.

On 29 June about 7,000 people took part in an "anti-fascist" rally in front of the Ostankino television centre in Moscow (see above).

On 16 September a hearing on antisemitism took place in the Moscow City Council building. The meeting was organized by the Council's Subcommittee on Human Rights, chaired by Valery Fadeev.

On 23 November, after several postponements, the Committee on Human Rights of the Russian Supreme Soviet held a hearing on the problem of antisemitism in the country. Among those testifying to the Committee, which was chaired by the former human rights dissident Sergei Kovalev, were Mikhail Chlenov, co-chairman of the Vaad (the main umbrella group of Jewish organizations in the former Soviet Union), the Moscow lawyer Genrik Reznik, and Valery Fadeev, chairman of the Human Rights Committee of the Moscow City Council. Testimony focused on possible amendments to Article 74 of the Russian Criminal Code, which prohibits incitement of ethnic and racial tension. The meeting was poorly attended. It was agreed that a further hearing would be held.

A curious development was the publication in the neo-Stalinist newspaper *Sovetskaya Rossiya* in August of a "letter" by a certain Avram Sholem. Sholem, described as a member of the Soviet Communist Party since 1989 and a member of the (neo-Stalinist) Working Russia movement, called on Jews and Russians to "stop the camapign of mutual antagonism". The publication of the letter was possibly a none too hopeful attempt by some conservative circles to provide a solid front on the part of the opposition to the Yeltsin government. However, there seemed little prospect that Shalom's—or *Sovetskaya Rossiya's*—extraordinary plea for "reconciliation" between Jews and Russians could lead anywhere.

LEGAL MATTERS

On 29 June the Moscow District Court upheld a charge of libel brought by Herman Branover against the literary monthly publication *Nash sovremmenik*. The Moscow periodical had two years previously published an article quoting Branover as stating, in his autobiography *The Return*, that one of the earliest accomplishments of Trotsky and other early Communists was the destruction of many representatives of "our most bitter enemy, Orthodox Christianity". Branover was also said to have written that this had "won the early Communists a place as heroes in Jewish history". The court found the periodical guilty of libel, but rejected the claim of 150,000 roubles in damages. The court also called for a public apology to Branover.

On 26 July Alexei Batogov, publisher and editor of the chauvinistic and antisemitic paper *Russkoye voskresenye*, was arrested under Article 74 of the Russian Criminal Code, which forbids incitement to racial or ethnic violence. The specific cause of Batogov's arrest was the publication in his paper of an article entitled "The murder of Chrsitian babies by Jews". In mid-September Batogov was released on bail.

On 1 August the independent daily newspaper *Nezavisimaya gazeta* reported that the Russian procuracy was investigating a total of sixteen cases of alleged violation of Article 74: besides that of Batogov, investigations were being conducted into the papers *Puls Tushina* and *Energiya*. On 16 August a spokesman for the Russian procuracy announced that criminal charges had already been brought against the publishers of two further antisemitic papers, *Russky klich* and *Russkiye vedomosti*.

On 27 October the Russian Federation Supreme Soviet Committee for the Mass Media found that an incident in which Pamyat representatives had forced their way into the offices of the newspaper *Moskovsky komsomolets* (see above) was a gross violation of the Russian Constitution, the law on the mass media and other legislation and proposed that the ministries of justice and of internal affairs, as well as the Russian procurator general, consider the legality of Pamyat operations by a fixed date and report the results to parliament.

There was much criticism in legal and political circles of the abovementioned Article 74 of the Russian Criminal Code, the Soviet-era law which still governed prohibition against incitement to ethnic and racial strife. In particular, according to Valery Fadeev, chairman of Moscow City Council's Human Rights Committee, the law was "written too narrowly, and it requires proof of intent, which is difficult to do". Fadeev's Committee submitted to parliament a draft law which would improve the chances for successful prosecution. The proposed legislation, backed by the Russian interior ministry, the procurator-general and the ministry of press and mass media, would prohibit "hurting an ethnic group's sense of dignity". It was hoped that the bill would be considered by the parliament the following spring. Fadeev's committee also proposed legislation which would expressly forbid distribution of unregistered periodicals, thus preventing vendors of antisemitic papers from claiming they were peddling their papers for profit alone.

Other impediments to the successful prosecution of hate-mongering publications were the fact that some prosecutors did not think the problem was sufficiently important and that some police officers were indifferent to the issue. There were also bureaucratic impediments, for example the press ministry said it had no budget for tracking down hate sheet printers, while the interior ministry had a budget, but claimed jurisdiction was with the former KGB.

Ukraine

General population: 52,000,000
Jewish population: 300,000-400,000
(mainly in Kiev, Kharkov and Odessa)

PARTIES, ORGANIZATIONS, MOVEMENTS

Some ultra-chauvinist groups such as the Ukrainian National Assembly, which was particularly active in Lvov, were distinctly xenophobic towards Ukraine's national minorities, principally the Russians but not excluding the Jews.

During the year a number of extremist organizations surfaced, carrying out antisemitic acts and threatening further provocations. In one instance, on 24 October, they set fire to, among other papers, *Khadashot*, a Jewish newspaper published in Kiev. The organizations included Bratstvo Skhidny Khrest (Brotherhood of the Eastern Cross), Legion Novogo Poryadka (Legion of the New Order), and Skhidna Ukrainska Molod (Conscious Ukrainian Youth). In the town of Poltava Jewish leaders complained of the activities of the Hitlerite National Socialist Party and the Petlyura Nationalists, both of which openly distributed pogromist literature.

In August the liberal newspaper *Nezavisimost* (Independence) carried an article by Aleksandr Shlaen, Chairman of the Baby Yar Centre. In the article Shlaen referred to the rise of Ukrainian Self-Defence para-military groups with branches in the Chernigov region, Gorlovka and elsewhere. The groups wore black, Pamyat-style uniforms and in Kharkov hoisted a swastika. The Kharkov branch was said to number 100 members.

MANIFESTATIONS

There were no reports of assaults on Jews. The principal acts of violence occurred during the independence referendum in December 1991 when a grenade was thrown at the Kiev synagogue although it failed to explode. Subsequently, there were attempts to set fire to the flat of the Chief Rabbi, Yaakov Bleich, and to the home of the Jewish writer Abraham Katznelson. The Baby Yar Memorial, the Kiev City Jewish Library and the Israel Cultural Centre were three of more than a score of Jewish memorials and buildings that were daubed with swastikas and antisemitic slogans. These crimes were invariably attributed to "hooligan elements".

The trial in Israel of Ivan Demyanuk for alleged war crimes reportedly continued to provoke some anti-Jewish rallies and pro-Demyanuk groups were set up in Lvov, Kharkov, Kiev and elsewhere.

PUBLICATIONS

While neither television nor mainstream press, both liable to censorship by the authorities, carried material which could be described as antisemitic, the same cannot be said for the press as a whole. Russian extremist papers such as *Russky vestnik*, *Zemshchina*, *Puls Tushina* and *Den* were on sale in Kiev outside factory gates and protests by both Jews and liberal elements in Rukh were made against such Ukrainian newspapers as *Natsionalist*, *Nova Ukraina* (New Ukraine), *Nezalezhna natsiya* (Free Nation) *Slovo* (The Word) and *Panorama* for carrying pogromist articles. The year saw a significant increase in the number and virulence of such publications, which also reprinted sections of *The Protocols of the Elders of Zion* and Holocaust-denial material and castigated Jews and other "foreign elements" as a danger to the "purity" of Ukraine.

OPINION POLLS

In October a poll conducted among Jews from seventy-two Ukrainian cities by the sociologist Leonid Finberg indicated that popular antisemitism had not noticeably diminished since independence. Respondents attributed this fact partly to historical reasons and partly to the long anti-Zionist and antisemitic propaganda under the Soviet regime.

COUNTERING ANTISEMITISM

In spring 1992 a section for the monitoring of antisemitism was set up in Rukh's Council of Nationalities by the Council's

Chairman, Alexander Burakovsky.

In June four Kiev city councillors called for action against *Slovo* (see above) for inciting intra-national discord.

Muslim Republics

Azerbaydzhan

General population: 7,137,000
Jewish population: 15,000-20,000

Kazakhstan

General population: 16,899,000
Jewish population: 20,000

Kyrgyzstan

General population: 4,400,000
Jewish population: 4,000-5,000

Tadzhikistan

General population: 5,358,000
Jewish population: 2,000-3,000

Turkmenistan

General population: 3,748,000
Jewish population: 1,200

Uzbekistan

General population: 20,000,000
Jewish population: 55,000

MUSLIM REPUBLICS: ISLAMIC FUNDAMENTALISM AND ANTI-RUSSIAN SENTIMENT

There was no Russian-style antisemitism in the Muslim republics. However, anti-Russian sentiment was directed against a part of the Jewish minority whom the indigenous population identified with the Russians. The resurgence of Islam and its growing role in public life were tied up with the national consciousness of the Muslim nations of the Caucasus and Central Asia as well as hopes for closer ties with, and assistance from, the Islamic states. The injection of Muslim fundamentalism was one aspect of these developments. A further element in the situation was ethnic and tribal strife.

In the Muslim republics the situation of the Jews was also bound up with the struggle between the supporters of a modern and more secular orientation and the partisans of an Islamic state. This question in turn was linked to the struggle for influence being waged between Turkey, which was regarded as a model modern Muslim nation, and Iran, which was regarded as a model Islamic state.

MANIFESTATIONS

Accurate information on anti-Jewish sentiment in the Muslim republics was difficult to come by. The following incidents were reported during 1992.

In April in Bishkek (Kyrgyzstan) a Jewish family was arrested and charged with murdering a three-year-old girl and making *matza* from her blood. The family was released on the same day; on the following day it received an apology from the police.

In Kazakhstan the editorial board of the newspaper *Birlesu* was ordered to appear in court on 27 August. The paper was charged with, among other things, insulting Jews. The editor claimed that the paper had been quoted out of context.

It was reported in November that a Tadzhik-language newspaper had published an article blaming the Jews, Israelis and "world Zionists" for "Russia's misfortunes during the Revolution and *perestroyka*".

FORMER SOVIET UNION: ASSESSMENT

The position of the Jewish minority in the former Soviet republics, as elsewhere in the former USSR and post-Communist Central and Eastern Europe, remained ambiguous. On the one hand, the Jewish population continued to enjoy a cultural and religious renaissance, unrestricted emigration, and the active support of the authorities, both nationally and locally. These gains were indisputable.

On the other hand, the economic and political situation in the countries of the former Soviet Union—specifically the three Slavic republics, which contained the highest proportion of the Jewish population—remained generally unstable. In Russia the position of President Yeltsin and his democratic supporters seemed to have weakened and the conservative opposition to have grown in confidence. Large sections of the population seemed either resentful of the government's reforms or at best apathetic.

Despite the existence of numerous grassroots chauvinistic and anti-Jewish groups and publications in Russia and the worrying new development of an antisemitic fringe movement in Ukraine, there was no indication that anti-Jewish sentiment was endemic among the rank-and-file of any of the populations of the former Soviet Union; besides, there was no shortage of ethnic scapegoats. While antisemitism did not presently appear attractive to the masses, the continuing economic, political and social dislocation accompanied by strong nationalist sentiments throughout the area of the former Soviet Union remained serious cause for alarm.

Former Yugoslavia

GENERAL BACKGROUND

Yugoslavia's disintegration into ethnic warfare, a process begun in 1991, continued into 1992. The barbarity of the ethnic warfare, in particular the practice of "ethnic cleansing", struck a chord of horror around the world, not least among Jewry. The Federation of Jewish Communities of Yugoslavia was succeeded by Jewish representative bodies of the new states which emerged. In the context of the violent disintegration of Yugoslavia, the governments of the new states intensified their campaigns to win friends on the international scene, including among world Jewry.

HISTORICAL LEGACY

There is no significant tradition of antisemitism in the former Yugoslavia.

In the 1930s and during the Second World War antisemitism (especially of the racial variety) remained a Nazi "import" which never became deeply rooted in the country.

Over 80 per cent of Yugoslav Jewry died in the Holocaust.

Published at the end of the 1980s, the book *Wanderings of Historical Truth* by Croatian President Franjo Tudjman has been subject to considerable criticism for its portrayal of aspects of the Holocaust (see below).

Croatia

General population: 4,700,000
Jewish population: 3,000 (most in Zagreb)

PARTIES, ORGANIZATIONS, MOVEMENTS

A disturbing development was the continued emergence of parties which glorified the wartime Ustashe movement. In the presidential and parliamentary elections which took place in August, fourth place went to the candidate of the Croatian Party of [Historic] Rights, Dobroslav Paraga, who won 5 per cent. The party, a neo-fascist group with a paramilitary arm, was arguably the most openly anti-democratic party represented in the elections. In December a second neo-Nazi party, the Croatian Pure Party of Rights (leader: Ivan Gabelica), was formed. No party openly condoned antisemitism.

"THE WANDERINGS OF HISTORICAL TRUTH"

The reputation of Franjo Tudjman, the President of Croatia, continued to suffer from the repercussions of his book "The Wanderings of Historical Truth". In the book, published in 1989, Dr Tudjman claimed, among other things, that Jews had taken part in the liquidation of gypsies at Jasenovac concentration camp and had taken the initative in preparing and provoking not only individual atrocities but also the mass murder of non-Jews, Communists, and Serbs. Dr Tudjman's book also minimized the number of Jewish (and Serbian) victims.

ASSESSMENT

The Jewish minority remained concerned, but not afraid, that mounting Croatian nationalism might prompt a resurgence of antisemitism similar to that which had recently emerged elsewhere in Central and Eastern Europe.

Slovenia

General population: 2,000,000
Jewish population: approx. 60

PUBLICATIONS

Between August 1988 and March 1989 *Tribuna*, a Ljubljana University weekly magazine financed by the Slovenian government, published the first Slovenian translation of *The Protocols of the Elders of Zion*. In November 1992 *Tribuna* reportedly began publication of Hitler's *Mein Kampf*.

Yugoslav Republic (Serbia and Montenegro)

General population: 10,500,000
Jewish population: 2,500-3,000 (mainly in Belgrade)

ATTEMPTED REHABILITATION OF WORLD WAR II FASCISTS

There was a continuation of attempts to rehabilitate fascists active in the Second World War period. In 1992 there were unofficial attempts to rehabilitate Dmitrije Ljotic, who was a theoretician of antisemitism and whose troops aided the Nazis in the extermination of Serbian Jewry, and Milan Nedic, a co-organizer of the murder of Serbian Jews in 1941-2. The Serbian Orthodox Church continued to publish antisemitic books written by Bishop Nikolaj Velimirovic, who was a prominent theologian, anti-Communist and antisemite. In all three cases, no mention was made of the anti-Jewish sentiments of the individual concerned.

PUBLICATIONS

Dragos Kalajic, who has acquired the reputation of a fascist and an antisemite, regularly published articles in the yellow press, especially the weekly *Duga*, on the subject of the so-called Jewish-masonic conspiracy.

Pravoslavlje, the bi-weekly organ of the Serbian Orthodox Church, included in its February issue an article entitled "The Jews are crucifying Christ again". Following intervention by the Jewish community, the magazine's editor-in-chief was dismissed.

On 22 June the yellow press weekly magazine *Horoskop*, which is published in Belgrade, carried an article entitled "All Jews are spies".

On 20 September *Dnevnik*, a daily published in Novi Sad by the ruling Socialist Party, contained the charge that a Jewish-masonic conspiracy was responsible for the disintegration of Yugoslavia.

ASSESSMENT

Antisemitism was not a serious problem in the Yugoslav Republic.

Middle East & North Africa

Introduction

Antisemitism has its origins in Europe and derives from a historical and cultural tradition which is distinct from that of the Muslim Arabs. However, there is no doubt that European antisemitism merged with indigenous Arab and Muslim anti-Judaism to produce a powerful and widespread form of vilification of Jews.

Jews living in Arab lands under Muslim rule had special status as *dhimmis*—protected minorities who were allowed their own communal organizations but who nonetheless lived under certain restrictions. They were not free from various forms of oppression but, before the modern era, they fared better than under Christianity.

In the 1920s, following the development of Zionism and the rise of secular Arab nationalism and Islamic fundamentalism, expressions of anti-Jewish sentiment took on a more virulent tone and became more influential. Although some Arabs claimed they distinguished between Zionists and Jews, this distinction was, and still is, barely tenable for the Arab masses.

Antisemitic propaganda broadcast from Berlin during the Second World War had a considerable impact in Tunisia, Morocco, Egypt and Iraq. Since the 1950s, blood libel myths (which were also spread by local Christians) and ideas of Jewish conspiracies to control the world have been spread widely throughout the Arab press, radio and school textbooks, and figured prominently in cartoons and caricatures. This material had become ubiquitous by the 1960s. *The Protocols of the Elders of Zion* is certainly to be found throughout the area and it is believed that its largest market is in the Middle East.

The use of Christian and Western antisemitic images is not arbitrary in the Muslim world. Negative images of Jews as evil, treacherous and conspiratorial have their own roots in Islamic thought, and have been given new force by the revival of radical Islam. Such images are found throughout the Arab world and Middle East, but also on the periphery—from the Maghreb and Sudan to Iran, Pakistan and Malaysia.

The continued existence of the state of Israel, which is perceived as a humiliation for Muslims and Arabs, is explained away by the attribution of demonic powers to Jews and Israel. Repeated defeats in war are attributed to Jewish control of governments, the media, the banks and so on. Persistent trauma and humiliation, as perceived by Muslims, have led to an ideological vacuum which Islamic fundamentalism has filled. Muslims have revived the blood libel and the denunciation of the Talmud (which, it is claimed, permits Jews to lie, cheat and steal from non-Jews) and mixed these with the image of a ruthless, oppressive Israel, making a dehumanized stereotype of the Jewish and Zionist enemy. No real differentiation is made between the Jews, Judaism and Israel—they are all part of a global conspiracy to create an alien body on Arab Muslim soil. For the fundamentalists, there can be no compromise—Israel will always be an alien entity in the heart of Muslim land.

Anti-Jewish stereotypes are not only used to explain the disappearance of the traditional hierarchy in the Arab Muslim world where Jews always lived as a tolerated yet dominated minority. In Algeria and Egypt, and in many other Arab countries, the Jews are also being used as scapegoats for the worsening economic situation. In addition, they are often seen as responsible for modernization and blamed for the corruption of morals.

At Islamic conferences and international Arab meetings, the anti-Jewish and anti-Zionist message is assiduously disseminated. The material produced in the Middle East is very often government sponsored, but the extent to which this is so differs from country to country. In Syria for example, editors of publications must be members of the Ba'ath Party. In Egypt and Saudi Arabia, control is less tight, but publications reflect government thinking. Antisemitic material can often be described as propaganda, but in some countries, Egypt especially, it can be seen as the free expression of certain attitudes.

Antisemitism in the Middle East and the Muslim world is primarily used in the ideological and political struggle against Israel—its expression is mostly linked to this purpose. The quantity of antisemitic literature and broadcasts is vast, and the status of those who are responsible for producing and sponsoring it is high. But it nevertheless appears to be ideological and political, literary and intellectual, rather than a true expression of popular attitudes. It may still be possible to say that antisemitism comes from above rather than below, although the irreversible poisoning of Arab society and culture may not be far off.

The anti-Jewish themes used by Arab establishments are also used by groups which challenge those establishments. The Islamic fundamentalist groups operating in the West Bank and Gaza, principally Hamas, account for the success of Zionism by referring to Jewish money power, secret societies and the ability of Jews to create havoc throughout the world and turn that to their interests. They regard the immigration of Soviet Jews as another example of Palestinian Arabs having to pay for the consequences of European antisemitism, which in turn appears to legitimize the use of antisemitic themes in Islamic fundamentalist propaganda. A leaflet issued in July 1992 referred to "the Zionist culprits who poisoned the water in the past, killed infants, women and elders". Although the official Palestinian movement makes a clear distinction between Jews and Zionists, this is not always appreciated at the grassroots level. For example, in January 1992, a leaflet issued by Fatah, the main constituent of the Palestine Liberation Organization, discovered near Khan Younis in the Gaza strip, responded to Hamas criticism of its role in the peace process: "The Fatah has entered the peace process with full awareness of the enemy's schemes. The Fatah realizes it is negotiating with Jews, and knows the Jews to be what they are: 'descendants of monkeys and pigs'."

Although more removed from the conflict with Israel, the Sheikhdoms of the Gulf are significant sources of antisemitic material. The press in Kuwait and the United Arab Emirates (UAE) carry the same accusations against Jews for causing the misfortunes of the Arabs and Islam.

Although Arab and Muslim antisemitism must be seen in the context of the Arab-Israeli conflict, this does not mean that peace will bring an end to antisemitic stereotypes and propaganda. Antisemitism did not disappear from Egypt after the signing of the Israel-Egypt peace treaty. The presence of the Jewish state will continue to be seen as an insult both to Arab nationalism and to Islam—an insult which must be explained.

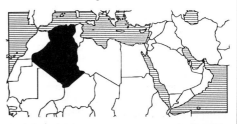

Algeria

General population: 25,798,000
Jewish population: 100

GENERAL BACKGROUND

The country continued to experience a severe economic, political and social crisis.

In December 1991, the Islamic fundamentalist Front Islamique du Salut (FIS, Islamic Salvation Front) won a majority in the first round of Algeria's first multi-party general election since achieving independence in 1962. In January 1992, the second round of the elections was cancelled in order to prevent a probable FIS victory. There followed months of sporadic violence which the government attempted to counter with stringent security measures.

In February, the High Committee of State (HCS), which had assumed presidential powers in January, decreed a state of emergency effective for twelve months. Suspected FIS activists and other militants were rounded up. In March, the FIS was officially dissolved, leading to further protests. All municipal councils were suspended and replaced by "executive delegations" in order to undermine the local political influence of the FIS, which had won control of over half the municipalities in the 1990 local elections.

In April, the HCS established a non-party political, sixty-member National Consultative Council with no legislative powers to replace the suspended National Assembly. In June, Mohammed Boudiaf, president of the HCS, was assassinated.

The HCS sought to curb press criticism: three independent newspapers were ordered to suspend publication in August and six more were banned in September, although restrictions on five of them were lifted in October.

Amid worsening violence linked to Islamic fundamentalist groups, in October the government issued a decree against "subversion and terrorism", which created secret courts, lowered the age of criminal responsibility from eighteen to sixteen and introduced sanctions, including longer prison terms and execution, without the right of appeal. The decree also included an amnesty for those who gave themselves up within a two-month period, but only 100 were said to have applied by the end of November. Prime Minister Abdessalam Belaid then declared "total war" on extremists.

By the middle of the year, about 7,000 people had been interned and, despite a number of releases, 4,000 were still considered to be in detention in November. Also in November, it was reported that 160 members of the security forces had been killed since February. The government consistently blamed all violence on the FIS, which had pledged to fight until an election was held but denied involvement in the assassination of Boudiaf and the bombing of Algiers airport in August.

HISTORICAL LEGACY

During the nineteenth century, traditional Christian antisemitism was introduced into parts of the Muslim world, including Algeria, by European clerics and missionaries. At the same time, the Jews received favoured treatment from the French colonists and, despite Muslim resentment, soon seized the new economic opportunities.

Following the 1894 "Dreyfus affair", leading French antisemite Edouard Drumont was elected as the representative for Algiers. Although the antisemitic movement of the time was short-lived in Algeria, Nazi propaganda in the 1940s brought about its resurgence. Under the Vichy regime, the Jews were treated with contempt by their French masters, who applied the Vichy laws in all their severity.

After Algeria gained independence from France in 1962, most of the country's 140,000 Jews emigrated. The Algerian Jews, almost universally gallicized, were viewed by Muslims not only as Zionists, and therefore as enemies of Arab national aspirations, but also as Europeans. The Jews were resented for their economic successes and the privileges they enjoyed under French rule. In 1960, during anti-French riots, the Great Synagogue of Algiers was destroyed. Jewish areas were attacked repeatedly and synagogues and cemeteries were desecrated. Large-scale emigration followed.

The 1967 Six Day war provided an occasion for further looting, attacks and desecrations.

PRESENT SITUATION

In the current disorder which afflicts Algeria, antisemitism exists at all levels of society, as reported in last year's *Antisemitism World Report*. The FIS leadership has developed antisemitic themes as a matter of policy and many newspapers have willingly echoed them. With only a tiny Jewish population (fewer than a hundred elderly people and a few businessmen), Algeria is an example of "antisemitism without Jews".

Recently, for example, much of the press accused Jewish journalists in France of being responsible for Algeria's poor image on the international stage. On 2 March 1993, the daily newspaper *al-Watan* published an article by Mokhtar Aniba, a former Algerian minister plenipotentiary, who asserted that "The Jews are able to worship God and gold at the same time; they are born super-materialists. . . . The Jewish character lies in the spilling of blood, in adultery, in the most inhuman usury, in gambling, in the most shocking speculation and in racial segregation. . . . Judaism is, fundamentally, a polytheistic religion."

ASSESSMENT

World Jewry, and French Jews in particular, are being used as scapegoats in a society which is facing severe economic and political problems. A *Protocols*-like vision of the world, coupled with more recent Holocaust "revisionist" theses, is being promoted as a way of explaining the country's misfortunes. This antisemitic campaign seems unlikely to cease in the near future.

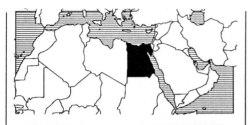

Egypt

General population: 53,087,000
Jewish population: 200 (mainly in Cairo)

GENERAL BACKGROUND

The major issues on the Egyptian agenda were the ongoing problems of confrontation with the Islamic fundamentalist movement, the budget deficit and related severe economic problems, and the Arab-Israeli peace negotiations.

The main resistance to the regime has come from the Islamic fundamentalist movement, which promises Egypt leadership of the entire Muslim world, with glory to be won in a sweeping surge rather than as the result of painstaking toiling over legalistic minutiae. In this alternative outlook, the West is a detested "other" rather than an ally, Jews are abominated and the Jewish state is an implacable enemy.

The Islamic fundamentalists have made capital of Egypt's economic predicament and, although the hardships suffered by the population cannot be seen as the only reason for the surge in support for Islamic fundamentalism, they have doubtless contributed to it. While President Hosni Mubarak was working to strike a balance between the pressures from overseas financial institutions to reform the economy and the need to safeguard minimum subsistence levels for his citizens, the Islamic fundamentalists were delivering immediate and direct economic help through the provision of health-care, education, banking facilities and clothing.

They were also able to play on the Israel-Arab relationship. Although the majority of Egyptians do not want war with Israel, they certainly do not recognize or accept what Israel and Zionism stand for. The Islamic fundamentalists' attitude towards Israel, which does not call for immediate war but rather favours an ardent, far-reaching and "sacred" antagonism, is more palatable than Mubarak's straightforward peaceful dealings with Israel.

The Islamic fundamentalist movement has been growing in recent years and 1992 witnessed an intensification in both its semi-institutional and its subversive branches—apparently with substantial financial and organizational support from Iran, Sudan and Pakistan. More importantly, the dialectics of this process in its interaction with the regime has led to an affirmation of militant Islam—its shifting from a marginal to a more central position—and, as a result, to a bolstering of the legitimacy of the movement and its message.

The radicals, represented mainly by al-Jama'a al-Islamiyya (Islamic society), a branch of the 1980s Jihad movement led by the New Jersey-based Sheikh Umar Abd al-Rahman, embarked on a course of assassinations of liberals such as the writer Faraj Foda and of European tourists, who were accused of turning Egypt into a place of illicit pleasures for foreigners. However, unlike the radical factions in the 1970s, who declared the whole of society "infidel" and proposed total disassociation from it, the Jama'a remained in and of society, centred on religious leaders in local mosques and involving the neighbourhood through preaching and welfare services—or, as opponents maintain, through forceful "persuasion".

The Islamic fundamentalist movement's main affirmation came from the pragmatists, the new regrouping of the Muslim Brotherhood. Its role as the principal provider of the extensive network of welfare services at a local level gained it the affection and the ear of wide sections of the population. More importantly, it continued its political activity within the limits set, although not formally adhered to, by the establishment. While not allowed to organize as a party—a right it still demands—the Brotherhood has been active in parliament and in professional associations. It has gained a foothold, even an ascendancy, in the most significant strata of Egyptian society—the syndicates of engineers, physicians and professors, and recently, and more importantly, the traditionally liberal Bar Association.

Thus the regime has had to compete with the Islamic fundamentalists to be seen as the upholders of "true" Islam, and has been forced to do so according to the fundamentalists' agenda, using their terminology and symbolism. The result has been an intensification of Islamic idiom and style in daily life and political dialogue, an affirmation of Islamic activism and an increase in Islamic power in defining criteria for public conduct.

HISTORICAL LEGACY

Following the establishment of Ottoman rule over Egypt in 1517, the position of the Jews deteriorated. But throughout the nineteenth and early twentieth centuries, with the advent of Western influence, their position improved and the foundations of the pre-1948 community with its economic and industrial pre-eminence were firmly established.

At the time of the Israeli-Arab war of 1948-9 the Jewish population of Egypt was 65-70,000 Jews. The economic situation of the Jews was good and there were many affluent members of the community. However, during the war hundreds of Jews were arrested; property and businesses belonging to Jews were confiscated; there were bombings in Jewish areas which killed or maimed hundreds of Jews. Between 1948 and 1950 about 25,000 Jews left Egypt, many of them for Israel.

In 1952 attacks were made on Jewish establishments causing millions of pounds of damage. After the 1956 war 3,000 Jews were interned and thousands of others were given a few days to leave the country while their property was confiscated by the state. By 1957 there were only 8,000 Jews left. After the 1967 war hundreds of Jews were arrested and tortured; Jews still in public employment were dismissed. Further emigration ensued so that by the mid-1970s, only 350 Jews remained.

PRESENT SITUATION

The involvement of the Islamic fundamentalists in public debates has brought antisemitism to the fore in Egypt. Their antagonism towards Israel is a fundamental

principle and, as is often the case in arguing against the Jewish state, anti-Jewish expressions are a convenient vehicle. The new element here, though, is increased reference to scriptural texts to support their arguments. Although Islam is in no way categorically anti-Jewish—it does provide for co-existence with *Ahl al-Zimmah* (monotheistic people who merit protection) in its global outlook—it harbours contempt, even condemnation, for Jews, and one can easily find holy verses and traditions capable of supporting a negative attitude. Such evidence was mobilized by fundamentalists to lend divine authority to imported European antisemitic material. Jews are not merely enemies but "enemies of Allah" and, if the Qur'an does not implicate them in the murder of Christ, then it does so as far as the "killing of the prophets" is concerned.

A conspicuous illustration of such Islamicization is the European-originated myth of a Jewish world conspiracy. The allegation has been avidly adopted in the Arab world and is already deeply ingrained in public writings, but with the ascent of Islam, it has been Islamicized as well. Thus a book by Ahmad Shalabi entitled *al-Yahud fi al-Zalam* (The Jews in the Darkness), which was published in Cairo in 1992, deals with this conspiracy theory, referring to *The Protocols of the Elders of Zion*. The publisher concludes, however, with what seems to him a relevant verse from the Qur'an: "Thou will find the most vehement of mankind in hostility to those who believe the Jews and the idolaters" (7: 82). Another book published in Cairo in 1992 that similarly Islamicizes *The Protocols* is *al-Nufuz al-Yahudi fi al-Aihiza al-I'lamiyyah wai-Mu'assasat al-Dawliyyah* (The Jewish Impact on the Media and International Organizations) by Fu'ad Bin Sayyid Abd al-Rahman al-Rifa'i. It is prefaced by another passage from the Qur'an: "O ye who believe! Take not the Jews and the Christians for friends. They are friends one to another. He among you who taketh them for friends is [one] of them. Lo! Allah guideth not wrongdoing folk." (7: 52). The copyright is "granted to any Muslim. God will reward him who will publish it or assist in distributing it, and shed his mercy on him, his parents and all Muslims."

Additional support comes from the academic world. A master's thesis completed in 1990 by a student in the Department of Religion at Cairo University, "*The Protocols of the Elders of Zion* and Their Threat for the Islamic Call", was reprinted by the department and used as a teaching aid (reported in *al-Liaw' al-Islami*, 29 March 1990). A professor in the Department of Muslim Philosophy at Cairo University, Muhammad Abdallah al-Sharqawi, published in 1990 *al-Kanz al-Marsud fi Fada'ih al-Talmud* (A Treasury of Talmud Infamies). A new book by Tahiyya Adb al-Aziz Isma'il, *Shar'aliah wal-Ishtirakiyyah* (The Divine Law and Socialism), reported in the establishment *al-Ahram* (14 November 1992), describes socialism as a destructive Jewish idea and relies heavily on "evidence" from *The Protocols* and the Talmud concerning "Jewish striving to control the world". A book by Khalid Muhammad Na'im, Professor of Modern History at Al-Minya University, *al-Juzur al-Ta'rikhiyyah li'irsaliyat al-Tansir al-Ainabiyyah fi Misr* (The Historical Roots of Foreign Missionary Activity in Egypt), reported in the establishment *al-Jumhuriyyah* (18 November 1992), dedicates a chapter to "the link between Zionism and missionary activity assisting it in order to undermine Islam".

Such a proliferation points to increased interest in, and acceptance of, antisemitism. Even the moderate leftist magazine *Rose al-Youssef*, in an article about the Rothschild family, having reluctantly admitted that Jews may be right in their claim that the conspiracy theory is libel, asks: "What are we to say—as Henry Ford [asked] at the turn of the twentieth century—about this intriguing congruency between what was written in *The Protocols* and what actually happened all through history . . ." (14 December 1992). And the author of a series of articles in the most liberal of all Egyptian government mouthpieces, *al-Wafd*, writes in a similar vein under the title "The intelligent citizen's guide to knowing the Jews and their affairs" (7-11 April 1992). The establishment *al-Akhbar* carried an interview (1 May 1992) with a "textile merchant in al-Hamzawi market" who is considered to be "one of the greatest experts on Israel and Jewish affair in the Middle East. His library contains more than 6,000 rare books, including 1,000 books on Jewish religion, Jewish history and the Jewish way of life. He wrote more than twenty books on Jewish religious law, Jewish history and comparative religious studies." This supposed expert repeats the perennial myths about Jewish espionage and betrayal and how the Jews derive their strength from the superpowers, and he goes on to anticipate Israel's demise.

The basic conspiracy myth lends credibility to a host of diverse allegations about the subversive nature of the Jews. A report in *Rose al-Youssef* (30 November 1992) suggested that Israel, in collaboration with Iran, created and planted in Egypt a weird Muslim sect by the name of al-Ahbash which, in addition to distorting Islam, was also working to win over Egyptians to supporting peace with Israel. Another favourite Jewish "subversive activity" is the "penetration" of the Egyptian mind in an effort to convey the legitimacy of Zionism. Books on the subject often focus on the activity of the Israel Academic Centre in Cairo—for example, *Tahwid Aql Misr* (The Judaification of Egypt's Mind) by Arafah Abduh Ali (Cairo, 1989).

Another "crime" against Muslim morals and Egypt in general is the modern version of well-poisoning—AIDS infection. A report in an Islamic fundamentalist-controlled journal on the increase of AIDS cases in Egypt blames contact with Jewish women of Polish and Arab origin who strive to infect with the disease "every Arab and Muslim" (*al-Sha'b*, 28 April 1992). Such messages are transmitted graphically as well. Egyptian illustrations tend to be bold, verging on the vulgar, and, as far as Jews are concerned, brutal. The cover of a classical edition of *The Protocols*, entitled *al-Khatar al-Yahudi: "Brutukulat Hukama' Sahyun"* (The Jewish Danger: *The Protocols of the Elders of Zion*, translated by Muhammad Khalifah al-Tunisi, which has a 1951 introduction by the venerable Dean of Letters Abbas Mahmud al-Aqqad and is always available in shops, sports an octopus intertwined with a Star of David. A pamphlet, *Al-Yahud fi al-Qur'an* (Jews in the Qur'an) by al-Sayyid Sabiq (Cairo, 1990), now in its third reprint and currently available, displays on its cover a hand marked with a

Star of David stabbing the globe and drawing blood. Similarly, *Bara'at Hitler wa Tazwir al-Ta'rikh* (The Innocence of Hitler and the Falsification of History) by Yasir Husayn (Cairo, 1990) shows an innocent-looking Hitler locked in the deadly embrace of a giant devil, with long nails, horns, fangs and eyes revealing Stars of David. Then there is a new rendition of the blood libel story entitled in letters of blood *Jarimah fi Harat al-Yahud: Fatirat al-Yahud Ajinah min Dam al-Masihiyyin* (A Crime in the Jewish Quarter: Jewish Matza is Made with Christian Blood!), prepared and prefaced by a popular moderate leftist writer, Adil Hamuda (Cairo, 1992). The list is seemingly endless.

No less pervasive is journalistic iconography, in which Israel and Zionism are depicted by all political shades of opinion regularly (though not exclusively) as a Stürmer Jew (for example, in the extreme leftist *al-Ahali*, 5 February 1992, the establishment *al-Jumhuriyyah*, 27 June 1992, the establishment *al-Ahram*, 28 April 1992); as a Nazi (for example, in *al-Ahali*, 15 January 1992, the moderate leftist *Rose al-Youssef*, 23 March 1992, *al-Ahram Weekly*, 24-30 December 1992); and as a snake (for example, in the leftist *al-Yasar*, 22 November 1992). Through constant denigration, the Star of David has come to signify a major unequivocal abomination and is often equated with a swastika (for example, in *al-Ahram*, 26 February 1992), while *Rose al-Youssef* shows it contaminating the whole world (15 June 1992).

ASSESSMENT

Together with other countries both inside and outside the Arab world, Egypt practises "antisemitism without Jews". However, it is unique in being a Muslim Arab country previously at war with the Jewish state and now in a relationship governed by a peace treaty. The significance of the latter is twofold. On the one hand, it demonstrates that practical, constructive policies can be dissociated from negative verbal/visual attitudes and exist independently. On the other hand— and less happily—it demonstrates that these negative attitudes also persist and flourish independently. Contrary to past experience, they are not being orchestrated by the powers-that-be; in fact, at present the

regime has a vested interest in preserving the peace, and so in theory should be encouraging public support. However, antisemitic constructs are so deeply ingrained in the population that, despite its own best interests, the regime chooses not to move against them. As a result, the peace policy is not as yet supported by a coherent underlying government strategy. Not only is this lack an obvious handicap to the development of peace but, should the peace process be stalled, or even reversed, its absence will leave the way open for existing antisemitic constructs.

Such an infrastructure consists of both negative imagery and plans for an ongoing battle. The Islamic fundamentalists are open about this. Their radical leader Umar Abd al-Rahman has declared that "peace with the Jews is prohibited" and that anyone who makes such peace puts themselves outside the community of Islam and is guilty of the gravest of sins (*al-Jazeera al-Arabiyyah*, November 1991). Such views are shared by the pragmatists (see article by Mustafa Mashhu, Egyptian Muslim Brotherhood leader, in the Hamas paper *Sawt al-Haqq wal-Huriyyah*, quoted in *ha-Aretz*, 3 May 1993; see also interview with Muhammad al-Sayyid Habib, Muslim Brotherhood member and Head of Faculty Organization of Asyut Universities, in the Lebanese *al-Bilad* (1 February 1992). The title of a recent book, *Alam bila Yahud* (A World without Jews) by Abd al-Mun'im al-Wifni (Cairo, 1992), says it all.

Another danger which springs from repeated antisemitic expression goes beyond the issue of Israel. The emergence of the Islamic fundamentalists as active proponents of antisemitism has led to the Islamicization of antisemitism, which then gains an aura of divine authority and practical urgency which was absent from traditional Arab antisemitism. Simultaneously, Islam itself—never previously virulently or lethally antisemitic—is being imbued with demonizing antisemitism and interpreted as such by militants. Given their zeal, it seems likely that they will leave their mark on Islam in a way that may prove hard to counteract.

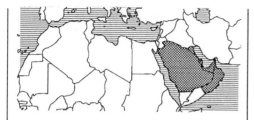

Gulf States

Bahrain

General population: 518,000
Jewish population: none

GENERAL BACKGROUND

The state of Bahrain became fully independent in 1971. It is an absolute monarchy, whose head of state—the Emir, Sheikh Isa bin Salman al-Khalifa—governs through an appointed cabinet. The 1973 constitution made provision for a National Assembly composed of the cabinet and thirty members elected by popular vote. However, the last National Assembly was dissolved in 1975 and has not been revived.

In 1992, there was little obvious progress towards the reintroduction of "democracy in the political life" which the Bahrain government promised after the 1990 Iraqi invasion of Kuwait. However, in December, the Emir announced plans to appoint a new consultative national assembly. In the meantime, political parties remained illegal and opposition members' movements were curtailed by the State Security Law, which permitted detention without trial and allowed conviction solely on the basis of a confession made by the accused.

The economy was badly affected by the 1990-1 Gulf crisis and showed few signs of improvement in 1992. In 1991, the 1990 trade surplus of nearly $7 million had become a deficit of over $85 million. Moreover, the annual grants received from Saudi Arabia and Kuwait were reduced.

Kuwait

General population: 1,200,000
Jewish population: none

GENERAL BACKGROUND

The state of Kuwait, which became independent in 1961, is governed by the Emir, Sheikh Jabir al-Ahmad al-Jabir al-Sabah, who is chosen by and from members of the al-Sabah royal family. From August 1990 to February 1991, when Iraq occupied Kuwait, the Emir led a government-in-exile in Saudi Arabia.

The Emir returned to power facing pressure for greater democratization both from opposition groups within the country and from the Western nations which had participated in the anti-Iraq coalition, particularly the United States. Some seven groups, ranging from liberal reformers to Islamic fundamentalists, formed an Opposition Front, which has called for separation of the posts of crown prince and prime minister, an end to domination of all key political posts by the al-Sabah family, a full disclosure of government finances, complete press freedom, the repeal of laws banning trade unions and political parties, and the extension of the franchise to naturalized Kuwaitis.

In October 1992, non-party elections were held for a reconstituted National Assembly. The majority of the fifty successful candidates were critics of the government. At the end of the year, the Democratic Front became the first group to defy the law and establish itself openly as a political party.

Economic decisions were determined largely by the aftermath of the Iraqi invasion. The 1991-2 budget raised total expenditure to almost double the 1990-1 figure, with the allocation for defence increasing almost six-fold. On the other hand, the devastation of the Kuwaiti oil-fields during the war led total revenue to fall by almost two-thirds, since oil receipts accounted for at least 80 per cent of the total.

Oman

General population: 1,618,000
Jewish population: none

GENERAL BACKGROUND

The Sultanate of Oman became independent from the UK in 1951. Sultan Qaboos bin Said rules by decree and is advised by his appointed cabinet. In common with its counterparts in other Gulf states, the Omani government moved towards limited political reform in the convening of an advisory fifty-nine-member Consultative Council, which replaced the fifty-five-member Consultative Assembly in January 1992. The Council members were appointed by the Sultan in 1991 from lists drawn up by Omani notables and sheikhs.

Qatar

General population: 402,000
Jewish population: none

GENERAL BACKGROUND

The state of Qatar became independent in 1971. It is an absolute monarchy, governed by the Emir, Sheikh Khalifa ibn Hamad al-Thani, who serves as both head of state and prime minister of an appointed cabinet. There is also a thirty-member Advisory Council.

As in other Gulf states, the Iraqi invasion of Kuwait helped to foster the development of a loosely organized opposition demanding political change. In January, a number of young members from prominent families submitted a petition calling for the formation of a legislative assembly,an end to the abuse of political power and economic, financial, educational and administrative reforms.

At the February meeting of the Organization of Petroleum Exporting Countries (OPEC), Qatar suffered the heaviest cut imposed on any member state when its production ceiling was set at 377,000 barrels per day.

Saudi Arabia

General population: 15,431,000
Jewish population: none

GENERAL BACKGROUND

The Kingdom of Saudi Arabia was established in 1932. King Fahd ibn Abdul Aziz rules as absolute monarch and heads a Council of Ministers which serves the royal family in legislative and executive matters.

Although King Fahd has said that the democratic systems of the West do not suit the region, a royal decree of 1 March 1992 provided for the creation of a sixty-one-member Consultative Council. Calls for political change came not only from proponents of greater liberalization but also from Islamic fundamentalists. There were reports, although officially denied, that the Saudi authorities had clamped down on fundamentalist dissent in December 1991 and January 1992.

The 1990-1 Gulf conflict cost Saudi Arabia nearly $50,000 million and forced the country to use foreign credit in 1991. In January, the 1992 budget was announced which set a record budget expenditure of $48,000 million, with a budget deficit of nearly $8,000 million. The largest single expenditure allocation was for defence and security ($14,400 million) and a further $13,900 million was allowed for "vital projects", thought to cover further spending on arms and military infrastructure.

The need to maintain oil revenue emerged when Saudi demanded at the February OPEC meeting that members cut production in order to boost world petroleum prices. With its commitment to reduce total oil output by 7.75 per cent. Saudi Arabia was one of the OPEC countries least affected by the quota system agreed at the meeting.

United Arab Emirates

General population: 1,630,000
Jewish population: none

GENERAL BACKGROUND

The United Arab Emirates (UAE), which is made up of the emirates of Abu Dhabi, Dubai, Sharjah, Ras al-Khaimah, Fujairah, Umm al-Qaiwain and Ajman, achieved independence from the UK in 1971.

Overall authority is vested in the Supreme Council of the seven emirate rulers, each of whom is an absolute monarch in his own state. Decisions of the Council require the approval of at least five of the rulers, including those of Abu Dhabi and Dubai. The president (currently Sheikh Zaid bin Sultan al-Nahayan of Abu Dhabi) and the vice-president (Sheikh Maktoum bin Rashid al Maktoum, who is also prime minister) are elected by the Supreme Council. The prime minister and the Federal Council of Ministers are appointed by the president and responsible to the Supreme Council. The forty-member Federal National Council, appointed by the emirates, considers legislative proposals from the Council of Ministers.

In the wake of the Iraqi invasion of Kuwait, the UAE embarked on a major programme to strengthen its armed forces and to build up its military supplies. It was reported in February that the UAE had also adopted a policy of making military purchases only from countries willing to make a proportional investment in the country's economy.

The national economy continued to flourish in 1992, based on oil production in Abu Dhabi and commerce in Dubai, which by 1992 had become the fifth most important gold trading centre. In the first six months of the year, the UAE's non-oil foreign trade showed a 47 per cent increase over the same period in 1991.

GULF STATES: HISTORICAL LEGACY

Notions of antisemitism in the Gulf states—Bahrain, Kuwait, Oman, Qatar, Saudi Arabia and the United Arab Emirates (UAE)—have been influenced by contradictory sources.

The influence of European antisemitism is deeply-rooted. With the exception of Bahrain, Gulf societies evolved without Jewish communities and without encountering a Jewish life-style and Jewish values. Their state of mind has been shaped by Western notions of antisemitism. Western travellers and businessmen, anxious to befriend Gulf Arabs for business purposes, relayed to them classical images of greedy, plotting and monstrous-looking Jews. Gulf societies accepted as facts such fabrications as *The Protocols of the Elders of Zion*. Due to state control of the media, many Gulf Arabs still do so. Moreover, the continuous and unconditional identification of the Gulf societies with Arab and Palestinian issues only entrenched among them a demonic image of Jews.

However, Israel's role in the 1991 Gulf War led Gulf societies to develop a more positive image of Jews. They were able to identify with Israeli society's position, which, like their own, had been attacked and victimized by Saddam Hussein's ventures. They appreciated Israel's restraint, in avoiding retaliation against Iraq, which helped facilitate the anti-Iraq coalition's victory. The Gulf states therefore started viewing Israel as a factor of stability in the Middle East and supported the US-initiated Arab-Israeli peace process. Israel's earlier image as the "Zionist enemy" was definitely improved. In addition, the Palestinians' support for Saddam Hussein earned them the animosity of many Gulf Arabs who resented their disregard for the hospitality and financial and material support which the Gulf states had always offered them. This caused a rupture in Palestinian-Gulf relations and contributed to the less hostile perception of Israel.

GULF STATES: PRESENT SITUATION

In 1992, the attitudes of the Arab Gulf states towards Jews reflected an interplay between traditional antisemitic stereotypes and more positive images developed in the wake of the Gulf War.

Gulf leaders and media focused on

Jewish issues mostly in the context of Israel's participation in the peace process. Israel and its Jewish society were thereby upgraded to a level of a legitimate partner in a peace process. However, Israel's interests and policies, often criticized as being too intransigent and offensive to the Arabs, were depicted and coined by Gulf Arabs in uncensored antisemitic terms and images. Saudi Arabia's mainstream papers, reflected the government's opinion of Israel's stubbornness in the peace negotiations, notably its unwillingness to give up the occupied territories.

Hence, former Israeli Prime Minister Yitzhak Shamir was depicted in caricatures as a huge spider spreading its web over the entire world (al-Sharq al-Awsat, 21 March 1992) and as a tiger breaking loose from UN Resolutions 242 and 338, running towards the land of new settlements (al-Madina, 13 March 1992). Israel was shown as a huge, ugly beast, with a Star of David hat, ready to swallow the small, innocent bird of peace ('Ukaz, 2 August 1992). In these caricatures, antisemitism was mainly evident in form and shape.

In other publications, Saudi antisemitism reached more substantial levels. Expressing Saudi lack of experience in any dealings with Israel, a Saudi intellectual, Dr Mustafa 'Abd Al-Wahid, wondered (al-Madina, 14 March 1992) how former Israeli Prime Minister Menachem Begin, in an article published after his death, could have been described by other Arabs as a credible person and even as a friend. According to the author, Begin was a Pole who had led terrorist bandits, became the leader of the terrorist Zionist entity and spilled Arab blood. He did not deserve to be buried on the Mount of Olives, in Palestinian soil. This article showed that at least certain Israeli Jews were regarded as illegitimate residents in the Middle East. Moreover, they are not judged as human beings of equal strength and weakness, but as bloodthirsty terrorists, whose only mission was to kill Arabs.

In spite of Saudi support for the peace process and the visit, in December 1991, of an American-Jewish delegation to Saudi Arabia, obtaining entrance visas to Saudi Arabia for Jews remained most difficult, if not impossible. There were allegations (such as in the Israeli daily Ma'ariv, 17

June 1992) that Saudi authorities still prohibited Jews from entering Saudi Arabia for business purposes, even if they were sent by US firms.

Qatar's acquaintance with Jewish or Israeli practices has been almost non-existent. The Qatari media's criticism of Israel has therefore reflected European stereotypes and images, transplanted into Middle East affairs. Hence, Israel's actions against Hizbullah's terrorism in South Lebanon were depicted in a caricature, where a bearded Jew, with a long nose and a black hat, was knifing Lebanon in the back. That the Jew was also being stabbed in the back, symbolized what was perceived to be Shiites'ite retaliation against Israel in the bombing of the Israeli embassy in Buenos Aires (al-Ra'ya, 25 March 1992). Another illustration showed Israel as a dog with a Star of David, storming the Arab world (al-Ra'ya, 16 January 1992).

In 1992, a book of over 600 pages was published in Qatar by Mohammed Qasim Mohammed of Qatar University, entitled "The Contradiction in the Annals and Events of the Torah from Adam to Babel". The book was a lengthy attempt to discredit the "historical" aspects of the Jewish scriptures and, thereby, Jewish history and historical experience itself. It was widely available throughout the Gulf and the Arab world.

The UAE-based paper al-Ittihad also published a series of caricatures which criticized Israel's policies vis-à-vis the Palestinians and what the UAE regarded as Israel's uncompromising attitudes towards Jewish immigration to Israel, the occupied territories and peace. Thus, in an illustration of a "Jerusalem airport", faceless, anonymous Palestinians were shown walking through the gate of expulsion with their belongings. At the same time, hairy, long-nosed monstrous-looking Jews were entering an immigration gate (8 January 1992). In another illustration, Arab calls for "land for peace" were being derided by a satanic-looking, bespectacled Jew, who while blocking his ears with his fingers, was shouting back "I can't hear you" (April 1992).

Another UAE caricature depicted a hairy rat, with a Star of David and razor-sharp teeth, consuming a dollar bill from the hands of the American people, thus updating the classical stereotype of Jews as parasites, living on US funds but behaving as financial usurpers (19 April 1992).

A Kuwaiti caricature showed an ugly, bald Jew with a curved nose who reciprocated his Arab counterpart's call for peace—symbolized in his lifting of an olive branch—by pointing a sub-machine gun at him (*Sawt al-Kuwait*, 12 November 1992).

There were a number of antisemitic books available in Saudi Arabia, Kuwait and Abu Dhabi, which were published in other countries. These included "The Greed of the Jews and the Scriptures" by Fuad Hussein Munazzer, which was published in Beirut, and "The Character of Israel" by Dr Hasan Zaza, published in Damascus. Both depicted the Jews as a people committed to material gain, expansion and aggression.

GULF STATES: ASSESSMENT

All these examples showed that the Gulf states, despite having learnt to treat Israel and its Jewish society as facts of life, nevertheless continued to de-legitimize its politics: they objected to Israel's encouraging of Jewish immigration, exercising self defence and bargaining over peace. Criticism of these policies took the form and shape of classical antisemitic illustrations, enriched with updated Arab concepts: the Jews were not shown only as twisted and deformed creatures, but also as blood-thirsty terrorists, war-mongers, and usurpers of Palestinian and Arab rights.

Iran

General population: 59,000,000
Jewish population: 15,000 (mainly in Tehran, Isfahan and Shiraz)

GENERAL BACKGROUND

In the aftermath of Ayatollah Khomeini's era—he was succeeded by Ayatollah Sayed Ali Khamene'i in 1989—more power was transferred to the president, currently Hujjat al-Islam 'Ali Akbar Hashemi-Rafsanjani, and in the amended constitution of the Islamic Republic, the president became the government's chief executive, as the post of prime minister was abolished.

Since assuming power, Khamene'i and Rafsanjani have joined forces to resist more conservative factions, with Rafsanjani more prominent in formulating policies. Rafsanjani has tended to adopt a conciliatory approach towards the West in an effort to resume economic co-operation and encourage the foreign investment desperately needed to repair the damage caused by fourteen years of revolutionary activity and eight years of war with Iraq. Even so, Iran remains determined not to restore relations with the USA, nor to recognize the state of Israel, and to maintain Khomeini's *fatwa* on Salman Rushdie.

HISTORICAL LEGACY

Throughout their long history in the region, the Iranian Jews have experienced more periods of persecution and discrimination than periods of relative equality.

Physical and spiritual persecution was intensified under the Safavid Dynasty (1501-1736), once Iran had developed into a united political entity based on Shiite principles. The Shiites saw Jews as unclean people who could be purified only by conversion to Islam. Between 1613 and 1662, many Jews were forced to convert, their property was looted and those who resisted were murdered. Further restrictions were enforced in the eighteenth century.

Even at times when Jews were not made to convert, they were obliged to wear a distinguishing sign on their clothes, could not build themselves houses or synagogues, were restricted in their movements, and were prohibited from testifying in court against Muslims.

Under the Qajar Dynasty (1796-1925), together with continuous persecution, various atrocities were perpetrated against Jews. Hundreds were murdered at the end of the eighteenth century in Tabriz after a Jewish merchant was accused of killing a

Muslim boy to use his blood at Passover. In 1839, Muslims killed thirty Jews in Mashhad, the pretext for this incident being that the Jews of the city had mocked the holy memory of the Imam Hussein. In order to save the remainder of the community, the Jews agreed to convert to Islam. These forced converts practised their faith in secret until 1925, when religious persecution was eased and freedom of worship was granted. In Tehran, the Jews also suffered at the hands of their Muslim neighbours and in 1897 the Jewish quarter was surrounded by Muslims, who forced the Jews to wear red patches on their clothes.

Changes in the status of Iranian Jewry began to take place at the beginning of this century as the 1907 constitution granted religious minorities civil and judicial rights, including the ability to send one representative to the *Majlis*. The more institutionalized forms of religious discrimination were eased, especially under the Pahlavi dynasty, although they did continue in sporadic fashion at a local level, especially during the years of close relations with Nazi Germany, at which time Jews were subject to continuous persecution.

Zionism and the establishment of the state of Israel have played key roles in the status of Iranian Jewry and its relations with Iran since 1948—the community's fate being determined by the country's relations with Israel. As co-operation between the Shah and Israel intensified, the Jewish community became increasingly identified with the regime and was detested by the opposition, especially the religious opposition.

The 1979 revolution dictated the future of the Jewish community in Iran. The basic antagonism of the Shiite religion in general and Khomeini in particular to Jews and Judaism left the community with two choices—either to leave the country or to conform with the changes by expressing vigorous support for the revolution and its ideas, including its animosity towards Israel and Zionism. In the first decade after the revolution more than 50,000 Jews fled the country; from a community of 80,000 at its height, no more than 15,000 remained.

Khomeini wrote: "From the very beginning, the historical movement of Islam has had to contend with the Jews, for it was they who first established anti-Islamic propaganda and engaged in various stratagems, and, as you can see, this activity continues down to the present." Furthermore, he described Jews as "wretched" people who "wish to establish Jewish domination throughout the world" and are trying to distort the Qur'an. "We see today the Jews (may God curse them) have meddled with the text of the Qur'an and have made certain changes in Qur'ans they have had printed in the occupied territories."

The regime has emphasized its implacable enmity to the state of Israel and to the very idea of Zionism (the words "Jew", "Zionist" and "Israel" are used interchangeably by the regime). When, in 1979, support for Israel and Zionism became a crime punishable by death, the leaders of the community were forced to declare publicly their rejection of these notions. In the two years following the revolution, the revolutionary court sentenced to death, on the grounds of Zionism, connections with Israel and collaboration with the Shah, a number of Jewish communal leaders and some dozens of other Jews were arrested and imprisoned.

In the wake of the 1979 revolution, the Islamic *komitehs* ordered the confiscation of property of those who had allegedly co-operated with the Shah. The confiscation of Jewish property, including factories, hotels, cinemas, houses and other assets, was said to have been more systematic than those among the rest of the population. Moreover, Jews who have left Iran report that over the years it became more and more difficult to obtain licences to run businesses and that, as the government was not employing non-Muslims, the well-being of the Jewish community had deteriorated considerably.

PRESENT SITUATION

As far as can be ascertained, there has been little change in the position of Jews in Iran over the last year. The situation remains tolerable, but there is constant fear for the future. Jews are not prohibited from practising their faith and are not subject to physical assault. Nevertheless, continual verbal attacks by the regime on Israel, Zionism and the role of the Jews in world affairs create a threatening atmosphere that

Jewish refugees claim was felt by the whole community. Moreover, articles of an antisemitic nature were published in various journals, accusing Jews of a range of crimes from undermining the revolution to offending Islam.

However, despite the fact that the Iranian leadership has expressed its hostility to the Jews, it has taken no steps to worsen their situation. The difficulties Jews have faced since the revolution remain, as far as education, contacts with Israel, emigration, running businesses and employment are concerned. The contradiction between their legal status as a recognized religious minority and official antagonism dominates the situation of Iranian Jewry.

ASSESSMENT

Attitudes towards the Jews in Iran typify the revolution's ambivalence in dealing with matters that have both internal and external implications. While the regime claims to make a distinction between the Jews on the one hand and Zionism and Israel on the other, since the revolution the Jewish community has frequently been accused of collaborating with Israel and the USA. As with other issues, a debate between the extremists and the pragmatists is taking place concerning the correct attitude towards the Iranian Jews. The more extreme clergy would like to see greater restrictions imposed, but as long as Iran is interested in improving her relations with the West, it is assumed that the position of the Jewish community will not worsen.

Antisemitism in speeches and publications continues to appear, but it is unlikely that any further action will be taken against Jews in Iran as long as the current balance of power inside the regime persists and no dramatic changes in Iran's international status occur. Traditional patterns of behaviour and ideological positions mean that the potential for more severe forms of antisemitism in Iran exists, but under current conditions they are unlikely to manifest themselves. However, the threat of danger remains and the situation will need careful monitoring.

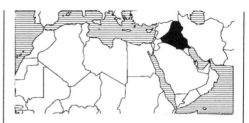

Iraq

General population: 19 million
Jewish population: 200-300 (in Baghdad)

GENERAL BACKGROUND

Political power in the Republic of Iraq is concentrated exclusively in the hands of President Saddam Hussein and his family, under the guise of the rule of a single party, the Ba'ath Arab Socialist Party, which has been in control since July 1968. From the early 1970s, Saddam has been the single most important decision-maker in Iraq, but he became president only in July 1979.

The supreme political decision-making, law-making and judicial body is the Revolutionary Command Council, a small and tightly-knit group. Second in importance is the regional leadership of the Ba'ath party. Third is the government, which is an executive body.

Saddam Hussein's power structure is arranged in concentric circles. Beyond him and his family, there is the tribal federation of albu-Nasir, which hails from the area in and around the town of Tikrit, north of Baghdad. The Sunni Arab population of Iraq, residing in a triangle between Baghdad, Mosul and the Syrian border in the west, forms a wider circle. The Sunni Arabs comprise only some 20 per cent of the total population of Iraq; most of the rest—some 18 per cent Kurds and 55 per cent Shiite Arabs—are hostile to the regime, or at least alienated from it. However, considerable numbers from these two communities have been collaborating with the regime since the early 1970s and this has increased resilience to Saddam's rule.

Iraq's eight-year war with Iran (1980-88), its invasion of Kuwait and the subsequent war (1991), and the massive

Shiites'ite and Kurdish uprisings that followed, caused severe economic hardship for the people of Iraq. The suffering was further augmented by the UN sanctions. However, Saddam's regime managed to ride the storm and by the end of 1992, despite many signs of decline, he was still securely in power. To achieve this, he ordered mass arrests, torture and executions, mainly of Shiites and Kurds but also of dissidents in the Sunni Arab community, including army officers. On 5 March 1992, the UN Human Rights Commission adopted a resolution condemning the Iraqi regime for human rights abuses of the "gravest nature". However, as Saddam Hussein understands that his rule cannot rely on bayonets alone for very long, he has also been careful to ensure that the population have had their basic needs—mainly food—provided. This, too, has followed the pattern of concentric circles: his entourage first, then the army, security apparatus and party officials, then the Baghdad area, then the Sunni Arab zone, and finally the Shiites and those Kurds who accept Ba'ath rule.

HISTORICAL LEGACY

A mere eight years after Iraq was created as a nation-state by the British colonial power, the Jews of Iraq were reminded for the first time of their vulnerability. In February 1928, in a protest against the visit to Baghdad of Sir Alfred Mond, a senior British politician who was involved in the formulation of the Balfour Declaration, some 40,000 Iraqis marched in the streets of Baghdad. The demonstration was directed against local Jews as much as against the Zionist movement and the British. Since then, most Iraqis have made no clear distinction between Jews and Zionists, and as a result, anti-Zionist propaganda has become inseparably intertwined with the ugliest sort of anti-Jewish diatribe.

During the 1930s and up to the Rashid 'Ali anti-British and pro-Nazi revolt of May 1941, Nazi influence in Baghdad further fanned racist anti-Jewish sentiments. Large segments of the Iraqi intelligentsia and many army officers and politicians (pro- as well as anti-British) gave vent to anti-Jewish sentiments and introduced such attitudes into the state education system. On 1-2 June 1941,

immediately following the collapse of the Rashid 'Ali revolt and with the victorious British troops encamped on the outskirts of Baghdad, the Muslim masses, aided by some military and police units, carried out a wide scale pogrom: 129 Jews were murdered, many hundreds were wounded and a huge proportion of Jewish property was looted and burned down. This pogrom (called the *Farhud*) marked the beginning of the end of 2,500 years of Jewish presence in Mesopotamia and Iraq.

In August 1948, the government declared it a crime to be a Zionist and many Jews were imprisoned. A few were executed for "espionage". In early 1950, Jews were allowed to leave the country for Israel, but to do so they had to relinquish their Iraqi citizenship and forfeit their assets. Initially, the Iraqi authorities had assessed that only a few thousand would leave, but the violent anti-Jewish atmosphere of Baghdad and the introduction of a series of anti-Jewish laws, making their stay practically impossible, encouraged even those who hesitated to leave. By mid-March 1951, some 104,000 Jews had already applied for immigration and been stripped of their citizenship. All in all, the 1950-51 exodus saw close to 120,000 Jews emigrating to Israel. After 1951, only around 6,000 Jews remained in Iraq; by 1964, this number had halved.

Under the Republican rule of General 'Abd al-Karim Qasim (1958-63), many Jews were released from prison and deported; the whole atmosphere was far less hostile. However, under the period of first Ba'ath rule, and that of the Arif brothers (February 1963-July 1968), the situation of the Jews deteriorated. In June 1963, for example, Jews staying abroad were told to return if they did not wish to be stripped of their citizenship and lose their property. Only a few did so. In August of the same year, Jews were forbidden to leave the country except under extraordinary circumstances. In 1964, Jews were forbidden, for all practical purposes, to sell their share in industrial and other companies.

The Six-Day War of June 1967 made things even worse. Jews were forbidden to leave their home towns. Most telephone lines to their businesses were cut off, they were excluded from all social clubs and some 300 Jewish businessmen and community leaders (that is, one in ten of the Jewish population) were arrested for "espionage" or for "economic support for Israel" and tortured. All Jews were sacked from government and public jobs without compensation. Jews were forbidden to sell, pawn or lease property. Banks were forbidden to pay a Jew a sum exceeding 100 Iraqi dinars per day. Jewish doctors and lawyers were forbidden to deal with non-Jewish clients. Finally, all the property of the Jewish religious endowment (*waqf*) was placed under government control and its income denied to the community. Jews were trapped in Iraq—indeed, even in their home town—and, at the same time, they were denied means of livelihood.

When the Ba'ath Party came to power, to demonstrate their nationalist credentials and indicate to the public what would be the fate of anyone opposing them, in January 1969 they conducted a mock espionage trial and public hanging of thirteen young Jews in a square in Baghdad. This was done to the cheers of hundreds of thousands of Muslim Iraqis, who turned the event into a national festival. By 1971, about forty Jews had either been executed or had died under torture, and many scores were jailed.

Due to rising international pressure (indeed, even Egypt's President Nasser denounced the public executions as inhumane), the Ba'ath regime was forced to change its course. Between 1971 and 1973, most of Iraq's remaining Jews were allowed to leave the country and only some 300 stayed behind. Since then, the Ba'ath regime has not initiated any attacks on the tiny Jewish community of Iraq, which has been generally left alone.

PRESENT SITUATION

During the war against Iran and the Kuwait crisis, despite some attempts to differentiate between Zionism and Judaism, anti-Jewish themes were quite widespread in the regime's war propaganda. Most conspicuous were claims that the Persian enemy had an ancient alignment with the Jews, dating back to the era of the Persian empire of Cyrus and his successors. Thus, for example, Dr Bahnam Abu al-Suf, one of Iraq's leading archaeologists and a one-time director of the Department of

Antiquities, argued in Saddam Hussein's daily *Babil* on 19 March 1992 that the Jews helped the Persians to conquer and destroy Babylon in 536 BCE and that they were also instrumental in the destruction of the Assyrian Kingdom (Babylon and Assyria are regarded in Saddam's Iraq as the forerunners of the modern nation).

Iraqi publicists have accused the "Zionists" of fabricating the Holocaust (for example, Sadiq Bakhan in the party daily *al-Thawra*, 1 November 1991). There is a widespread belief (or a claim to such belief) in the authenticity of *The Protocols of the Elders of Zion* and, more generally, in a Jewish conspiracy to dominate, and even destroy, the world (for example, Mu'min al-Sharif in *Qadisiyya*, the daily paper of the ministry of defence, 20 March 1992). In the same context, it has been frequently claimed that the USA and Europe are totally controlled by Jewish money and that the Allied attack on Iraq following the invasion of Kuwait was nothing short of a Jewish-Zionist plot (indeed, Saddam himself asserted as much to CNN's Peter Arnet in his famous interview during the Gulf War). Dr Jabir Ibrahim al-Rawi, when objecting to the UN resolution rescinding an earlier one equating Zionism with racism, claimed that the Talmud, *The Protocols* and the clandestine programme of the freemasons ware all racist and served as the Jewish "constitution" (*al-Thawra*, 30 March 1992). More seriously, an anonymous publicist, writing under the pseudonym "TS", claimed that Jews use human blood in their religious rites (*Qadisiyya*, 15 February 1992).

Occasionally, there have been claims that Jews belong to a different race from all other human beings and that they have a particular physique. Contrary to official party doctrine, it is sometimes claimed that Judaism and Zionism cannot be separated. Finally, when the Iraqi publicists want to humiliate the Saudi family, the most decisive and devastating insult they can come up with is to claim that the royal family of Saudi Arabia is, in fact, descended from a Southern Iraqi Jewish family by the name of Sa'id.

ASSESSMENT

Antisemitic imagery and themes are clearly significant in the propaganda produced by

Saddam Hussein's regime.

In the Iraqi context, antisemitism appears to be used more in defence of Iraqi interests and in attacking those responsible for military action against Iraq, than in a direct campaign against Israel and Zionism.

Lebanon

General population: 2,700,000
Jewish population: 100 (in Beirut)

GENERAL BACKGROUND

Lebanon's first general election since 1972 was held in August and September. The election was boycotted by the leading Maronite Christian parties and groups who had called for a postponement "until the right circumstances and national conditions exist". The Shiite Muslim parties and groups, principally Amal and Hizbullah, emerged as the largest bloc of deputies in the new National Assembly.

With the appointment of Rafiq al-Hariri, a Lebanese-born Saudi businessman and billionaire, as prime minister, prospects for the country's economic reconstruction improved. Hariri's appointment halted the decline of the Lebanese pound, which had depreciated by 60 per cent in the nine months prior to the general election, although it increased to only about half of its December 1991 value. Since Hariri took over, some $500 million was given in foreign aid and the prime minister's links with Riyadh encouraged considerable Saudi investment.

HISTORICAL LEGACY

The Lebanese Jewish community, which numbered 10,000 in 1952, was treated more tolerantly than in any other Arab country. Jews left Lebanon in two waves, after the

Six-Day War in 1967 and following the civil war of 1976.

Eleven Lebanese Jews, including the president and secretary-general of the community and a local paediatrician, were taken hostage between 1984 and 1986 by a group called the Organization of the Oppressed of the Earth which has links with Hizbullah. The bodies of four of them, killed because Israel had failed to release all Lebanese and Palestinian prisoners in South Lebanon, have been recovered. The Organization of the Oppressed of the Earth has claimed to have "executed the sentence of Allah" on a total of nine of these hostages. On 28 December 1985, the terrorist group threatened that unless its demands against Israel were met it would not only kill the remaining hostages but also any other Jews "upon whom we can lay our hands". Forced out of its traditional quarter in West Beirut, the remnant of the Jewish community still lives in Christian East Beirut.

PRESENT SITUATION

As mentioned in last year's *Antisemitism World Report*, Lebanese newspapers have used, and continue to use, antisemitic themes of money, drugs and AIDS in their articles against Israel. An article in *al-Diyar* in October called upon the Syrian nation to fight the "Jewish enemy" which "had not built a civilization nor made any visible impression on history in its name" and believes in a God which "allows them to murder other nations and lay claim to their property, honour and land".

Libya

General population: 4,714,000
Jewish population: none

GENERAL BACKGROUND

Libyan politics have been dominated for over two decades by Colonel Muammar Gaddafi, who came to power in a military coup in 1969. Libya remains in diplomatic isolation because of its support of international terrorism. In 1992, the political scene was overshadowed by the imposition

of UN sanctions over the government's refusal to extradite two Libyan citizens believed to be responsible for the 1988 Lockerbie bombing. Indicators of a possible flexibility on the part of the regime were seen in the printing of articles critical of Gaddafi's handling of the issue in the state-controlled media in July and the appointment of a new official in charge of foreign affairs in a November reshuffle.

In recent years, Libya has witnessed a rising tide of Islamic fundamentalism. Between 1988 and 1991, the regime frequently resorted to the detention of its critics. In 1992, it was estimated that between 600 and 800 people were still being held.

Although the economy remained centralized and under state control, measures permitting privatization of some state concerns and free investment in public-sector ventures were announced in September.

HISTORICAL LEGACY

From the fifteenth century onwards, Jews in Libya went through many periods of persecution. Libyan Jews were subjected to Italian racial laws in 1936. During the Second World War, the Jewish quarter of Benghazi was sacked and 2,000 Jews were deported across the desert, many dying *en route*. In November 1945, more than 100 Jews were murdered in anti-Jewish riots in Tripoli. This was carefully planned, and took place against the background of the anniversary of the Balfour Declaration and stories of violence in Palestine.

Before independence in 1951, a majority of the 38,000 Libyan Jews emigrated to Israel. Those who stayed were deprived of their right to vote in 1963 and were forbidden to hold office. During the 1967 Six-Day War, about 118 Jews were killed and there was widespread destruction of Jewish property. When Gaddafi came to power, he announced the seizure of all Jewish property without compensation.

PRESENT SITUATION

Gaddafi has played a major part in financing the spread of negative Islamic perceptions of Jews and in his speeches he has often used antisemitic and anti-Jewish stereotypes to substantiate his extreme anti-Zionism.

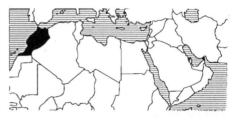

Morocco

General population: 27,731,000
Jewish population: 6,000-7,000 (mainly in Casablanca)

GENERAL BACKGROUND

King Hassan II has ruled continuously since 1961. In 1992, the main political development was the introduction of constitutional reforms in preparation for general elections, originally due in 1990.

In March, King Hassan announced that a referendum would be held in September on proposed constitutional changes to establish a better balance between legislative and executive bodies. In May, the main parties of the legal opposition—the nationalist Istiqlal (Independence Party), the Socialist Union of Popular Forces, the Organization for Democratic Popular Action and the centre-left Union Nationale des Forces Populaires—formed a Democratic Bloc to press for fundamental reforms. Despite the announcement in June of measures to ensure a free electoral process, the opposition parties called for a boycott of the September referendum. The official result of the 4 September referendum showed a 97.25 turnout and a vote of 99.96 per cent in favour of the changes.

Allegations of intimidation of opposition candidates and supporters prior to the local elections on 16 October cast doubt on the government's claims of democratic progress.

Despite the releases and pardons of a number of political prisoners during the year, there were continued reports of human rights abuses. In mid-January 1992, the European Parliament refused to approve aid to Morocco on human rights grounds.

Although a programme to improve the country's economy was agreed with the International Monetary Fund in February, Morocco still faced the problems arising from a highly inequitable distribution of wealth. The World Bank reported that one in three Moroccans lived below the level of "absolute poverty".

Historical legacy

Jews were massacred in Fez in 1033 and in Marrakesh in 1232. Despite some periods of revival, the condition of the Jews deteriorated until the establishment of the French Protectorate in 1912. The Jews then entered an era in which, for the first time, they began to enjoy real equality with their fellow citizens. Under the Vichy regime, Jews suffered discrimination but King Muhammed V did much to ensure that they were not deported. By 1948, there were some 270,000 Jews in Morocco but thereafter the population decreased rapidly.

Following the declaration of the state of Israel, there were numerous attacks on Jewish individuals and premises. In June 1953, forty-three Jews were murdered. Pogroms and other violence persisted until Morocco gained independence in 1956. Following independence, Jews were treated in some respects better than they had ever been. They were granted full suffrage and complete freedom of movement. On the other hand, legislation was introduced making emigration illegal (although thousands of Jews continued to leave for Israel clandestinely). After the 1967 Six-Day War, a worsening of conditions, including a virulent press campaign against the Jewish community as well as against Israel, led many middle class Jews to emigrate.

Present situation

With the diminution of the Jewish community by successive waves of emigration, mainly to Israel, France and Canada, the "Jewish problem" has become less of an issue. Certain ministers have even publicly expressed regret at the way the Jewish community has been treated in the past. The Jewish community now appears to maintain good relations with the regime and antisemitic sentiment has not been evident in the government or in the media. This positive climate has been reinforced by King Hassan's appointment of a Jew, André Azoulay, as his advisor on economic affairs. Moroccan-born Israelis have been allowed into the country and a recent visit to Casablanca by a former French chief rabbi received extensive and positive coverage in the Moroccan media.

Generally good relations exist between the Jewish and Muslim communities. However, antisemitic themes have emerged in sermons by Islamic fundamentalist clerics. Since the regime seeks to quell the spread of Islamic fundamentalist ideas, particularly in view of the situation in neighbouring Algeria, any expression, antisemitic or otherwise, by these circles tends to be made clandestinely.

Assessment

Moroccan Jewry currently enjoys the tolerance of King Hassan's regime. However, the situation of the Jews is potentially precarious in view of the threat posed by Islamic extremism and, although there did not appear to have been antisemitic repercussions arising from anti-Zionism in the media in 1992, a further armed conflict in the Middle East involving Israel could have grave consequences for Morocco's Jews.

Syria

General population: 12,824,000
Jewish population: 1,450 (mainly in Damascus)

General background

With the demise of the Soviet Union, Syria lost its principal patron. As a result, it began to adopt a pragmatic foreign policy, with the aim of improving relations with the West, in particular the USA. Syria

participated in the anti-Iraq coalition in the 1991 Gulf War and joined the Middle East peace process, where it entered into direct negotiations with Israel.

Changes in foreign policy were not matched in domestic policy. In spite of promises to liberalize the political system, Syria remained an autocratic regime propped up by the military and the secret services.

A number of economic liberalization measures contributed to Syria's improved economic situation, which saw inflation drop from 35 per cent in 1989 to 12 per cent in 1992 as well as a substantial increase in foreign investment. However, the economic improvements were largely due to healthy oil revenues.

Senior Syrian officials were still thought to be involved in the cultivation and trafficking of drugs, and Amnesty International believed that several thousand political prisoners remained incarcerated in Syria's jails.

HISTORICAL LEGACY

The Jewish community in Syria dates back to the Seleucid period of the third century BCE. The community prospered then, and under the Romans, even at the time of the great rebellion and the destruction of the Second Temple in 70 CE. The situation deteriorated with the advent of Christianity in the fourth century CE. Restrictions were imposed on the Jewish community and in many cases Jews were subjected to religious and economic persecution.

The Arab conquest of 636 saw a considerable improvement in the situation of Syrian Jews, particularly during the Umayyid Caliphate (661-750). During the Abbasid Empire (750-1258), however, Jews were obliged to pay higher taxes than non-Jews and were pressurized to convert to Islam.

The Crusades and attendant struggles between Muslims and Christians did not affect Jewish communities in the interior of Syria but caused considerable damage to, and sometimes the destruction of, Jewish communities in coastal regions.

Under the Mamluks, who ruled Syria from 1260 to 1516, the Jews suffered various forms of discrimination. Influenced by fanatical clerics, the Mamluks forced many Jews to convert to Islam and imposed religious and economic restrictions on others. Persecution by the Mamluks, and the instability that prevailed in the country after their demise, resulted in the further depletion of the Syrian Jewish community.

The fate of the Jewish community changed once again with the Ottoman conquest of 1516. Although Jews were occasionally persecuted and were subject to economic restrictions, on the whole they were treated well by the regime. The Jewish community developed and prospered in cultural, political and economic terms—aided by the absorption of Jews who had been deported from Spain.

In 1840, the Jews suffered particularly as a result of the "Damascus affair": they were accused of murdering a Capuchin friar and using his blood for the manufacture of Passover bread—perhaps the first time this weapon of doctrinaire Christian European antisemitism has been used in the Muslim Arab world.

In the second half of the nineteenth century, the legal position of Syrian Jews improved—probably as a result of pressure from Europe. The Ottoman government introduced a series of reforms known as the Tanzimat, which in theory gave Jews virtual equality before the law. But by the end of the century, partly for economic reasons, many Jews started leaving Syria to settle elsewhere.

In 1947, there were about 30,000 Jews in Syria. A wave of hostility towards Israel, culminating in officially orchestrated riots in Aleppo and Damascus, left hundreds of Jewish homes and several ancient synagogues in ruins. Many Jews were killed and 15,000 fled the country, a sizeable proportion finding their way to Israel. A further 10,000 were able to leave between 1948 and the early 1960s, during periods when restrictions on emigration were temporarily lifted.

Once the Ba'ath regime had consolidated its hold on power during the 1960s, Syrian Jews became hostages of the state. They were subjected to strict supervision by the Syrian security services, denied most of their civil rights, economically harassed, and in many cases their lives were endangered.

The physical and economic situation of the Jews gradually improved after President Asad assumed power in 1970. Nevertheless, they were still denied the right to emigrate and their movements within the country were restricted. They continued to be "supervised" by the security services and in a number of cases they were the victims of murders and robberies.

The plight of Jewish women was of particular concern. As many more Jewish women than men remained in Syria, often they could not find husbands within the Jewish community and in most cases were denied the right to emigrate and seek them elsewhere. Some of these women were among the groups who attempted to leave Syria illegally; they were often detained and paid with their lives.

Over the past few years, considerable pressure has been exerted on the Syrian regime to improve the situation of the remaining members of the Jewish community and to lift emigration restrictions. These issues were repeatedly raised in discussions between Syria and US officials and by the Israeli delegation to the peace talks in 1991.

PRESENT SITUATION

In April 1992, President Asad met with representatives of the Syrian Jewish community, headed by Rabbi Ibrahim Hamra. This event was highlighted in the Syrian media, with the intention of showing a positive attitude towards Jews and demonstrating to the USA that Syria was honouring the rights of minorities. Also in April, the Syrians told the US administration that they had lifted all restrictions on the departure of Jews from Syria, provided that their destination was not Israel and their departure was defined not as emigration but as a trip for the purpose of study, tourism or business.

Since May 1992, Jews have been leaving Syria in groups of up to several dozen. By early 1993, some 2,400 Jews had left. Most of them travelled to the USA, where there is a large community of Syrian Jews.

Towards the end of 1992, the Syrians temporarily stopped Jewish emigration, apparently in order to express dissatisfaction with what they saw as the slow pace of the development of Syrian-US relations and of the Middle East peace process. Syrian spokesmen denied, however, that the departure of Jews from Syria had been suspended, promising that restrictions on such departures would not be imposed again.

Most of the remaining Syrian Jews are businessmen and merchants who prefer to remain in Syria for the time being and take advantage of the improved conditions, both for the economy in general and for the Jewish community. Nevertheless, some of the restrictions on Jews appear to be still in force: Jews are still subject to the "supervision" of the security services and are not allowed to contact foreigners visiting Syria.

Although there has been some improvement in the Syrian regime's treatment of its Jews and Syria is participating in the peace process with Israel, its attitude to Israel and Jews remains hostile as reflected in the media and in speeches by the country's leaders.

Changes in Syria's foreign policy are perceived by the government-controlled media as a necessary evil, and therefore there has been no accompanying change in the regime's attitude towards Israel (which is implicitly identified with the Jews). Israel was represented as aggressive and expansionist.

In the media, antisemitic caricatures, especially in cartoons, appear frequently. They tend to show deformed Jews, Jews with money-bags and, typically, a Jew holding a globe in his hands (*al-Thawra*, 27 November 1991, 8, 27 July 1992; *Tishrin*, 2 August 1992).

In a series of antisemitic publications in the late 1980s, Jews were accused of using blood for ceremonial purposes and of sowing seeds of hate towards members of other religions. Most prominent among these publications was the book by Syrian Minister of Defence Mustafa Tlass', "The Matza of Zion", which attempted to prove the blood libel against the Jews of Damascus in 1840. In 1992, articles containing hints and explicit accusations in the same vein continued to be published in the Syrian media, for example, in *al-Sha'ba*, an army periodical.

ASSESSMENT

Syria's process of change, mainly in foreign policy, has brought about an improvement in the situation of Jews in the country, mostly because they are now able to emigrate. These improvements are, however, contingent on developments in Syria's relations with the US administration, and the changes in foreign policy have not brought about any change in Syria's basic perception of Israel and Jews at large. This remains deeply hostile, as evidenced by antisemitic representations in the media.

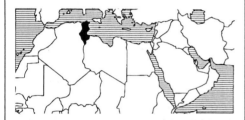

Tunisia

General population: 8,233,000
Jewish population: 3,000 (in Tunis and Djerba)

GENERAL BACKGROUND

General Zine el-Abidine Ben Ali replaced President Habib Bourguiba in a bloodless coup in 1987, and, as sole candidate, was elected president in 1989. In November 1992, President Ben Ali failed to introduce a timetable for multi-party democracy but he announced that opposition parties would be allowed to run in the legislative elections scheduled for April 1994.

The government's campaign to restrict the activities of the Islamic fundamentalist opposition movement Nahda led to renewed allegations of human rights abuses in the country, in particular the charge that torture had become routine.

The economy experienced a recovery from the effects of the Gulf War, partly as a result of a bumper harvest and a sharp upturn in tourism, although the growing trade deficit was still a cause for concern.

HISTORICAL LEGACY

In the early years of Islam, at least in certain periods, the Jews were tolerated and even respected. By the nineteenth century, most Jews lived in squalor in one of the sprawling ghettos of the Tunisian cities. The conditions of the Jews of southern Tunisia and those on the island of Djerba were considerably better.

Tunisia was occupied by France in 1830 and a French Protectorate was established in 1881. By and large, the Jews were beneficiaries of the French presence. The so-called fundamental Pact of 1857 gave equality under the law to non-Muslims, and other liberal measures were introduced even before the Protectorate. During the Second World War, the brief German occupation of Tunisia led to the establishment of forced labour camps for thousands of Jews.

Since independence in 1956, the country has followed the path of moderation in its dealings with Israel. Up to the 1967 Six-Day War, the condition of the Tunisian Jewish population was tolerable. After the Six-Day War, several Jewish shops were burned in Tunis while the monumental Star of David on the front of the great synagogue in Tunis was destroyed. The authorities did their best to keep the peace.

Despite the authorities' concern to allay the fears of the Jewish community, occasional attacks on Jews and Jewish property have occurred, among them the destruction in 1979 of a synagogue on the island of Djerba and in 1983 that of a synagogue in Zaris near the Libyan border.

PRESENT SITUATION

The Tunisian authorities have recently adopted a more welcoming policy towards Tunisian-born Jews who emigrated to France or Israel. Several Tunisian-born rabbis have been invited to visit the country with the apparent aim of attracting Jews as tourists. The French chief rabbi, who was also born in Tunisia, was invited to Tunis as part of a delegation and was received by the president. During this meeting, the president assured his visitors of his country's feelings of friendship towards the Jews and his determination to do everything possible to ensure that the remaining members of the community would be able to live undisturbed by antisemitism.

ASSESSMENT

Despite their liberal treatment by the Bourguiba and Ben Ali regimes, Tunisian Jews have always felt vulnerable. Strong elements in Tunisia have supported the more extreme Arab regimes and there is the potential threat posed by the Islamic fundamentalist movement. Although the regime has pursued policies to limit the influence of Islamic radicals, the latter have a substantial infrastructure which may result in violence against foreigners and Jews identified as foreigners should the domestic situation worsen.

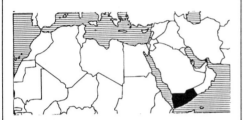

Yemen

General population: 12,533,000
Jewish population: 1,000 (mainly in the Saada region and Raydah)

GENERAL BACKGROUND

The Republic of Yemen was founded in 1990 by the unification of the Yemen Arab Republic (North Yemen) and the People's Democratic Republic of Yemen (South Yemen).

In 1992, the country continued to suffer the repercussions of its pro-Iraq stance in the 1991 Gulf crisis, when Western and Gulf aid donors withdrew support. The economy remained in deep recession throughout the year with high unemployment, mainly due to the sudden return of a million migrant workers driven out of Saudi Arabia. An atmosphere of

political tension and violence developed, with a series of apparently politically-motivated murders, anti-government rioting, and lawlessness, which the government failed to tackle.

Yemen's holding of the first genuine multi-party elections in the Arab world in April 1993 may go a long way to warming relations with the US and help to reverse the country's post-Gulf War isolation.

HISTORICAL LEGACY

Traditionally, Jews have been known in Yemen as silversmiths, producing world-famous jewellery. Their position as artisans resulted largely from a messianic belief that the "return to Zion" was imminent, and that they should therefore not be too attached to the land. Restrictions on their ownership of land and property also pushed the Jews into commerce and trade.

An edict, passed during the Ottoman period but still in force, made it mandatory for Jews to grow side-locks and forbade them from wearing bright colours so as to distinguish them from Muslims. They were also forbidden to carry weapons or wear the ceremonial daggers worn by all Yemeni Muslim men.

Since the 1962 Revolution, Jews have been forbidden to leave Yemen. In addition, Yemeni suspicions of Israel and Zionism have led to further restrictions—Jews' contacts with Jewish and other visitors were strictly limited. They lived under a permanent curfew which prevented them leaving their homes between midnight and dawn. They also had different identity papers from Muslims.

In 1986, two Jews were killed in Raydah in separate incidents by local residents. It has also been alleged that Jews have been forced to convert to Islam and that those who refused were put to death, but there is no evidence to support this. Newspaper articles have told of Yemeni Jews being sold into slavery.

PRESENT SITUATION

Since the recent forced return of hundreds of thousands of Yemeni workers, the government has attempted to show a more "moderate" face to Western powers, from whom aid is sorely needed. It has permitted foreign funds to be used for the construction of a Jewish school and a *mikveh*

(Jewish ritual bath). When Muslim fundamentalists destroyed the foundations of a
Jewish school in January 1992, the government committed itself to facilitate its
reconstruction. Various external Jewish
groups have been working on educational
and cultural projects with the Yemeni
Jewish community but some Yemeni Jews
who have been seen to be too closely
associated with these activities have
received threats from local Muslims.

Criticism was made of Yemen's
treatment of its Jewish community at the
UN Committee on the Elimination of
Racial Discrimination in August 1992.
There have been persistent rumours that
the remnant of this ancient community
may be permitted to emigrate and recent
statements by government ministers have
reaffirmed the right of Jews to travel,
though not to Israel.

Assessment

While antisemitism is apparent in some
extreme fundamentalist circles, Jews now
have greater freedoms: the curfew and
special identity papers no longer apply, and
Jews can now have freer contact with
foreigners, including Jews.

Africa

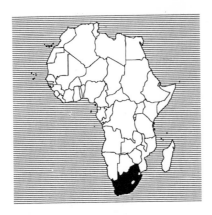

South Africa

General population: 39,400,000
Jewish population: 112,000-116,000 (in Johannesburg, Cape Town, Pretoria, Durban and Port Elizabeth)

GENERAL BACKGROUND

Hopes for a speedy transition to democracy were given a boost when a whites-only referendum in March 1992 gave President de Klerk an overwhelming mandate to pursue negotiations. In May, however, multi-party negotiations broke down. Increased social and political violence, including massacres at Boiphatong and Bisho, and a rise in crime and economic hardship, characterized the second half of the year. According to the South African Human Rights Commission, 3,500 people—including 129 members of the security forces—died as a result of political violence. The year ended on a more positive note with a series of bilateral meetings between the major parties.

HISTORICAL LEGACY

Jews were denied the right to settle at the Cape during the rule of the Dutch East India Company (1652-1795). This practice was abrogated under the relatively enlightened Batavian administration (1803-6) and the British, who inherited the administration, continued to allow Jews into South Africa. In the South African Republic (Transvaal), established by the Voortrekkers in the mid-nineteenth century, non-Protestants (including Jews) remained disenfranchised until after the British occupation in 1902.

Jews, mainly from Lithuania, were among the influx of fortune-seekers following the discovery of diamonds and gold in the late nineteenth century. Their presence generated considerable antisemitism. By the outbreak of the First World War, there were calls to restrict Jewish immigration from Eastern Europe.

During the First World War, Jews were accused of shirking military responsibilities and, in the post-war years, were popularly associated with Bolshevik subversion. By the mid-1920s, the "racial quality" of the Jews and their ability to assimilate were questioned, culminating in the 1930 Quota Act which virtually ended Jewish immigration from Eastern Europe.

There was a surge of popular antisemitism during the 1930s and 1940s against a background of fervent Afrikaner nationalism. It was particularly evident in the rhetoric and actions of "Shirt" movements (most notably Louis T. Weichardt's Greyshirts), the Ossewabrandwag (Oxwagon Sentinel) and Oswald Pirow's New Order. Many key theoreticians in the Afrikaner nationalist movement had imbibed German National Socialist views. Anti-Jewish feeling prompted the governing United Party to introduce the 1937 Aliens Act which curtailed German-Jewish immigration. National Party publications during the Second World War, which were influenced by European fascism, emphasized the racial exclusivity and antisemitic nature of Afrikaner nationalism.

Antisemitism declined rapidly after 1945, although Prime Minister Jan Smuts opposed large-scale Jewish immigration. The Greyshirts and New Order disbanded and, in 1951, the ban on Jewish membership of the Transvaal National Party (the National Party was structured along federal lines) was lifted. Nonetheless, the National Party, in power since 1948, expressed dissatisfaction with disproportionate Jewish involvement in liberal and Communist activities. Anti-Jewish feelings were compounded among the white population by Israel's support for the African bloc at the United Nations in the early 1960s.

Close ties between South Africa and Israel developed in the 1970s, engendering favourable attitudes towards Jews on the part of the white population, although antisemitic outbursts, including Holocaust denial, were prevalent among elements of the white far right.

The majority black population felt betrayed by Israel's close relations with South Africa and were particularly disappointed at alleged military co-operation between the two countries.

Notwithstanding sympathy for the Palestinian people, black leaders have made a clear distinction between anti-Zionism and antisemitism. Nevertheless, there are indications of problems between blacks and Jews, including anti-Jewish attitudes among black élites.

In August 1990, the South African Zionist Federation commissioned a survey in which a sample of 1,031 black and 1,014 white "élites" were questioned about Jews. The survey was widely condemned for its methodology which incorporated a range of misleading questions.

The main findings among blacks were: 17.5 per cent said the Jewish community "irritated" them because, in descending order, they were parasites, snobs, racists, anti-Christian and unpatriotic; 16.5 per cent approved of right-wing antisemitic actions and one-third were uncertain whether or not they approved; and 30 per cent considered the Jewish community to be "mostly a liability" to South Africa. Percentages of whites giving the same responses were: 5.7 per cent, 0.7 per cent and 3.2 per cent respectively.

PARTIES, ORGANIZATIONS, MOVEMENTS

In 1969 the Herstigte Nasionale Party (Reconstituted National Party) was formed to counter deviation from Apartheid philosophy. Although not avowedly antisemitic, the party's official organ, *Die Afrikaner* (circulation 8,000), has featured numerous anti-Jewish articles as well as Holocaust denial material.

In 1981 the Afrikaner Weerstandsbewegig (Afrikaner Resistance Movement, AWB) became active. Its leader, Eugene Terre'Blanche, pursues exclusivist, racist and antisemitic policies. The movement includes a paramilitary outfit, the Storm Falcons, and a crack guerrilla unit, the Ystergarde (Iron Guard).

Antisemitic views are also expounded in numerous small white supremacist movements and cells, including the Blanke Bevrydingsbeweging (White Liberation Movement, or the BBB), the World Apartheid Movement, the Israelites and the Church of the Creator. In terms of membership and influence, these movements are of little consequence.

MANIFESTATIONS

In December, a synagogue in Kimberley was daubed with Nazi slogans. There were a few similar incidents but none of major significance. A register of these is now being kept by the South African Jewish Board of Deputies.

PUBLICATIONS

A range of extreme right-wing newspapers, including *Die Afrikaner* and the *South African Observer* (circulation unobtainable), continue to revile Jews and Israel. Offensive jokes about Nazi concentration camps were published in a Potchefstroom University "rag" (fundraising) magazine. The incident was followed by an apology from the university.

DENIAL OF THE HOLOCAUST

Extreme right-wing groups have close links with Holocaust-deniers. Thus, for example, David Irving undertook a lecture tour which included a visit to Pretoria University, where he was well received by a small group of academics. Irving's most controversial claim was that Israel would be annihilated within eight to ten years, thus putting an end to the "Jewish problem". One of Irving's lectures was cancelled due to threats from the South African Union of Jewish Students. Pressure led to Irving's visit being curtailed.

COUNTERING ANTISEMITISM

The work of the Outreach Programme continued. It was established in 1991 by the South African Jewish Board of Deputies to foster dialogue with opinion-makers in the wider community and to explain Jewish concerns.

Cape Town's Holocaust Memorial Council hosted a Holocaust Educational Project for matriculation pupils. Twenty-one schools from all racial sectors participated.

Substantial contacts existed, and continued to be developed, with the national and regional leadership of various black organizations including the African National Congress, the Pan-African Congress and the Inkatha Freedom Party. Representatives of the Jewish community were present and warmly received at conferences and funerals. The community also participated in the activities of the multi-faith World Conference on Religion and Peace (South African Chapter), particularly in the drawing up of a charter of religious rights and responsibilities which were to be suggested as an addendum to the proposed South African Bill of Rights.

ASSESSMENT

Antisemitism was of marginal significance in South African public life. Ultimately, the fate of South African Jews is tied up with that of the white population as a whole.

The new constitution is almost certain to include a Bill of Rights. This, at least in theory, would be in the interest of all citizens, including the Jewish population, as it would safeguard communal organizations and provide the necessary context within which Jews may continue to flourish.

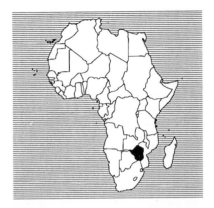

Zimbabwe

General population: 10,000,000
Jewish population: 1,000 (mainly in Harare and Bulawayo)

GENERAL BACKGROUND

The main economic activity is agriculture and the devastating drought in the Southern African region forced a previously food-exporting country to import maize in 1992. Various industries, including steel manufacturing contribute to the economy.

PRESENT SITUATION

President Robert Mugabe, during a tour of peasant areas in July 1992, made a remark that "commercial farmers are hard-hearted people—you would think they were 'Jews'", which created a stir in the Jewish community. The president subsequently apologized to the Zimbabwean Jewish community and good relations between the community and the presidency were restored.

Asia

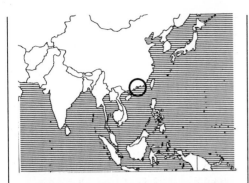

Hong Kong

General population: 6,003,000
Jewish population: under 2,000

GENERAL BACKGROUND

Hong Kong, a British Crown Colony, will revert to China by agreement in July 1997. A major business and financial centre, its economy has flourished through significant integration with China's Guandong province. Many in Hong Kong's intellectual and professional groups are deeply concerned about the future under Chinese control, particularly in the light of Beijing's hostile reaction to Governor Chris Patten's proposals for expanding the franchise.

PRESENT SITUATION

Hong Kong has little history of antisemitism. Most Chinese residents have virtually no information about Jews or Judaism. Nevertheless, occasional manifestations of anti-Jewish prejudice appear in the Chinese-language publications. These occur mainly, but not always, in response to some action taken by Israel. For instance, an article in the Chinese-language "Hong Kong Economic Journal" on 25 February entitled "Is the Gulf War a fraud?" blamed Israel for creating chaos and stirring up trouble in the Middle East.

The author quoted a foreign source as saying "No wonder in the past everybody hated the Jews in Europe and Hitler killed them in concentration camps". The author added that the Jews "don't get along with other people and even their ideas are weird. They stir up trouble here and there and

cause agitation everywhere in the world. The Jews have lots of money and powerful influence in the US and other countries".

For the most part, however, both in Hong Kong and China, the main problem is philosemitism. Many Chinese believe that Jews have great influence in the world and are a conduit to American Jewry and thus to a seat of power. In Hong Kong this is manifested by the view that it is a good thing to have a Jew to advise you on financial matters.

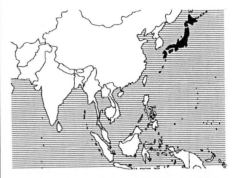

Japan

General population: 124,100,000
Jewish population: fewer than 1,000
(mainly in Tokyo)

GENERAL BACKGROUND

Japan has been making efforts to become a political as well as economic superpower. It has long been a major purveyor of foreign aid, especially to under-developed countries in Asia and Africa. Japan's efforts to assume a greater leadership role are, however, hampered by a slow-moving political process which makes decision-making complicated and, sometimes, impossible. In 1992 the country's domestic political environment was made even more uncertain by ongoing political corruption scandals. Japan's enormous trade surpluses continued to grow leading to further hostility on the part of nations suffering from negative trade balances with Tokyo. Added to all this was an economic crisis fueled by a major decline in stock market values, over-extended banking institutions and a multitude of bankruptcies.

HISTORICAL LEGACY

The Japanese are keenly interested in Jews although most have never met one and they have little or no knowledge of Jewish matters. Jews have been coming to Japan since the mid-nineteenth century with an early Jewish mercantile settlement in Nagasake, followed by small numbers of refugees from the Russian Revolution and Nazi Germany. Antisemitism is not new in Japan and appears in Christian fundamentalism, right-wing nationalist propaganda and Leninist-Stalinist ideologies.

Following the Russian Revolution *The Protocols of the Elders of Zion* was translated into Japanese and, over a number of decades, led to the publication of a number of books portraying a Jewish world conspiracy.

There has also been a philosemitic literature that encourages the Japanese to emulate the Jews in gaining wealth. Readers are advised to follow the supposed Jewish characteristics of shrewdness in the business and financial fields in the context of the influence of "international Jewish capital". Some of these writers subscribe to the "common ancestry" theory which seeks to coopt the history of the Jews in order to promulgate forms of Japanese superiority and imperialism.

PRESENT SITUATION

There has been a marked increase in the publication of anti-Jewish books since the mid-1980s, when Masami Uno's works sold almost a million copies and became best-sellers. Uno and a number of other "experts" argue that the so-called international Jewish conspiracy has led to Japan's current economic difficulties. They also advance a "revisionist" version of the Holocaust.

Although new titles continue to appear, the volume of sales of such books has declined dramatically, leading many to believe that this was a passing fad in the realm of Japanese sensationalist literature. However, we are now entering a new phase in the expression of antisemitic attitudes in Japan through the appearance of articles in weekly journals of the Japanese "yellow press". A June 1992 article in the *Shukan Post*, a tabloid with a readership of 800,000, carried the headline "Stock price manipulation by Jewish capital". The article blamed Jewish-led investment banking firms for causing the crash of the Tokyo stock market and contributing to the serious decline of Japan's economy. In an article in the December issue of the *Shukan Gendai* entitled "Clinton's Jewish strategy towards Japan" it was claimed that the Jews had elected President Clinton and would control his administration to the detriment of Japan.

In January a Japanese television network broadcast a CNN report presented by Cairo-educated commentator Mari Nishimori. She said that if you did not have a Jewish name you could not get into the entertainment business because it was controlled by Jews.

Two major Japanese corporations agreed to co-sponsor in July, August and September a series of lectures by Masami Uno devoted to such topics as the "lies" of Anne Frank's diary and the "myth" of the Holocaust. The seminars were cancelled following a protest to Japan's foreign ministry by an American Jewish source.

ASSESSMENT

All of the above should be seen in the context of the general perception of foreigners in Japan. As the Japanese seek to preserve their homogeneity through conformity to strict cultural and societal codes, they reinforce a sense of uniqueness by making positive and negative comparisons with other highly distinctive ethnic groups such as the Jews. It should also be recalled that many positive books written about Jews, or translated from foreign works, are prominently displayed in major Japanese bookstores. While most Japanese know little or nothing about the Jews, for many they have become a symbol of what the Japanese can aspire to or what they need to fear.

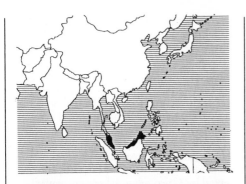

Malaysia

General population: 18,000,000
Jewish population: under 10 (in Penang)

GENERAL BACKGROUND

The prime minister, Dr Mahathir bin
Mohamad, heads the United Malays
National Organization (UMNO), the
leading faction in the governing coalition,
the Barisan Nasional. Since he assumed
office in 1981 he has attempted, with
success, to accelerate economic development and to make Malaysia a leading
spokesman for the Third World. Politics
has become increasingly suffused with an
Islamic content to uphold UMNO's
dominant position and also increasingly
authoritarian.

The Malays (who are Muslims)
comprise a bare majority of the population.
The Chinese account for 35 per cent, and
Indians and other minorities about 13 per
cent. By enforcing an economic policy
which ensures the political dominance of
the "Bumiputras" (ethnic Malays) over the
Chinese and Indian populations, Malaysia
is distinguished by classes of citizenship.

Despite discrimination in economic
and social policy, racial violence has not
erupted for almost a quarter of a century.

HISTORICAL LEGACY

Antisemitic sentiment in Malaysia has been
identified specifically with Prime Minister
Dr Mahathir Mohamad, who in 1986
charged that Zionists and Jews (without
distinction) were attempting to destabilize
the country through a campaign in an
allegedly Jewish-controlled international

media.

In his treatise on the Malay identity,
The Malay Dilemma (Federal Publications,
Malaysia 1970), Dr Mahathir observed that
"The Jews for example are not merely
hook-nosed, but understand money
instinctively. . . . Jewish stinginess and
financial wizardry gained them the commercial control of Europe and provoked an
anti-semitism which waxed and waned
throughout Europe through the ages."

In 1984 the Kuala Lumpur authorities
banned a performance of Ernst Bloch's
work *Schlomo*, which is based on Hebrew
melodies, by the visiting New York
Philharmonic orchestra. Following a
worldwide protest the orchestra omitted
Malaysia from its tour of Asia.

In September 1986 Dr Mahathir said
"The expulsion of Jews from the Holy
Land some 2,000 years ago and the Nazi
oppression of the Jews have taught them
nothing. If at all, it has transformed the
Jews into the very monsters that they
condemn so roundly in their propaganda
materials. They have been apt pupils of Dr
Goebbels."

In recent years Malaysian politics has
been influenced by the role of Islam in
determining the identity of the Malay
community, who have long felt vulnerable
to vigorous Chinese and Indian communities of migrant origin. Dr Mahathir's
attitudes to Israel and the Jews are a
mixture of personal prejudice and political
opportunism. As the Islamic factor became
more central to Malay identity, the
Palestinian cause became increasingly
understood as a co-religionist struggle. In
the light of the role of Islam in intra-Malay
politics, Dr Mahathir's support for Palestinian nationalism and his strictures against
Zionism serve the domestic political
function of upholding the dominant
position of UMNO.

In 1991 Mahathir used UMNO and
the domestic news agency Bernama to
allege that leaders of the Australian Jewish
community were conspiring to overthrow
his government and cause instability. His
allegations of a Zionist plot became
increasingly bizarre. Bernama reported an
anti-Malaysian campaign "orchestrated" by
Australia's "powerful Zionist lobby",
"many of whose leaders have direct and
intimate contact with Prime Minister Bob

Hawke".

Mustapha Yaakub, a spokesman for an UMNO branch, ascribed the alleged "Zionist" motive in destabilizing Malaysia to envy of Malaysia's achievements in the Islamic field.

At a press conference shortly after a summit meeting in Singapore in January 1992 of the Association of Southeast Nations, Dr Mahathir was asked if he continued to believe that a Jewish conspiracy existed in Australia against Malaysia. He replied that he was still gathering evidence.

PUBLICATIONS

The Protocols of the Elders of Zion was in wide circulation in 1983, but then largely disappeared from bookshops. In November 1991 a new edition was published and distributed together with the equally defamatory *A History of Jewish Crimes*. It is inconceivable that a racially offensive publication should survive on public display in Malaysia without the knowledge and consent of the authorities (see entry on **Singapore**). Both these publications remained available for about US $5 throughout Malaysia and copies were on sale at a book shop in Kuala Lumpur's international airport. The shop was reportedly owned by Dr Mahathir's daughter.

Pakistan

General population: 123,000,000
Jewish population: under 10 (in Karachi)

GENERAL BACKGROUND

Pakistan has one of the lowest rates of life expectancy and one of the highest birth rates of natural increase in Asia. The country is poor and relies heavily on imports, especially of petroleum, vehicles and machinery.

Following the rise to power of President Zia in 1977 Islam became increasingly central to the identity of the state. Prime Minister Nawaz Sharif heads a coalition government held hostage by fundamentalist elements.

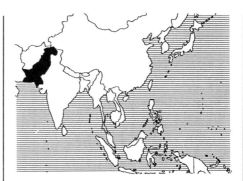

HISTORICAL LEGACY

Until 1947, under the British, the Jewish community felt reasonably secure. Within a year of independence, Pakistan revoked their rights, denying them political representation in the legislative chambers and in all official functions. In 1948, when fighting broke out between the Arab countries and Israel, a mob attacked the Karachi synagogue, looting its contents and destroying the Torah scrolls. There are reports that shortly afterwards the president of the congregation was summarily dismissed from his hereditary position of Justice of the Peace. Many Jews then sold their possessions and fled. The government, fearing the effect on foreign aid and sensitive to international opinion, restored him to his office and provided protection to the remaining community.

By 1964 only 350 Jews were left in Karachi, scratching a living as petty tradesmen and artisans. Records do not show how many resided elsewhere in Pakistan—probably there were few.

The Chel Shalom B'nai Israel Synagogue, which stood behind tenements at the corner of Lawrence Road and Jamillah Street, had been a symbol of pride to a flourishing B'nai Israel community. By 1987 it was in ruins. The community had declined to no more than two or three families.

PRESENT SITUATION

Information about antisemitism in Pakistan is scant and difficult to obtain. It is reported that antisemitic publications originating in the Middle East find their way to Pakistan. The atmosphere in Pakistan remains generally hostile towards Israel and Jews.

The Islamicization of the country,

Iranian influence, has focused more attention on Israel and anti-Zionist articles occasionally appear in the press. The population is largely illiterate and easily swayed by Islamic fundamentalists. The educated classes, who comprise less than 10 per cent of the population appear unconcerned whether there are relations with Israel or not; the fundamentalists are opposed to relations with Israel.

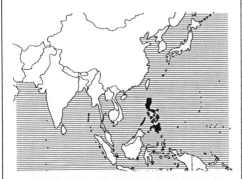

The Philippines

General population: 60,000,000
Jewish population: 100-200

GENERAL BACKGROUND

Widespread poverty and institutionalized corruption continue to characterize life in the Philippines. Nevertheless, the country has acquired a new constitution, the power of Congress has been restored, the labour unions have been re-established and the Supreme Court is an independent arm of government.

PRESENT SITUATION

The intelligentsia and the middle class generally are aware of the Holocaust and sympathetic towards the Jews and Israel.

In 1989 Senator Leticia Shahani called on the Senate to declare the Israeli ambassador, Yoav Behiri, persona non grata after he had criticized Shahani's support for the PLO. According to local press reports, Behiri had used "undiplomatic language". Shahani was championed by the head of the influential Foreign Relations Committee on the grounds that Behiri was interfering in the country's internal affairs.

The local media were divided in their reaction. The leader in the *Daily Globe* read that "The racist notion that Jews are God's privileged chosen people must have gotten into Behiri's head so much that he thinks he holds the privilege, as a mere visitor, to tell Filipino official and the Filipino people what they can and cannot do."

It should be noted that Behiri was a highly controversial ambassador, frequently at odds with his staff and the Jewish community.

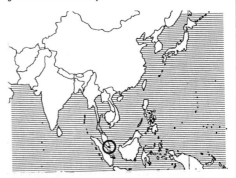

Singapore

General population: 2,800,000
Jewish population: 300-600

GENERAL BACKGROUND

Singapore is a city state with virtually no natural resources. An authoritarian government under Lee Kuan Yew proclaimed independence in 1965. Lee ruled as prime minister until 1990, when he stepped aside for Goh Chok Tong, his selected interim successor. Singapore is widely regarded as being a corruption-free environment, an unusual achievement in Southeast Asia.

The country has benefited economically from strong one-party rule. Political opposition is tolerated but disadvantaged. Lee, ever wary of the delicacy of racial imbalance, has outlawed racially offensive language and material. He has been instrumental in providing stability and prosperity. The media operates under strict guidelines, and guidance.

HISTORICAL LEGACY

Jews in Singapore are not identified by race or given special status as a religious community. There has never been any antisemitism on the part of the administration or in the media. The wider community is largely unfamiliar with Jews, though an increasingly educated population is becoming better informed.

The Jewish community has declined in number since the turn of the century, when two synagogues supported about 2,000 members. There are presently signs of a numerical revival.

MANIFESTATIONS

In 1992 a local "country-and-western" band at Singapore's premier hotel, the Shangri La, included a Nazi song in its repertoire, adapting *The Rodeo Song* to antisemitic and obscene lyrics. The management stepped in when it was brought to their attention.

Also in 1992 a Chinese entrepreneur decided to publicize a discotheque sub-leased by the Pan Pacific hotel by decorating it with Nazi memorabilia. For example, he provided beer mats with pictures of Hitler. After protests from the expatriate community all offensive material was removed. The owner argued that he was unaware that such items could give offence. An editorial in the English-language *Straits Times* considered the affair a fuss over nothing.

PUBLICATIONS

The Protocols of the Elders of Zion and *A History of Jewish Crimes* were found in 1992 to have been printed by a Muslim fundamentalist publisher in Singapore for distribution in Malaysia. It may be presumed that the authorities in Singapore had no prior knowledge and intervened when the matter was brought to their attention.

ASIA: ASSESSMENT

In Asia, antisemitism is essentially an epiphenomenon, except in Malaysia, where Prime Minister Dr Mahathir Mohamad clearly believes that allegations of Jewish conspiracies serve a useful domestic purpose, and in Japan, where the popularity of antisemitic books—a kind of anti-semitism without Jews—is given some significance because of the country's international importance.

Antisemitism in India and Sri Lanka, two countries covered in last year's *Report* is so marginal that they are not included in this year.

Australasia

Australia

General population: 18,500,000
Jewish population: 90,000-100,000
(mainly in Melbourne and Sydney)

GENERAL BACKGROUND

In 1992, the governing Australian Labor
Party was beset by a series of scandals and
forced resignations, and opinion polls
recorded high levels of unpopularity for
Paul Keating's administration.

By the end of the year, however, the
government appeared to have closed the
gap on the Liberal National Party opposition in the opinion polls to such an extent
that a fifth successive election victory in
1993 seemed a distinct possibility. This was
in part due to Keating's willingness to take
strong and popular positions on issues such
as republicanism and Aboriginal land
rights.

Although the Australian economy
remained sluggish throughout 1992.,
Keating's attempts at economic expansion
produced some results. The rate of growth
of GDP was estimated at 2.1 per cent, one
of the highest figures among OECD
countries, while the estimated inflation rate
of 0.8 per cent was one of the OECD's
lowest. However, at 11.3 per cent, unemployment was at a post-1945 high, and was
thought likely to remain at that level for
most of 1993.

HISTORICAL LEGACY

Jews first came to Australia as convicts
with the first Europeans in 1788 and thus
have a considerable historical legitimacy,

perhaps unique in the Diaspora. Until the
1930s most Australian Jews were from
Britain and were English-speaking and thus
met little or no organized antisemitism.
General Sir John Monash, a Melbourne
Jew, was Australia's Commander-in-Chief
during the First World War, while Australia's first native-born Governor-General
(head of state) was another Melbourne Jew,
Sir Isaac Isaacs.

Between 1933 and 1955 about 30,000
Jewish refugees arrived from Europe. There
was some intensified antisemitism just after
the Second World War, but in general the
level of antisemitism has remained low,
with racial and ethnic conflict centred far
more on British Protestant/Irish Catholic,
white/Aboriginal, and (in recent years)
white/Asian divisions.

PARTIES, ORGANIZATIONS, MOVEMENTS

Since the Second World War probably the
most constant antisemitic body has been
the Australian League of Rights (ALR), a
group which propagates a thesis of world
domination engineered by "Zionists" and
"Fabian socialists". The ALR is the
primary distributor in Australia of
antisemitic literature, including Holocaust
denial and "Jewish-Bolshevik conspiracy"
material. It also advocates a programme
based on patriotism, maintenance of links
with Britain and family issues. The ALR
has a following in rural areas, especially in
Victoria and Queensland.

A number of other white supremacist
bodies exist, such as National Action, an
anti-Asian skinhead group; there are also
some antisemitic Christian fundamentalist
bodies. In addition to these groups, there
are a number of individual far right activists
including a Melbourne lawyer, John
Bennett, who has achieved publicity for his
Holocaust denial activities. Other sources
of traditional antisemitism are some East
European ethnic groups which (as in
Canada and elsewhere) migrated after 1945
with antisemitic stereotypes intact. Partially
dormant in recent years, these stereotypes
re-emerged strongly during the Australian
debate on war crimes (see below).

The Lyndon LaRouche movement (see
United States) is coming close to rivalling
the League of Rights in the promotion of
conspiracy theories, especially in rural
Australia.

MANIFESTATIONS

Although there were no acts as serious as the fires set in synagogues in 1991, there were still a number of examples of assault and serious harassment. Although the total number of incidents in 1992 was lower than that for 1991, the tally was still over ten incidents a month and actually increased in the areas of personal harassment and threatening letters. There was a decrease in the number of offensive telephone calls reported, which could well be related to police action to stop this form of harassment in 1991, and a dramatic decrease in reports of anti-Jewish or neo-Nazi graffiti, the most statistically unreliable of categories.

An Australian film entitled *Romper Stomper* opened with considerable publicity. The film depicts with brutal frankness the rise and fall of a violent neo-Nazi gang in a Melbourne slum, although the targets of the gang are Vietnamese rather than Jews. Local spokesmen in the slums insisted that they did not know of the existence of such gangs.

PUBLICATIONS

In recent years the Arabic-language and Muslim press has emerged as a new, disturbing source of open antisemitism. For example, *an-Nahar* of 16 July 1992 carried an article entitled "His blood be upon us and our children". The article, by Michael Haddad, made repeated references to the alleged folly of some Christians who "exonerate today's Jews from the crime of spilling the blood of Christ" and argued that "the presumed Holocaust has been disproved by great writers and historians", and that "the grandchildren" of those who took "the blood of Christ" today "crucify the Arab followers of Christ day and night" and "shed their blood".

RELIGION

At the end of 1991 elements in the Uniting Church in Australia (a 1970s merger between Methodists and most Presbyterians) issued a harsh anti-Israel document which many Jews regarded as antisemitic and certainly as ill-informed. The Moderator of the church apologized for the pain the document had caused to Jews and intensified efforts at interfaith dialogue.

In 1992 the Catholic Church in Australia issued a set of guidelines for relations with the Australian Jewish community which included a strong condemnation of antisemitism. The Anglican Church set in motion moves towards a similar policy. The main concern in this area has been a large number of examples of "triumphalism" and anachronistic discussions of Jews and Judaism in newspapers published by a number of churches and the use by far-right groups of individual churches as places to propagate anti-Jewish myths.

LEGAL MATTERS

Most Australian states have enacted legislation on racial vilification and group defamation in recent years, the chief exception being Victoria (Melbourne), whose Labor government had promised such legislation, as has the federal government. However, in October 1992 the Victorian Labor government lost an election and the new government, the Liberal National Coalition, was reluctant to introduce any legislation. The Jewish community strongly supports such legislation, especially in view of the increased level of attacks on Jewish properties. On the other hand, no prosecutions relating to Jews have as yet been made under these laws in Australia, and most Jews are also aware that they are unlikely to be of major importance except in extreme cases. It is fair to say that anti-defamation specialists have concentrated, with some success, in keeping the mainstream media and political sphere voluntarily free of antisemitism.

In 1992 the federal government announced plans to enact a Racial Vilification Act which would make many antisemitic statements and publications illegal, although Jewish groups were seeking assurances that Jews would be considered an ethnic group by the Act rather than a religious one since religions would not be included within the scope of the Act. A provision of this Act would also give the government wider powers to exclude foreign racialist speakers from Australia.

The first of the anti-racist laws introduced in Australia, in the State of New South Wales, was under review in the past year due to a common belief that it is ineffective. The Jewish community has lodged a complaint over an antisemitic article in the Arabic newspaper *an-Nahar* and this could produce the first result in favour of a complainant.

Legislation relating to the media was amended considerably in 1992 and one of the positive outcomes has been a revised code regarding the broadcasting of racially gratuitous and offensive material by television stations.

In December draft national anti-racism legislation was introduced by the Labor government which, prior to its re-election in March 1993, promised to introduce final legislation early in the life of the new government.

WAR CRIMES ACT

In July the federal government announced that it was unwilling to proceed with further prosecutions under the War Crimes Act, although the two already launched were proceeding slowly with neither case coming to trial in 1992. The government was criticized for this decision by the man chiefly responsible for supervising these prosecutions, Robert Greenwood QC, and by the Jewish community, but the enormous expense of these efforts (an estimated $20 million) and the meagre results convinced the government to bring them to an end.

ASSESSMENT

The level of antisemitism in Australia is unquestionably low, the exception to this state of affairs being a greatly increased number of attacks on Jewish properties in Melbourne and Sydney in 1991. There is no evidence that anyone other than extremists is engaged in peddling antisemitic propaganda. Also of concern is the fact that antisemitic articles appeared in the Arabic press in Australia.

Australia has seldom seen sharp ideological debate and is most unlikely to develop a significant audience for antisemitism at this stage. Any survey of antisemitism in the country must also, in fairness, include those elements which contribute to philosemitism, such as the work of the Council of Christians and Jews, the general awareness in the country

of the Holocaust as a universally-known symbol of supreme evil and considerable popular admiration for the Jewish people and their achievements. The recession which affected Australia in the early 1990s did not appear to produce new sources of antisemitism.

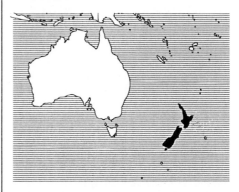

New Zealand

General population: 3,400,000
Jewish population: 5,000 (mainly in Auckland and Wellington)

GENERAL BACKGROUND

As with other countries which have moved to deregulate production and labour markets, New Zealand is experiencing substantial economic, social and political change. The negative effect of a growing level of unemployment and other social problems has been exacerbated by the reduction in welfare provisions, and major social tensions which are expected to grow during the 1990s. There are serious political tensions. The Labour government of 1984-90 adopted a monetarist approach to economic policy, thus confusing traditional political alliances. Green parties and Maori nationalists have grown in strength in the face of this political confusion.

HISTORICAL LEGACY

Unlike similar societies such as Australia and Canada, New Zealand did not have fascist groups in the 1930s. However, antisemitism was to be found among some small farmers and business people who looked to Major C. H. Douglas and Social

Credit for a political answer to their economic woes in the 1930s and later. Here they found arguments about a Jewish conspiracy. This antisemitism proved, however, to be relatively insignificant because Social Credit allied itself with the Labour Party which gained power in 1935.

In the post-war period Social Credit developed two quite different camps. One sought to retain the antisemitic arguments of Douglas; the other rejected them. By 1970 the latter had succeeded in gaining control of Social Credit, which by this time was a political party in its own right. The Douglasites found refuge in the Australian-based League of Rights led by Eric Butler. Butler had been involved in the Australian Social Credit movement in the 1930s and had written an antisemitic book, *The International Jew*, in the late 1940s. He continues to tour New Zealand at regular intervals, and discussed the Holocaust on local "talk-back" radio during 1992.

The League of Rights has been the main vehicle for antisemitic arguments in the sense that it has provided the only link with the limited antisemitism which did appear in the 1930s and its members have sought to maintain arguments about a Jewish conspiracy. The New Zealand League of Rights operates, like its Austral-ian parent, as a pressure group. At their height in the late 1970s, their newsletter was probably sent to around 1,000 people, but currently they are small in number, though committed.

PARTIES, ORGANIZATIONS, MOVEMENTS

The first explicitly fascist groups appeared in New Zealand in the 1960s and they gained new adherents in the 1980s. There are two sorts. The New Zealand Nazi Party invokes a German Nazism for the 1930s and 1940s, while groups such as New Force or the Conservative Front identify with the neo-fascism of the British Na-tional Front. Both wish to retain links with Britain and things British. As organiza-tions—and there are probably less than ten such bodies active at any given time—they attract a very small membership (probably less than 200 for all groups currently active) but they have helped encourage younger New Zealanders, notably skinheads, to adopt racist and antisemitic arguments. This can be observed in antisemitic graffiti,

desecration of Jewish graves, antisemitic pamphlets and, occasionally, threats or attacks on Jews. Attacks are rare but a cause for concern given recent incidents when skinheads or "white power" groups expressed their views publicly and vio-lently. The New Zealand National Front became more active in publishing in 1992 and produced two magazines, *Skinhead* and *Viewpoint*.

RELIGION

Other expressions of antisemitism take a variety of forms. Fundamentalist Christian-ity grew considerably in the 1980s, and some representatives of the trend express a Christian antisemitism. Typical is Barry Smith, a fundamentalist preacher who, in a popular lecture tour in 1991, said he foresaw a world government, a world church exerting "evil influences", and a cashless society based on microchips which would allow "demonic forces to track and programme people to worship the devil". Needless to say, Jews play a major role in instituting this new world order.

Another Christian fundamentalist, Phil Young, talks of "Jewish international bankers who believe that they are God's Israel but reject Christ". He has also described *The Protocols of the Elders of Zion* as the work of Talmudic Jews, "mainly Rabbis" and that "Jews believe in Satan". His most recent book (1992) is entitled *Jesus Says "Go", But the Pharisees Say "No"*.

Young, a New Zealander born in the post-war period, is university-trained and runs a financial advisory service in a provincial town. His arguments echo those of the Social Creditors of the 1930s and probably reflect the economic uncertainty and political changes which occurred in New Zealand in the 1980s.

CONTEMPORARY ISSUES

In addition to the ongoing activities of the above groups, the main issue during 1992 was the findings of the Special Unit on war criminals in New Zealand. The Solicitor General established the Unit in 1991 and, after a year-long investigation, the *Report on War Crimes Investigations* was released in December 1992. The Unit had acted on seventeen names supplied by the was released in December 1992. The Unit had acted on seventeen names supplied by the Wiesenthal Centre, and fourteen of these individuals were investigated. The Unit investigated material from a variety of countries and sources. The final recommendation was that there were no grounds for bringing prosecutions against any of those identified, and that it was very unlikely that there would be reasons for further investigations in the future. The president of the Wellington Jewish Council, Stephen Levine, said it was difficult to disagree with the recommendations given that the evidence gathered by the Special Unit could not be examined. He was disappointed that the matter could not be re-opened if new information came to light. Some public comments questioned the need to spend time and money ($NZ190,000) investigating the claims in the first place.

The issue of the approximately 400 Palestinians deported by Israel to Lebanon at the end of the year gave some individuals an opportunity to attack Israel and a New Zealand event involving the Jewish community. One letter-writer attacked "massive state terrorism conducted daily . . . against all non-Jewish inhabitants in Palestine". This letter appeared in the *Evening Post*, a major daily newspaper. The issue of the deportees was further invoked as grounds for halting a gathering involving the Governor-General of New Zealand and the Wellington Jewish community as part of the 150th anniversary of the Wellington Hebrew Congregation. Israel was said to be a "barbaric state" and Palestinians were described as "slave labour".

Such letters, and radio "talk-back" programmes, have long been a concern among the New Zealand Jewish community. The above letters provoked a response from leaders of the Wellington and national Jewish communities, who protested about their publication. There was further concern that David Irving, the British Holocaust denier, was given airtime on radio in July to state his views.

Early in 1990, a member of the Jewish community had noted Jewish concern at what was described as anti-Jewish material and had complained to the Press Council about anti-Jewish letters published in the New Zealand media. The Press Council invited editors to consider the issue but it appears to have had little effect and radio "talk-back" callers and letters to editors remain a major vehicle for anti-Jewish views.

ASSESSMENT

Debates such as the above, and antisemitic views in general, are a minor part of New Zealand's mainstream politics. There is an audience for such views but they are most likely to be found among those who support a Social Credit tradition or those who are involved in neo-fascist politics. What is disturbing is the way in which the mass media at times uncritically give publicity to those who would trivialize the Holocaust and express antisemitic opinions.

North America

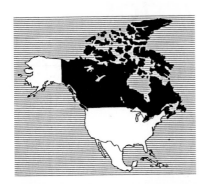

Canada

General population: 26,500,000
Jewish population: 340,000 (main centres: Toronto, Montreal, Vancouver and Winnipeg)

GENERAL BACKGROUND

Canada continued to face major constitutional and political problems in 1992. In the aftermath of the failure in 1990 to ratify the Meech Lake constitutional agreement, secessionist sentiment in Quebec was at record levels. A new constitutional initiative, involving the federal government and the ten provinces, was begun in 1991. This eventually led to the Charlottetown Accord in August, which held out the promise of resolving the outstanding constitutional issues between Quebec and the rest of Canada through the recognition of Quebec as a distinct society, the shifting of powers from the federal to the provincial governments and some structural changes to the federal government, including reform of the Senate. The matter was put to a national referendum in October but was defeated by a combination of opponents who voted against it for different reasons. The failure left the constitutional dilemma unresolved and increased apprehension that Quebec might separate within the next five years. The Jewish community, which is strongly federalist, generally supported approval of the Charlottetown Accord and was very disappointed at its defeat.

Economically, the recession persisted and took a heavy toll. The economic downturn had an adverse effect on the resources of the Jewish community,
resulting in budgetary restraint by communal organizations. Even though the economy was improving by the end of the year, there was continuing concern about attitudes towards minorities.

HISTORICAL LEGACY

Jews have lived in Canada for over 200 years, but most trace their roots to twentieth-century immigrants from Eastern Europe or North Africa. The achievement of equal rights in all respects has required a long struggle by the community. Public and private manifestations of antisemitism were common before the Second World War. Perhaps the worst of these was the government's stubborn refusal to admit refugees from Nazism before and during the war. Since then there has been great progress in eliminating antisemitism. The Jewish community has worked with the government to develop legal tools to combat antisemitism. Nevertheless, antisemitic incidents continue to occur.

PARTIES, ORGANIZATIONS, MOVEMENTS

The Ku Klux Klan, although neither numerous nor consequential, attracted a great deal of attention through various activities. In Quebec three men were arrested for importing 1,250 copies of the American KKK newspaper, while in Manitoba two Klansmen faced criminal charges for promoting genocide after a large amount of Klan material was seized. Even though the men in Quebec were fined, the authorities found additional material in April, prompting Jewish organizations to charge that the fines were too small to be a deterrent. The charges in the Manitoba case were dropped during the trial because key evidence was ruled inadmissible. Late in the year there was a flurry of Klan activity in Nova Scotia, particularly the distribution of hate literature.

Canadian Liberty Net, which allegedly used telephones to spread hate messages in Vancouver, was investigated by a tribunal of the Canadian Human Rights Commission after complaints by the Canadian Jewish Congress (CJC) and others. Examples of the taped messages demonstrated that fostering hatred against Jews and non-whites was the major purpose of the enterprise. Two of the Liberty Net people were convicted of contempt of court for violating an injunction that prohibited them from offering their messages while the tribunal was conducting hearings. Liberty Net was fined $5,000 and Toby McAleer $2,500 for the violations. McAleer admitted that contributors to the messages included a number of well-known American and Canadian hatemongers.

The Heritage Front is the latest and possibly the most significant of the neo-Nazi/white supremacist organizations in Canada. Headed by Wolfgange Droege, a long-time neo-Nazi and supporter of David Duke, the Heritage Front was founded in Toronto some three years ago and has had some limited success in manipulating the media for its own purposes.

The Church of the Creator is potentially the most dangerous racist and antisemitic group in the country. Although the group is extremely small in numbers, its ideology, which emanates from the racist work *The White Man's Bible* and its magazine *Racial Loyalty* (both of which are prohibited material in Canada) advocate everything from white supremacy to racial genocide. Its Canadian leader, George Burdie (otherwise known as the Rev Eric Hawthorne) is a twenty-three-year-old semi-articulate individual with significant links with the Heritage Front.

In other matters, the Aryan Resistance movement of British Columbia, whose leader admires Hitler, set up headquarters in a Vancouver suburb. In July American neo-Nazis Tom and John Metzger were deported for lying to immigration officers when they entered Canada. They tried to conceal their intention to attend a meeting of the white supremacist Heritage Front.

MANIFESTATIONS

According to B'nai Brith Canada's annual audit of antisemitic incidents, the total number of examples of either harassment or vandalism declined after rising annually since 1987. On a countrywide basis there were 150 incidents of harassment and 46 of vandalism, for a total of 196, compared to 251 in 1991. Despite the overall decline, there was continued reason for concern. First, the 1990 and 1991 figures were inflated by a number of incidents sparked

by the Iraqi invasion of Kuwait and the Gulf War. In fact, the total number of incidents for 1992 was still the third highest in the eleven years for which B'nai Brith's League for Human Rights has been conducting its audit. Secondly, there was an outbreak of antisemitic vandalism in Montreal at the beginning of 1993, too late to be counted in the 1992 statistics, but an indication that 1992's decline may have masked the persistence of an underlying phenomenon.

By far the bulk of the incidents (97) occurred in Toronto while Montreal and Ottawa experienced 25 each. There was a decline in the western part of the country which was attributed to tougher law enforcement. Ontario and Quebec remain the focal points of hate group activity.

Desecrations of Jewish cemeteries and houses of worship continued to be a popular activity among antisemitic groups. In January it was discovered that a computer bulletin board containing antisemitic messages and hate propaganda was being run out of Montreal. The man behind the bulletin board was affiliated with the racist Canadian National Party. Various forms of legal action were undertaken in order to shut it down. In February eight tombstones were defaced with graffiti in a Jewish cemetery near Montreal. Antisemitic slogans were written on the monuments. Again in Montreal posters depicting a worldwide Jewish conspiracy were discovered in the downtown and east end areas during Passover. A B'nai Brith spokesman blamed a lax judicial system for emboldening hatemongers. In Winnipeg the large Rosh Pina synagogue was vandalized by neighbourhood teenagers in April. Three Toronto synagogues were defaced with swastikas and antisemitic slogans in June.

Neo-Nazis planned a rally for the town of Ste Anne de Sorel, Quebec, at the end of July. The Aryan Festival was sponsored by White Power Canada and a KKK group. Various anti-racist groups urged the provincial government to stop the event. The rally was held nevertheless, but only about seventy people participated. Vigorous action by the authorities, including local officials in the region, helped to discourage attendance.

A vacant house in Kitchener, Ontario, owned by a Jewish woman who publicly opposed the speaking activities of British Holocaust-denier David Irving was burned down in November. Also in Kitchener a young man was charged with uttering a death threat against one of the anti-Irving protesters. Toronto police seized a large cache of weapons that belonged to a man connected to white supremacist groups; the weapons included submachine guns and a rocket launcher. In December many Ottawa Jews and Jewish organizations received antisemitic material in the mail. Antisemitic stickers were also affixed to Jewish-owned businesses in the city.

PUBLICATIONS

B'nai Brith filed a complaint with the Quebec Press Council against articles and cartoons which appeared in the Montreal newspaper *La Presse* in 1988-89. It alleged that the articles, which dealt with difficulties in the relationships between Hasidim and French Quebecois in the suburb of Outremont, lacked fairness and sensitivity. In February the Press Council rejected the complaint. Afterwards a B'nai Brith spokesman reiterated his objections to the use of "vicious ethnic stereotypes". Early in October *La Presse* was compelled to apologize for a front-page cartoon that linked controversial Canadian Jewish writer Mordecai Richler with Hitler. In Vancouver a columnist in a weekly paper expressed some support for James Keegstra's contention that there was a world Jewish conspiracy and suggested that Jews might be responsible for the Holocaust. Keegstra had recently been convicted for promoting hatred against Jews. CJC protested in October to the Canadian Radio and Television Commission (CRTC) because the Toronto radio station CJCL had used an antisemitic stereotype in a commentary on high parking prices near the baseball stadium. The station declined to apologize on the air pending the CRTC's resolution of the complaint. The station subsequently issued an apology. In another radio incident CJC in Montreal protested against CJMS broadcaster Claude Jasmin, who had a history of uncomplimentary comments towards Jews, for describing Hasidic Jews in Outremont as racist in a Radio-Canada television programme. Further, it should be noted that National television broadcaster Dini Petty

uttered the remark "Hymie" during one of her interview shows in regard to divorced couples in which the husband refuses to pay alimony. Following complaints by the CJC, Ms Petty issued a nationally-broadcast apology.

MAINSTREAM POLITICS

The relatively new Reform Party, which has yet to win a seat in the House of Commons, has been plagued by reports of hostility towards minorities. In an interview with the *Canadian Jewish News* in January, party leader Preston Manning tried to dispel such fears. Manning disavowed the extremists in his party and welcomed Jewish members as the best way to "inoculate the party from the problem". Nevertheless, shortly afterwards accusations were made by a Toronto newspaper that members of the racist Heritage Front had infiltrated the local branch of the Reform Party. The Front's leader, a former KKK recruiter, joined and two Front members were appointed to the board of a local Reform association. Manning reaffirmed that "there is no room in the Reform Party for people who hold racist positions". The controversial members were expelled in the wake of the unfavourable publicity. Yet in June the highest ranking Jew in the party, Michael Lublin, resigned, charging widespread racism and antisemitism in the rank and file and even among some officials. He cited "routine" racist and antisemitic remarks by members and organizers, asserting that "unless you're white and Christian, you're not really going to get anywhere in Reform". Party spokesman Tom Flanagan responded that the party had rooted out racists vigorously and in a timely manner and was determined to stamp out racism within the party.

Norman Spector was appointed Ambassador to Israel in January, the first Jew to hold that post. There was an outcry in some quarters when he was named. The Canadian Arab Federation's president was particularly vehement in his objections, asserting that Spector's "primary interest will be in serving the interests of the international Zionist movement and in supporting Israel". He also suggested that Spector's first loyalty might be to Israel rather than Canada. The new ambassador stated that he had "no doubt" that the Department of External Affairs had excluded Jews from high diplomatic appointments in Israel. And foreign service officer Aharon Mayne said that Jews were still discouraged from applying for Middle East postings.

The publication of Mordecai Richler's *Oh Canada! Oh Quebec!* raised a storm, in part because of his contention that anti-semitism was a longstanding and continuing force in Quebec politics. Several Quebecois politicians and commentators called on the Jewish community to disavow Richler's positions. Richler, in return, asked whether "Jews have to cleanse themselves because I have written what I consider to be a fair book?". He criticized CJC for having felt compelled to distance the community from him and defended his allegations about antisemitism in Quebec. CJC, for its part, questioned the facts upon which Richler based his antisemitism charges.

BUSINESS AND COMMERCE

The big issue during the year concerned allegations by a Jewish employee of the New York subsidiary of a major Canadian brokerage house that antisemitic attitudes and practices were tolerated in the company. The employee, Simon Israel, was dismissed from his job amid much controversy. He contended that he and other employees had been the target of ethnic slurs on more than one occasion. Jewish organizations in Canada intervened forcefully with ScotiaMcLeod Inc. and its parent company, the Bank of Nova Scotia. One Toronto synagogue threatened to move its account with the Bank unless a satisfactory solution was reached. The main concern was that the company had not disciplined those employees who had been charged with antisemitism by Israel. He contended that the head office had been dilatory in dealing with his accusations, which dated back to 1989. Eventually a settlement was reached between the company and Israel, which involved the demotion of two employees who had been accused of making antisemitic remarks. But several Jewish community officials claimed that such action came only after adverse media publicity and that the company was interested only in damage control, rather than rooting out discriminatory attitudes.

GRASSROOTS

A doctoral dissertation in political science at Université Laval in Quebec created a controversy. The author, Esther Delisle, wrote on the subject of "Anti-Semitism and Extreme Right-Wing Nationalism in Quebec from 1929-39". She was subjected to an inordinate delay in having the thesis accepted, presumably because of dissatisfaction over her contentions regarding the centrality of antisemitism in the intellectual life of Quebec, especially due to the influence of the late Lionel Groulx, a priest and historian who had a great influence on the development of Quebec nationalism. She also documented the frequency of antisemitism in the Montreal newspaper *Le Devoir* during the 1930s, stating that "Richler was right; it was like *Der Sturmer*". The thesis was eventually accepted over objections by some members of her committee and then published as a book. Many Quebec intellectuals were outraged by her charges against Groulx, making her the object of considerable opprobrium. In a community near Toronto teacher Paul Fromm was investigated for alleged links to white supremacist organizations. CJC called for his dismissal on the grounds that he was unfit to teach. In a similar case, New Brunswick teacher Malcolm Ross, who had earlier lost his teaching job because of his antisemitic publications, tried to convince an appellate court that his removal by a human rights tribunal was unconstitutional.

DENIAL OF THE HOLOCAUST

The visit to Canada by David Irving focused a great deal of attention on his Holocaust-denial efforts. Immediately his speaking tour for November was announced, efforts were made by the Simon Wiesenthal Centre in Toronto to have him barred from the country on the grounds that the German law under which he was convicted was equivalent to Canada's anti-hate law. CJC also opposed the visit. The government agreed and notified Irving, then in the USA, that he would not be admitted, thus jeopardizing planned speeches in at least seven cities. Irving sneaked in, but was eventually deported to Britain. However, he did speak in Victoria and Toronto before being apprehended. In a separate matter, Irving sued the federal minister for multiculturalism, Gerry Weiner, for defamation in connection with an earlier visit.

In July, the *Phoenix Liberator*, a Holocaust-denial publication, was mailed to several hundred Jewish leaders. B'nai Brith and the CJC called on the government to declare it as hate propaganda and act accordingly against the distributors under the criminal law.

OPINION POLLS

Sociologists Robert Brym and Rhonda Lenton published a study entitled *The Distribution of Anti-Semitism in Canada in 1984* which was based on a random sample survey of the Canadian population. Among their findings were the following: antisemitic attitudes were more common in Quebec, New Brunswick, and Newfoundland than elsewhere in the country; Catholics were twice as likely to dislike Jews as Protestants; about a quarter of Francophone Catholics disliked Jews compared to the national average of about 14 per cent; and that antisemitism was inversely related to socioeconomic status.

LEGAL MATTERS

Cases of vital interest to the Jewish community made their way through the courts during the year. Most of them had been in litigation for years. James Keegstra, former high school social studies teacher and mayor of Eckville, Alberta, was convicted for the second time of promoting hatred against Jews. His first conviction was overturned by the Supreme Court of Canada. Keegstra was fined $3,000 but planned to appeal. The Crown also appealed, asking for a prison term. On the other hand, Toronto printer Ernst Zundel had his conviction for spreading false news (i.e., Holocaust denial) reversed because the Supreme Court found the law to be unconstitutional on freedom of expression and vagueness grounds. Jewish organizations both condemned the decision and looked for new legal avenues so that Zundel might again be prosecuted. Zundel had been convicted twice and had been in the courts for seven years, but emerged with no conviction that would stick.

In New Brunswick the Court of

Queen's Bench upheld the decision to dismiss Malcolm Ross from his teaching post on account of his antisemitic writings. Ross planned to appeal. In another matter, Al Waddell, a member of the racist Posse Comitatus, was arrested in British Columbia in January and held for extradition to the USA on a variety of weapons charges.

Alleged war criminals were the other main focus of legal proceedings. Jacob Luitjens, a former professor in British Columbia who had collaborated with the Nazis in his native Holland during the Second World War, was stripped of Canadian citizenship and deported to the Netherlands to stand trial, thereby concluding a lengthy immigration case in Canada. Nazi rocket scientist Arthur Rudolph, who tried to visit Canada, was also deported. Imre Finta, who had been acquitted of charges under Canada's war crimes legislation, faced an appeal by the Crown to the Supreme Court. Charges against Michael Pawlawski, accused of participating in the killing of nearly 500 Jews and Poles in Belorussia in 1942, were dropped by the Crown after adverse rulings on the admissibility of evidence by the judge that made it impossible to present a case. In a new case, Radislav Grujicic, originally from Yugoslavia, was charged with ten counts of murder and other crimes for his activities between 1941 and 1944 while a police officer. In an analysis of the government's handling of the war criminals' matter during the five years since the passage of the war crimes legislation, B'nai Brith's David Matas was highly critical of lack of action by the prosecutors and unsatisfactory progress in dealing with actual and potential cases. "There is no area of the law where action is more lethargic", he charged.

COUNTERING ANTISEMITISM

Canadian Jews were not alone in the fight to combat racism and antisemitism. In Winnipeg the Coalition for Human Equality was formed at the end of 1991. B'nai Brith's League for Human Rights was a key member. A top priority of the coalition was Manitoba's school prayer policy. In Ontario the CJC forged a coalition with the Native Canadian Centre in fighting both the Heritage Front and Paul Fromm. British Columbia Jews began to work together with anti-racist organizations on issues of minority rights. Quebec's department of education encouraged students to participate in an international essay contest on antisemitism organized by the Israeli government. The city of Ottawa adopted a regulation banning the use of its facilities by groups likely to incite discrimination, contempt, or hatred of identifiable groups. In September the government of Ontario announced a plan to combat antisemitism. The Ontario Anti-Racism Secretariat declared antisemitism a form of racism and initiated educational and political action to create barriers to racist activity. Finally, Canadian MPs joined colleagues from fifty-three countries to form the Inter-Parliamentary Council Against Antisemitism.

ASSESSMENT

Antisemitism remained a problem in Canada, though it was limited in scope. Incidents of vandalism were particularly vexing for Jews. The existence of anti-hate legislation is helpful in combatting antisemitism, though the protracted nature of legal proceedings may be a deterrent to the use of the Criminal Code. Generally antisemitism seemed to be at the fringes of society and did not constitute a major problem in mainstream social, cultural, and political life. On the other hand, accusations of antisemitism in the Reform Party and the nature of some debates in Quebec, especially those concerning Mordecai Richler and Esther Delisle, were disturbing. The recognition of the seriousness of antisemitism by governments suggests that existing threats can be contained.

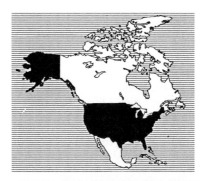

United States of America

General population: 248,710,000
Jewish population: 5,800,000 (mainly in New York, Los Angeles, Chicago, Philadelphia, Miami, Boston and Washington DC)

GENERAL BACKGROUND

Nineteen hundred and ninety-two, a presidential election year, signaled a new emphasis on domestic policy on the part of elected officials, candidates and in the general body politic. The election of Bill Clinton as president was viewed by many observers as heralding opportunities for movement in a number of areas, including the domestic legislative arena, the Arab-Israeli peace process and US-Israel bilateral relations. At the same time, questions were raised with respect to the re-emergence as a potential political force of a fundamentalist Christian "religious right". Additionally, salient in the public affairs picture was the urban agenda, which many felt had been neglected during the Reagan and Bush years, including issues related to a perceived increase in bias and bigotry in society.

HISTORICAL LEGACY

Owing to the singular nature of American society—a society based on the principles of democratic pluralism, with the separation of church and state firmly entrenched as constitutional law—antisemitism did not take root in the United States in the same manner or to the same degree as it did in Europe, where it was embedded in the institutions (often the formal institutions) of power.

During the seventeenth and eighteenth century—the periods of colonial America and the new nation—there were few manifestations of antisemitism: indeed, the Jews were but a tiny proportion of the total population. During the early years of the Republic a certain degree of exclusion from public office did exist. But as protective measures were constitutionally incorporated in both federal and state jurisdictions, these restrictions were ultimately removed.

Antisemitism was not a serious issue until the Civil War. In 1862 General Ulysses S. Grant, at the time commander in the Tennessee district, issued the infamous General Order Number 11 in which he unfairly identified Jews as being the worst offenders in a smuggling operation and expelled all Jews "as a class" from all territory under his jurisdiction. Jews were singled out because antisemitism, previously almost non-existent in the USA, had been aroused—in a classic pattern of Jewish scapegoating—by the turmoil of war.

Antisemitism of a racialist bent emerged during the highly nationalistic 1890s, a period during which the large-scale immigration of Jews that characterized the next three decades began. The incorporation of overt racism in American antisemitism followed the European nineteenth-century pattern and informed "nativist" moves to restrict immigration. A leading nativist, Madison Grant, condemned the Jews for allegedly mongrelizing the nation in his 1916 book *The Passing of the Great Race.*

Another result of the nativist trend was the re-emergence in the early twentieth century of the Ku Klux Klan, which promoted antisemitism and became a potent force in a number of communities.

In the early twentieth century antisemitic stereotypes proliferated in the popular culture of vaudeville and the stage and later in motion pictures. But two events during the early decades of the twentieth century galvanized Jewish reaction to antisemitism. In 1913 Leo Frank, a Jew, was wrongfully convicted of the murder of a Christian girl in his factory in Atlanta, Georgia. In 1915 Frank, a victim

of rumours, slanders, and calls to anti-Jewish prejudice, was removed from his prison cell by a vigilante mob and lynched.

In the 1920s automobile-maker Henry Ford, picking up from an American edition of *The Protocols of the Elders of Zion* the libel of an international Jewish conspiracy, conducted a seven-year-long propaganda campaign through his newspaper, the *Dearborn Independent,* against what he termed *The International Jew.*

The 1930s, the era of the American depression, was a time of distinct anti-Jewish bias in many areas of the social order. Economic and social antisemitism (that is, large-scale discrimination against Jews in employment, higher education, and housing) combined with virulent political antisemitism resulting from the rise of Nazism and fascism in Europe. The last major burst of antisemitism in America came during this period, with an upsurge of ideologically-motivated and political anti-Jewish activity. The era gave rise to domestic anti-Jewish bigots such as Father Charles Coughlin, Gerald L.K. Smith and William Dudley Pelley, leader of the Silver Shirts. It also witnessed the rise of the German-American Bund and its leader Fritz Kuhn and the notorious anti-Jewish speech of the aviator-and American hero-Col. Charles A. Lindbergh to an "America First Committee" rally.

Especially influential was Father Coughlin, a Catholic priest whose weekly radio broadcasts which contained an openly antisemitic message reached millions in the 1930s. Coughlin's campaign paved the way for isolationist organizations such as the America First Committee to attract antisemites to their banners.

The 1930s also witnessed the establishment of community relations councils in Jewish communities around the country, organized for the prime purpose of serving as "fire brigades against antisemitism" and supplementing the work of national Jewish "defence" agencies that had been founded earlier in the century.

The 1940s, a period of cohesiveness as America went to war against Nazism, fascism and Japanese imperialism, saw a diminution of some forms of overt antisemitism. Nonetheless, there was continuing anti-Jewish bias in employment and housing and in social clubs and other "polite" forms of discrimination. Quotas on Jewish students also remained at many major universities.

The 1950s was an era in which the American Jewish communal agenda was almost synonymous with the civil rights struggle. In the years following the 1954 decision of the US Supreme Court in the case of *Brown v. Board of Education*, efforts to end official racial segregation of blacks in the United States caused serious social turmoil and led to some scapegoating of Jews, a re-emergence of the Ku Klux Klan and the growth of "White Citizens Councils", and the proliferation of antisemitic groups, mostly on the extremist fringe.

The general experience during the post-war years has been that antisemitism lost much of the ideological strength it had achieved during the previous decades. Serious manifestations of behavioural antisemitism have not been a factor in the United States. There has been little political antisemitism—arguably the most virulent form of the disease—and discriminatory barriers have continued to fall in all areas of American society, including the corporate world. Perhaps most significant is the continued decline, as measured over the past thirty-five years, of negative attitudes towards Jews in all areas of the society.

Notwithstanding these trends, there have been some noteworthy manifestations of antisemitism during the past three decades. In 1960, during a two-month swastika-daubing epidemic, 643 desecrations of synagogues and other Jewish property throughout the United States took place.

The late 1950s and 1960s also witnessed the rise of radical right-wing groups promoting a theory that included, on the part of some, the notion of a Jewish world conspiracy.

In recent years elements on both the far right and far left have articulated antisemitic rhetoric. Some black nationalists, in the guise of anti-Zionism—a transparent camouflage since often the target was not Israel but American Jews—have espoused antisemitism as well. Much anti-Zionist rhetoric at the United Nations in New York, and some of its agencies elsewhere, challenged the legitimacy of the state of Israel, was thus a challenge to the peoplehood of the Jews, and therefore antisemitic. But UN-based rhetoric had little influence in increasing antisemitism in the USA.

Also during the latter part of the 1980s and continuing into the 1990s the number of incidents of antisemitic vandalism and harassment rose steadily around the country. Notwithstanding these manifestations, the general diminution of most forms of antisemitic expression, and of attitudinal antisemitism, continued. Analysts suggest that there is no contradiction between the rise in the number of acts of antisemitic vandalism and the decline in attitudinal antisemitism: those relative few who hold antisemitic views have been in recent years—a period of general decline of societal taboos—more likely to express these feelings in a destructive manner.

It is important to note that the pattern has been that "conflict" situations that carry with them the expectation of an increase in expression of antisemitism—for example, the oil crisis of the 1970s, the farm crisis of the 1980s and, most dramatically, the Pollard affair, which invoked clearly the question of "dual loyalty"—did not result in increased expressions of antisemitism or antisemitic attitudes. This was not the case in America before the Second World War, when "conflict" situations did lead to antisemitic expression.

Two recent events suggest that certain inhibiting factors may be weakening. President George Bush at his 12 September 1991 news conference, referring to pro-Israel activists who had converged on Washington to press for loan guarantees, characterized the legitimate Jewish grass-roots advocacy as "powerful political forces". And syndicated columnist Patrick J. Buchanan, commenting in August 1990 on the then-developing Gulf crisis, characterized American Jews as the "'amen' corner" for the Israeli defence ministry. These two sets of remarks were direct responses to "conflict" situations and were troubling.

PARTIES, ORGANIZATIONS, MOVEMENTS

There has been a general diminution in both the membership and influence of racist and antisemitic organizations. The estimated total membership of all "hate groups" in the United States is 20-25,000. The number of discrete hate organizations totaled 346. Such groups for the most part remained on the fringes of society. Nonetheless, extremist groups remained a source for concern as they have been progenitors of occasional manifestations of violence. The following were active in 1992:

Liberty Lobby: the major antisemitic propaganda organization in the USA, Liberty Lobby, founded in 1955 by Willis A. Carto, a professed admirer of Adolf Hitler, continued its pre-eminent position as a propagator of anti-Jewish bigotry in the garb of patriotism or "populism". The organization's newspaper, *Spotlight*, which once reached 300,000 readers, still maintains a circulation of approximately 100,000. In recent years Liberty Lobby has built a sizable broadcasting base: its talk-show, "Radio Free America", is carried on more than 300 US radio stations and on short wave to Europe, the Middle East, and elsewhere. Also, Willis Carto is the key American figure in Holocaust denial in the USA being the founder and prime mover of the Institute for Historical Review.

Ku Klux Klan: the total membership of the different factions collectively known as the Ku Klux Klan is slightly over 4,000, with the ten-year decline in membership having come to a halt in 1991 and with perhaps a small upswing in 1992. The two major Klan organizations are the Knights of the Ku Klux Klan, based in Arkansas, and the Invisible Empire, Knights of the Ku Klux Klan, based in North Carolina. The two groups have a combined membership of 3,000.

The old Protestant fundamentalism in the KKK religious bias—and that of a number of other extremist groups—is in large measure being replaced by the doctrine propagated in the "Identity" churches, whose hallmark is antisemitism (see below). This has increased the various Klans' emphasis on antisemitism. As one means of furthering their antisemitic agenda, the Klans have viewed Nation of Islam leader Louis Farrakhan as a black whom they can support. According to the *Klansman*, unlike "Jew-controlled puppets like Martin Luther King", Farrakhan "is well aware of the Jewish menace".

"Identity" Churches: prominent among purveyors of antisemitism are the various branches of a racist pseudo-religion known as "Identity", which preaches that Jews are "children of Satan" and "a race of vipers, Anti-Christs who have been a curse to true Israel". "True Israel" are, according to Identity doctrine, the Anglo-Saxons, descendants of the Ten Lost Tribes who are the "chosen people". (This doctrine is derived from Anglo-Israelism, a doctrine that originated in Great Britain in the nineteenth century.) The pre-eminent Identity-related group in the USA is Aryan Nations, a Nazi-like organization based at Hayden Lake, Idaho, where annual "world congresses" provide instruction on urban terrorism and guerilla warfare.

The Identity doctrine and its antisemitism have been extremely influential with members of the contemporary Ku Klux Klan groups, replacing traditional Protestant fundamentalism.

American Nazis: "neo-Nazis" in America—the remainders and/or imitations of George Lincoln Rockwell's American Nazi Party—are still present, although in small numbers. Their input with respect to antisemitism in the USA is negligible.

Neo-Nazi "Skinheads": neo-Nazi skinheads have menaced numerous American communities over the past eight years. The membership figures of hard-core Nazi skinheads, as of 1992, stood at approximately 3,000 nationwide. Violence committed by skinheads has been racist in nature, targeting blacks, Jews, Asians, other groups and gays.

White Aryan Resistance (WAR) is a racist organization headed by a former Klan leader named Tom Metzger.

The LaRouche Cult: the bizarre pseudo-political activities of the fanatical followers of Lyndon LaRouche continued during 1992. Antisemitism is a mainstay of the LaRouche network and its rhetoric. His publications—the *New Federalist* (formerly *New Solidarity*) and *Executive Intelligence Review*—single out prominent Jews, Jewish families and Jewish organizations for special abuse and he finds a "hard kernel of truth" in the antisemitic forgery *The Protocols of the Elders of Zion*. In 1988 LaRouche and six of his followers were convicted of conspiring to defraud the US Internal Revenue Service and of deliberately defaulting on loans from contributors. LaRouche is currently serving his sentence in a US federal prison.

MANIFESTATIONS

The Anti-Defamation League's annual audit of antisemitic incidents reported a decline, for the first time in six years, in the number of such incidents in the USA in 1992. A total of 1,730 antisemitic incidents were reported during the year, 8 per cent fewer than in 1991. The most serious acts—assaults against individuals and acts of harassment—declined by 8 per cent from 1991 to 874 in 1992.

Other than the reported acts of antisemitic vandalism and harassment, there were few noteworthy manifestations of behavioural antisemitism during 1992.

PUBLICATIONS

Unlike a generation ago, there are no major national publications that espouse antisemitism. Among the more important antisemitic periodicals are:

Spotlight, Washington DC, Liberty Lobby (weekly)

Klansman, North Carolina, Invisible Empire, KKK (bi-monthly)

Journal of Historical Review, California, Institute for Historical Review (quarterly)

Robb's Victory Report, Arkansas, Knights of the Ku Klux Klan (monthly)

The Truth at Last, Georgia, independent publisher (monthly)

Liberty Bell, West Virginia, independent publisher (monthly)

National Vanguard, Virginia, National Alliance (irregular)

WAR, California, White Aryan Resistance (irregular)

The most recent published circulation figure for *Spotlight* is approximately 100,000, significantly lower than its readership a decade ago. Figures for the others are not available but a reasonable estimate would be within a range of 2,000-3,000 at the lower end and 12,000-15,000 at the upper end.

Numerous books with antisemitic content were on sale in 1992.

MAINSTREAM POLITICS

Political antisemitism, arguably the most virulent form of antisemitic expression, was not a factor in the USA during 1992 and has not been a factor in American politics for many decades. Nonetheless, antisemitism was a factor, albeit a marginal one, in the candidacies of David Duke and Patrick J. Buchanan for the American presidency.

Pat Buchanan, a columnist and former White House staffer, had over the years articulated numerous anti-Israel and Jew-baiting remarks—including his famous August 1990 "'amen'-corner" comment, his defence of Nazi war criminals, and other assertions—characterized by many as antisemitic. Although his vote fell far behind that of the incumbent president, George Bush, Buchanan received high visibility at the Republican National Convention in August 1992 with a nationally-televised address in which he articulated many of his anti-inclusivist themes.

Duke, a veteran antisemite and political extremist who had been a neo-Nazi and Klan leader and founder of the National Association for the Advancement of White People, dropped out of the race in April 1992.

The candidacies of Buchanan and Duke raised the question of the willingness of a segment of the American body politic to embrace a candidate's programmes and vote for that person, despite his or her antisemitism and racism. These candidacies raised questions about the ability of societal taboos to inhibit, at the level to which the American Jewish community has become accustomed, political and other forms of antisemitism.

Also of concern was a comment by President Bush, at a 12 September 1991 news conference on the Israeli loan guarantees matter, in which, conjuring up classic antisemitic stereotypes of Jewish manipulation, power, and control, he characterized Jewish activists who had come to Washington to press for the guarantees as "powerful political forces", while "we've got one lonely little guy down here". President Bush later apologized for this remark.

CULTURAL LIFE

While the lyrics of a number of pop music artists raised some questions during 1992, this was not a significant area of concern. An emerging issue was that of "talk-radio" programmes that provide a forum for often

unchallenged antisemitic and racist rhetoric. Additionally, through public-access
television channels, racist and antisemitic
groups had the opportunity to air programmes preaching their message of
bigotry in a number of large cities and
numerous smaller communities around the
country.

ANTISEMITISM ON THE CAMPUS

The most widely publicized vehicle for the
expression of antisemitism on the campus
in late 1991-early 1992 was the submission
of Holocaust-denial advertisements to
campus newspapers around the country by
Bradley R. Smith, a Holocaust "revisionist"
(see **Denial of the Holocaust**). The spate of
advertisements raised questions about the
efficacy of campus institutions in responding to and counteracting antisemitism.
Jewish campus organizations—particularly
B'nai B'rith-Hillel—proved effective in
responding to this issue.

Most Jewish students and faculty
members on college and university campuses feel secure. Nevertheless, many
among the Jewish student leadership
continue to feel uneasy, as antisemitic
expression occurs around "flash points",
such as invited speakers—for example,
Nation of Islam leader Louis Farrakhan
and black activist Kwame Toure (formerly
Stokely Carmichael)—who carry an
antisemitic message. Additionally, in the
current climate on many campuses, Jewish
students bear the brunt of the reality that
expressing pro-Israel sentiments is not
"politically correct". The misuse of
"political correctness", while not
antisemitic in itself, often deligitimizes
Jewish values and concerns.

In Los Angeles, after months of delay
and amid rising indignation in the Jewish
community, the administration of the
University of California, Los Angeles, took
action in May 1992 against the black
student magazine *Nommo* for its persistent
"Highly-offensive and blatantly antisemitic
statements". *Nommo* had approvingly cited
excerpts from *The Protocols of the Elders of
Zion* and Henry Ford's *The International
Jew: The World's Foremost Problem* and
had published other antisemitica. The
university action came as result of an
approach spearheaded by the Los Angeles
Jewish Community Relations Council, the

Los Angeles Hillel Council, the Anti-
Defamation League and a faculty "teach-
in".

As a means of enhancing the counter-
action of antisemitism on the campus, and
providing for other intergroup-relations
needs, a number of campus-based community relations councils—cooperative efforts
between local Hillel groups and Jewish
community relations councils—were
organized.

With respect to the total number of
antisemitic incidents on college campuses,
according to the Anti-Defamation League
114 such incidents were reported on sixty
campuses in the USA during 1992, a 12 per
cent increase over 1991.

DENIAL OF THE HOLOCAUST

In the United States as elsewhere, Holo-
caust "revisionism" is used as a vehicle for
antisemitic expression. The vanguard of
Holocaust deniers in the USA is the
California-based Institute for Historical
Review, founded in 1979 as an offshoot of
Liberty Lobby by Willis Carto, Liberty
Lobby's head. Holocaust denial plays a role
in virtually every antisemitic organization
in the USA.

Holocaust denial found its main
vehicle of expression in 1991 and early 1992
in a series of advertisements offered for
placement in campus newspapers around
the country by Bradley R. Smith, head of
the so-called Committee for Open Debate
on the Holocaust. The antisemitic ads did
appear in some newspapers but, following
exposure by university-based Hillel groups,
were rejected by a majority of editorial
boards.

EFFECTS OF ANTI-ZIONISM

The question of anti-Zionist rhetoric and
antisemitism is in large measure connected
with the "threshold" question—at which
point does this expression become, in the
eyes of American Jews, antisemitism? Most
Jewish groups continued to maintain the
stance that criticism, including harsh
criticism, of the policies of the government
of Israel was legitimate and did not
constitute antisemitism. The point at which
anti-Israel rhetoric becomes antisemitism is
the point at which the legitimacy of
Zionism and the state of Israel—and by
extension the legitimacy of the peoplehood

of Israel—is challenged, or when the Holocaust is invoked in anti-Israel rhetoric. While there was some increase in antisemitic incidents related to the Gulf War, these manifestations decreased sharply following the end of the war in 1991 and during 1992.

OPINION POLLS

In the first comprehensive survey of American attitudes towards Jews since the 1960s, the polling firm Marttila and Kiley, under the auspices of the Anti-Defamation League, found a continuation of the gradual long-term downward trend of attitudinal antisemitism that has characterized American society for the past forty years. The ADL/Marttila survey re-enforced two well-accepted principles: (a) the correlation between education and antisemitism: more-educated people are less likely to accept antisemitic beliefs than are less-educated people; and (b) that the change in attitude is generational: each succeeding generation of Americans in a given age-group is less likely to hold antisemitic views than the same age group of the preceding genera-tion. One surprising finding of the Marttila survey, refuting conventional wisdom, was that the amount of contact an individual has with Jews has little bearing on propen-sities to holding antisemitic beliefs.

The American Jewish Committee in 1992 sponsored an intergroup-relations public opinion survey of New York City conducted by The Roper Organization. While the AJC/Roper survey probed ethnic and racial relations generally in New York, some of the poll's findings with respect to antisemitism were disturbing. For example, 47 per cent of New York City residents responded affirmatively to the "Jewish power" question, with 66 per cent of Hispanics and 63 per cent of blacks affirming this view. Questions remained as to how representative is a poll of New York City vis-à-vis the rest of the country. Nonetheless, the study is noteworthy if for no other reason than the fact that more than one-third of America's Jews reside in New York.

LEGAL MATTERS

It is the nature of the American constitu-tional system that bigotry—including antisemitic attitudes or verbal expression—

cannot be proscribed by law. Constitution-ally—protected freedom of expression is unusually broad in the USA. (Free-speech protections guaranteed under the Bill of Rights First Amendment to the Constitu-tion are not unlimited. For example, "fighting words"—conduct which itself inflicts injury or tends to incite violence—do not merit protection under the free-speech clause of the First Amendment to the Constitution.) Nonetheless, there has been significant activity in recent years in the US Congress and in numerous state legislatures in introducing and passing "hate-crime" statutes. Forty-seven states, and the federal government, have some form of "hate-crime", ethnic intimidation, or bias-motivated violence legislation. The constitutionality of many of these laws was called into question, however, by the US Supreme Court in 1992, when the High Court, in *RAV v. St Paul*, struck down a municipal statute on the grounds that the law in question selectively "silenced speech on the basis of content". Most Jewish groups favoured an approach to drafting hate-crime laws based on a "penalty-enhancement" approach, which might pass constitutional muster.

ANTISEMITISM IN THE BLACK COMMUNITY

One of the major sources of anxiety in the American Jewish community derives from antisemitism in the African-American (black) community. This anxiety was fueled by the July 1991 speech of City College of New York Professor Leonard Jeffries, Jr, who claimed that Jewish conspiracies controlled, among other things, the slave trade and negative depictions of blacks in Hollywood movies, and the August 1991 black-Jewish disturbances in the Crown Heights section of Brooklyn, in which an antisemitic murder was committed. These two events crystallized for many Jews the questions with respect to black anti-semitism. The verdict in October 1992 acquitting the accused murderer of Yankel Rosenbaum, the Australian Hasid who was slain during the Crown Heights turmoil, rekindled questions among many American Jews about black antisemitism.

At the same time, statements were made by a number of prominent blacks, analyzing and repudiating antisemitism in their community. An article in the *New*

York Times in July 1992 by Harvard University Professor Henry Louis Gates was noteworthy in this respect and received significant attention. These individual expressions were, however, denounced by others in influential black positions. While to American Jews the key dynamic with respect to antisemitism is repudiation by community leaders of the antisemitism in a community's midst, to many blacks the controlling principle is solidarity.

The few available data suggest that much of the conventional wisdom about black antisemitism is unfounded. For example, antisemitism drops for blacks—as it does for whites—as education levels rise, contrary to common belief and expectation. (Blacks do, however, appear to be relatively more antisemitic than whites at the same education level.) The 1992 Martilla and Kiley/Anti-Defamation League poll confirmed this finding (see above, **Opinion polls**). There are few data, and little clarity, on the nature and extent of antisemitism in the black grass-roots in the USA; a serious, comprehensive study of the black population is needed.

COUNTERING ANTISEMITISM

One index of a society's response to antisemitism is the extent to which public officials and official bodies publicly reject any expression or manifestation of anti-semitism. A significant development in the David Duke campaign for Governor of Louisiana occurred on 6 November 1991— ten days before a crucial run-off election— when President Bush denounced Duke, asserting "When someone has an ugly record of racism and bigotry, that record simply cannot be erased by the glib rhetoric of a political campaign." While the president and other Republican leaders had disavowed Duke after the October primary (Duke ran as a Republican), Bush's vigorous denunciation was especially welcome.

With respect to the response to most forms of behavioural antisemitism, the experience in most communities in the United States was that the public entities of the community—the law enforcement agencies, the mayoralty, and so on—took the lead in counter-action. Local police departments were for the most part vigorous in pursuing antisemitic activity

that manifested itself in criminality, such as acts of vandalism; and police departments in larger cities established "bias units", whose task was to focus on the investiga-tion of any crime in which it appeared that bias or bigotry was an element that informed or motivated the crime.

The activities of church bodies were noteworthy as well. The national bodies of a number of major Protestant denomina-tions, including the Presbyterian Church (USA), the United Church of Christ, the Lutherans and others, have issued state-ments in recent years rejecting and repudi-ating antisemitism and calling for active counter-measures. The formal structures of the Roman Catholic Church in America, the National Conference of Catholic Bishops and the United States Catholic Conference, have likewise been forthright in their condemnation of antisemitism. And in local communities, it has often been the church federation or the Catholic bishop that has taken the lead in denouncing antisemitic expression.

ASSESSMENT

Antisemitism is assessed along a range of evaluative criteria, most of which show a continuing gradual diminution in levels of significant forms of antisemitism in the United States, particularly of a virulent nature, such as political antisemitism or widespread discrimination. National survey data on attitudinal antisemitism released in 1991 and 1992, including polls conducted by the American Jewish Committee/ National Opinion Research Center and the Anti-Defamation League/Marttila and Kiley, reflect this pattern of gradual decline in antisemitism. These studies also revealed a sizable repository of good feeling towards Jews.

Nonetheless, there has been an increase in some forms of behavioural antisemitism in recent years, notably the number of incidents of antisemitic vandalism, which, according to the Anti-Defamation League, increased for five years, through 1991, and declined in 1992. The apparent contradic-tion between a decline in attitudinal antisemitism and an increase over a period of years, until this year, in the number of antisemitic incidents is easily explained: among those relatively few who profess antisemitic attitudes, there has been in recent years a greater propensity to "act out" their beliefs in various forms of expression. Clearly the erosion of traditional taboos against the expression of antisemitism continued during 1992.

Also, brought into question during 1992, in the aftermath of the US Supreme Court's *RAV v . St. Paul* decision, was the ability of states and municipalities to prosecute bias-motivated "hate crimes".

Overall, analysts suggest that for the USA in 1992 a distinction should be made between whatever manifestations of antisemitism do exist and must be monitored and countered, and the state of Jewish security in the country, which is strong, because of the continued strength of democratic institutions and constitutional protections inherent in the society. Further, antisemitism must be countered wherever it poses a real threat. But to posit antisemitism where it does not exist—or where its effect is minimal—is often counterproductive and may prevent the realization of other Jewish communal goals.

Finally, there remain serious gaps in our knowledge and understanding of antisemitism in the United States. For example, we know very little about the nature and extent of antisemitism in the black community. Further, other areas— thresholds at which individuals experience or perceive antisemitism, the mechanism of taboos that inhibit the expression of antisemitism, a "hierarchy" of antisemitism, and other questions—suggest the need for further data collection, study, and analysis.

Latin America

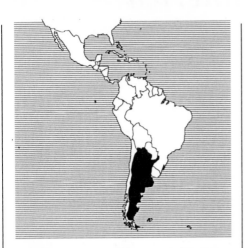

Argentina

General population: 32,300,000
Jewish population: 213,000-225,000
(mainly in Buenos Aires city and vicinity)

GENERAL BACKGROUND

The economy continued to benefit from
the belt-tightening measures introduced by
the Menem government. According to the
Inter-American Development Bank,
inflation, which had reached 4,512 per cent
in 1989, when Menem assumed power,
dropped from 173 per cent in 1991 to 23
per cent during 1992.

For the second consecutive year, GDP
grew at the relatively high rate of about 9
per cent. The government's continued
commitment to the convertibility scheme
adopted in 1991 meant that the Argentine
currency's parity with the US dollar
remained unaltered. This, and the restruc-
turing of the country's foreign debt,
fostered a degree of business confidence
which translated itself into a record net
inflow of capital, $11.3 billion.

These achievements were useful for
Menem's aspirations to seek re-election in
1995, an act which would require amending
the country's constitution. However,
economic adjustment also resulted in rising
labour unrest and the first general strike
against the Menem government.

HISTORICAL LEGACY

From the beginnings of mass immigration

into Argentina in the nineteenth century,
the country's élites did not consider the
arrival of certain groups, including Jews, to
be desirable. The intolerance inherited from
the Spanish colonial period coupled with
Jewish efforts at ethnic self-preservation
meant that Jews were seen as undesirable.
While this did not prevent the unhindered
arrival of Jews until the 1930s (Argentina
had the largest number of Jewish immigrants, legal and illegal, in Latin America in
the crucial 1933-41 period), the nationalist
reaction against immigration in general
which surfaced in 1910 transformed Jews
and other undesirable groups into victims
of xenophobia.

The antisemitism of the Argentine
élites became part of a more general
xenophobic reaction, which successively
borrowed ideas from French right-wing,
Falangist, fascist and Nazi sources. Jews
were perceived as social revolutionaries and
parvenus whose faith, culture and social
habits threatened the society the élites
sought to preserve. In the 1930s, such
influences made themselves strongly felt in
the upper and middle strata of Argentine
society, from which the armed forces drew
their officer corps.

During the most recent military
regime (1976-83) the government encouraged and/or tolerated antisemitism. It was
therefore not surprising that this implied a
higher possibility of torture and murder for
those Jews who were detained and/or
disappeared. Several hundred Jews (out of
nearly 9,000 victims of state terrorism)
were killed. Some argue that the leadership
of the Jewish community felt mostly
unable to speak out against the regime.
However, documents released by Argentine Jewry's umbrella organization, the
Delegation of Argentine Jewish Institutions
(DAIA), show that it did make representation and issued statements, both written
and verbal, on the fact of the detained and/
or disappeared. The constraints under
which the DAIA operated resulted in the
silencing of almost all of the bodies with
which it was in contact.

PARTIES, ORGANIZATIONS, MOVEMENTS

The far-right Movement for Dignity and
National Independence (MODIN),
founded in 1991 and led by Aldo Rico,
probably remained the third largest party

in the Buenos Aires province, although this was not tested in an election. Since 1991, MODIN's leaders have deliberately distanced themselves from anything that appears anti-Jewish in order to be able to participate as a seemingly respectable force in the electoral process. But observers believe this respectability is only skin deep. The more extreme neo-Nazi Nationalist Workers' Party (PNT) continued to exist. In addition, a human rights monitoring body, CELS (Centre for the Study of Social and Legal Issues), found evidence of the existence of thirty neo-Nazi groups at the end of 1991. These organizations were also listed in *La Ultraderecha Argentina y su Conexion Internacional* (The Argentine Far Right and its International Connection), a book by Claudio Diaz and Antionio Zucco which was published in 1991.

MANIFESTATIONS

During 1992, the DAIA recorded dozens of antisemitic incidents: several Jewish cemeteries were desecrated, there were thirteen attacks on Jews, telephone threats were received, and the walls of over twenty Jewish institutions were daubed with graffiti including swastikas and antisemitic slogans. The police did not apprehend any of the perpetrators.

In March a bomb exploded at the Israeli embassy in Buenos Aires. Thirty people died and 250 were injured. Most casualties were Argentines.

Whereas some Argentine and other press comment sought to present the outrage as anti-Jewish, or at least one which was not devoid of anti-Jewish overtones, there is insufficient evidence to justify this claim.

The possibility that Middle East terrorists could have subcontracted part of the operation to local anti-Jewish elements was hinted at by President Menem soon after the bombing. He suggested that there was a connection with discredited dissidents within the armed forces. This link has remained unproven. Heeding the advice of members of his party, as well as the opposition, not to jump to conclusions, Menem thereafter did not pursue this thesis further.

In the wake of the bombing, the Jewish community organized a march,

which attracted between 60,000-130,000 people, in condemnation of the attack. Among those present were President Menem and senior cabinet members, former President Raul Alfonsin, legislators from various parties, representatives of trades unions, and the Archbishop of Buenos Aires, Cardinal Antonio Quarraccino.

Prior to the march, the lower house of the Argentine Congress issued a statement urging legislators to take part. The statement, which was supported by all major political forces, expressed the chamber's strongest condemnation of the attack.

Among those who condemned the attack was Aldo Rico, leader of the far-right Movement for Dignity and National Independence. Rico ascribed the attack to the government's decision to contribute ships to the 1991 Operation Desert Shield in the Gulf. This charge was, however, described as unsavoury opportunism by Atilio Cadorin, a respected columnist of the conservative daily *La Nacion*.

A number of Arab institutions and personalities also condemned the attack. These included the Buenos Aires Islamic Centre, which is aligned with Saudi Arabia and other conservative Arab states, the Coordinating Entity of Argentine Arab Youths, and three Syro-Lebanese organizations. The Syrian Ba'ath-inspired Federation of Arab-American Institutions, however, repudiated this "grave episode", while insinuating that the blast could have been caused by explosives stored at the embassy.

SPECIAL FACTORS

There was concern among members of the Jewish community that anti-Arab sentiments as expressed in particular by journalists such as Horacio Verbitzky could have a boomerang effect on Jews, both in terms of racism being transferred to the Jewish population and increased tension between the Jewish and Arab populations.

This problem was illustrated in July 1992 in an incident involving the Jewish-owned opposition paper *Pagina/12* and Amira Yoma, President Menem's appointments' secretary and former sister-in-law. *Pagina/12* alleged that there was a cover-up of Yoma's involvement in the laundering of narcodollars. One of those reportedly implicated, Jorge Antonio, who is of Arab descent, described himself as the victim of "racial persecution" by "a group of Jews". According to Antonio, those harassing him were linked to *Pagina/12*. *Pagina/12* reached the "categorical conclusion" that Menem, Antonio and magistrate Maria Servini de Cubria had colluded to protect Yoma. This "conclusion" was described by federal judge Nestor Blondi as wholly unwarranted and Blondi was quoted in *Pagina/12* as saying that the paper's references to the case were "premature and tendentious".

A statement by the DAIA on the so-called "Yomagate affair" was critical of anti-Arab bigotry in parts of the media and warned against facile generalizations concerning the traffic in narcotics. The DAIA also condemned Antonio's remarks.

LEGAL MATTERS

Following the participation of the Buenos Aires authorities in the Jewish community's commemoration of the Warsaw Ghetto uprising in August 1992, ruling party members drafted a council ordinance banning the exhibition and sale at newsstands in underground stations of any publication that "promotes, publicizes or argues for racist, antisemitic or discriminatory views, ideas and theories in general". The proposed decree was immediately supported by the council's socialist bloc. Subterraneos de Buenos Aires, the underground transport company, was authorized to revoke the licences of news-stand owners who ignored the decree.

WAR CRIMINALS

In February the government released documents concerning the arrival of alleged war criminals in the Plate in the post-war years. They also transferred the police files on Walter Kutschmann, Josef Mengele, Edward Roschmann and Josef Schwammberger and others to the Archivo General de la Nacion.

Disappointingly for historians and other interested parties, out of a total of 250 pages over 80 per cent of the files in question were press clippings, thereby lending credence to accusations of concealment. While sanitizing cannot be ruled out *a priori*, the part played by inter-agency

rivalries has been generally neglected as an explanation for the seeming inconsistency of President Menem's declared objective, and Foreign Minister Guido di Tella's intellectual authorship of, a policy which might lead to greater access to government records.

In any event, the commonly held view of Argentina as the world's foremost sanctuary for Nazi war criminals is not backed by any comparative study. Some scholars have argued that most war criminals remained in Germany and Austria.

OPINION POLLS

The preliminary results of a DAIA-sponsored investigation into prejudice and discrimination caused by ethnic religious and racial heterogeneity were released in 1992. The investigation highlighted a hostile attitude towards certain groups, including Jews.

The investigation was conducted among university students in Buenos Aires. Seventy-seven per cent of the nearly 1,000 interviewees perceived Jews as working exclusively in their own group's interest, while 24 per cent believed Jewish involvement in Argentine politics was excessive. Over 45 per cent of those interviewed admitted to having Jewish friends. Moreover, respondents listed Koreans, Jews, Mestizos, Japanese and Arabs in descending order as the groups without which Argentina would be better off. Whereas 63 per cent of respondents did not believe Argentina would be better off without Jews, the latter were still among the stigmatized groups.

A broader survey, sponsored by the American Jewish Committee and the DAIA and conducted in Buenos Aires as well as the provinces of Cordoba, Sante Fe and Tucuman, is still being analysed and will be covered more fully in next year's *Antisemitism World Report*. However, the preliminary findings established that a third of the 1,900 interviewees considered Jews and Arabs among those least integrated into the country, and less than 40 per cent considered that both groups belonged to a separate people (that is, not the Argentine people). Moreover, 41 per cent declared that they would not vote for a presidential candidate if he were Jewish; the figure rose to 45 per cent if the candidate were Muslim. Despite this, 69 per cent were in favour of the diversity of religions, customs and origins of the country's population, while 82 per cent indicated that the origin, nationality and creed of the people with whom they were in contact at work or in their neighbourhood were not important.

More then 70 per cent of the respondents indicated that Jews did not behave in a way that provoked hostility, a result corroborated by the same proportion of respondents who did not object to having Jewish neighbours. Eighty per cent had no objection to their children or next of kin marrying into a Jewish family. Unlike the survey sponsored solely by the DAIA, this one indicated that the economically disadvantaged, the least educated and least satisfied with themselves of the interviewees, showed greater intolerance towards Jews and groups perceived as different.

COUNTERING ANTISEMITISM

The government's release of documents relating to alleged war criminals, in accordance with President Menem's declared desire to see his country repay a "debt to humanity", led the DAIA to establish a Testimony Project through its Centre of Social Studies. The project is intended to provide an archive of documents and oral accounts on the arrival and activities on Nazis in Argentina, the ideological influence of Nazism and the response of the democratic sectors of society.

ASSESSMENT

Though not *prima facie* an antisemitic attack, the bombing of the Israeli embassy gave rise to an unparalleled display of sympathy for Argentine Jewry on the part of the government and Argentinean society at large. Many Argentineans of Arab descent were concerned that the ensuing anti-Arab atmosphere in the country might be exacerbated by Islamic Jihad's claim that an Argentine convert to Islam had blown himself up in the car bomb attack.

The government's attempts to win the support of US public opinion-formers resulted in the release of documents on alleged Nazis who took refuge in the country during the presidency of Juan

Domingo Peron. Bringing war criminals to justice, however, runs the risk of losing credibility due to unproven claims and exaggerations. There was concern in the Jewish community that this could have damaging consequences for Argentine Jewry.

Moreover, some of the results of the DAIA-sponsored investigation among Buenos Aires university students, especially the perception of Jewish interference in Argentine affairs, threw light on the ease with which irresponsible exaggerations relating to the Nazis in Argentina could be counterproductive.

Regardless of the merits of Menem's aspirations for a second term of office, the constitutional reform needed to allow him to run for immediate re-election might yet put an end to the impermissibility of non-Catholics from aspiring to the presidency. If such a constitutional reform were sanctioned—and this is highly dubious— the findings of the American Jewish Committee-DAIA opinion survey suggested the Argentine people were not ready for a Jewish head of state—even less so for a Muslim one.

Despite the appearance of antisemitic publications after the collapse of the military regime, the return of democracy has led to a steady improvement in the position of the Jewish community because antisemitism was closely linked to the former regime.

Brazil °

General population: 145,000,000
Jewish population: 100,000 (mainly in São Paulo, Rio de Janeiro and Porto Alegre)

GENERAL BACKGROUND

Fernando Collor was democratically elected President in 1988 following more than two decades of brutal military rule. Collor's presidency was marred by charges of corruption and, in mid-1992, he was suspended from office for six months pending an investigation. On 29 December,

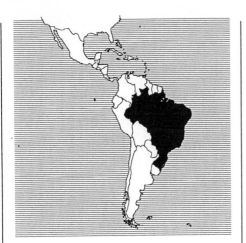

immediately before Senate impeachment proceedings were to begin, Collor resigned and was replaced by Vice-President Itamar Franco. The smooth transition of power from Collor to Franco followed the rules set out in Brazil's constitution and suggested that democracy had taken hold in Brazil.

Brazil's economy continued to suffer from very high inflation and recession. Thus many of the privatization schemes the government encouraged in order to modernize the economy failed. Brazil's economic growth in 1992, as in 1991, was negative.

HISTORICAL LEGACY

Antisemitism has never been a major social problem in independent Brazil because most Brazilians have had little contact with Jews or images of them. Antisemitic policies have largely been created by a tiny élite and supported by a relatively small urban middle and upper class.

Brazil remained a colony of Portugal into the early nineteenth century and therefore inherited the traditions of the Inquisition.

Modern antisemitism in Brazil dates from 1930 when, following the Depression, a new nationalist and nativist regime led by Getúlio Vargas came to power. At that time, nativism, of which antisemitism was one component, became popular among intellectuals and the élite press. Groups which regularly attacked Jews and Jewish immigration, for example the Society of the Friends of Alberto Torres, also had access to the corridors of power. The antisemitism

of many members of the Vargas government was, however, inspired by modern Central European, and not Iberian, antisemitism.

From the mid-1930s and onwards, the government tolerated antisemitic acts and, during the early years of Vargas's rule, the green shirts of the Ação Integralista Brasileira (Integralist Party) initiated a virulently antisemitic campaign which was tolerated by the government. At their height, the Integralists claimed one million members. When Vargas created the proto-fascist Estado Novo (New State) in 1937, groups like the Integralists were banned but secret anti-Jewish immigration policies were regularized and formalized, a pattern that continued until Vargas was overthrown in 1945.

There was no indication of state-sponsored antisemitism in Brazil following the end of the Vargas regime in 1945. Indeed, when Vargas was elected President in 1950 by popular vote, he chose an important member of the Jewish community, Horacio Lafer, as his finance minister.

PARTIES, MOVEMENTS, ORGANIZATIONS

There are a number of explicitly antisemitic movements in existence. The Integralist Party, revived in 1988, is based in Rio Claro, a city in the state of São Paulo. It appears to be supported by a few hundred people at most.

The growing neo-Nazi skinhead movement, modelled on those which exist in North America and Europe, has a number of affiliate groups. These include the Skinheads, the Carecas do Suburbio, White Power and the neo-Nazis. Most are based in the industrial suburbs surrounding Brazil's largest cities where the economic crisis has created enormous levels of unemployment.

The neo-Nazi Brazilian National Revolutionary Party, established in 1992, is not legally registered and appears to have only about 200 sympathizers.

Most of these neo-Nazi groups have revived the use of the old Integralist symbol, the sigma, in spite of the fact that they are not supporters of the Integralist movement, which they find too conservative. The neo-Nazi movement in Brazil targets Jews, those of African descent, migrants from Brazil's impoverished north-eastern states, and homosexuals.

In October, the daily mass-circulation newspaper *O Estado de São Paulo* reported that Brazilian neo-Nazi groups were in contact with similar groups outside Brazil, possibly in the United Kingdom, Holland, Portugal, Germany and the USA.

Neo-Nazi groups did not focus exclusively on Jews. They also painted swastikas on the inside of churches and attempted to burn down one of Rio de Janeiro's premier concert halls.

MANIFESTATIONS

Most antisemitic incidents were confined to publications and neo-Nazi marches to celebrate Hitler's birthday. In late September and early October, however, two Jewish cemeteries in Porto Alegre, home to Brazil's third largest Jewish community of about 15,000, were vandalized. While the perpetrators have not been found, the governor of Rio Grande do Sul, Alceu Collares, publicly condemned the incident and granted police protection to the city's synagogues and cemeteries.

In mid-September the Jewish Telegraphic Agency reported that two Jewish boys wearing skullcaps had been physically attacked in Santo Andre, in greater São Paulo.

PUBLICATIONS

In October, the mass-circulation daily *Folha de São Paulo* reported that two pamphlets with a minimal circulation, "Determination and Courage" and "São Paulo Pride", had been found in a number of locations in the state of São Paulo. Both promoted the killing of Jews, blacks and north-eastern Brazilians. It is not known who published them.

MAINSTREAM POLITICS

In September, a member of the Integralist Party, Anésio de Lara Campos, who is also the half-brother of Senator Eduardo Suplicy, the Worker's Party candidate for mayor of São Paulo, was shown on the national television network SBT in a library filled with Nazi literature. Inexplicably, Suplicy took Lara Campos to a meeting against racism held at São Paulo's Jewish Federation headquarters. During the meeting, Lara Campos is reported to have said that the Nazis did not exterminate Jews and that the gas chambers were simply prisoners' showers. Suplicy's refusal to condemn his brother's statements is thought to have resulted in the loss of Jewish votes in his candidacy for mayor.

DENIAL OF THE HOLOCAUST

Virtually all Holocaust denial material published in Brazil is written by sixty-four-year-old Siegfried Ellwanger Castan, a wealthy industrialist living in the state of Rio Grande do Sul. Castan's publishing company, Editôra Revisão (Revision), distributed free of charge an unknown quantity of Holocaust-denial books to Brazilian politicians. However, there were no indications that this has had any detrimental effect.

Castan's "Holocaust: Jewish or German?" is said to have reached its twenty-ninth edition but the number which has actually been printed is unknown.

Also published in 1992 was Castan's "The Lie of the Century" in which he claims that the Nazi murder of Jews during the Second World War did not happen and is the fabrication of "Zionist lies". Castan's books were not available in any of the major bookshops, but could be found in small second-hand bookshops.

In spite of its small circulation, Holocaust-denial literature has been widely condemned by politicians, the media, academics and religious leaders, and thus received publicity disproportionate to its circulation.

LEGAL MATTERS

In 1992, attempts to stop the distribution of Holocaust-denial literature in accordance with Brazil's anti-racism laws were not actively supported by politicians and failed under Brazil's freedom of speech and press guarantees. When Editôra Revisão was removed as a member of a publisher's consortium in Rio Grande do Sul, a local judge reinstated it. Attempts to prosecute Castan for defamation and injury were unsuccessful.

The 1988 Brazilian Constitution makes the public expression of religious or racial prejudice a crime for which imprisonment is mandatory and no bail is allowed. Many members of Brazil's Jewish community, however, remain cautious about using the new constitutional laws as a means of combating antisemitism since they do not appear to have resulted in any diminution of antisemitism or positive action by the government and the legal establishment. Brazil's Jews fear that it may even indicate a growing sophistication in masking antisemitism and other forms of bigotry behind "acceptable" rhetoric. The law, however, was used twice in 1991 by the City Council of Porto Alegre, Rio Grande do Sul's largest city, to ban the public display of swastikas.

COUNTERING ANTISEMITISM

The response to the upsurge in anti-semitism was rapid and widespread. The Jewish Federation of São Paulo created a permanent commission to fight racism. In addition, the Movement of Democratic Entities was formed to oppose the growing neo-Nazi movement. At the group's opening meeting in October, São Paulo state governor Luiz Antonio Fleury Filho, São Paulo city Mayor Luiza Erundina and José Roberto Batochio (President of the Brazilian Order of Lawyers) joined with Jewish, black and north-eastern Brazilian civil rights groups to proclaim that "São Paulo has 1,000 peoples: Say yes to solidarity, say no to racism".

ASSESSMENT

There was little popular or open anti-semitism, mainly as a result of the limited contact between the relatively small Jewish community and Brazil's impoverished population. However, the growing neo-Nazi movement continued to be of concern to the Jewish community.

Brazil's rhetoric of ethnic, cultural and racial tolerance has been backed up by law, thereby making the public expression of antisemitism a potential crime. This, however, was difficult to implement because it conflicted with laws guaranteeing freedoms of speech and the press.

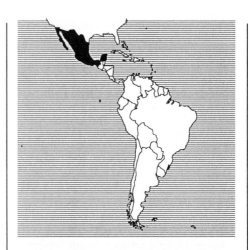

Mexico

General population: 88,600,000
Jewish population: 38,000-50,000 (mainly in Mexico City)

GENERAL BACKGROUND

Since Carlos Salinas de Gortari was elected president in July 1988, he has attempted to move away from the revolutionary nation-alism of the past towards a liberal and pluralistic society. The ruling Institutional Revolutionary Party (PRI) won a large majority in the August 1991 mid-term congressional elections but opposition parties accused it of vote-rigging.

President de Gortari had instituted radical reforms in the economy, agriculture, education and religion and carried out further privatization of state-controlled companies. In spite of trade deregulation and low interest rates, poverty remained widespread.

Human rights groups severely criti-cized alleged abuses by the Mexican government. This issue and calls for a more open and democratic political system formed part of the debate surrounding ratification of the North American Free Trade Agreement (NAFTA) and acted as external pressure for furthering the cause of democracy. The negotiated, though not yet ratified, NAFTA generated growing expectations and much uncertainty about the influence it will have on Mexico. Open borders have already had a disruptive effect on Mexican industry.

HISTORICAL LEGACY

Antisemitism in Mexico can be traced back to the sixteenth century with the establishment of the Inquisition. However, the absence of a significant Jewish population in the nineteenth century and the liberal struggle for tolerance diluted its impact.

Antisemitism in contemporary Mexico has generally not been government-sponsored. It was initially prompted by the debate surrounding immigration policies from the second half of the 1920s onwards. Groups such as the Anti-Chinese and Anti-Jewish National League, founded in 1930, and the Association of Honourable Traders, Industrialists and Professionals lobbied the government to implement restrictive immigration policies towards the Jews. The activities of these groups reached a climax with the expulsion in May 1931 of 250 Jewish peddlers from the La Lagunilla market and the proclamation of 1 June of that year as the National Day of Commerce. On that date, Mexicans protested about the Jewish presence in Mexico's commercial life.

In the 1930s, Mexico experienced outbursts of antisemitism centring on economic and racial themes. Gradually, racial themes became the dominant tenet of right-wing groups. Among them, the Mexican Revolutionary Action, a group created in March 1934, operated through its paramilitary units, the Golden Shirts. The Pro-Race Committee and the Middle Class Confederation expressed their antisemitism by exerting pressure on the government and by antisemitic press campaigns. These reached their peak in 1938-9.

In the following decades, antisemitism was confined to minority groups with marginal national influence.

In the second half of the 1960s, there emerged a new, quasi-Marxist anti-Zionism and antisemitism which saw Israel as a spearhead of "imperialism". Gradually, the antisemitism became more pronounced than the anti-Zionism.

The financial chaos of 1982 and the social upheaval caused by the 1985 earthquake in Mexico City were used by the media as a pretext for the expression of anti-Jewish sentiment, accusing Jewish businessmen of exploiting their workers.

PARTIES, ORGANIZATIONS, MOVEMENTS

Throughout Mexico's modern history, with the exception of the 1930s, antisemitism has not been a central issue for political parties or movements. However, the extreme right has proved fertile ground for the expression of antisemitic attitudes. Some of the more significant groups are the Partido Laboral Mexicano (Mexican Labour Party-LaRouche) (on Lyndon LaRouche, see **United States**), Editorial Tradición (Tradition Publishing House), Falanges Tradicionalistas Mejicanas (Mexican Traditional Falangists), Federación Mexicana Anticomunista (Anti-Communist Mexican Federation) and Tecos. The number and strength of these groups are hard to assess, but they may be regarded as marginal in national terms.

In 1992, some Muslim fundamentalist cells were detected in Torreon, the capital of the Northern state of Cohauila. Though very few Muslim families live in Mexico, this city has a mosque which apparently serves as headquarters for these as yet unidentified groups. Letters from Torreon denouncing the "Zionist-Jewish conspiracy" appeared regularly in *Excélsior*, one of Mexico's most influential dailies. Several were published in December and were sent by, among others, Federico Campbell Peña and Augusto Hugo Peña, both closely associated with the PLO. The letters included such arguments as "orthodox Jews are the true power in the United States".

MANIFESTATIONS

Much anti-Jewish graffiti, in particular swastikas, continued to appear in Mexico City, especially in Jewish neighbourhoods. It also appeared in downtown Mexico City, where some businesses are owned by Jews.

PUBLICATIONS

Antisemitic publications included *La Hoja de Combate* (Combat Newsletter), which is published by Tradition Publishing House and run by Salvador Abascal; the monthly *Surge* (Emergence); the monthly *Verdades* (Truth); and the bi-monthly *Solidaridad Iberoamericana* (Ibero-American Solidarity), which is published by the Mexican Labour Party-LaRouche.

Tradition Publishing House also published works by the prolific antisemitic writer Salvador Borrego, including *World Defeat* (1950) and *America in Danger* (1960), which are now in their thirtieth and eleventh editions respectively.

With the perception that the extreme right has stepped up its activity world-wide, Mexico has felt its effects especially in the written media. Editors like Mauricio Gonzàlez de la Garza, who in the past has expressed xenophobic feelings, nowadays are more blatant. During 1992, de la Garza wrote eight editorials in *El Sol de Mexico*, a well known Mexico City daily, in which he denounced Jews as being foreigners, arrogant and seeking economic and political power.

DENIAL OF THE HOLOCAUST

In 1991, the California-based Institute for Historical Review, seeking a foothold in Mexico, began to distribute propaganda in selected areas such as the German School in Mexico City. No further activity of this nature was detected in 1992.

Literature by British Holocaust-denier David Irving, such as *The War Against the Jews*, was sold in some of Mexico's prestigious bookshops indicating that this subject was growing in popularity.

EFFECTS OF ANTI-ZIONISM

The most significant channel for anti-Zionism and antisemitism is the press; its impact on public opinion cannot be overstated. The rescinding of the UN resolution equating Zionism and racism seems to have quieted the anti-Zionist rhetoric which reached its peak during the Gulf crisis of 1991. Rabin's rise to power in Israel contributed to improving Israel's and Zionism's image.

Israel's removal of the Hamas fundamentalists to Lebanon in December resulted in dozens of hostile articles. The most pervasive arguments were that Zionism is racism (José Enrique Gonzalez Ruiz, "Despite it, it's racism", *El Dia*, a conservative daily, 24 January 1993) and that Israel is a fascist state, (Daniel Herrendorf, "Fascist Jews", *El Nacional*, a government daily, 4 January 1993).

COUNTERING ANTISEMITISM

Jewish writers who work on Mexico's most prestigious newspapers, *Excélsior, El Nacional, El Financiero*, and *El Universal*, published articles which put into perspective references used in anti-Zionist arguments. Furthermore, the public relations campaign conducted at different levels of Mexican society by Tribuna Israelita, an agency of the Mexican Jewish community, forged close links between Mexican opinion-formers and Jewry.

Between October and December, more than fifty newspaper articles denouncing racism and antisemitism were published, reflecting a tendency in Mexican intellectual circles to accept Judaism as a legitimate cultural and historical entity, even while distancing themselves from contemporary Jewish existence, Israel included.

There was concern at all levels of Mexican society with racism, antisemitism and neo-Nazism. President de Gortari condemned the resurgence of far-right tendencies through Mexico's representatives in international forums. In the framework of the Third Commission of the forty-seventh General Assembly of the United Nations in September and October, Mexico condemned racism and suggested the proclamation, starting in 1993, of a third decade of fight against racial discrimination. In meetings with Mexican Jewish leaders, the President noted that the expressions of xenophobia occurring in Europe were alien to Mexico's liberal tradition.

ASSESSMENT

Positive developments have occurred in recent years regarding a more pluralistic approach to cultural, religious and ethnic diversity, which may be seen as new and strong sources of Jewish legitimacy. These, as well as the country's new international alignment, have been expressed in a lessening of the traditional anti-imperialist and anti-foreign rhetoric which has been related to anti-Zionist and antisemitic expressions in the past.

Although there were great expectations for the success of economic and political projects, which would act as stabilizing influences, there remained much uncertainty about the future. Failure to bring about economic and political change may result in a resurgence of nationalistic rhetoric and anti-foreign attitudes.

Panama

General population: 2,300,000
Jewish population: 5,000-7,000 (in
Panama City)

GENERAL BACKGROUND

In December 1989, US troops invaded
Panama and overthrew the discredited
regime of General Noriega. The democratically elected President Guillermo Endara
and his government assumed office in the
wake of the invasion. The economy began
to improve but inflation was 56.7 per cent
in 1992 and the unemployment rate
remained among the highest in Latin
America with more than half the population living in poverty. Opposition to the
government's austerity policies and offical
corruption led to demonstrations.

PRESENT SITUATION

There have been no physical attacks on
Jews since they first settled in Panama 140
years ago. Antisemitism is found, in the
main, at the grassroots level. Antisemitic
pamphlets are sometimes distributed at
universities and there have been some
reported incidents of antisemitic messages
written on blackboards. Occasionally, the
small weekly sensationalist newspaper *El
Camaleon* publishes caricatures of, and
jokes about, Jews. These usually revolve
around traditional stereotyping of "Jewish
greed". The media generally presents a

positive and informative view of Jews and
Judaism. Antisemitism was not a major
concern in 1992.

Peru

General population: 21,600,000
Jewish population: 3,000 (mainly in Lima)

GENERAL BACKGROUND

On 5 April, President Fujimori dissolved
Congress claiming that Congress members
were sabotaging efforts to adopt legislation
fundamental to the restoration of calm to
the political and social spheres and to the
modernization of the economy. He also
accused the judiciary of corruption and of
using the law to obstruct government
reforms. Dozens of judges and prosecutors
were dismissed and the constitutional court
was closed down.

As a result of international pressure,
fresh elections were held on 22 November
in which the Fujimori government won 44
of the 80 parliamentary seats. This majority
gave the President the opportunity to draw
up a new constitution and adopt the
legislation needed to implement his
policies. However, human rights violations
by the armed forces continued despite
government assurances that individual
freedoms would be safeguarded.

HISTORICAL LEGACY

Antisemitism in Peru has been largely

tenuous and sporadic and invariably prompted by external factors. During the Second World War, antisemitic leaflets were circulated. Peru's most prominent newspaper, *El Comercio*, expressed sympathy for Nazism and Peru's Jews were accused in Congress of hoarding food and conspiring against the goverment (these accusations were accompanied by calls to expel or control them).

In 1990, at the time of the presidential election campaign, conservative elements in society led a campaign designed to stir up nationalist, racist and religious prejudice. Fujimori and his wife, both of Japanese descent, were singled out as Asians and foreigners. Furthermore, the president's inclination towards evangelism—he and his party were supported by evangelist leaders—despite his being a Catholic, clearly represented a serious threat to the traditional power and hegemony of the Catholic church. Against this backdrop, a country which is traditionally racist in its dealings with the native Indians, whom it blames for Peru's current deep economic crisis, could have been expected to be the scene of antisemitic outbursts. However, nothing exceptional took place.

PARTIES, ORGANIZATIONS, MOVEMENTS

Tercios Nacional Socialista de la Nueva Castilla (National Socialist Corps of New Castille) is a small neo-Nazi group. Its members are in their early twenties, mostly of Spanish and German descent and live in Lima's Chosica district. They look to German neo-Nazism for inspiration, deny that the Holocaust took place and give credence to *The Protocols of the Elders of Zion*. They operate on a small scale within higher education institutions. It is possible that they are wealthy youngsters with links to Ortiz Acha, the editor of *Temple*, a neo-Nazi newspaper with a small circulation.

There also exist tiny groups of right-wing extremists such as Orden Celta (Celtic Order) and the Frente Nacional Socialista del Peru (Peruvian National Socialist Front), but these groups have no significant impact on a national level.

MANIFESTATIONS

There was a substantial increase in neo-Nazi activity in Lima, especially in the

second half of the year. Swastikas were displayed by supporters of the popular Universitario de Deportes football team and were daubed on the walls of the stadium as well as in Lima's main streets. Notices about "aryan" gatherings were published in *El Comercio*. Threatening telephone calls were made to Jewish businesses and organizations.

MAINSTREAM POLITICS

At a meeting of former members of parliament on 31 May, Roberto Ramirez del Villar, one of the founding leaders of the Partido Popular Cristiano and President of the Chamber of Deputies before the dissolution of Congress, accused the Jewish owners of the Channel 2 television station of being servile to the Fujimori regime and of forgetting their fate under Hitler. He also accused the Peruvian Jewish community of helping to bring about the end of democracy in the country, selling themselves to the government, and not respecting the independence of the media.

PUBLICATIONS

The left-leaning weekly journal *Si* (circulation: 60,000) emphasized the Jewish origin of public figures close to the government or of those who buy privatized state industries, and drew attention to the Jewish ownership of the Channel 2 television station, private business transactions between President of Congress Jaime Yoshiyama and Jewish businessman Efraim Goldemberg, and Jewish involvement in the field of security.

The accusation of Jewish collaboration with the regime on security matters was a theme which appeared so frequently in political and journalistic circles that it became a significant cause of concern to the Jewish community.

At the beginning of the year, *Panorama*, a programme on the Channel 5 television station, disclosed that Israeli companies based in Lima were involved in security concerns and the arms trade, and that these enabled Israeli equipment and arms to reach Peru. As the media makes little or no distinction between Israel and Jews, the association of Israel with the intelligence services, which are perceived to be corrupt, created a negative image of the

Jewish community in the eyes of the general public. This was compounded in August when the former Minister of Defence, General Jorge Torres Aciego, was appointed ambassador to Israel.

On 22 June, the weekly centrist magazine *Caretas*, (circulation: 281,700) compared President Fujimori to the High Priest Caiphas (that is, a Jew) and blamed him for the death of Jesus (that is, democracy).

COUNTERING ANTISEMITISM

On 15 December, there was a public demonstration against racism, xenophobia and antisemitism. Confronted with the resurgence of these phenomena in Europe, as well as increased political racism in Peru, the Third World Committee of the World Jewish Congress and the B'nai B'rith International organized a public meeting on the theme of "Human Dignity". It was held under the auspices of the Jewish community and was of great historic value for a number of reasons—the joint participation of over 600 mainly young Jews and non-Jews; the fact that the most important leader on the left, Gloria Helfer of the Movimiento Democratico Izquierdo, and a number of her supporters, took part in a Jewish communal activity for the first time in decades; and that the heads of the four leading parliamentary lists in the Congress (Jaime Yoshiyama—Officialists, Lourdes Flores—PPC, Rafael Rey—Renovacion, Gloria Helfer—MDI), which account for over 80 per cent of all parliamentarians, spoke in support of the cause.

ASSESSMENT

Incidents of antisemitism were sporadic and were contained by the self-censorship of Peruvian politicians, intellectuals and journalists as well as by actions taken by individuals within the Jewish community.

Although Jews were not singled out for racist attacks, there was a fear in the Jewish community that the attacks could easily be transferred to them.

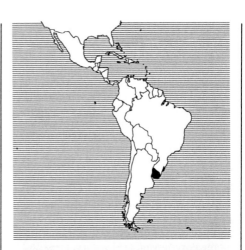

Uruguay

General population: 3,100,000
Jewish population: 24,000-30,000 (mainly in Montevideo)

GENERAL BACKGROUND

Uruguay is one of the most stable parliamentary democracies in Latin America. Since the mid-nineteenth century, the political system has been dominated by the Colorado Party and National Party. However, in 1971, the left-wing Broad Front coalition emerged as the third political force. Uruguay has had a high, though slowly decreasing, annual inflation rate—55 per cent in 1992. The unemployment rate in 1992 was 8.9 per cent.

HISTORICAL LEGACY

Uruguay has no serious tradition of antisemitism. However, on several occasions during the first half of the twentieth century, government action indicated anti-Jewish attitudes. In January 1919, several hundred workers, many of them of Jewish origin, were arrested and charged with "subversive" activities: all were released within a month. By the end of the 1930s, there were several incidents of Jewish refugees from Central Europe having been refused entry at the port of Montevideo. In the early 1960s, left-wing Jews and non-Jews in Montevideo were attacked with razor blades and marked with swastikas.

Those responsible were never identified. Equally, those responsible for the defacement of the Jewish cemetery in La Paz in September 1990 were never identified.

In December 1990, a lone gunman attacked members of the Jewish community, leaving two dead and three severely wounded. The perpetrator, a neo-fascist supporter, remains in prison under special security measures.

PRESENT SITUATION

In 1992, antisemitic incidents were minimal with the exception of isolated daubings of swastikas and slogans on walls in the Montevideo suburb of Pocitos. The attitude of the government, civil service, press and general population remained positive towards the country's Jewish population and Israel. This position reflected the generally positive attitude towards minority groups, with the exception of the 7,000-strong black population, which was the main target of racist sentiment in Uruguayan society.